W9-ACE-919

HOSTELS SERIES

hostels
european cities

the only comprehensive, unofficial, opinionated guide

6th edition

Paul Karr

gpp®
travel

Guilford, Connecticut

South Huntington Public Library
145 Pidgeon Hill Road
Huntington Station, NY 11746

914.06
HOS
2014

The prices and rates listed in this guidebook were confirmed at press time. We strongly recommend, however, that you check online or contact hostels directly before traveling to confirm up-to-the-moment pricing, directions, office hours, and other information.

To buy books in quantity for corporate use or incentives, call **(800) 962-0973** or e-mail **premiums@GlobePequot.com**.

Text for Brussels, Paris, Marseille, Lyon, Dublin, Rome, Milan, Florence, Pisa, Venice, Luxembourg City, Amsterdam, Edinburgh, London, Cardiff, Glasgow, and Manchester copyright © 2014 by Paul Karr

Text for Vienna, Prague, Copenhagen, Berlin, Munich, Athens, Budapest, Oslo, Lisbon, Barcelona, Madrid, Seville, Stockholm, Geneva, and Zürich copyright © 2014 Morris Book Publishing, LLC

ALL RIGHTS RESERVED. No part of this book may be reproduced or transmitted in any form by any means, electronic or mechanical, including photocopying and recording, or by any information storage and retrieval system, except as may be expressly permitted in writing from the publisher. Requests for permission should be addressed to Globe Pequot Press, Attn: Rights and Permissions Department, P.O. Box 480, Guilford, CT 06437.

Editor: Kevin Sirois
Project Editor: Staci Zacharski
Text design: Sheryl P. Kober
Maps: M.A. Dubé © Morris Book Publishing, LLC; Maps updated by Alena Joy Pearce © Morris Book Publishing, LLC
Co-concept and Other Editorial Assistance: Evan Halper

ISSN 1541-8065
ISBN 978-0-7627-9204-7

Printed in the United States of America
10 9 8 7 6 5 4 3 2 1

Contents

About the Author

Paul Karr is an award-winning journalist, musician, and author or co-author of more than 25 travel books covering the US, Canada, and Europe; he has twice been named a writer-in-residence by the National Parks Service and can usually be found bouncing around Hawaii, Italy, Japan, and/or Canada when he's not home.

Acknowledgments

Many people have contributed to this book. Thanks to the editors at Globe Pequot—including Amy Lyons, Mike Urban, the late Laura Strom, and legions of others—for championing this series, editing it well, and giving the writers the freedom to write what they *really* think.

Thanks to our fearless team of freelancers once again, for traveling all those miles, turning taps, sleeping in every sort of bunk known to humankind, and contributing some wickedly funny (yet accurate) write-ups.

Thanks to all hostel associations of Europe who helped provide basic information for this and previous editions, including (but not limited to): Danhostel in Copenhagen, NHJC in Amsterdam, LAJ in Belgium, AIG in Rome, FUAJ in Paris, YHA in London, and American Youth Hostels in Washington. All supplied a world of help as well as continuous encouragement and assistance.

Thanks again to friends and family at home and abroad for bringing light and joy to our travels, and for providing a home away from home.

And thanks, finally, to a world (literally) of new friends met or made on the road. So many of you have taught us about your corner of the world or otherwise made this work enjoyable and useful.

Thank you all.

How to Use This Book

What you're holding in your hands began more than a decade ago as the first attempt of its kind: a full listing and truthful rating of hostels in Europe's most popular cities. Dozens of hostellers from countries all over the globe were interviewed during the course of putting that first guide together, and their comments and thoughts ran through its pages. We weren't sure if anyone would read it, but we were reasonably happy with the results. For the first time, hostellers heading to Europe had all the information at their fingertips. They could sleep cheap and risk a noisy, chilly night—but at least they'd know that going in.

During the years since, this book has gained momentum like a powerful snowball: More and more contributing freelance writers (and regular people with opinions) began writing in to give us tips, complaints, and new info. Who knows? You yourself might be quoted somewhere inside.

We set out to write this guide for two pretty simple reasons: First, we wanted to bring hostelling to a wider audience. Hostels continue to grow in popularity, but many North American travelers still don't think of them as viable options when planning a European trip—partly thanks to their poor reputation, partly due to ignorance.

Yet Europeans have traveled hostel-to-hostel since they were schoolkids. And you should think about it, too; at its best, the hostelling experience brings people of differing origins, faiths, and points of view together in a convivial setting. They learn about one another, and about the place in which the hostel is located, in a very personal way that no guidebook or textbook could ever provide.

So there was an altruistic reason. But there was also a practical reason. We wanted very much to create a database of honest opinions of European hostels. You wouldn't send your best friend to a fleabag, and we don't want readers traveling great distances only to be confronted with filthy kitchens, nasty managers, or dangerous neighborhoods. At least, we thought, we could warn them about unsafe or unpleasant situations ahead of time. Of course we would also tip our friends off to the truly wonderful hostels—the ones with tree houses, cafes, free breakfasts, and real family spirit. So that's what we've done.

Time after time on the road, we heard fellow travelers complaining that the guidebooks they bought simply listed places to stay but didn't rate them. Or the online message boards and travel sites' reviews sounded suspiciously positive (or negative).

Well, we've done the work for you—visited all these places and collected all the info. And we haven't pulled a single punch or held back a bit of praise.

How We Wrote This Book

The author, along with a cadre of assistants, has been fanning out across Europe with notebooks and laptops in hand since 2001. We count beds, turn taps, thump bunks. We sleep. We cook breakfast. We talk with managers and staff. And before we leave, we also take time to interview lots of the hostellers in private and get their honest opinions about the hostels.

The results are contained within this book: actual hosteller quotes, opinions, ratings, and more.

What Is a Hostel, Anyway?

If you've picked up this book, you probably know what a hostel is. A surprising number of people interviewed for this book, however, weren't sure at all what it means.

So let's check your knowledge with a little pop quiz. Sharpen up your pencils, put on your thinking caps, then dive in.

1. **A hostel is:**
   A. A hospital.
   B. A hospice.
   C. A hotel.
   D. A drunk tank.
   E. None of the above.
   (correct answer worth 20 points)

2. **A hostel is:**
   A. A place where international travelers bunk up.
   B. A cheap sleep.
   C. A place primarily dedicated to bunks.
   D. All of the above.
   (correct answer worth 20 points)

3. **You've just turned 30. Word on the street has it that you'll get turned away at the front desk for being too old. Do you tell the person at the hostel desk your true age? Or do you try to keep it a secret and bribe some 18-year-old to book your bunk for you?**

A. Bribe, because hostels only take students under 27 years old.

B. Buy a fake ID and a white wig, because hostels are restricted to guests over 65.

C. They don't care about my midlife crisis. But still, there's that 27-years-old thing. Solution: bribe-o-rama.

D. No sweat. I tell the truth.

(correct answer worth 10 points)

4. **You spy a shelf labeled "FREE FOOD!" in the hostel kitchen. What do you do?**

A. Begin stuffing pomegranates in your pockets.

B. Ask the manager how the food ended up in jail.

C. Run for your life.

(correct answer worth 5 points)

5. **Essay question: Why do you want to stay in a hostel?**

(extra credit; worth up to 45 points)

Done? Great! And the envelope, please . . .

1. **E. None of the above.** The word *hostel* has German origins, and it means "country inn for youngsters," or something like that.

2. **D. All of the above.** You got that one, right?

3. **D.** Normally there are no age limits or restrictions at a hostel. However, in Bavaria— the south of Germany—there is an age limit; if you're 27 or older, you can stay only under special conditions. Some hostels in Berlin also enforce this old-fashioned restriction. And other places tack on a surcharge for persons over age 26. But in nearly all of the world's hostels, you can stay no matter your age.

4. **A.** Free means free.

5. Give yourself 15 points for every use of the word *friends, international,* or *cool,* OK? But don't give yourself more than 45. Seriously. Don't make us turn this car around right now. We will. We mean it.

What? All you wrote was "It's cheap"? OK—give yourself 20 points.

So how did you do?

100 points:	Born to be wild
80–99:	Get your motor runnin'
40–79:	Head out on the highway
20–39:	Lookin' for adventure
0–19:	Hope you don't come my way

Don't be embarrassed if you flunked this little quiz, though. Even hostel operators get confused and blur the lines sometimes, too. You'll occasionally find a campground or retreat center or college setting aside a couple bunks—and calling itself a hostel anyway. (In borderline cases like this, we've used our own best judgment to decide whether a place is or isn't a hostel.)

Also, we have excluded some joints—no matter how well-meaning—if they exclude either men or women; serve primarily as university residence halls (with a few, very special exceptions); or serve you a heavy side of religious doctrine with the eggs in the morning. Again, we've allowed for just a few exceptions to this rule, notably in Italy, where if you struck all the religious hostels in that country from this book, there might not be any left!

In a few cases our visits didn't satisfy us either way about whether the place was truly a hostel; those places have either been left out, set aside for a future edition, or briefly described here but not rated.

The bottom line? If it's in this book, it is a hostel. If it isn't, it's not, and don't let anyone tell you otherwise. There. 'Nuff said.

Understanding the Ratings

All the listings information in this book was current as of press time. Here's the beginning of an entry in the book, from a hostel in Denmark.

Wombat's Backpackers

Grangasse 6, A-1150 Vienna

Phone: 01-897-2336

Fax: 01-897-2577

E-mail: office@wombats-vienna.at

Website: wombats.at

Rates: €10–€28 (about $13–$35 US) per person; doubles €50–€58 (about $63–$73 US)

Credit cards: No

Beds: 296

Private/family rooms: Yes

Kitchen available: Yes

Season: Open year-round

Office hours: 24 hours

Affiliation: None

Extras: Breakfast ($), Internet access, laundry, bike rentals, roller skate rentals, in-line skate rentals, bar, bicycle tours, lockers, games, darts, movies, terrace, kitchen

*F*irst things first. See those little pictures immediately above? Those are icons, and they signify something important we wanted you to know about the hostel. We've printed a key to these icons on page TK.

The overall hostel rating consists of those hip-looking thumbs sitting atop most entries. It's pretty simple: Thumbs up means good. Thumbs down means bad. One thumb up, and one thumb down? So-so, mixed bag, meh.

We've used these thumbs to compare the hostels with one another. Only a select number of hostels earned the top rating of two thumbs up, and a few were considered unpleasant enough to merit a thumbs down. You can use this rating as a general assessment of a hostel.

Often we didn't give any thumbs at all to a hostel that was a mixed-bag experience. Or maybe for one reason or another—bad weather, bad luck, bad timing, remoteness, an inability to get ahold of the staff, or our own confusion about the place—we just didn't feel we collected enough information to properly rate that hostel for you.

That said, here's a key to what these ratings mean:

Cream of the crop; recommended

Pretty good

OK; average; jury's still out

Only if you're desperate

Bad news; don't even THINK of calling

Note that hostels in our "at-a-glance" charts are ranked according to quality—that is, if there are eight hostels all with a one-thumbs-up rating, we consider the one listed at the top of the pile to be the best (and the one at the bottom to be the, er, least) of the bunch.

The rest of this listing information is pretty much self-explanatory:

Address is usually the hostel's street address; occasionally we add the mailing address if different from the physical address.

Phone is the primary telephone number.

Fax is the primary fax number.

E-mail is the staff's e-mail address, for those who want to get information or (sometimes) book a room by computer.

Website indicates a hostel's website address (URL, for you techies).

Rates are the cost per person to stay at the hostel—when all the currency converting's said and done, expect to pay somewhere around $15 US per person, more (sometimes considerably more) in cities or popular tourist areas. For private or family rooms, we've listed the total price for two people to stay in the room; usually it's higher than the cost of two singles, sometimes considerably so. Single or triple room rates will vary; ask ahead if you're unsure what you'll pay.

Note that these rates sometimes vary by season or by membership in a hostelling group such as Hostelling International (HI); we have tried to include a range of prices where applicable. Most HI member hostels, for instance, charge $2 to $4 extra per day if you don't belong to one of Hostelling International's worldwide affiliates.

Also, many European hostels might charge you the equivalent of $1 to $5 US to supply sheets and/or towels if you haven't brought your own, a charge that can add up fast over time. (Sleeping bags, no matter how clean you think they are, are often frowned upon.) Finally, various local, municipal, or other taxes might add slightly to the rates quoted here.

Key to icons

Attractive natural setting

Ecologically aware hostel

Superior kitchen facilities or great cafe/restaurant

Offbeat or eccentric place

Superior bathroom facilities

Romantic private rooms

Comfortable beds

A particularly good value

Wheelchair-accessible

Good for business travelers

Especially well suited for families

Good for active travelers

Visual arts at hostel or nearby

Music at hostel or nearby

Great hostel for skiers

Bar or pub at hostel or nearby

Editors' choice: Among our very favorite hostels

Credit cards can be a good way to pay for a bed in a foreign country (you get the fairest exchange rates on your home currency); here we have mentioned whether cards are accepted by the hostels. More and more hostels are taking them, and even if we haven't listed a hostel as accepting credit cards, things may have changed. When in doubt, call ahead and ask.

Beds indicates the number of beds available at the hostel.

Private/family rooms are rooms for a couple, a family with children, or (sometimes) a single traveler. Sometimes it's nice to have your own room on the road—it's more private, more secure, and your snoring (or your kids' sudden happy and unhappy unbursts) won't bother anyone else. Private rooms are becoming more and more common in Europe, but they're still pretty hard to snag during the busy season in some cities. So book *months* ahead for one if you're going to a popular place like Berlin or London. Seriously.

Kitchen available indicates whether the hostel allows hostellers to cook in a kitchen. In North America and the UK, almost every hostel has a kitchen—but the situation changes in Europe. Very few of these hostels have a kitchen setup. Almost all, however, serve a delicious meal instead, so take advantage and fill 'er up. Breakfast is often included with the price of your bed; if it is, we have noted this under "Extras" (see next page).

Season indicates what part of the year a hostel is open—if it's closed part of the year. We've made our best effort at listing the seasons of each hostel, but schedules sometimes change according to weather or a manager's vacation plans. Call if you're unsure whether a hostel will be open when you want to stay there.

Office hours indicates when staff are at the front desk and answer the phones, or at least would consider answering the phones. Although European custom is to use military time (23:30 for 11:30 p.m.), we've used "American" time throughout this book.

Keep in mind that nothing is set in stone, however; some hostel staffs will happily field calls in the middle of the night if you're reasonable, while others can't stand it. Try to call within the listed hours if possible.

A good rule to follow: The smaller a place, the harder it is for the owner/manager to drag him/herself out of bed at four in the morning just because you lost your way. Big-city hostels, however, frequently operate just like hotels—somebody's always on duty, or at least on call.

Do keep in mind that some Europeans are notorious for their strict attitudes toward time and punctuality. Don't expect the front desk to stay open a few minutes late or end the lockout 10 minutes early. Don't knock it; adapt and deal. It's just their way.

Lockout and curfew is useful to know at those hostels that sometimes lock you out of the place for part of a day (in other words, you're not permitted on the premises) while they clean, balance the books, sack out, etc. Though rare in cities, some hostels do have a curfew; be back inside before this time, or you'll get locked out for the night.

Affiliation indicates whether a hostel is affiliated with Hostelling International (HI), the nonprofit global association of world hostels. For more information about what HI organizations do (and do not do), see "A Word About Affiliations" (page 13).

Extras lists some of the other amenities that come with a stay at the hostel. Some—but not all—will be free. There's an amazing variety of services, and almost as big a variety in managers' willingness to do nice things for free. Laundries, for instance, are never free, and there's almost always a charge for meals, lockers, bicycle or other equipment rentals, and other odds and ends. On the other hand, some hostels maintain free information desks, and a few will pick you up at rail stations and the like.

Tips & Tricks

Along with each hostel review, we've also given you a little more information about the hostel, to make your stay a little more informed—and fun. The sidebar below is part of the hostel entry that began above.

Best bet for a bite:

Schwejk (Bohemian cuisine)

What hostellers say:

"Let's rock it."

Gestalt:

Wombatmobile

Safety:

Hospitality:

Cleanliness:

Party index:

What does all that stuff mean? Let's take a look.

Best bet for a bite tells you where to find food in the area; usually we'll direct you to the cheapest and closest supermarket. But sometimes, in the interest of variety—and good eatin'—we'll point you toward a surprising health food store, a farmers' market, a place rich with local color, or even a fancy place well worth the splurge.

Insiders' tip is a juicy secret about the area, something we didn't know until we got to the hostel ourselves.

What hostellers say relates what hostellers told us about a hostel—or what we imagine they would say.

Gestalt is the general feeling of a place, our (sometimes humorous) way of describing what it's about.

Safety rates city hostels on the quality of the neighborhood, the condition of the locks, doors, and windows, *and* the security precautions taken by the hostel staff. (Keep in mind that you should take normal safety precautions at *any* hostel, no matter its rating.)

Here's how this rating breaks down:

No worries

Panic a little bit

Dial 911

Hospitality rates the hostel staff's friendliness toward hostellers (and travel writers).

Smile city

Passive-aggressive

Very hostile hostel

Cleanliness rates, what else, the general cleanliness of a place. Bear in mind that this can change—rapidly—depending on the time of year, turnover in staff, and so forth. Use it only as a general guide.

Spic-and-span

Only span

Don't let the bedbugs bite

The **party index** is our way of tipping you off about the general scene at the hostel:

Rage all night

Party hearty

Lively

Mellow

Downright quiet

Finally, **how to get there** includes directions for how to get to the hostel—by car, bus, train, plane, or, in some cases, even ferry. Subway directions are given in big cities if applicable. Often these directions are complicated, however; in those cases, managers have asked (or we recommend) that you call the hostel for more precise directions.

A Short History of Hostelling

*H*ostelling as we know it began around 1907 when Richard Schirmann, an assistant schoolteacher in the little town of Altena, Germany, decided to make one of the empty classrooms a space for visiting students to sleep. That was not a completely unique idea, as Austrian inns and taverns had been offering reduced rates and bunk space to students since 1885. But Schirmann would develop much grander plans. He was about to start a movement.

His idea was to get students out of the industrial cities and into the countryside. Schirmann was a strong believer that walking and bicycling tours in the fresh air were essential to adolescent development and learning. But such excursions were impossible without a place to spend the night. His logic was simple: Since rural schoolhouses were deserted during weekends and holidays, why not make use of those spaces?

The caretakers of the school he chose agreed to serve as houseparents, and some fast ground rules were established. Students were responsible for piling up the tables and benches in the classroom and laying out thin straw mats on the floor. At some ungodly early-morning hour, the students were to stack the straw mats back up and organize the classroom as they had found it. Boys and girls slept in separate rooms but were treated as equals. Detractors cried scandal, wondering aloud what was going on in these schoolrooms after dark.

The experiment worked, sort of. Altena became a haven for student excursions into the countryside, but finding shelter in other communities proved difficult. Sometimes the situation would become dire. Late one night in the summer of 1909, Schirmann decided it was time to expand his movement beyond Altena. His goal was to establish a network of hostels within walking distance of one another; beginning in a schoolhouse with straw mats, Schirmann eventually acquired the use of a castle. It still stands—the Ur-hostel, if you will—in Altena, and it's still used as a hostel.

After World War I the movement really began to spread. By 1928 there were more than 2,000 hostels worldwide. Today tens of thousands of hostellers stay at HI-affiliated hostels each year, hailing from everywhere from Alaska to Zaire. Thousands more stay at independent hostels. The goal of a single association of hostels located within a day's walk of one another will probably never be realized in the US. But it is reality in many places in Europe.

You may never get to every hostel in Europe. But wherever you do end up, you're likely to find a promising brew of cultural exchange and friendship over pots of ramen noodles and instant coffee almost anywhere you go.

In that sense, perhaps, Richard Schirmann's dream has been realized after all.

A Word About Affiliations

A majority of hostels in this book are affiliated with **Hostelling International (HI);** the rest we've labeled independent hostels.

Hostelling International–affiliated hostels are part of the International Youth Hostel Federation (hihostels.com), which oversees thousands of member hostels in about 70 countries worldwide. Member hostels are held to a number of regulations, such as maximum number of beds per shower, even a minimum amount of space that must exist between top bunks and the ceiling. To get into an HI hostel you must sometimes have an HI membership card (see next section).

Overall, these HI hostels generally earn higher marks from our reviewers than independently run hostels. That's because they usually are in nicer buildings (sometimes purpose-built as a hostel), and the floors are kept cleaner—with staff doing the cleaning, not the hostellers. On the other hand, this organization's mission statement trumpets its contribution to "the education of young people," so be warned that some of its most popular hostels attract youth groups en masse. These places are also usually pretty strict with rules (what did you expect?), curfews, and the like, and some big-city joints—located in huge, suburban tenement-like blocks—seem to thrive on packing in busloads of schoolkids. That said, they also are uniformly clean, safe, informative—if a little blah.

English isn't always spoken well in these hostels, but it is usually spoken by at least one staff member. HI-affiliated city hostels in Europe are generally open 24 hours and year-round. Also take note that many of these *kick you out for part of the day* while they clean, as we've noted above. (There are some exceptions, especially for couples paying extra dough for a double room.) Breakfast is often included in the rate at an HI hostel, and dinner—which you pay for—is usually cheap and filling.

Independent hostels are what we call all the rest. They have no affiliation at all. Some independent owners opted not to join Hostelling International because the dues are high and the rules are strict. Such a decision—in and of itself—does not reflect on the quality of the hostel. It would be foolish to write a hostel off simply because it's not affiliated.

But there's no denying that life in an independent hostel is more laid-back—and that's not always a good thing. Some of them are Party Central, 24 hours a day and night. Liquor isn't always officially off-limits at these places. (In HI joints, you must buy it at either the hostel bar or restaurant, or forget about it.) On the upside: Some independent hostels lock you out, but it's far less common or long-lasting than the lockout at HI hostels. Rooms are homier, but also more crowded or smoky, or less likely to be perfectly clean. Standards vary wildly from place to place. Some are outstandingly fun; some are grungy beyond belief.

As well, a few independent hostels are run by church organizations, such as convents. These obviously have strict lockouts, curfews, and no-alcohol rules. Some of them even ban unmarried couples from sharing a bed. (If they do, we have banned THEM from this book.)

Hostel Memberships & International Booking

First things first. We advise you to get a Hostelling International membership before you set out on your trip.

How do you do that? Easy. Contact the home office of your country's Hostelling International chapter and get a membership card plus other goodies, such as individual country hostelling guides. Membership costs $28 for American adults—cost varies in other countries—and is good for one year. If there's a Hostelling International hostel in your neck of the woods, ask about buying the card there instead. (US residents can also order online at hiusa .org.) Seniors receive a discount: In the US, 55-and-up memberships cost $18 annually. And if you're (or your kids are) under 18? Free, baby.

If you want to try some hostels before committing to the responsibility of owning a card, you can also try before you buy. Just pay a small supplement (about $4 USofficially, this is known as a guest membership). After you've gotten six of those stamps, presto! You're a member by default. As a bonus, many hostels have established discounts for hostellers at businesses in the towns where hostels are located; you might get 10 percent off a meal at a local restaurant, discounted train tickets or museum entrance fees, or other perks. Check with HI to find out before you travel.

If you're the type who needs the security of knowing where you're staying each night of your trip, you might also want to take advantage of HI's international booking network. Not all HI hostels are part of this network, but many are; participating hostels (usually located in big cities or major tourist areas) will call ahead to another international hostel and book your bunk—even in high season if it's humanly possible. It can save you time and stress. Most participants ask for an advance notice of three to seven days; if there's any room, you'll get priority for a bed—you have to prepay with a Visa or MasterCard (plus a $5 US booking fee, converted into the local currency) and you're in. The system is fairly straightforward. However, be prepared to eat the whole cost of the bed if you need to cancel on short notice. There are *no* refunds at HI hostels for cancellation within less than 24 hours, or if you don't like the hostel once you get there.

You do get back all your dough if you cancel more than a day ahead of time. On the other hand, if you never call to cancel a multiday stay, you eat the entire cost of the stay (versus one night's rack rate if you canceled less than a day in advance).

How to Hostel

*H*ostelling is, generally speaking, easy as pie. Plan ahead a bit and use a little common sense, and you'll find that check-in goes pretty smoothly.

Reserving a Bed

Snagging a good bunk will often be your first and biggest challenge, especially if it's high season. Here's our quick primer to getting one.

Summer is high season in Europe, thanks to loads of college students on summer break; Christmas can be a tough bed to book, too, even in chilly cities like Copenhagen or Stockholm. Popular places like London, Paris, Rome, and Berlin seem to be busy almost year-round, so you need to book early in any of those. Want to visit Oktoberfest in Munich? You might have to book a year in advance. Hostellers often have an amazingly laissez-faire attitude about reservations; many simply pull into town on a midnight train, expecting that a bed will be available. No. Sometimes it is. But often it isn't.

Almost every Hostelling International abode takes advance reservations of some form or another, so if you know where you're going to be, use this service. Be aware that you will need a credit card number to hold a bed (some hostels might even require you to send a check in the mail for a deposit). You might need to show up by a certain hour, such as 6 p.m., to check in.

Independent hostels are sometimes stricter and sometimes more lax about reservations. They're often much faster to fill up than HI joints, just because of the wild popularity of these no-rules places. But a growing number of these independent joints now take online reservations.

If you can't or won't reserve in advance, then you must get there early. How early? Office opens at 8 a.m.? Get there at 7 a.m. Hostel's full, and you notice that checkout ends around 11 a.m.? Be at the front desk at 11:05 a.m. in case of cancellations or unexpected checkouts. Doors are closed again till 4:30 p.m.? Come back around 4 p.m. with a paperback and camp out on the porch.

Paying the Piper

Once you're in, be prepared to pay for your night's stay immediately—before you're even assigned a bunk. Take note ahead of time which hostels take credit cards, checks, and so forth. Learn the local currency (mainly euros now), and don't expect a small hostel to be able to change your huge-euro bill for tons of coins so you can do the laundry. (Think it through: You can get coins ahead of time by buying some gum at the airport or train station.)

You will almost always be required to give up your passport and (if you have one) Hostelling International card for the night. Don't panic; sometimes it's a police requirement that a hostel or hotel take your passport. Also, if an emergency happens, the passport helps hostel staff locate your significant others and contact them quickly.

Pay in advance if you want a weekly stay. Often you can get deep discounts, though the downside is that you'll almost never get even a partial refund if you decide you can't stand the place and want to bail before the week is up.

If you're paying by the day, rebook promptly each morning; hostel managers are very busy during the morning hours keeping track of check-ins, checkouts, cleaning duties, and loose cash. You'll make a friend if you're early about notifying them of your plans for the next day. Managers hate bugging guests all morning or all day about whether they'll be staying on. Don't put the staff through this.

All right, so you've secured a bed and paid up. Now you have to get to it. This may be no easy task at some hostels, where staff and customers look and act like one and the same. A kindly manager will probably notice you bumbling around and take pity. As you're being shown to your room, you're also likely to get a short tour of the facilities and a briefing on the ground rules.

On checkout you'll get your card and passport back. You might need to pay a small amount if you lose your room key—usually about $5 but sometimes as much as $25 US.

Knowing the Ground Rules

There's one universal ground rule at almost every hostel in Europe: You are responsible for serving and cleaning up after yourself. And there's a corollary rule: Be courteous. So while you're welcome to use the kitchen facilities (if a kitchen's available), share that space with your fellow guests—don't spread your five-course meal all over the counter space and ran-getop burners if other hungry folks are waiting. And never, ever leave a sink full of dirty pots and pans behind (unless it's one of those rare hostels where staff do the dishes). That's just bad form.

Hostel guests are often asked to mark their names and check-in dates on any food they store in a refrigerator. Do it. Only a shelf marked "free food" is truly up for grabs; anything else belongs to other hostellers, so don't touch it. (Some hostellers get touchy about people stealing their grub.) Some of the better-run hostels have a spice rack and other kitchen essentials on hand—if spices and oils are in the cupboard or on the counter without markings, those are probably communal. If you're not sure whether something is communal, ask someone who looks official.

Then there's "the lockout," a source of bitter frustration among non-European hostellers. A few hostels do indeed kick everybody out in the morning and don't let them back in until mid-afternoon or even early evening; big-city hostels are less likely to do this, but some still do it. Lockouts tend to run from around 9:30 a.m. (which is ungodly, but pretty typical) until 5 or 6 p.m., during which time your bags might be inside your room—while you're out on the streets. A few places let you back in around 2 or 3 p.m.

This practice has its pros and cons; managers justify a lockout by noting that it forces travelers to interact with locals and also allows a hostel's staff to "meticulously clean" the rooms. The *real* reason is often that the hostel can't or won't pay staff to hang around and babysit you all day. On the other hand, we've never seen official European hostels become quasi-residential situations stuffed with couch potatoes living there for weeks and months at a time, like some North American hostels do. So maybe these lockouts do some good, after all.

Curfews are surprisingly common in Europe in smaller cities and towns; usually the front doors lock between 11 p.m. and midnight, and they won't give you a key if you want to party later. Big-city hostels generally have some system in place to let you get in 24 hours a day: a guard, numbered keypad, or room key that also opens the main door. We have noted hostels' opening hours in this book, but check anyway if you're unsure or plan to burn the midnight oil.

In our reviews we've tried to identify the hostels that enforce lockouts. Usually you wouldn't want to be hanging out in a hostel in the middle of the day anyway, but after several sleepless nights of travel—or when you're under the weather—daytime downtime sure is appreciated. So read the listings carefully. Note that even if we haven't listed a lockout or a curfew, it might exist. It's safest to assume you will get kicked out at 9 a.m. for part or all of the daylight hours, and (except in big cities) will need to be back in the building by midnight.

Finally, some hostels enforce a limit on your stay—anywhere from three days, if the hostel is really popular, to about two weeks.

Savvy budget travelers, of course, have learned how to get around this rule: They simply suck it up, spend a night at a local inn (or competing hostel)—then check right back into the original hostel first thing in the morning.

Etiquette & Smarts

To put it simply, use common sense. Hostellers are a refreshingly flexible bunch. All these people are able to make this system work by looking after one another; remember, in a hostel you're a community member first and a consumer second. With that in mind, here are some guidelines for how to act:

- The first thing you should do after check-in is get your bed made. When you're assigned a bed, stick to it. Don't spread your stuff out on other bunks, even if they look empty. Someone's going to be coming in late-night for one of them; you can bet the backpack on it.
- Be sure to lock your valuables in a locker or safe if one is available. Or in the trunk of your car, if you have one. Or stuff it deep in your sleeping bag. Good hostels offer lockers as a service; it might cost a little, but it's certainly worth it. Always bring at least one padlock over to Europe in your suitcase in case the hostel has run out of 'em or charges an arm and a leg for one.
- Set toiletries and anything else you need in a place where they are easily accessible. This avoids your having to paw through your bag late at night, potentially disturbing other guests from their slumber. Same goes for early-morning departures: If you're taking off at the crack of dawn, take precautions not to wake the whole place. People don't like it.
- If you're leaving early in the morning, try to make all arrangements with the manager before going to bed the night before. Managers are usually accommodating and pleasant folk, but guests are expected to respect their privacy and peace of mind by not pushing things too far. Dragging a manager out of bed at four in the morning to check out, call a taxi, settle a bill, or for some other matter is pushing it.
- Do a little bit to keep your bathroom and kitchen area clean. A quick wiping off of the shower floor with a towel after you use it takes just a second and makes a big difference. Spilled shaving cream on the sink, some pasta sauce on the stovetop? Grab a towel or some Kleenex and scrub it off. Again: takes just a second.
- Finally, be sure to remember the quiet hours (after 10 p.m., basically). Some hostels have curfews, but very few force a lights-out. If you're up after hours, be respectful. Don't crank the television or radio too loud; don't scream in the hallways late at night; don't chat on a cell phone at top volume with your girl/boyfriend back home. We all need sleep.

Packing

Those dainty hand towels and dapper shaving kits and free soaps you get at a hotel won't be anywhere in sight at the hostel. In fact, even some of the base essentials may not be available—even kitchens are not a given in European hostels, for instance, so check our listings carefully for places that lack one.

You're on your own, so bring everything you need to be comfortable. There are only a few things you can reliably expect a hostel to supply:

- a bed frame with a mattress and pillow
- shower and toilet facilities
- a common room with some spartan furniture
- maybe a few heavy blankets

More and more hostels are edging closer to full-service, "upscale" hostelling. But they are still the exception rather than the rule. So bring stuff like this to keep your journey through hostel territory comfortable:

- If you're traveling abroad from the US, you need a passport. Unlike US hostels, a European hostel will often take your passport as collateral when you check in. Don't get nervous; this is normal. It's the European equivalent of taking down your driver's license number when you write a check. However, in the unlikely event someone loses your passport, make sure you've got a backup copy (with the issuing office, date, and passport number clearly visible) in your luggage and also back home with friends or family. That's the only quick way to get a new passport issued fast.
- Hostelling International membership cards are a good thing to have on hand—most of the official European hostels require one just to stay. They can be purchased at many foreign HI hostels at the local rate (usually about $28 US annually per adult; free for under-18s); you can also buy cards at HI-affiliated US hostels ahead of time, or from the American Youth Hostels headquarters in Washington, DC. Log on to hiusa.org for more information. If you can't get a card before you arrive in Europe and you'll be there at least a week, don't panic: You can buy an HI "guest stamp" for about €3 (about $4 US), and when you collect six of those, you get a free card. This card identifies you as a certified superhosteller and gets you the very cheapest rate for your bed in all HI (and also some unaffiliated) hostels. At $2 to $4 US per night, the savings can add up fast. Sometimes that membership card also gets you deals at

local restaurants, bike shops, and tours. Again, it will be easier to deal with the front desk at some of the more cautious hostels (even nonmember ones) if you can flash one of these cards.

- **Red alert!** Do not plan on using your sleeping bag at every hostel. Lots of places simply won't allow them—problems with ticks and other creatures dragged in from the woods created that prohibition. The alternative is a "sleep sack," basically two sheets sewn together with a flimsy makeshift pillowcase. You can find them online, at travel stores, or make your own. Personally we hate these confining wraps, and we rarely get through the night in one without having it twist around our bodies so tight that we wake up wanting to charge it with attempted manslaughter. Our preferred method is to bring our own pair of sheets (though that might be too much extra stuff to carry if you're backpacking or traveling light).

  Some hostels give you free linens; most that don't will rent you sheets for about $1 to $3 US per night. You don't get charged for use of a hostel's standard army-surplus blankets and all the musty charm that comes with them.

- Some people bring their own pillows, as those supplied tend to be on the frumpy side. This is a good idea if you're traveling by car and can afford the space. Small pillows are also useful for sleeping on trains and buses.
- We definitely suggest earplugs for light sleepers, especially for urban hostels—but also in case you get caught in a room with a heavy snorer.
- A small flashlight is a must—not only for late-night reading but also to find your bed without waking the entire dorm. And they're very handy in power outages and emergencies.
- A little bit of spice is always nice, especially after one too many nights of bland pasta meals. The cost of basil, oregano, and the like in convenience stores on the road is way too high. Buy it cheaply before you leave and pack it in jars or small plastic bags. It weighs next to nothing.
- Check which hostels have laundry facilities. Some don't, so you'll need to schlep your stuff to the local Laundromat from time to time. It'll be expensive, so bring lots of money. If you do stay in a hostel with a laundry, take advantage, absolutely. There's nothing more liberating than traveling in clean clothes.
- Wearing flip-flops or other plastic sandals in the shower might help you avoid a case of athlete's foot.

- Finally, be sure your travel towel is the quick-drying type. Otherwise you'll wind up with mold and mildew and muck in your pack—which means your socks, your notebook, and your breakfast-purloined snacks. Yuck. A ShamWow-type cloth or two can be a lifesaver not only on the road, but also when you've spilled something in the communal kitchen. (Camera guy, you gettin' this?) But dude, remember: Don't toss those babies in the dryer. That destroys their miraculous absorbency powers in a heartbeat. Dryers are like Kryptonite . . . if your towel . . . were Superman.

Traveling in Europe

GETTING THERE

Take a careful look at your transportation options when planning a hostel journey. You should be able to hop from city to city by bus or train without a problem, but you could have some serious trouble getting to many rural European hostels without a rental car.

From North America by Plane

The airline business is crazy: Great deals and rip-off fares come and go with a regularity that is frightening to behold—supply, demand, season, the stock market, and random acts of cruelty or kindness all appear to contribute to the quixotic nature of fares.

As a result, there is no one simple piece of advice we can give you, other than this: Find a darned good travel agent who cares about budget travelers, and trust him/her with all the planning. You can cruise the Internet if you like, too, and you might find an occasional great deal your agent doesn't know about. Just make sure the sellers are reputable before giving out that credit-card number.

A couple tips:

- Charters are often the cheapest way to go, but it's no-frills all the way. You'll need to do some serious Web cruising and calling and Sunday newspaper reading to find the best deals, though.
- Phoning a student travel agency in your hometown or city is a great first call—they know more about cheap flights than anyone.
- Obviously, if you have any Web savvy at all, the very best way to score cheap tickets is to cruise the Web, using sites like Orbitz, Kayak, Expedia, and Hipmunk. We're not endorsing any one of these over the others; they all work, to some extent, and they all fall short in some areas. Mix 'n' match, we say.

From Europe by Plane

Flights within Europe used to be fantastically expensive. However, times are changing: A raft of cut-rate short-hop airlines have sprung up, such as Easyjet, Ryanair, and Virgin Express (there are plenty of others, too). Check Sunday papers, travel agents, glossy travel magazines, and websites for the latest-breaking deals, and be prepared to sometimes fly into or out of a weird airport to save dough. But any airport in London or Paris is fine; even if it's an hour from the city, it's worth it.

From Europe by Train

Most folks travel by train around Europe, and it's a sensible choice. Services and connections are generally good, so getting around by rail is normally a straightforward matter of booking and then taking a long-distance journey, possibly with a change or two en route. You've got two choices: (1) Buy point-to-point tickets for every leg of the journey, or (2) buy a Europe-wide pass.

If you're math- and map-friendly, buy a copy of the *Thomas Cook European Rail Timetable* (yes, it's a *real book,* just like this one) before you go—or in an English-language bookstore in London, Paris, or elsewhere in Europe after you arrive. It's an invaluable reference to the changing train schedules of Great Britain and Eastern and Western Europe. Of course, you can use the Web to research fares and schedules—but that's not as much fun. And you can't get online when your train's speeding through a tunnel in the Alps.

From England by Train

There's only one way to get to Europe from England by train: on a **Eurostar** (eurostar.com). They've got a monopoly on the sub-Chunnel service that takes you from England to Brussels or Paris in under three hours. They advertise that you can have breakfast in Soho and lunch in Paris—without the delays of airport check-in and checkout and with pretty minimal customs and immigration formalities—and it's pretty much true. From either Paris or Brussels, you can then take a daytime or overnight train directly to most other European capitals.

Of course, you pay extra for the privilege. Round-trip tickets can run as inexpensive as about £100 (about $125 US), if you book more than three weeks in advance, and they can also cost much more (say, £300 or more, about $400 US, round-trip) if you book on short notice or travel during a summer weekend. Note to self: Plan ahead. Also, take note that buying a one-way ticket isn't usually cheaper than purchasing a round-tripper. So you might as well go whole hog.

At least there are big discounts for Eurail and BritRail pass holders, as well as for travelers under age 26. The Eurail discounts vary, so check with Eurail when you book.

It's easiest to book ahead through your travel agent at home or online, but Eurostar also has offices in London's Waterloo Station, Paris's Gare du Nord, and Brussels's Gare du Midi.

One extra plus with Eurostar: If you somehow miss your train, they will let you reschedule your ride for another convenient and available time—within certain limits—at no extra penalty. Wouldn't it be nice if the airlines worked that way? (Dream on.)

Getting Around Europe by Train

Using trains in Europe is an absolute snap, and damned fun. You've got a few options on how to do it: (1) Buy point-to-point tickets for every leg of the journey at stations, (2) get a regional pass, or (3) buy a Europe-wide pass.

Obviously the easiest way is behind door #3. Eurail passes are key if you're touring the Continent and to avoid lines and hassles. Plus you'll usually save money, assuming you're traveling widely. These passes are a great deal for covering big distances. (For small trips or countries, get local tickets or passes instead.)

Rail Europe (800-622-8600 in the US; 800-361-7245 in Canada; raileurope.com) sells the passes via phone and the Internet. Eurail passes aren't cheap, but they're super-convenient and cover almost everything. Just remember that you've gotta play by certain rules. Wait until the first day you're going to use it, then go to the station earlier than your departure time and have the pass validated (stamped) by a ticket agent. Write the current date into the first square (it should have a "1" beneath it)—and remember to put the day (not the month) first (on top).

Now it gets easier. Just show your pass to ticket agents whenever you want to reserve a seat on a train—which is crucial in summer season, on weekends, and during rush hours. The ticket agent, hopefully smiling, will print you out a seat reservation, which you will then show to the conductor on the train. (If you can't or won't get a reservation, just show your pass to the conductor. Sometimes he'll let you get on anyway if the train's not full.)

The pass is long and made of cardboard; don't fold, bend, or otherwise mangle it (which can be difficult to achieve while fumbling for your money belt at the station as the train whips in). For some reason, that might invalidate the whole thing if it's not in pristine condition. Washed it in the wash? You're probably out a few hundred bucks. Don't let that happen.

The cost of these passes depends on a few things, including how long you're traveling and how much comfort you want. First-class passes, which anyone over 27 is required to buy, cost more and give you a little more legroom. Call one of the railpass vendors listed above for the very latest pricing information.

The full Global pass currently costs about $460 US for 15 consecutive days of travel if you're under 26 years old, with prices going up from there for 21-day, one-month, two-month, and three-month (about US $1,275) passes. If you're over 26, you pay a lot more: $710 US for the same 15-days-in-a-row pass, and you've gotta ride second class on all trains. Children ages 4 to 11 get half off the regular adult prices, while children under 4 ride free. A flexible Global pass (formerly known as the Flexipass) may be a smarter bet: it gives you 10 to 15 days over a two-month period for $740 to $970 US. Those over age 26 will pay $1,135 to $1,500 US for the same 10- to 15-day flexible pass, but once again, for those folks it's all second class, all the time. You can't sneak into first class. Don't sweat it, though: Usually you can't tell the difference between first and second class on a European train anyway.

- Point-to-point tickets are the best route to go if you're just blowing through a single country in a hurry and won't keep traveling to other countries shortly. Get them at stations at ticket windows or—if you have cash or credit cards—automatic machines.
- Combo passes: Eurail also offers three- to five-country and one- to two-country combo passes in a bewildering variety; check the Eurail website for the current offerings and prices.

A few more tips on cross-European train travel:

- If you're just buying point-to-point tickets, go for second class.
- For longer distances and overnight trips, you might want to take a sleeper car (also known as a *couchette*). At around $30 to $50 US extra—a railpass covers a seat, not a sleepable *couchette*—it saves you a night in a hotel or hostel and gets you closer to where you want to go. The downside is that you sleep four or six to a little bunkroom. On a moving, noisy train. You can also pay a lot more (usually $100 to $200 or more US) for a private double compartment for you and your sweetie. Not cheap, but I've used that option a few times, and it was well worth it for the time savings. Plus, it was nice to have a little private space for a change. Europe's not a very private place.

- Remember that trains don't run as frequently on weekends. Saturday is usually the worst day to travel due to light schedules. International trains and sleeper cars usually run seven days a week, but Friday and Sunday are feast or famine—thin scheduling or packed-full trains. Check schedules and think like a local.

From Europe by Bus

Eurolines (eurolines.com) is a Europe-wide company running comfortable long-distance buses around Europe for very competitive rates, certainly cheaper than trains and cheaper than planes if you're booking on short notice. They serve quite a network of cities.

GETTING AROUND
By Train

Trains are still king in Europe. Sure, the car dominates everyday life for locals, but when you're a tourist you just can't beat the iron horse.

Though these rail systems cross an incredible variety of landscapes, even the iron horse can't get everywhere. It's likely, at some point, that you will need to supplement your train travel with some form of gondola, lift, bus, cog railway, or steam train—all part of the fun.

Tickets & passes

What to buy? If you're going to be doing lots of short city-to-city hops, just buy tickets each day; it's cheaper. If you'll be in the area for a week or two, get a pass.

Always remember to punch your train ticket before you get on the train; there will be a machine in every station that stamps the current date and time on the ticket, showing the conductor that it has been "used up."

By Bus

Buses can be cheaper than the train or more expensive, depending on where you are; it's not a given that the bus is much cheaper. They're extremely useful in places where trains simply don't go—reasonably on time, scenic, and with lots of locals riding alongside you happy to give advice or opinions or soccer scores.

It might take you all day to make connections, but most bus drivers are helpful and knowledgeable. As a bonus, they'll sometimes let you off where you want to go even if there isn't an actual bus stop there. They are also quite accustomed to hostellers asking "Where's my stop?" and handle the situation calmly and professionally. Usually. (In small towns and rural areas, though, sometimes anything goes. Smile and deal with rudeness or incompetence calmly. We're all human.)

In many cities, you can also buy tickets in bus or subway stations, at newsstands and cigarette shops, even right on the bus—it's usually more expensive to buy 'em directly from the driver than anywhere else, however.

In most countries, you will need to punch your ticket at the start of a local bus ride; there will be a machine either at the bus stop or in the front or back of the bus. This can be confusing; don't panic. Single-ride city bus tickets are usually good only for the next one hour (if you don't use it by then, try to get a refund at a ticket window), while most transit passes are good for a day or more.

You can purchase Eurolines bus passes allowing free travel among 35 European cities served by the line; these are available for periods of either 15 or 30 days and cost from €175 (about $230 US) per under-26 traveler—for a 15-day pass in the low season (early and late winter, early spring)—up to €385 (about $480 US) for a 30-day pass in the high season (basically, summer plus the week between Christmas and New Year's). Buy the passes online at eurolines-pass.com. Travelers over age 26 pay about 20 percent more above those rates.

By Boat

On a few occasions you might be cruising lakes or rivers; your Eurail pass covers part or all of some of these journeys. Usually you get a discount, not a free ride. You get a 20 percent discount on ferries to the crazy Spanish island of Ibiza, to take one example, and a 30 percent discount on Irish Ferries boats to Wales or France. Other Eurail-discounted ferries run between England and the Netherlands, Denmark and Sweden, and Greece and Italy (some of these are free!).

By Car

Renting a car is definitely the most expensive way to travel in Europe, but it does have its advantages. You've got privacy with a few of your well-chosen buds. You can cover the countryside in more depth (contrary to popular belief, European trains don't go everywhere, and neither do buses). Best of all, you have almost complete freedom to go where you want, when you want—no more waiting for the 9:10 from Brussels or that idiosyncratic British bus driver winding his way among the Peaks.

Gas isn't cheap—it can cost 1½ times more than what it costs in North America. At least those tiny Euro-cars get terrific mileage. Watch out for traffic jams, too. Even on the open highway, weekends, holidays, and rush hours can bring things to a grinding halt. Do your driving during lunchtime or on a Sunday to minimize traffic (but Sundays at the end of holiday weekends are busy, too).

How to save money renting? Try these strategies:

- Rent in Germany. It's the cheapest country in Europe in which to rent a car, with plenty of opportunities to rent in one city and drop off—with little or no penalty— in another (within Germany). That country's high-speed autobahns are free, too, which is remarkable—the high-speed highways in most other European countries are toll roads, and pretty expensive compared per mile with US highways.

- Rates in France and Austria aren't too bad, and deals can sometimes be had in the UK or Ireland with advance booking while still in the US. (Expensive places to rent a car? Denmark, Sweden, Norway, Switzerland, and Italy. We didn't rent in Spain, Portugal, or Greece—spend a day alongside daredevil locals and you'll see why.)

- Learn how to drive a stick shift, for gosh sakes: It can cost you up to twice as much per day for an automatic-transmission car.

- Book your rental ahead, from your home country. It's cheaper. Rentals will set you back $40 to $70 US a day for a small car, and that might or might not include heavy local taxes and insurance costs tacked onto the price. (Automatic transmission will be more expensive.)

- Think about renting or leasing for a few weeks to a month, rather than just a week-end. Often you save a boatload of money (on a per day basis) by booking one long rental. Check with a US-based company such as Kemwel (877-820-0668 or kemwel .com), which offers long-term rentals for a fraction of the daily rate if you book ahead from your home country. They do short-term rentals, as well. All the standard chain car rental outfits do business in Europe, though rates are usually quite a bit higher than they are in the US.

- Speeds and distance in Europe are usually measured in kilometers. (But in Ireland, England, Scotland, and Wales, miles still rule.) To remind you, 1 kilometer is a little less than 0.6 mile, and 100 miles equal roughly 160 kilometers. Here are some common speed limits and distances you might see on road signs, with their US equivalents:

$$40 \text{ kph} = 25 \text{ miles per hour}$$
$$100 \text{ kph} = 62 \text{ miles per hour}$$
$$50 \text{ kilometers away} = 31 \text{ miles away}$$

Gas is measured in liters (spelled "litres" in Europe and abbreviated "l") and there are about four liters to one US gallon. Gas prices are listed per liter, so multiply by four and then convert into your home currency to estimate the price per gallon you'd pay back home—you'll probably be shocked. (Wish you'd brought a bike yet?)

It's important to know the driving rules. In the UK (England, Scotland, and Wales) and Ireland, you drive on the left, which takes a lot of getting used to, especially at rotary intersections. In continental Europe, however, you always drive on the right. Local laws must be paid attention to: Swiss traffic laws require you to stop at all crosswalks, for example, if someone's waiting to cross. European drivers tend to be fairly aggressive, especially in open-highway situations—that supercharged car in your rearview might have just been doing 100 miles an hour. Pull over and let him by. And don't give the finger or make other obscene gestures. You could get tossed in the pokey or fined heavily for it on the spot. Yes, really.

PHONES

You've got a cell phone, obviously—and it should work in Europe, though you'll have to do one of two things to make it so.

1. Contact your carrier about a European add-on plan. This assumes your phone can actually work in Europe. (Not all can; sometimes different customers of the same carrier even get different treatment, we hear. Ask nicely.)
2. Purchase a local SIM card (a little square data chip) before you leave, online, or at the local airport when you arrive, then plug it in. (Note to iPhone users: According to Apple support, if the phone's iTunes software doesn't function correctly after you plug in a new SIM, you may need to *restore the entire freaking phone.* Translation: You may need to *erase* the phone. Be careful, and get good technical advice before you decide to do the SIM swaparama.)

So a jacked-up cell's the most convenient way to call while on the Continent, but is it the cheapest? Not always. Believe it or not, people still use real phones and phone cards in this region. Buy local phone cards at tobacco shops, train station windows, or corner markets and stick 'em into the slots in the pay phones that are still peppered throughout the European continent. Don't bother trying to call Mom and Dad back home with these cards, though—they're best for short chats within a country (to the next hostel, for instance) or emergencies.

MONEY

You'll need it, that's for sure.

First things first. Remember this simple rule about cash: Get it from an ATM whenever possible, because that's almost always the easiest and lowest-cost way to get it.

Second, pay attention to where you are. All of the European countries used to have their own unique bills and coins, which was quaint but also something of a pain. You often had to pay big fees to change money when traveling from one country to another. And you also had to get rid of all your loose change before you left each country, since change bureaus don't change coins. Basically it was a use-it-or-lose-it situation.

However, in 2002 most European countries—including most, but not all, of the countries covered in this book—changed over to a single unified currency called the euro. Though it was a shame to see lire, schillings, and francs disappear, this change did make life quite a bit easier for travelers. They no longer needed to stand in long lines and change money while traveling between European countries. And it became suddenly easy to compare prices for an item or a meal from country to country, which was a real chore before the switchover.

In this book, we have listed prices in euros for the countries that use them. The euro symbol looks like this: €. It's easy to estimate costs in euros, because one euro is worth just a little more than one US dollar. To convert when you're in a hurry, just switch the price to dollars in your mind, then add a tiny bit extra. Ten euros = about 13 bucks. In this book, we have used an exchange rate of €1.00 = $1.25 US, though the value may fluctuate year to year.

For all countries that still use their own currencies, such as England, we have printed prices in the local currency and converted the prices to US dollars. Our favorite quick-and-dirty website for performing currency conversions is xe.com. Click on "currency converter" and convert to your heart's content; you get exchange rate calculations using live, up-to-the-minute rates.

Having trouble remembering which countries use the euro? So did we, until we made up a little memory aid: "BAFFLING PIGS are IN." Look at the first letters of those first two words: They remind you that Belgium, Austria, France, Finland (not covered in this book), Luxembourg, Italy, the Netherlands, Germany, Portugal, Ireland, Greece, and Spain are now IN the euro game. Who's out? Norway, the UK (including Northern Ireland), Denmark, Sweden, Switzerland, and all the Eastern European countries—including Hungary and the Czech Republic, which are covered in this book—are still using their own money, though that could change. (We didn't make up a memory aid for this. But use NUDSSEE if you like. It just sounds a little too dirty for a PG-rated book like this one.) Some countries, like Denmark and the Czech Republic, have debated converting to euros in the near future—but that's hardly a certainty.

If you must change money—let's say you're traveling from England to Switzerland (which still use their own money), won't be coming back to England, and want to get rid of all your English pounds and get Swiss francs—try to find a big bank instead of a tourist office, train station, currency exchange office, or small bank. Their rates are all terrible, and they figure you won't know the difference. But a big bank usually has something like fair rates.

SAFETY

As exciting as hostelling your way through European cities might be, you've got to be on the alert at all times and remember that you're traveling in cities. Avoid wandering unfamiliar streets at night, and try to stay in well-lit areas with plenty of foot traffic. Expect to be jostled by crowds, assaulted by noise, panhandled, and pickpocketed. Guys: If you carry a wallet, keep it in your front pants pocket instead of your back pocket. Gals: If you carry a purse, carry it across your body rather than over your shoulder. (Even backpacks aren't fail-safe: Thieves occasionally use razors to slash off the straps and grab 'em on the go. While riding scooters. Rad.) Above all, get a good map and study it before you go out—the worst feeling in the world is that of being utterly lost, late at night, in a dicey area without a cop or friendly face in sight.

Pack your prescription medications carefully in separate bags so customs officials can easily examine them. Make a photocopy of your passport and carry it separately from the real thing. (Also leave a copy with your folks or best friend back home.)

Don't walk alone late at night. Bring a whistle or other noisemaker for emergencies. Don't flash your cash around in bars. Don't challenge the guys on the train to an argument over competing religious doctrines. Etc. ibid. et al.

OK, now that we've got you completely paranoid, don't forget to have a good time! None of these imagined terrible things will probably ever happen to you.

TRAVEL INSURANCE

Travel insurance might seem like a useless expenditure, but it can come in handy when the worst happens. This insurance typically covers everything from baggage loss and injuries in an air travel accident to medical expenses incurred while you're traveling. It's also helpful if someone puts a dent in that rental car and you waived the necessary collision/damage coverage to save a couple bucks.

It's not even expensive—often something like $15 to $50 US, depending on the length of your trip and where you're going, for some basic medical coverage. One emergency visit to the doctor and you've made back the cost already.

We strongly recommend buying some form of travel insurance before you go.

SPEAKING EUROPEAN

English will get you by in touristed areas and cities of Europe, which likely covers most of the places you're going. However, you'll occasionally want to get way off the beaten track, and in those places you might have a little more trouble. Just think: This might be your only chance to forge a meaningful bond while getting the right bus tickets.

So learn a little language before you go, and don't despair. You'll be OK with a bit of brushing up and a little sign or body language where necessary. Hereforth, a short primer on the Big Four: French, Italian, German, and Spanish.

Bon courage! Buona fortuna!
Viel glüeck! ¡Y buena suerte!

Français (French)

What they say	How they say it (approximately)	What they mean
oui	we	yep
non	no!	nope
peut-être	put-Ed	maybe
un	uh	one
deux	do	two
trois	twa	three
quatre	cat	four
billet/billets	B.A.	ticket/tickets
première classe	premier class	first class
deuxième classe	doozie "M" class	second class
autobus	aw toe booze	bus
non fumer	naw foo may	non-smoking
passe d'Eurail	pass door rail	Eurail pass
train	tren	train
quai/voie	kay/vwa	platform/track
voiture	vwa-choor	car number of a train
voiture-lit	vwa-choor leet	sleeping car of a train
place	plass	seat
pardon	par don	excuse me/I'm sorry
de Nice	de niece	from Nice
à Paris	ah, pear "E"	to Paris
je voudrais	zhuh food ray	I'd like . . .
j'ai besoin de	J.B. swan, duh	I need . . .
merci	mare "C"	thank you
merci bien	mare CBN	thanks a lot!
bonjour	bon sure	good morning, good afternoon
bon soir	bon swar	good evening, good night
au revoir	oh, vwar	good-bye
à bientôt	ah, be in tote	see ya soon
de rien	darien	you're welcome
monsieur	miss yew	sir
madame	ma damn	ma'am

mademoiselle	madam was hell	miss
mesdames	may damn	ladies, girls
messieurs	may sure	sirs, guys
ceci	sir see	this one
cela	sir la	that one

Italiano (Italian)

What they say	How they say it (approximately)	What they mean
si	see/she	yes
no	no	no means no
una/uno	ooh nah/noh	one
due	do "A"?	two
tre	tray	three
quattro	kwa-tro	four
biglietta/biglietti	Billy Etta/Billy A.T.	ticket/tickets
prima classe	preema class "A"	first class
seconda classe	sick on da class "A"	second class
non fumatori	naw foo ma tory	nonsmoking
passa di treno	passa the traino!	train pass
treno	traino	train
binario	beanario	platform/track number
scusami	skoo-za-mee	excuse me
mi dispiace	me "D" spee-ah-chee	I'm sorry
grazie	gratsy	thank you
grazie mille	gratsy mealy	thanks a lot!
bongiorno	Bon Jovi	good morning
buona sera	wanna Sarah	good afternoon, good evening
ciao	chow	hi; bye
ciao-ciao	chow-chow	bye-bye
arrivaderci	a-riva-dare-chay	good-bye
prego	prego	you're welcome
pronto	pronto!	yes?
da Roma	d'aroma	from Rome
per Firenze	pear friends, ah	to Florence

vorrei	vhooray	I'd like . . .
ho bisogno di	obi sanyo "D"	I need . . .
questa	kwest-ah	this one
quella	kwell-ah	that one

Deutsch (German)

What they say	How they say it (approximately)	What they mean
Guten tag	Goo ten tag	hello, good day
bitte	beetah	please [or] excuse me; may I help you?
danke	donkey	thanks
danke schöne	donkey shame	thank you very much
ein	ine	one
zwei	dzvye	two
drei	dry	three
zug	zoog	train
U-Bahn	oo baan	subway
S-Bahn	S baan	commuter/suburban train
Bahnof	baaaa-noff	train station
Hauptbahnof	how baa-noff	main train station
Bus	booze	bus
Ich möchte	Eek mookta	I'd like . . .
ein Fahrkart	eine far carta	a ticket
Jugendherberge	you get her burger	hostel
Doppelzimmer	dopple zimmer	double room
platz	plats	city square
sprechen	spricken	speak
Sie Englisch	zee English	English

Español (Spanish)

What they say	How they say it (approximately)	What they mean
sí	see!	yes
no	no	Nanette
buenos dias	Wayne O's DS	good day; hello

señor	say NYOUR	sir; mister; dude
señora	say NYOUR-a	ma'am; Mrs.
señorita	seen yer EATer	miss; dudette; cutie
¿Como está?	comb "A" star?	how's it hanging?
Esta bueno	"A" star WAYNE-O	goin' great
¿Como se llama?	Como say ah, Ma?	what's your name?
soy Pablo	soy PAH-blow	I'm Paul
se habla	say HAH-blah	do you speak . . .
Inglés	een-GLAY-say	English
iglesias	"E" CLAY-see-us	I can be your hero [or] church
donde está	One day, a STAR!	where's . . . .
la estación de tren	la stash he OWN, day TRAIN	. . . the train station
uno	oooooh, no	one
dos	dose	two
tres	trace	three
boleto	bow LAY toe	ticket
boletos	bow LAY toast	tickets
tren	train	train
pista	PEE-stah	train track
numero	NEW mare O	number
a Madrid	ah, my DREDS!	to Madrid
de Barcelona	day BARTH a LOANer	from Barcelona
hoy	oy	today
mañana	money ANNA	tomorrow
por favor	pour fah-VOUR	please
gracias	GRASS, see us	thanks
muchas gracias	MOOCH us, GRASS see us	thank you so so much
obrigado	oh Brie? GOD! Oh . . .	thank you (Portugal only)
de nada	day NAH dah	you're welcome
plaza	plaza	public square
buenas noches	Wayne O's Nachos	good night
hasta la vista	Ah stah la VEE stah	bye, baby
hasta luego	a star Lou EGGO	so long!

The HOSTELS

Austria

*O*nly a shred of its former size and glory, Austria is somehow still one of Europe's best-kept secret travel getaways—cheap, safe, friendly, unbelievably scenic, and even a little exotic, with reminders of various empires, good and bad, that passed this way. You can also ski like a banshee (experts only, please), surrender to Vienna's urban mishmash of architecture and coffee, experience Salzburg's almost too-perfect *Sound of Music* cuteness and classical music, admire Innsbruck's position at the foot of the towering Alps, soak in Bregenz's lakeside quiet . . . and those are just the places you've heard about. There are many more towns and cities you never dreamed existed.

Contact ANTO, the Austrian National Tourist Office (austria.info, 212-944-6880 in the US), for lots more information on this wonderful, mountainous country; they have tons of info on skiing, snowboarding, food, rustic hotels, golf—just about everything.

And remember: Austria remains a good value for your travel dollar; the conversion to euros hasn't changed that one bit, and a typical dorm room here can cost as little as €12 (about $16 US) a night. Given the amazing scenery, it's well worth a stop or side trip on your cross-European jaunt.

Practical Details

Austrian trains are good, not great. Many of the cars have six-seat compartments, where for the next six hours you're staring down five people you don't know. And distances are long; definitely bring a book. It's also likely that at some point you will need to supplement your train travel with some form of gondola, lift, bus, cog railway, steam train—something. That can add to the fun. The Austrians also have an interesting system of getting you to really rural areas called a "postbus." Long, sleek, and comfortable, these buses take you up mountain passes and into tiny hamlets where no train would dare venture. They're cheap, too.

You can even get around nicely by boat. The DDSG (you don't need to know the full name; we don't have all day here) runs one ferry per day on summer Sundays from Vienna up the Danube to Krems and Dürnstein and then back. It leaves Vienna (on the river, obviously, just on the bridge next to the U-Bahn stop) at 8:30 in the morning, starts back in midafternoon, and finally arrives at around 9 p.m. A round trip is about €30 ($37.50 US) per adult, about €15 ($19 US) for children age 10–15. (Younger kids cruise for free.) Other ferry companies run boats along the pastoral stretch of the river between Krems and Melk, and around Lake Konstanz (also known as Lake Constance and the Bodensee)—that big lake connecting Switzerland, Austria, and Germany.

Austria's country code is 43. To call most Austrian hostels from North America, dial 011-43 and DROP THE INITIAL ZERO from any number printed in this book. To call most Austrian hostels from within Austria, dial the number and SUBSTITUTE 0 as the international long-distance code. But Vienna has special rules—see below. To call home from Austria, dial 001 and then the number you are calling.

VIENNA (WIEN)

For most travelers, eastern Austria can be defined in just one word.

Vienna.

It's actually supposed to be pronounced "Veen," or something close to that, in German. But no matter. This city is one of Europe's most distinctive places—as instantly recognizable as Venice. And yet, it's not a place thoroughly stuck in the past. Beer, wine, chocolate, lingerie, ice cream, clubs, discos, cafes . . . neighborhood after neighborhood of university students, well-heeled locals . . . cool architecture. This is not just some frumpy 19th-century town where guys looking like Beethoven and Freud wander around town in powdered wigs looking for pianos to play and libidos to psychoanalyze on a couch. (The city does have an amazing history, though. Hapsburg emperors once ruled this part of Europe with iron fists from the Hofburg Palace and assorted villas around town. There are also some Roman ruins downtown.)

Independent travelers and backpackers flocking to Vienna can be divided into two camps: those seeking the old, historical city centered on palaces and cathedrals, and those in the know who realize this town is shaking off its formerly dusty image with an explosion of trendy restaurants and cafes, clubs, and provocative fashion sense.

Those in the latter camp will be found snuffling through the district west of the city center, near the largest concentration of hostels. The area is dominated by Neubaugasse and Neustiftgasse Streets, and is one of the most interesting and entertaining neighborhoods in Eastern Europe. You can do your grocery shopping, check out a cafe or bar, browse through a bookstore, even convert to a different faith. Hostels here are nearly always full at all times of the year, so it's best to call well ahead of your scheduled arrival. We recommend at least six months to a year ahead if you're coming during the high seasons of June, July, and August. We're not saying you won't find a bed on short notice; we're just saying it's a lot more likely if you plan ahead.

Those who come to see what it was that made Vienna a rival to Paris and London during the 18th and 19th centuries? You can find plenty to do, too. Wander past the stupendous

Vienna (Wien)

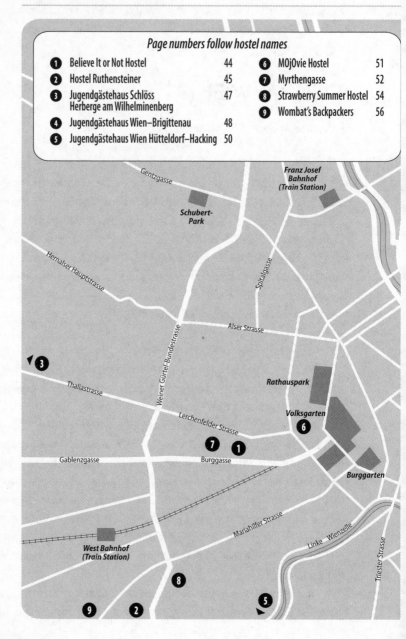

Page numbers follow hostel names

Gentzgasse

Franz Josef Bahnhof (Train Station)

Schubert-Park

Hernalser Hauptstrasse

Spitalgasse

Alser Strasse

Weiner Gürtel-Bundestrasse

3

Thaliastrasse

Rathauspark

Volksgarten
6

Lerchenfelder Strasse

7 **1**

Gablenzgasse

Burggasse

Burggarten

Mariahilfer Strasse

Linke Wienzeile

West Bahnhof (Train Station)

Triester Strasse

8

9 **2**

5

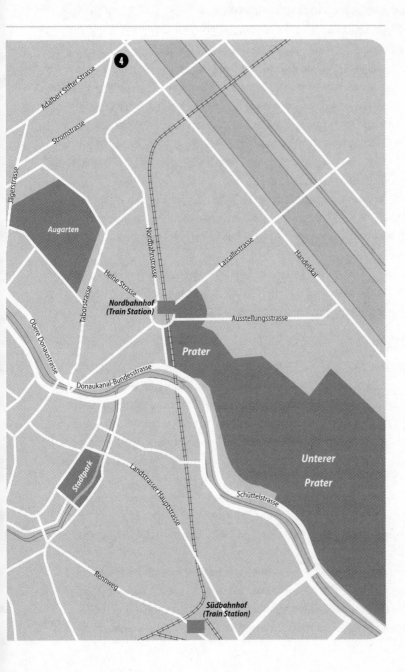

architectural achievements brought to you courtesy of the Hapsburgs, saving yourself a lot of hassle by simply taking the #1 and #2 trams that circle Ringstrasse in opposite directions, giving a quick overview of the big sights. If you take the U-Bahn to St. Stephan's Cathedral, just walk upstairs to the exit and you'll be within easy walking distance of the cathedral— which manifests itself immediately upon exit—and the pedestrian Kartnerstrasse, where you can watch the human parade in all its glory (and lameness). Be prepared for milling crowds watching in awe as some guy manipulates a faux piano-playing puppet to the strains of Beethoven's Fifth Symphony, or Kurdish political groups stage a demonstration. (Either way, with milling crowds come the usual pickpockets, always on the lookout for clueless Americans stepping away from a handy ATM, stuffing their wad of newly acquired bills into their already bursting wallets.)

Other places to hit in Vienna include the Prater amusement park and the beaches on the Danube. Because Vienna gets more sun than western Austria and is usually blessed with pretty warm weather, sightseeing isn't normally marred by rain or snow the way it is in, say, England or the Alps.

Finally, if you've really got some serious problems, there's always the Sigmund Freud Museum (freud-museum.at) in the ninth district, at Berggasse 19. Check out the world's most famous sofa and reflect upon the meaning of cigars.

Getting Around

Getting around Vienna is ridiculously easy. A comprehensive network of streetcar ("tram"), subway, electric railway, and bus lines crisscrosses the city, ensuring that you'll never have to walk too far to anything. Even late at night, after most of the normal transit stops running, a series of "night buses" ferry partygoers from the action back to their homes (or hostels) in the burbs. It's a good system. People drive cars here, too, of course, but they just aren't as thick on the ground as they are in most other European cities. Walking around town is actually a pleasure.

A single ticket costs €2.20 (about $2.75 US). But to get the most out of the transit network, you may want to buy a 24-hour pass from a station, online, or a tobacco and cigarette shop (*Tabak*); at this writing, it costs €6.70 ($8.50 US). You can also buy a weekly ticket for €15 (about $19 US).

Stamp your ticket before you use it. You push the ticket into a blue machine (on buses, on streetcars, and at train station entrances) and stamp the time and date on it just before your first ride (not sooner), and then for the next 24 hours you can ride anywhere on the city transit system without a bother. Unlike in most other European cities, you don't have to keep buying tickets or even showing your ticket to the conductor—it works on the honor system. (If you get caught without a proper ticket during a surprise inspection, though, you could be fined the equivalent of hundreds of US dollars. Ouch!)

Public transportation is very advanced in Vienna. Dig this, for instance: Cars *must* stop for pedestrians in crosswalks. (But if the walk signal's red, *don't cross*—it's dangerous.) They also must stop for any child or elderly person crossing, even if it's *not at a crosswalk*. The city's network of trams, U-Bahns, and buses (which bear the Austrian flag) is cheap and efficient.

Stephansplatz is the city's central node for subway lines going into and out of the historic center, and the West Bahnhof train station is handy for most other destinations. All the instructions are usually in German, though—the only drawback to this city—so make sure you get the correct information before the train leaves. Ask someone trustworthy to confirm train, track, or subway information.

VIENNA HOSTELS AT A GLANCE

	RATING	PRICE	IN A WORD	PAGE
Wombat's		€10–€28	zany	p. 56
HI-Ruthensteiner		€11–€38	central	p. 45
HI-Wilhelminenberg Castle		€21–€50	scenic	p. 47
Believe It or Not		€25–€29	tiny	p. 44
HI-Myrthengasse		€1	good	p. 52
Strawberry Summer Hostel		€22–€42	pricey	p. 54
HI-Wien-Brigittenau		€18–€20	huge	p. 48
HI-Hütteldorf-Hacking		€12.50–€50	remote	p. 50
MOJOvie		€15	rubble	p. 51

Believe It or Not

Myrthengasse 10, Apartment #14, A-1070 Vienna

Phone: 0676-55-000-55

E-mail: believe_it_or_not_vienna@hotmail.com

Website: believe-it-or-not-vienna.at

Rates: €25–€29 (about $31–$36 US) per person

Credit cards: No

Beds: 10

Private/family rooms: No

Kitchen available: Yes

Season: Open year-round

Office hours: Vary; call ahead

Lockout: 10 a.m.–12:30 p.m.

Affiliation: None

Extras: Kitchen, Internet access, lockers, TV

f you're into communal living situations—everything's a little tight here, and all rooms are mixed-sex—this is a better-than-OK place to bunk down for the night, smack in a neat area of Vienna. You've got to like the fact that they state their non-party intentions right up front, too: "You looking for a big hostel with a bar, partys, free drinks . . . ? WELL THEN YOU'RE WRONG HERE!"

We'll pardon the grammatical and semantic liberties. Point made.

This small place with the unusual name is located just across the street from two massive and group-filled "official" hostels. The crowd here, though, is vastly different. Most guests are youthful adults traveling singly or in pairs; it's more like an apartment run by the owner, who has gotten better at answering the door and the phone during the day. It's important that you call during the evening and ahead of arrival; a week before you plan to come to town isn't too early to secure a bed.

It's basically an apartment packed with 2 rooms of laid-back hostellers. Most people love this place for such a cozy and real-life-like atmosphere (some say a little too cozy—those triple bunks are quite a climb if you've been assigned one on the top level). It's usually kept surprisingly clean. There's a self-catering kitchen, with all you'll need for a spaghetti or ramen noodle feed. And perks like Internet and TV have also been added. You may have to present proof of age since word on the street is that guests under age 30 sometimes aren't allowed, but our spies tell us the rule is rarely (ever?) enforced. People tend to drift in and out of the place—we're just hoping they're hostellers—and traffic noise can get a bit annoying when windows are left open, but the (female) owner's so friendly and personable you might not care.

How To Get There:

By bus: Take #5 streetcar or #13 bus to hostel.
By car: Call hostel for directions.
By subway: Take U-Bahn U2 or U3 line to Volkstheater stop, or U6 line to Burggasse stop.
By train: From West Bahnhof Station, take U-Bahn U6 line to Burggasse stop and change to #48A bus to Neubaugasse. From Südbahnhof Station, take #13A bus toward Haltestelle to Kellermanngasse stop.

Best bet for a bite:
Naschmarkt
Insiders' tip:
Knock on the correct door!
What hostellers say:
"Like sleeping with friends! Um, 10 friends."
Gestalt:
Believable
Safety:
Hospitality:
Cleanliness:
Party index:

Hostel Ruthensteiner

Robert Hamerlinggasse 24, A-1150 Vienna

Phone: 01-893-4202
Fax: 01-893-2796
E-mail: info@hostelruthensteiner.com
Rates: €11–€38 (about $14–$48 US) per HI member; doubles €44–€52 (about $55–$65 US)
Credit cards: Yes
Beds: 74
Private/family rooms: Yes
Kitchen available: Yes
Season: Open year-round
Office hours: 24 hours
Affiliation: None
Extras: Courtyard, Internet access, breakfast ($), kitchen, laundry, bar, lockers

*T*his hostel's in a bit of an odd position. It's practically right next to Vienna's main train station, yet tucked away in a decently quiet location on a little side street. You simply sleep much closer to this city's transit points, and that's helpful when you're turning in late, late at night or heading out for lands unknown early in the morning. The private rooms are nice, the attitude is laid-back, and you might hear lots of foreign languages here.

Family-owned and -operated for years, it is a welcome relief from (a) the usual huge, institutional HI places and (b) the occasionally rancid independent hostels you run across in your travels across the Continent. This one gets almost everything right: It's friendly, it's relatively quiet, it's good-sized. Older travelers in particular will appreciate it as a way station while exploring one of Europe's most intriguing, museum-piece cities.

Is there a drawback? Well, there's one enormous dorm room (30 beds? You've gotta be kidding us) where hostellers are simply crammed in where needed. Try to book in advance and avoid that one. We can report to you that the very friendly staff cares about your discomfort— but that's just more sweaty socks than we usually care to commune with in a night. You have to pay a bit extra here for breakfast, too; it's not included for free, as it is at many Euro-hostels.

Still, there are plenty of smaller rooms—with 2, 3, 4, and 8 beds, plus the rare, coveted (and more expensive) single room. A smallish kitchen enhanced by an outdoor patio with a grill, computer terminal, and lively courtyard have to be counted as positives, and this is certainly a very convenient place to sleep when you've gotten to town very late. The bar gets raves, too; quaff a local brew and stay awhile. The all-night reception is happy to let you in—it's just great to find the place open and convenient. Internet access is free. There are no curfews, and it's both sparkly clean and full of good vibes. All in all, excellent for an "official" hostel and not at all what we expected.

Since it's so small, though, book well ahead of your arrival.

How To Get There:
By bus: Call hostel for transit route.
By car: Call hostel for directions.
By train: From West Bahnhof Station, walk out the extreme right side, cross busy street, and continue to Robert Hamerlinggasse on right. Turn right and walk down street to hostel on left.

Best bet for a bite:
Pizzeria Mafiosi
Insiders' tip:
Local ice cream is good
What hostellers say:
"Pretty groovy."
Gestalt:
Ruthless
Safety:
Hospitality:
Cleanliness:
Party index:

Jugendgästehaus Schlöss Herberge Am Wilhelminenberg (Wilhelminenberg Castle Guest House Hostel)

Savoyenstrasse 2, A-1160 Vienna

Phone: 01-4810300
Fax: 01-4810300-13
E-mail: shb@hostel.at
Rates: €21–€50 (about $26–$63 US) per HI member; doubles €62–€70 (about $78–$87 US)
Credit cards: Yes
Beds: 164
Private/family rooms: Yes
Kitchen available: No
Season: Open year-round
Office hours: 7 a.m.–10 p.m.
Lockout: 9 a.m.–2 p.m.
Affiliation: HI-ÖJHV
Extras: Minigolf, table tennis, TV, laundry ($), breakfast, meals ($), Internet access

*T*his nice though way-out-of-the-way hostel, owned by Vienna's tourist board, gets big points for its stunning surroundings and beautiful rooms. On the other hand, being waaay out in the burbs, it sure does attract busloads of school groups—who have the benefit of bus drivers to schlep them out here. So consider yourself forewarned: Kids will abound, and your journey here will entail at least three changes of transportation unless you're rambling around Europe in a car. Also keep in mind that you'll turn into a pumpkin if you stay out past 11:45 p.m., as that's the last bus out to this remote location. Thankfully, a key-card system means there are no curfews.

All the rooms here are quads with their own bathrooms (cool), and you can wash your clothes in a hostel laundry for a nominal fee. They've got a television lounge, meal service, really good free breakfast included with the (expensive) rack rate, and even a sort of miniature golf course adjacent. Woods? Views? Birds? Tree? Yes: This is Vienna's best hostel for visiting families and/or nature lovers. It's super-friendly, clean, and quiet.

Best bet for a bite:
Heurigen (wine cellars)
Insiders' tip:
Get a 1- or 3-day transit pass
What hostellers say:
"Thought I'd never get here!"
Gestalt:
Savoy special
Safety:
Hospitality:
Cleanliness:
Party index:

However, if you have an early train to catch, or you're a different sort of animal—the party kind, not the woodsy kind—you may want to consider one of the more central Viennese hostels instead.

How To Get There:

By bus or train: From West Bahnhof, take the U3 to Ottakring, then the #46B or #146B bus to Schloss Wilhelminenberg. Look for hostel on the left of big hotel. From Südbahnhof, take D tram to Volkstheater and follow bus directions as above.

By car: Call hostel for directions.

Jugendgästehaus Wien-Brigittenau (vienna brigittenau guest house hostel)

Friedrich Engelsplatz 24, A-1200 Vienna

Phone: 01-332-8294-0

Fax: 01-330-8379

E-mail: jgh.1200wien@chello.at

Rates: €18–€20 (about $20–$25 US) per HI member; doubles €42 (about $53 US)

Credit cards: Yes

Beds: 410

Private/family rooms: Yes

Kitchen available: No

Season: January 1–31; February 14–December 31

Office hours: 24 hours

Lockout: 9 a.m.–1 p.m.

Affiliation: HI-ÖJHV

Extras: TV, foosball, pool table, vending machines, in-room lockers, Internet access

---

*T*his hostel usually has tons of decent beds—that's good, in a pinch—but it's also overrun with school groups and is located in a somewhat depressing, bland suburban neighborhood alongside a major traffic artery. It's a huge edifice with zero character but also a lot of frills, including vegetarian meal options, some rooms with private bathrooms, and, for the most part, friendly and helpful staff—some of whom are native English-speakers, which can be a relief for some. You make the call, but this place won't win any design awards; the words *cell block* do come to mind.

The hostel is actually situated in 2 buildings, one of which is newer and is designated for families and couples. The main building is where those kiddie groups stay. Noise tends to travel through the walls here, and double rooms consist of a bunk bed instead of the two twins one would expect. At least some of the rooms are fairly spacious.

Given the out-of-the-way and bland location, you're not going to be hanging out in the neighborhood, so hop the U-Bahn or the S-Bahn (you get endless rides on both if you buy a 24-hour pass) to other points. The Donauinsel, a riverside beach and park, isn't far, for instance, nor is the Prater amusement park—fun for an afternoon—just a couple stops away by suburban train, which is covered by the city's 24-hour tickets. Also of note: A huge office tower with large-screen theater, bowling, bars, mall, and food court is just a few blocks away.

Still hungry for nightlife? Catch one of the night buses that runs out of the heart of the city and stops right here in Friedrich Engels Platz, steps from the hostel. Just make sure you have a map and an understanding of how to use the night bus first.

Best bet for a bite:
Zielpunkt supermarket
Insiders' tip:
Pack lightly
What hostellers say:
"Too far from town."
Gestalt:
Outer space
Safety:
Hospitality:
Cleanliness:
Party index:

How To Get There:
By bus: Take the #11A or #5A bus to Friedrich Engels Platz and, following hostel logo sign, walk 50 yards to hostel.

By ferry: Take boat to Reichsbrucke dock, then walk 1½ miles to hostel.

By subway: Take U-Bahn subway U6 line to Handelskai stop and walk ⅓ mile to hostel, or take the #5A bus at the Handelskai stop for 3 stops, exit, and walk under overpass to hostel.

By tram: Take N, #31, or #32 streetcar to Friedrich Engels Platz and walk 50 yards to hostel.

Jugendgästehaus Wien Hütteldorf-Hacking (Vienna/Hütteldorf-Hacking Guest House Hostel)

Schlossberggasse 8, A-1130 Vienna

Phone: 01-877-1501

Fax: 01-877-02632

E-mail: jgh@hostel.at

Rates: €12.50–€50 (about $16–$63 US) per HI member; doubles €40–€72 (about $50–$90 US)

Credit cards: Yes

Beds: 307

Private/family rooms: Yes

Kitchen available: No

Season: Open year-round

Office hours: 24 hours

Affiliation: HI-ÖJHV

Extras: Laundry, TV, VCR, foosball, table tennis, meals ($), Internet access, lockers, information desk, garden, playground

A huge 6-story bunker on leafy grounds near Hütteldorf Station, this place remains ruthlessly efficient, if distant from the center and at times a little cool on the hospitality front. It's not the greatest place in town—only so-so—so let the buyer beware.

A key-card system lets you into the place, where you'll find 4 singles, 11 doubles, 3 triples, 11 quads, 24 sixes, and 6 eight-bed dorms—none of 'em with private bathrooms. Bummer. They serve breakfast, maintain a television lounge, and really cater to families more than indy travelers on the make. Witness the playground area, game room, and meal service; college kids will love the Internet access, but if you're not yet at the family-creating age, consider giving this one a pass. It's not hip and happening, just comfortable for kiddies.

Best bet for a bite:
Duran sandwich joints

Insiders' tip:
Use the satellite train station

What hostellers say:
"Good place, so-so location."

Gestalt:
Huttel house

Safety:

Hospitality:

Cleanliness:

Party index:

How To Get There:

By bus: Take #53B bus and walk 20 yards to hostel.

By car: Call hostel for directions.

By subway or train: Take U-Bahn U4 line to Hütteldorf stop and walk ⅓ mile to hostel.

MOjOvie Hostel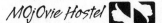

Apt. 8, Kaiserstrasse 77, A-1070 Vienna

Phone: 0676-55-111-55

Website: panda-vienna.at/index.html

E-mail: accommodation@mymojovie.at

Rates: €24–€38 (about $30–$48 US) per person; doubles €56–€80 (about $71–$100 US)

Credit cards: No

Beds: Number varies

Private/family rooms: Yes

Kitchen available: Yes

Season: Open year-round

Office hours: 8 a.m.–11 p.m.

Affiliation: None

Extras: TV, luggage storage, free WiFi, laundry ($)

---

*F*ormerly known as the Panda, this shut-down-then-reopened hostel is kind of the same deal as the Believe It or Not Hostel (see p. 44)—this one's also in an apartment building, it also doesn't hold very many folks, and it's pretty funky with the rules and organizational skills.

Whenever the place is open (which is not always; call ahead to confirm any reservation), the expensive doubles here actually pretty good (they're in apartments separate from the main building). Dorms themselves, however, consist of 30 bunks squashed into a room, three-high—which is a big buzzkill. There are lockers to stash your stuff in, although you'll have to supply your own lock. If you stay in the off-season, which

Best bet for a bite:
Supermarkets in the neighborhood

Gestalt:
Panda bear

Safety:

Hospitality:

Cleanliness:

Party index:

runs from November to Easter, you'll be charged a reduced rate, so there is that. The kitchen is too minimal, and desk staff got a few complaints for being evasive about bunk prices—watch out for the ol' bait-'n'-switch.

The street the hostel is located on is full of restaurants and other diversions. It's basically an extension of the Neubaugasse/Burggasse area, only slightly closer to the West Bahnhof Station, into and out of which you'll very likely be traveling.

How To Get There:
By train: From West Bahnhof Station, take #5 tram 4 stops to Burggasse. From Südbahnhof, take #18 tram to West Bahnhof, then change to #5 to Burggasse.
By bus: From central bus station, take U3 subway line to West Bahnof, then follow directions above.
By car: Call hostel for directions.

Myrthengasse (Vienna Myrthengasse Hostel)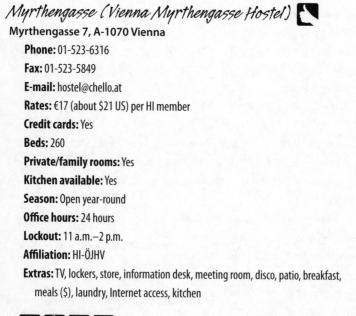
Myrthengasse 7, A-1070 Vienna

> **Phone:** 01-523-6316
> **Fax:** 01-523-5849
> **E-mail:** hostel@chello.at
> **Rates:** €17 (about $21 US) per HI member
> **Credit cards:** Yes
> **Beds:** 260
> **Private/family rooms:** Yes
> **Kitchen available:** Yes
> **Season:** Open year-round
> **Office hours:** 24 hours
> **Lockout:** 11 a.m.–2 p.m.
> **Affiliation:** HI-ÖJHV
> **Extras:** TV, lockers, store, information desk, meeting room, disco, patio, breakfast, meals ($), laundry, Internet access, kitchen

*O*K, if the last hostel was not hip and happening, this one is. And if you're like most other hostellers, you'd probably think a hostel with this many beds (more than 250) would be easy to waltz into and grab a bunk at the last minute.

Well, you couldn't be more wrong. You'll have to book it at least 6 months in advance if you have any hope of gracing its bunks during the summer. But it's not individual travelers who are booking the place out. It's groups from all over Europe, sometimes in numbers totaling 50 or more. Multiply that by six, and there is no chance you'll get a bed. In fact, management prefers groups because they bring in more money, what with the meals and all. So you'll just have to be really forward-thinking, because this is among the best-located hostels in town: It's right smack in the middle of the hippest district in Vienna, otherwise known as Neustiftgasse.

Best bet for a bite:
Pizza joints on Neustiftgasse
Insiders' tip:
Book six months ahead
What hostellers say:
"No beds next July? But it's only February!"
Gestalt:
Group mentality
Safety:
Hospitality:
Cleanliness:
Party index:

Staff are surprisingly laid-back and lack that authoritative look we've come to expect from a place dealing with gangly rugrats. Rooms are pretty clean and accommodating, though the place has been remodeled to eliminate doubles. All the 2-, 4-, and 6-bed dorms come with their own shower and toilet—and there are more than a dozen private rooms here, though most are 4-packs—as do the bigger 8- and 10-bed rooms. Staff are variably friendly, but certainly not terrible. Some of them have even left to create their own independent hostels in the city. So the place does sprout a certain conviviality.

Hostel staff have organized a really useful information board, including stuff like nearby ATM locations and transportation information; ask about it. Common areas include a cool, tranquil back patio with picnic tables, ivy-covered walls, and one of those antique-looking water fountains so common in Europe and so uncommon everywhere else. There's a television lounge with cable TV. The dinners (weekdays only) are basic—stuff like spaghetti, soup, and a few local Viennese specialties—but they've added vegetarian and organic options, and you can legitimately eat dinner here if you're just too tired to explore the surrounding neighborhood (or if the weather sucks).

Overall, management runs a good hostel here despite a preference for booking in groups. Maybe they can apply this efficiency and good cheer and open up a satellite "official" hostel for funkier travelers and backpackers. 'Til then, though, this one is pretty good, safe, clean, and well-run.

How To Get There:

By bus: Call hostel for transit route. At night, take the N46 bus to Skodagasse.

By car: Call hostel for directions.

By subway: Take U-Bahn U2 or U3 line to Volkstheater stop, or take U6 line to Burggasse stop.

By train: From West Bahnhof Station, take U-Bahn U6 line to Burggasse stop and change to #48A bus to Neubaugasse. From Südbahnhof Station, take #13A bus toward Haltestelle to Kellermanngasse stop.

Strawberry Summer Hostel Mittelgasse

Mittelgasse 18, A-1060 Vienna

Phone: 01-5997-9660

Website: strawberryhostels.com

Rates: €22–€42 (about $28–$53 US per person); doubles €56 (about $70 US)

Credit cards: No

Beds: 80

Private/family rooms: Yes

Kitchen available: Yes

Season: July 1–September 12

Office hours: 24 hours

Affiliation: None

Extras: Laundry, storage, TV, free Internet access, bicycle storage, movie nights

---

This Strawberry's not a perfect peach, but it's definitely not a lemon, either. And you've got to love a place where they include free breakfast.

A summer-only hostel from the same folks who run the Strawberry in Salzburg, this basic, functional place does deliver decent-enough beds plus some extras. Sure, it's expensive—one of the most expensive hostels in the whole damn city, in fact—but worth it, especially when you're stuck for a safe bunk late at night and the better places in town are already fully booked. Its position close to the big West-bahnof train station is key, too.

They tout the bathrooms and showers in each room, the lack of curfews/lockouts, the 24-hour reception, the luggage storage, a laundry, and activities such as regular movie nights, and these are all laudable amenities. It has to be said, though, that the cleanliness of this place has always been variable—sometimes it's clean, and sometimes it's hurting.

Other than that, we can't find anything else bad to point a finger at. Wait, here's one complaint: How come they don't open it year-round?

Best bet for a bite:
Reinthalers
What hostellers say:
"Fun place."
Gestalt:
Strawberry bunks forever
Safety:
Hospitality:
Cleanliness:
Party index:

How To Get There:

By car: Contact hostel for directions.
By bus: Contact hostel for transit route.
By train: From Westbahnhof, exit and walk along Bürgerspitalgasse 2 blocks to Mittelgasse. From Südbahnhof, take #18 streetcar 9 stops to Mariahilfergürtel, then walk 5 minutes to Mittelgasse.

Attractive natural setting

Ecologically aware hostel

Superior kitchen facilities or cafe

Offbeat or eccentric place

Superior bathroom facilities

Romantic private rooms

Comfortable beds

A particularly good value

Wheelchair-accessible

Good for business travelers

Especially well-suited for families

Good for active travelers

Visual arts at hostel or nearby

Music at hostel or nearby

Great hostel for skiers

Bar or pub at hostel or nearby

Editors' choice: Among our very favorite hostels

Key to Icons

Wombat's Backpackers

Grangasse 6, A-1150 Vienna

Phone: 01-897-2336

Fax: 01-897-2577

E-mail: office@wombats-vienna.at

Website: wombats.at

Rates: €10–€28 (about $13–$35 US) per person; doubles €50–€58 (about $63–$73 US)

Credit cards: No

Beds: 296

Private/family rooms: Yes

Kitchen available: Yes

Season: Open year-round

Office hours: 24 hours

Affiliation: None

Extras: Breakfast ($), Internet access, laundry, bike rentals, roller skate rentals, in-line skate rentals, bar, bicycle tours, lockers, games, darts, movies, terrace, kitchen

This is one of the consistently best hostels in Vienna, year in and out, but be prepared: It's not like any of the others—in any way, shape, or form.

What kind of place is Wombat's? You get a free drink as soon as you walk into this place (well, not the very moment, but you know what we mean), and that should tell you something—though not everything—about it. There's more to this cool independent entry than just booze, and it's conveniently located almost right behind the city's main international train station. Hey, you've got to give props to a place that sometimes rents roller skates, right? But they do like their parties here, too.

Room arrangements consist of about 20 doubles, a few triples, about three dozen quads, and almost 20 six-bed dorms—with a shower and bathroom inside every room. People frequently write in the guestbook that the rooms are clean and the beds are comfy, so it must be true, right? Right: We concur, for the most part. The kitchen's decent, there's a free (yes, free) laundry for your use and abuse, and staff and management seem very receptive to hosteller comments, complaints, and suggestions. You just don't find this sort of openness in the hostelling world. The guys who run the place have loads of character, too. Nice to see.

The pub with its terrace is the most popular place in the joint, of course. It's one great party spot, that's for sure. But they do other stuff: You get your own locker and key for storage safety. Breakfast costs a little bit; they've got a few Internet terminals and a laundry. And even better, they rent bikes and those previously noted skates for exploring this wonderful city. Reception also helps arrange ad hoc local walking tours from May through Oct (figure around $12 per person, if we are converting the price correctly), as well as longer tours extending to the Wachau region and even Budapest.

Best bet for a bite:
Schwejk (Bohemian cuisine)
What hostellers say:
"Let's rock it."
Gestalt:
Wombatmobile
Safety:
Hospitality:
Cleanliness:
Party index:

OK, Vienna's train-station neighborhood may not be the most luxurious (or the safest) in town, but it certainly does provide a selection of ethnic eateries to pick from when you're famished. And the hostel's close to Vienna's great city transit, a linked network of buses, streetcars (often called "trams"), and a short, rudimentary subway. Wombat's buzz continues to spread, so book ahead or try to arrive before noon if you're intent on staying—this is among Vienna's top hostels, and Euro-travelers come here as a destination now.

If this place is full, be sure to ask the receptionists about booking a room at Wombat's 2 satellite hostels in the city, one known as The Lounge and the other known as the Naschmarkt, named for that wonderful market. Both are adequate.

How To Get There:
By bus: Contact hostel for transit details.
By car: Contact hostel for directions.
By train: From West Bahnhof, exit station and turn right onto Mariahilfer Strasse. Follow to #152 (at the corner of Rosinagasse); bear right at Rosinagasse and continue to Grangasse, then make a left and continue to hostel on right.

Belgium

*I*f you've never been to Belgium, you might be in for a bit of a surprise: Though it has a blah image, it's actually a fun place to visit despite the mostly flat terrain and frequently drab weather. Kick back and enjoy the friendly people, low cost of traveling, and good food and drink.

The famous squabbling between the Dutch-speaking half of Belgium (the north) and the French-speaking part (the south) has even spilled over to hostelling: There are actually two separate hostel organizations in this country, and—to make matters worse—if you're Belgian you have to declare allegiance to one or the other. Pretty silly. But as a hosteller you can pretty much ignore that turf war.

Given a short period of time in Belgium, we'd probably head first for Brugge, which is a beautiful little city with tons of sights to offer and a likable, small-town feel within the compact city center. Then we'd go for Brussels—a noisy, sprawling place that makes up in culture what it lacks in physical beauty. Finally, we'd skip down to the Ardennes for a few days of back-roading.

Oh, and if you happen to find yourself in the country on July 21, good for you. It's Belgium's National Day, sorta like our Fourth of July. And they celebrate it the same way, too, with fireworks and general merriment.

Practical Details

Lots of airlines fly into Brussels; Virgin Express has the best selection of cheap flights to and from here, because this city is a Virgin hub. Brussels Airlines (formerly Sabena) has more daily choices—from the most foreign airports—because it's Belgium's national airline carrier.

To get to Belgium from London, you can also take a Eurostar (see p. 23) train from London directly to Brussels, no change of trains required. Or take a train to Dover (on the southeastern tip of England), then catch a ferry across the English Channel to the Belgian coast—note that these ferries and trains are timed to meet each other, but once in a while they don't. And if the boat runs late because of weather, the train won't wait. Be prepared.

Once you're here, Belgian trains are comprehensive, comfortable, and inexpensive, though not especially speedy. You can get from anywhere to anywhere else, just about, in this small country—but count on making lots of stops in every town along the way.

Brussels is the main rail hub for the country, and also for much of Europe. The city's Midi/Zuid Station (confusingly, it has two names) connects quickly to London, Paris, Nice, and other distant points; too bad it's in an odd, unattractive neighborhood far from the city center and the hostels. If you're heading right into town, get off at Centraal Station if possible. Nord (North) Station is another good option, handy for most of the Brussels hostels, though, again, not in a particularly attractive area—especially at night.

The local Benelux Pass costs under-26 travelers about $165 to $225 US for a three- to five-day pass (you have to use it up within two months) and $200 to $425 US for older folks for the same length of time (the first-class pass, which is pretty useless, costs a lot more than the second-class pass). "Partners" traveling with over-26ers get a 33–40 percent discount on the pass if you buy both together. If you want to take a bus to the countryside, buses fan out (and depart for international destinations) from Gare du Nord, not Midi. Because of Belgium's density, buses can take even longer than trains: one hour to get from Brussels to Ghent, for example, which is twice as long as the train takes. But they do cost less. And Eurolines buses travel from Brussels to Paris, London, Germany—heck, even all the way up to Copenhagen.

The unit of currency in Belgium is the euro. A large bag of fries purchased late at night might cost you €1.80 plus another €0.25 for curried ketchup on top. (You gotta try it—trust us.) That's about $2.50 US. Your €16 dorm room is also pretty cheap, about $20 a night.

Belgium's phone code is 32. To call Brussels hostels from the US, dial 011-32 and then DROP THE ZERO from the numbers listed in this book. To call Brussels hostels from within Belgium, dial the numbers EXACTLY AS PRINTED in this book.

BRUSSELS

Belgium's capital city, Brussels (also spelled Bruxelles, in French), is centrally located in the country and is a good mix of the two cultures that make it up—plus, there are lots more people who come here to work for the EU's home offices and various European governmental, quasi-governmental, and nonprofit organizations. Though the city can be gray and bland—it seems that these people never met a green park they liked as much as a new store or parking garage—it's also quite hip and happening these days if you go to the right places. As a city, you're not going to do much better than this—once you overlook the place's physical appearance, which can border on the ugly in spots. Get past that, and you'll find food that's as good as Paris's, beer that's as good as Munich's, people as friendly as in your hometown, and costs that are surprisingly low.

Brussels

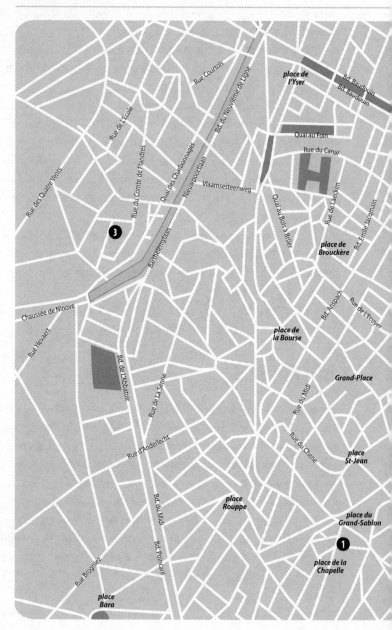

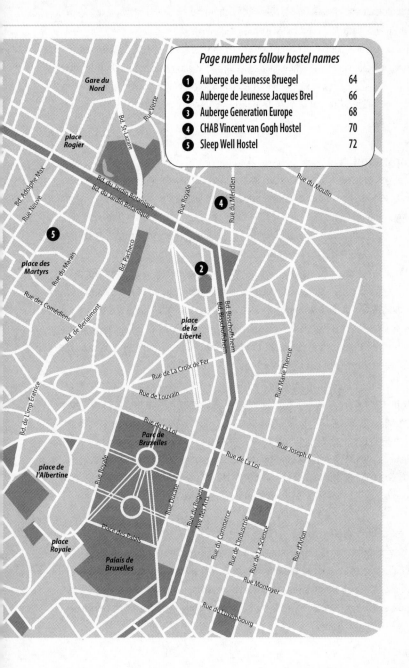

Gare du
Nord

place
Rogier

place des
Martyrs

place
de la
Liberté

Parc de
Bruxelles

place de
l'Albertine

place
Royale

Palais de
Bruxelles

Place des Palais

Bd. St-Lazare
Rue Vierte
Bd. Adolphe Max
Rue Neuve
Bd. du Jardin Botanique
Bd. du Jardin Botanique
Bd. Pacheco
Rue Royale
Rue du Méridien
Rue du Moulin
Rue du Marais
Rue des Comédiens
Bd. de Berlaimont
Bd. de l'Imp Eratrice
Bd. Bisschoffsheim
Bd. Bisschoffsheim
Rue de La Croix de Fer
Rue de Louvain
Rue Marie Thérèse
Rue de La Loi
Rue de La Loi
Rue Joseph II
Rue Royale
Rue Ducale
Rue du Brabant
Ave des Arts
Rue du Commerce
Rue de l'Industrie
Rue de La Science
Rue d'Arlon
Rue Montoyer
Rue du Luxembourg

The hostel situation here is amazingly good, too: For once, four of five hostels here are centrally located—no more than a 10-minute walk from the main downtown square known as the Grand-Place. And almost all of them are high-quality.

Hostels near Gare du Nord (the Jacques Brel, the Sleep Well, and the CHAB) are all fine, although located in blah, slightly dodgy areas. There used to be a botanical garden here but it's been mostly paved over. Auberge Generation is beautiful, but pretty far north of the center in a slightly bad part of town. The Bruegel Hostel is the most central, best-located of the five-pack.

Transportation

To help you get around, Brussels operates loads of mass transit under the name of STB. This system takes a little figuring out to master. There are Metro subway lines, augmented by a system of streetcars that dip and dive above and beneath ground. There's also a pretty good bus system. Transit isn't cheap, but a *carte du jour* (day pass) can reduce your costs; for a few dollars, the pass gets you all-day access to the web of buses, trams, and subways around Brussels.

Maps in the stations and signs on the trains aren't much help, though; it's best to ask a ticket vendor, hostel staffer, or conductor first what's going where before climbing aboard anything. Make special note of where your train ends—that's critical. The train or tram or bus will have its final destination posted on the front, and that's the only clue you'll have about where it's going. Get that basic fact wrong, and you could spend an hour riding the wrong direction before you figure out your mistake.

At least all the options are quick and efficient. It's easy to buy a ticket, too; you can get one from ticket sellers in the Metro stations or from automatic machines scattered around town and concentrated inside the stations. The tickets are good on any kind of transit, plus a transfer in the same direction within one hour; one ride in town costs about €1.90–€2.50 (about $2.50–$3 US), but buy a five-ride card and the per-ride price drops by about 25 percent. Buy a 10-ride card (€12–€13, about $16–$17 US) or a daily pass (€6.50, about $8 US) that you use a lot, though, and your PPR (price per ride) drops quite a bit more.

Attractions & Nightlife

Most tourists come here for the obvious sights: the EU's home offices, the offices of NATO, stuff like that. But to our eye, the hippest places to get a bite here are in the Ixelles neighborhood, which isn't right downtown but is very reachable—it's got a melange of veggie, ethnic, and Belgian eateries—and in the burgeoning Sainte-Catherine neighborhood close to the downtown square.

Ixelles is where Brussels's nouveau-riche kids (if this were London, we'd be calling them "trustafarians") boogie the nights away in bistros and discos. Otherwise it's rather dull, with the European Union's massive edifices and a couple museums and administrative buildings for company. Most eateries around here cater to diplomats' tastes, and thus probably aren't gonna be in your price range. That's OK. Hike down to the Grand-Place and its surrounding maze of streets for ethnic options of every sort instead. Sainte-Catherine is livelier and more interesting, livened up by a number of strip joints, student-y bars, and the like.

Though a lot more touristed, there are also plenty of good bars and restaurants in the streets around the *Mannekin Pis* (an inexplicably popular statue of a boy peeing). The Port-Namur area is Brussels's Fifth Avenue, good for those looking to lighten their wallets before heading onward to the next European destination.

No matter where you're going, though, this is an easy city to get lost in—there are absolutely no central arteries or grids to orient yourself by—much like Paris. Except about 10 times worse. So get a good map, head for the Grand-Place or some other obvious landmark, and begin fanning out from there. Note that all the streets and stations in Brussels are schizophrenically named, both in French and Flemish, and the names often bear no resemblance to each other. This can be a circle of hell if you're not sure where you're going. Best strategy? Recruit/befriend/bring a local. Second best? Pay close attention to maps and signs.

BRUSSELS HOSTELS AT A GLANCE

	RATING	PRICE	IN A WORD	PAGE
CHAB Hostel		€19–€34	fun	p. 70
Bruegel Hostel		€19–€36	modern	p. 64
Jacques Brel Hostel		€16–€34	good	p. 66
Sleep Well Hostel		€22.50–€41.50	central	p. 72
Auberge Generation Europe		€26–€34	distant	p. 68

Auberge De Jeunesse Bruegel

2 Heilig Geeststraat/rue Saint-Esprit 2, Brussels 1000

> **Phone:** 02-511-0436
>
> **Fax:** 02-512-0711
>
> **E-mail:** brussel@vjh.be
>
> **Rates:** €19–€36 (about $24–$45 US) per HI member; doubles €46–€51 (about $57–$64 US)
>
> **Credit cards:** Yes
>
> **Beds:** 135
>
> **Private/family rooms:** Yes
>
> **Kitchen available:** No
>
> **Season:** Open year-round
>
> **Office hours:** 7 a.m.–1 a.m.
>
> **Lockout:** 1–2 p.m.
>
> **Curfew:** 1 a.m.
>
> **Affiliation:** HI-VJ
>
> **Extras:** Currency exchange, TV, breakfast, meals ($), conference rooms, disco, lockers, patio, bar

B y far the best located of Brussels's 5-pack of hostels, the "official" Bruegel is certainly a good bunk—and, unlike almost all the rest of the city's budget lodging, is actually in a halfway interesting area: central, even if the actual street it's on is so tiny that it's almost impossible to locate unless you're a local. Which you're not.

Anyway, this hostel perches on top of a little hill that leads to Brussels's so-called upper town: the part, of course, where the richest folks lived/live, where European Union officials have met for eons to hash out details of integrating the euro and bad pop music, and so on and so forth.

However, an interesting thing happens right around the corner from the hostel. Before you get to the hoity-toity, beautiful-homes-of-diplomats district, you hit a little working-class area at the base of the beautiful Notre Dame de la Chapelle church. This is a place where you can still get a beer for just a couple bucks instead of the rip-off prices they'll charge you up in the richer area. After all, this is beer country! Inquire about happy hour specials, and drink to your heart's content (if you're a drinker). Afterward, stumble uphill—there's something poetic in that, though we're not sure what—to your bunk.

Inside, the hostel's the usual HI-Europa situation. They serve decent meals daily, often featuring chicken or pasta but also sometimes slipping a regional Flemish specialty into the mix just to see if you're paying attention. (Hint: When you start going, "What the heck is that on my plate?" then whatever you're eating is probably a local specialty.)

After dinner there are 3 main areas to congregate in. Outside, there's a beautiful little nook of a terrace, enclosed in ivy-covered brick walls and laid out with tables for hanging out. That would be our first choice. There's also a good television lounge, although who cares? Downstairs there's a bar/disco area that features a combination of Euro-pop, strobe lights, and the usual Belgian bar with a couple great (local) and wishy-washy (American) beers on tap. In the past, the bartender has sometimes even played CDs our hostellers brought him. Can't beat that for service.

The beds are pretty good; some hostellers rave that they're hotel-quality, though we don't know if we'd go quite that far. (Question: How many hotels ask you to shower with strangers?) Oh yeah, the room layouts. There are 4 singles, 22 doubles (all of them twin bunk beds, of course, not real double beds), 1 triple, and 21 quads. They're all nicer than you'd expect for the price, and some rooms (but not all) even come with TVs, sinks, showers, and en-suite bathrooms. (Other rooms share bathrooms.) They've got lockers for your valuables, too.

There is a drawback to all this; it isn't perfection. Staff could be a lot friendlier and more helpful. But they're not rude; they simply match the impersonal quality of the place. Also, it's hard to find, as we noted. Look sharp as you're walking, and follow the directions below carefully. All in all, it's a good, adequate, slightly bland place—not a perfect one.

The interesting pocket neighborhood around the hostel is OK for browsing, and if you continue walking uphill you'll be in Armani (and also Notre Dame) territory. You're also—perhaps the best reason of all to stay here—maybe 5 minutes' walk from the city's central train station, a little bit farther than the famous Grand-Place at the center of the city with all its associated eateries. You think they have Belgian food in New York and Montreal and L.A.? Pshaw. Grand-Place is the nerve center of the world's Belgian cuisine, so dive into those beers, mussels, *frites,* and gamey other specialties with everything you've got.

Best bet for a bite:
Snack La Chappelle or Chez Leon
What hostellers say:
"I can see for miles . . ."
Gestalt:
Back to Bruegal-oo
Safety:
Hospitality:
Cleanliness:
Party index:

How To Get There:

By bus: Take #20 bus to La Chapelle and walk 50 yards to hostel.
By car: Call hostel for directions.
By train: From Centraal Station, walk 300 yards down Boulevard de l'Empereur to hostel.
From Midi Station, take #20 bus to La Chapelle and walk 50 yards to hostel.

Auberge de Jeunesse Jacques Brel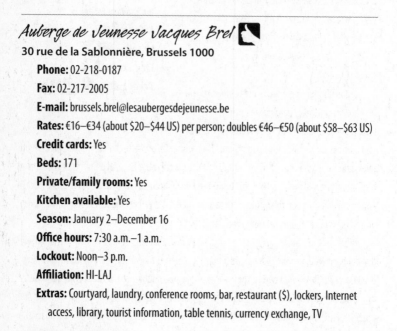

30 rue de la Sablonnière, Brussels 1000

> **Phone:** 02-218-0187
> **Fax:** 02-217-2005
> **E-mail:** brussels.brel@lesaubergesdejeunesse.be
> **Rates:** €16–€34 (about $20–$44 US) per person; doubles €46–€50 (about $58–$63 US)
> **Credit cards:** Yes
> **Beds:** 171
> **Private/family rooms:** Yes
> **Kitchen available:** Yes
> **Season:** January 2–December 16
> **Office hours:** 7:30 a.m.–1 a.m.
> **Lockout:** Noon–3 p.m.
> **Affiliation:** HI-LAJ
> **Extras:** Courtyard, laundry, conference rooms, bar, restaurant ($), lockers, Internet
> access, library, tourist information, table tennis, currency exchange, TV

---

*T*his hard-to-find hostel sits not too far from Brussels's Gare du Nord on a quiet side street just off the bustle near the city's former botanical gardens. (Today it's more of an arts and entertainment complex; you'll see more guitars and concrete than flowers.) The Jacques Brel's wing is the real star—and it shows that this Hostelling International chapter has paid close attention to the services and design quirks that have made independent backpacker-style hostels so competitive over the past decade.

Outside, the unassuming 3-story building looks as prim and proper as a schoolhouse. Inside, though, you enter a very mod-looking reception area decorated with movie posters, sleek furniture, and other cool stuff. This part of the hostel doubles as a travel store, honor-system lending library, and game room with Risk and other multilingual favorites—not to mention a major hangout area. A jovial staff calls out requests on an intercom and generally keeps this very busy hostel moving; the guests often are groups—American, French, or German—plus the usual motley crew of good-hearted backpackers. Slackers don't tend to stay here, we noticed.

They have 4 meeting rooms with TVs, VCRs, and flipcharts, in case you've brought the entire soccer team along with you and want to diagram plays in secret. Forget that and head instead for the sitting areas, with plenty of neato furniture like glass tables, hipper than hip Eurochairs, skylights, and the like. The exposed rooftop terrace gets lots of action during the summer, when Polish girls work on their tans to the appreciative *oohs* and *aahs* of working-class Belgian guys walking by on the street. There is no curfew of any kind here—a big plus and frankly quite surprising given that this is a Hostelling International–affiliated joint.

Best bet for a bite:
Head downtown
What hostellers say:
"Magnifique! Mais où est la centre-ville?"
Gestalt:
Brel done
Safety:
Hospitality:
Cleanliness:
Party index:

One big drawback, however: There is neither a kitchen for hostellers to cook in, nor cooked meals for sale (unless you've come along with a big group, in which case they will do you this catering service). That leaves you in a bit of a squeeze. The only food is served in the beautiful little bar, all freshly painted and clean and serving brews on tap. They've got toast and snacks like that, so you could probably make a meal of it if you added a couple great Belgian beers to the mix. (Beer, after all, is just liquid bread.) But if you want to shop 'n' cook, as you can in most every other city hostel in Europe, you're outta luck.

But we digress. The bar—painted in a pleasing stars, angels, and moons motif—comes complete with a piano and other instruments, such as a tambourine, congas, shakers, and more.

Rooms, as you would expect, come in a variety of configurations: There's 1 single room, about 20 doubles, 5 triples, 11 quad rooms, 6 six-bed dorms, and 3 larger dorms of 13 and 14 beds in the older wing. (You don't want to get stuck there.) You get into rooms with key cards, which is nice, and most have lockers and cupboards for arranging your stuff; many come with showers, as well. Cleanliness is just so-so, not pristine.

As for the neighborhood, that's one minus in an otherwise good hostel. It's not a bad area, and it's not a great area, safety-wise. There's just little of interest. At least there are a couple bars and cafes and a bit of shopping as well on the ring highway that encircles Brussels. To get there just take the Metro a couple of stops, or during the day hike a half mile or so.

Note that some hostellers complained of security issues—not sure if hostellers or outsiders are to blame for that, but keep an eye on your stuff.

Hey, things could be worse.

How To Get There:

By bus: Take #61 bus to Botanique and walk to hostel, or take #92, #93, or #94 streetcar to Botanique and walk 200 yards to hostel.

By car: Call hostel for directions.

By train: From Gare du Nord, walk 1 mile north up rue Royale to hostel. From Centraal Station, take Metro Line M2 to Botanique or Madou stop and walk to hostel; or take #91, #92, #93, or #94 streetcar and walk to hostel.

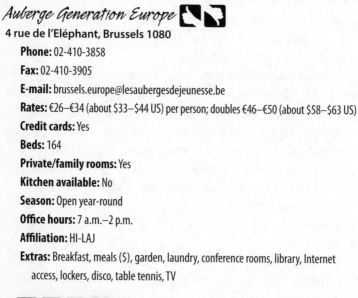

Auberge Generation Europe

4 rue de l'Eléphant, Brussels 1080

Phone: 02-410-3858

Fax: 02-410-3905

E-mail: brussels.europe@lesaubergesdejeunesse.be

Rates: €26–€34 (about $33–$44 US) per person; doubles €46–€50 (about $58–$63 US)

Credit cards: Yes

Beds: 164

Private/family rooms: Yes

Kitchen available: No

Season: Open year-round

Office hours: 7 a.m.–2 p.m.

Affiliation: HI-LAJ

Extras: Breakfast, meals ($), garden, laundry, conference rooms, library, Internet access, lockers, disco, table tennis, TV

*T*his place was once a foundry; now it's a hostel. It's not elaborate, and it's the least central of the city's five—though it is packed with welcome extras like a garden, laundry, and Internet access. Too bad the neighborhood is seriously unsafe (sorry, but it has to be said), and this unsavory element even seeps into the hostel itself. (Also note that the front-desk hours are incredibly short—gotta check in before midafternoon.)

The 3-story converted building features modern, airy architecture—think lots of arching windows open to the gray sky—and newish, mostly quad rooms. The dining area is roomy enough to hold a small dance in—if you've cleared away the homey tables, that is—and they've got 5 meeting rooms here, too, in case you need 'em.

There are an unusual number of private rooms here—10 doubles and 24 quad rooms—plus 2 six-bedded dorms and 4 bigger ones. The facilities here are incredibly modern: Try Web cruising, a disco (well, that's actually retro, but in Europe it's modern), meeting rooms, and lockers, for starters. You get the picture. It's well done.

Unfortunately, the place isn't near any train stations; it'll require a Metro ride plus a good-size walk to get here. And the neighborhood is just plain terrible. Absolutely take a taxi here at night; you walk at your own risk. (Group tourists stay here because they've got a bus to safely ferry them to and from the city's central attractions.) Lone hostellers just really need to be careful here, and there's nothing of interest to do in the area. You're paying for a so-so bed, in a beautiful building, smack in the middle of Skid Row.

> **Best bet for a bite:**
> *Once again, head downtown*
> **What hostellers say:**
> *"Allo? Police?"*
> **Gestalt:**
> *Generation Ex*
> **Safety:**
> **Hospitality:**
> **Cleanliness:**
> **Party index:**

How To Get There:
By bus: From Midi Station, take #18 streetcar to Porte de Flandre stop and walk ⅓ mile to hostel.
By car: Call hostel for directions.
By train: From train station, take Metro to Comte-de-Flandre stop and walk to hostel.

Chab Vincent Van Gogh Hostel

8 rue Traversière, Brussels 1210

Phone: 02-217-0158

Fax: 02-219-7995

E-mail: info@chab.be

Website: chab.be

Rates: €21–€36.50 (about $29–$46 US) per person; doubles €57–€59 (about $71–$74 US)

Credit cards: Yes

Beds: 210

Private/family rooms: Yes

Kitchen available: Yes

Season: Open year-round

Office hours: 7:30 a.m.–2 a.m. (check-in 2-3 p.m. only)

Lockout: 10 a.m.–2 p.m.

Affiliation: None

Extras: Kitchen, laundry, pool table, courtyard, breakfast, Internet access ($), solarium, garden, lockers, bar

Note: Must be age 18 to 35 to stay, unless booking as an entire group.

This is one of the best of the Brussels Fun Bunch—OK, we'll give it a nod and call it the best; better than it has to be. But not perfect. (For one thing, there should be *a lot* more bathrooms. And the check-in hours are ridiculously short.)

A pretty central hostel, it's not too far from town, either. It's close to the city's northern train station and no more than a leisurely half-hour stroll from the central square—though it isn't a terribly exciting walk and we'd probably end up taking the expensive city subway instead of being bored out of our minds.

Best bet for a bite:
Fries, of course

Insiders' tip:
De Ultieme Hallucinatie (bar)

Gestalt:
van Go!

Safety:

Hospitality:

Cleanliness:

Party index:

The main reception area opens onto a bar area (here's a tip: a cheap bar) with a small but fun pool table and a lounge with a nicely designed solarium. They serve those great Belgian beers, of course, and the kitchen is also aces. Then there's a kiosk for Internet access, a credit-card phone, and a free locker room for your stuff (the room itself is locked, giving double security). Out through the back is the best part of all—a pretty enclosed courtyard, surrounded by ivy, with a rose garden that blooms in spring.

That's where most of the kiddies are groovin' and mingling.

The crowd doing that mingling is a real melange of cig-smoking French girls, youth groups, young Americans, rasta guys . . . just think young. We didn't see anybody over the age of 20 when we stopped in, so it's not really the sort of place where lots of families with kids show up.

Rooms are standard and nothing to write home about—usually 6 to a room but sometimes 4 or 8 to a room. Amazingly, some doubles come with private bathrooms. But the cheapest dorms are packed and the bathrooms are shrimpy overall. These are downtown city hotel rooms at hostel prices, folks; snap 'em up quick if you can. But remember: Hostellers under 18 or over 35 may not stay here unless they have booked as part of a group (contact the hostel directly for details about group-booking requirements).

How To Get There:

By bus: Take #91, #92, #93, or #94 streetcar to hostel.

By car: Call hostel for directions.

By train: From Nord (North) Station, walk or take Metro to Botanique stop and then walk down rue Royale to rue Traversière; take a right and walk to hostel. Or take #61 bus to Botanique Metro stop and walk down rue Royale to rue Traversière; take a right and walk to hostel. From Centraal Station, take Metro Line 1 to Arts-Loi stop and change to Line 2, then continue to Botanique stop. Walk down rue Royale to rue Traversière; take a right and walk to hostel.

 Attractive natural setting

 Ecologically aware hostel

Superior kitchen facilities or cafe

Offbeat or eccentric place

Superior bathroom facilities

Romantic private rooms

Comfortable beds

 A particularly good value

Wheelchair-accessible

Good for business travelers

Especially well-suited for families

Good for active travelers

 Visual arts at hostel or nearby

 Music at hostel or nearby

Great hostel for skiers

 Bar or pub at hostel or nearby

Editors' choice: Among our very favorite hostels

Sleep Well Hostel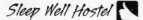

23 rue du Damier, Brussels 1000

> **Phone:** 02-218-5050
> **Fax:** 02-218-1313
> **E-mail:** info@sleepwell.be
> **Website:** sleepwell.be
> **Rates:** €22.50–€41.50 (about $28–$52 US) per person; doubles €52 (about $65 US)
> **Credit cards:** Yes
> **Beds:** 240
> **Private/family rooms:** Yes
> **Kitchen available:** No
> **Season:** Open year-round
> **Office hours:** 7 a.m.–midnight
> **Lockout:** 11 a.m.–3 p.m.
> **Affiliation:** None
> **Extras:** TV, tours, currency exchange, bar, garden, Internet access, restaurant ($),
> breakfast

*A*nother decent place? Yes—Brussels may be a bit of a bore, but this town knows hostels. This is the newest joint in town of the five we've reviewed here, and it's good enough for government work—if big, impersonal, and at times filled to the rails with European schoolkiddies.

Also, the surrounding area looked a little like a bomb shelter when we rolled in to check it out. At least this is the closest hostel to the Grand-Place square, where you'll probably be spending your time.

Lots of work has been done to spruce up this hostel. Beds come in singles (8), doubles (11, not counting the annex; see below), triples (8), quads (9), six-bed dorms (7), and 2 eight-bed dorms. The hostel also has a hotel-like 32-room annex of all-double rooms called the Star. All have private bathrooms, TVs, and no lockout! This site also has a bar, club, and other upgrades. In other words, you're probably going to have a cozy, small room, and that's a nice feeling. There are a surprising number of other amenities here for the traveler as well: Try an Internet bar/cafe and fax service, in the main hostel, for starters. They do breakfast and meals, too, and store luggage for you during the day. There's even an outdoor terrace. It's all doled out by mostly friendly staffers who don't lean on rules to keep you out.

We found only one drawback to this place, in fact: a long 11 a.m. to 3 p.m. lockout, a bit discouraging in tiring Brussels. Sure, the city is fun and has some attractions—but not that much fun. We needed a rest after hours of pounding the pavement. (While we're complaining, can we say a word about those well-meaning, low-flowing, push-button-style showers, too? Argh! Those are so 1980. Get some real low-flow showers, will ya?)

Best bet for a bite:
Grand-Place
Insiders' tip:
Lop Lop (bar) near Grand-Place
What hostellers say:
"It's OK."
Gestalt:
Sleeping beauty
Safety:
Hospitality:
Cleanliness:
Party index:

But we digress. There's one other problem when you've got such a successful hostel: popularity. This place requires advance booking, especially during the European school holidays (generally speaking, in May, July, Aug, and Sept)—during which times the place is absolutely swamped, not only by German and French schoolkids but the occasional American group as well. Don't show up here on short notice, even a day ahead, during those months expecting to find a bed, 'cause it just won't happen.

How To Get There:
By bus: Take #91, #92, #93, or #94 streetcar to hostel.
By car: Call hostel for directions.
By train: From Gare du Nord, walk down rue du Progrés to rue de Malines, then make a right onto rue du Damier. Or take Metro to Rogier stop and walk to hostel.

Czech Republic

Part of the former Czechoslovakia, the Czech Republic remains one of the most popular visitor destinations in the former Soviet bloc—mostly thanks to the lovely, you've-gotta-see-it city of Prague.

Hostels aren't nearly as prevalent here as they are in some other European countries, but the low cost of lodging in hotels means you probably won't need one—until you get to Prague, that is, where a recent spike in tourist traffic and hotel prices is now making hostels a very good business to get into.

Practical Matters

The unit of currency in the Czech Republic is the koruna (crown), abbreviated as Kč. There are 20 Kč per US dollar, so a 300 Kč dorm room costs about $15 and a 60 Kč beer costs $3.

The country code, if you're dialing ahead from the US or elsewhere in Europe, is +420. When dialing the numbers listed here from abroad, do NOT drop the initial zero as you normally do when calling Europe. (You don't need a double zero, though, just one.)

The Czech Republic is served by its own decently efficient train company, but this is NOT a Eurail country. You'll need to buy either a special pass or tickets right from conductors and at train stations. There's a Czech pass, a Czech-Germany pass, and an Austria-Czech pass.

PRAGUE (PRAHA)

We think of two words when we think of Prague: *beautiful* and *changing*.

Prague is a city on the move. Prices are going up, phone numbers change constantly, political figures come and go, and capitalism is on a serious upswing.

Must-see sights here range from the grand (Hradčany Castle) to the sobering (the wonderful Jewish neighborhood known as Josefov) to the various mazes of streets, bars dispensing pilsner, and the character-filled merchants and children. It's best to just dive in—with a good map—or else hire a reputable city tour guide, available through many of the hostels listed below.

There's one downtown hostel run by the Hostelling International affiliate CKM, but at least a dozen others run by independent owners and outfits. Most notable among them is the Travellers chain, which currently includes about a half dozen hostels, some open only during the summer months and some more apartment than hostels. We haven't included those adjunct-type hostels in this guide, but you can get all the details from the main Travellers hostel, which is open year-round.

Note that Prague's hostels are particularly finicky, and any hostel listed in these pages could well be closed by the time you get there. CALL OR E-MAIL AHEAD before you visit.

Orientation & Getting Around

Hlavní Nádraží, less than a mile east of the river that splits the city, is the main train station and your likely arrival point. It's also a good orientation point. From here, going directly west and a little north, you soon pass through Old Town; go west and a little south, and you pass through New Town. Most of the hostels are in these two neighborhoods. Just north of Old Town lies Josefov, another neighborhood you'll surely want to see.

Once here, the best way to get around the city is to use public transit. Prague's subway system consists of three lines—labeled A (green line), B (yellow line), and C (red line)—that run about every two minutes (yes, every two minutes) from approximately 5 a.m. until midnight. Fast streetcars (also known as trams) and buses supplement the subway, running about every 10 minutes, though less frequently at night or on weekends. Big maps at the stations show you where the lines run; it's important to know which end point your subway car is heading toward before you get on, because the train will be labeled according to end point.

During the night you must use night buses or night trams (streetcars), most of which pick up every forty minutes or so from downtown. Many of these lines pass through the Metro Station Lazarská, one of the main hubs of the entire transit system. For more-out-of-the-way places, a few bus lines run out to the city's outlying districts, usually with numbers in the 300s; these are more expensive rides, but you can buy these tickets (and these alone) right on the buses.

Buy local transit tickets at ticket offices, Information Centers of the Prague Public Transit Company, selected stores, or from bright yellow-orange ticket machines. For almost all practical purposes, you will always be within "the zone," the central fare area. (There is also another zone in Prague, the "finishing zone," and four suburban zones; prices below apply only to the two central zones.) There are several kinds of tickets: a more expensive ticket (about $1.50 US) allows 75 minutes of riding and free transfers among Metro, bus, and tram (streetcar) lines. And then a normal single ticket (about $1 US) gives you 20 or 30 minutes of riding or up to four subway stops; get them at machines in the stations. (If you need to travel farther than four stops, you have to buy the more expensive ticket.) There are half-price discounts for children ages 6 to 15 and seniors age 60 and up.

Prague (Praha)

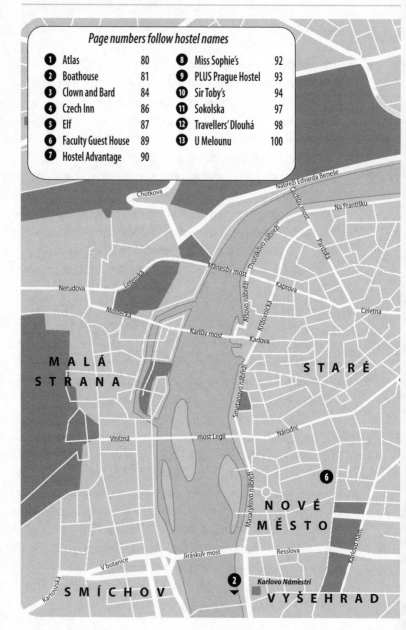

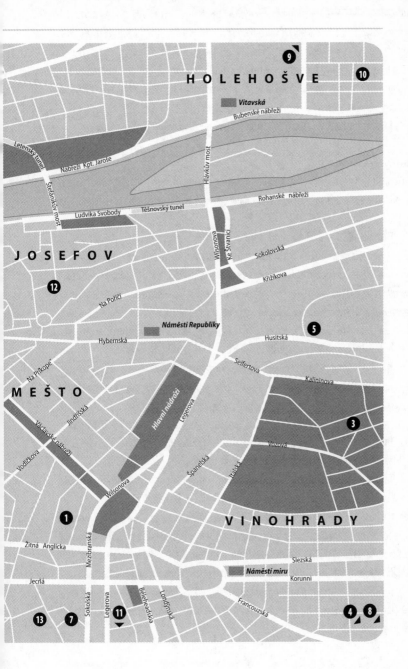

If you'll be around for a while, offices also sell passes valid for 24 hours or three, five, and 30 days. They cost from 110 Kč (about $5.50 US) for one day to 300 Kč (about $15 US) for three days; that's a deal only if you'll be riding around a lot. Also remember that if your luggage is bigger than about 10" x 18" x 28"—and many backpacks are—you'll also need a cheap (less than a buck) supplemental ticket for it. Don't try to ride without a ticket, either: Cops are much more common here than on other European transit systems, and fines can be steep.

To find out more, visit the transit system's website: dpp.cz/en.

Safety & Crime

You'll need to be careful in Prague to avoid getting separated from your cash: Bad hostels, pickpockets, dishonest taxi drivers, and bogus currency exchangers are just a few of the potential pitfalls.

First, the hostels. You'll be surrounded by "touts" or "runners"—guys who get paid to rope in hostellers for a hostel—at the train station or even on the train going to Prague. Ignore them; you've got this book as a guide, and we're unbiased. NEVER get in a car with a "hostel representative" at the station. If you're truly interested in one of those places, ask to see on a map where the hostel is located, then take public transit or a cab by yourself later. More often than not, these places are located way out of town (which they don't tell you up front), and they're very poor quality (which they obviously also don't tell you). Exceptions are rare.

There are lots of pickpockets here, especially active in crowded buses and subway cars. If you feel a hard shove, grab your wallet and backpack pronto—it could be a thief distracting you for a second so he can go for the goods. Better yet, take off your backpack and hold it tightly in front of you, even if there isn't much space on the subway; thieves could use knives to cut them off your back. Crowded public squares like Charles Bridge, Old Town Square, or at the Hlavní Nádraží (main train station) also require caution.

Taxis are another problem; rip-offs are unfortunately more common than they should be, so we recommend avoiding them altogether while in Prague. They're not worth the potential hassle of arguing with some burly dude very late at night in a bad neighborhood. If you're taking one from the airport, bear this in mind before agreeing to a ride: The lift should start at 30 or 40 Kč ($1.50–$2 US) and add only about 30 Kč ($1.50) per km; your total fare shouldn't exceed 700 Kč ($35). If the driver's talking higher numbers, find another cab.

Finally, you'll also find gambling cons and prostitutes in Prague. Try to avoid all that—and keep your eyes open whenever in the Third District or Wenceslas Square—and focus on why you came: the city.

Communications

To dial Prague hostels from within Prague, dial the numbers as printed.

To dial Prague hostels from elsewhere within the Czech Republic, dial 02 plus the number printed.

To dial Prague hostels from outside the Czech Republic but within Europe, dial +00-42-02 plus the number printed—KEEP THE ZERO, unlike in most other European countries.

To dial Prague hostels from the US, dial +011-42-02 plus the number printed. Again, KEEP THE ZERO.

PRAGUE HOSTELS AT A GLANCE

	RATING	PRICE	IN A WORD	PAGE
Boathouse		350–400 Kč	communal	p. 81
Miss Sophie's		420–575 Kč	chic	p. 92
Sir Toby's		207–380 Kč	comfy	p. 94
Czech Inn		285–990 Kč	hip	p. 86
PLUS Prague Hostel		270–410 Kč	relaxing	p. 93
Hostel Advantage		470–1,880 Kč	improving	p. 90
Faculty Guest House		750–1,200 Kč	collegiate	p. 89
U Melounu		450–990 Kč	plush	p. 100
Elf Hostel		240–1,250 Kč	groovy	p. 87
Clown and Bard		250–500 Kč	fun	p. 84
Atlas Hostel		300–1,100 Kč	conservative	p. 80
Travellers' Dlouhá		270–850 Kč	rockin'	p. 98
Sokolska Hostel		160–500 Kč	OK	p. 97

Atlas Hostel

Ve Smečkách 13, Praha 1

   Phone: 222-210500

   Fax: 602-262215

   E-mail: hostel@atlas.cz

   Website: hostelatlas.cz

   Rates: 300–1,100 Kč (about $15–$55 US) per person; doubles 800–1,400 Kč (about $40–$70 US)

   Credit cards: No

   Beds: 50

   Private/family rooms: Yes

   Kitchen available: No

   Season: Open year-round

   Office hours: 8 a.m.–8 p.m.

   Affiliation: None

   Extras: TV lounge, Internet access

   Neighborhood: Staré Město (Old Town)

*V*áclavské náměstí (Wenceslas Square) is the dominant influence in this part of Prague, yet it's quite surprising how quiet this hostel's street is. Though the square itself used to be the city's main red-light district, it has gradually transformed itself into one of Prague's most exclusive shopping and business places.

And that's the best thing about this hostel: the location. You're directly in the heart of downtown, a place that's full of street life, shops, theaters, pubs, and more—a place for window-shopping and party-hopping all night long, if you want.

The hostel itself? It used to be one of our prime picks in the city, but it has slowly been downsliding. Again, the main selling point now is that it's within walking distance of the main train station and not a complete Party Central.

Best bet for a bite:
Cafe around corner

What hostellers say:
"Like a rehab center for dudes."

Gestalt:
Atlas rugged

Safety:

Hospitality:

Cleanliness:

Party index:

It has been renovated fairly recently. But on the downside, there's no kitchen in the common areas, only in the private apartment section. That's 5 floors up . . . and no elevators. Other complaints? Showers are balky, and the dorms are a bit cramped. Upkeep isn't what it once was.

It's easy to feel at home here, though. The lounge TV gets prominent news channels, and if you pay more you can stay in an attached apartment with a small kitchen. Then you'll really feel at home. There's no curfew, no lockout, and the owners are amazingly friendly, so that's something. And they added slowish Internet access.

Note: Be sure not to confuse this hostel with the nightclub called Atlas on the same street. The hostel's street number is #13. The club is at #13. No confusion there. Nope.

How To Get There:

By bus: Contact hostel for transit route.
By car: Contact hostel for directions.
By train: From Hlavní Nádraží, walk or take Metro subway one stop to Muzeum.

Boathouse Hostel

1 Lodnická, Praha 4

Phone: 2417-70051
Fax: 2417-76988
E-mail: boathouse@volny.cz
Website: hostelboathouse.com
Rates: 350–400 Kč per person (about $18–$20 US)
Credit cards: No
Beds: 58
Private/family rooms: No
Kitchen available: No
Season: Open year-round
Office hours: 24 hours
Affiliation: None
Extras: Breakfast ($), shop, lockers, luggage storage, games, laundry ($), Internet access ($),
Neighborhood: Braní

Best bet for a bite:
Right here, right now
What hostellers say:
"We are family . . ."
Gestalt:
Love Boathouse
Safety:
Hospitality:
Cleanliness:
Party index:

*T*he "Boathouse Gang" runs this very unconventional hostel, located right next to the Vltava River in a green area with stupendous views. (The area was hit so hard during Prague's 2003 floods that it practically became an island in the river, for a time.) It takes work to get here, but do get here. 'Cuz this is the city's top hostel; it might be one of Europe's top hostels; and it's cheap.

The owners and the crew ensure a great stay with incredible customer service. Yes, you have to walk through the woods and climb stairs to a dark wood building to get here. But as soon as you open the door, you'll like the look of things: The interior is amazing, from the colors to the photos on the walls showing previous guests in the big lounge. By the time you've wandered into the reception area—a living room, really—you've got the full flavor of the place. It's as laid-back as can be, and staff try to initiate personal contact with each guest (but not in an annoying way).

This is a true hostel, not a hotel, so beds are simple. You won't find any double rooms at all—just 2 big nine-bed dorms and a collection of 3-, 4-, and 5-bed rooms. All are spic-and-span clean. There are lockers in these rooms, every guest gets a key, and in fact you can't get in without it—thumbs up again. Luggage storage at the reception is free. The free breakfast is hot and almost too good to be true—and they serve 'til noon. Whaaaat? Yes; we are not lying. (They'll also pack you one to go. Are we dreaming?) The hostel's in-house shop is basically a convenience store, stocked with everything from beer and smokes to film, tissues, gum, and local transit tickets.

The focus here is on creating an ad hoc family of travelers. A glance at the photos on the wall makes that point: One features loads of guests sitting together on Christmas Eve for dinner. In other shots people are playing music or singing together. The whole place seems like a giant summer camp where hostellers stay in rather than go out at night, sitting in the lounge or on the terrace playing cards or chess, talking, or writing some of the free postcards you get as a welcome present. In summer they sit singing around a fire, work the grill, or play guitar—all with a pilsner in hand, of course.

As we've said, this place is all about fun; no worries that it might get rowdy, as the helpful staff keep everything running smoothly. They know what they expect—and they will tell you. For example, dinner is at 7:30 p.m. sharp and you've gotta order it by afternoon—so do it! It's cheap, good, hearty Czech food, with some additions they got from guests, and nobody tries to miss it. (Much of the cuisine uses poultry, if that's any help. The house tomcat undoubtedly forages carnivorous leftovers.)

Curfew? Lockout? Please! This place is way too cool for all that stuff, and the streetcar ride from downtown—the only mild drawback to this place—might mean people getting locked out. They'd never let that happen.

All in all, a great pick—the best. Just be careful walking to the boat late at night, OK? We don't want them finding you in the river.

How To Get There:
By bus: Contact hostel for transit route.
By car: Contact hostel for directions.
By streetcar: Take #54 streetcar from the Charles Bridge, or #17 streetcar from Holešovice Station to Černý Kůň; follow yellow signs to river and hostel.
By train: From Hlavní Nádraží Station, cross through the park and walk straight through to Jeruzalemská Street. Catch #3 streetcar Line 3 at Jindřišská to Černý Kůň stop, then walk toward river several hundred yards, following signs. From Nádraží Holešovice Station, take #17 streetcar to Černý Kůň stop and follow yellow signs to river and hostel.

Attractive natural setting
Ecologically aware hostel
Superior kitchen facilities or cafe
Offbeat or eccentric place
Superior bathroom facilities
Romantic private rooms

Comfortable beds
A particularly good value
Wheelchair-accessible
Good for business travelers
Especially well-suited for families
Good for active travelers

Visual arts at hostel or nearby
Music at hostel or nearby
Great hostel for skiers
Bar or pub at hostel or nearby
Editors' choice: Among our very favorite hostels

Key to Icons

Clown and Bard Hostel

Bořivojova 102, Praha 3

Phone: 222-716453

Fax: 222-719026

E-mail: clownandbard@clownandbard.com

Website: clownandbard.com

Rates: 250–500 Kč (about $13–$25 US) per person; doubles 900-1,200 Kč (about $45–$60 US)

Credit cards: No

Beds: 142

Private/family rooms: Yes

Kitchen available: Yes

Season: Open year-round

Office hours: 24 hours

Affiliation: None

Extras: Currency exchange, city tours, bar, laundry service, ski information, luggage room, Internet access

Neighborhood: Žižkov

The hoppin' Clown and Bard, here since 1995, may be the most famous hostel in Prague. It got most of its reputation for the kavárna (basically, a bar) that is run on the same premises—and also for the offbeat people working the reception or staying as guests. It certainly deserves its reputation as an offbeat place.

Staff are friendly and cool, though, and the hostel has hugely expanded (80 new beds) in recent years. But upkeep has slid downhill a lot, and there's a bit of a strangeness to the place as well. The rooms themselves are on several floors of a typical Prague house; you'll find everything from small twin rooms to a big dorm in the attic holding more than 30 beds. All of these rooms have enough daylight and make a clean and comfortable (if bare) impression, what with the whitewashed walls and such. There's a lot of wood here—in fact, the whole place looks half-timbered.

The attic dorm is a little odd, though. There are bunk beds and even overhead beds—3 layers of snoring people in one hosteller sandwich—plus a lot of screeching sounds from the wooden bunks. You don't even get lockers here, so deposit your valuables in the safe at the reception or try to avoid that dorm if you can. Other rooms may not look as cool, but they are actually much quieter and safer, and bathrooms are modern, even futuristic.

While the linens and the rooms are nice, the state of the showers of the large dorm is bad—not nearly clean enough, and bordering on scuzzy at times. Who's been cleaning this place? (Nobody, apparently.) Also on the downside, there are a lot of long-term guests here (the hostel offers

Best bet for a bite:
Pizzeria Mestre
Insiders' tip:
Pl@neta Internet cafe nearby
What hostellers say:
"Fun, fun, fun."
Gestalt:
Class Clown
Safety:
Hospitality:
Cleanliness:
Party index:

discounts for long stays), and they tend to be possessive of public areas and such. Not a good thing for a hostel. The breakfast, though technically cheap, is overpriced for the quality, and terrible, too.

On the upside, the attached kavárna is mighty popular in the evenings, and justly so. Hostellers enjoy the draft beer and atmosphere, and the place is so good that even locals blend in regularly—come to Czech out the Czechs. Watch for live music nights with bands, too; there are even some open-mike nights if you're feeling inspired.

There's a kitchen with very minimal equipment, so you'll probably need to go out to eat. And the costs-extra hostel breakfast, while cheap, is nothing at all special; have a backup plan. Fortunately, the location here in Žižkov is one of the few pluses. Starting from the Flora Metro station, there are some interesting cemeteries, including a small Jewish one, as well as a park in Vozová next to the hostel with a green area for hanging out. You'll find a large choice of shops and restaurants here, as well. Lost in the back streets? Just look for the big TV tower, one of the most prominent buildings in the hostel neighborhood.

How To Get There:
By bus: Contact hostel for transit route.
By car: Contact hostel for directions.
By streetcar: Take #55 or #58 night tram.
By train: From Hlavní Nádraží Station, catch any streetcar (#5, #9, or #26) one stop to

Husinecká. Take the first right on Krásova Street, up the hill, then take second right down Bořivojova Street. (Entrance is through a metal door; descend stairs into the kavárna to find reception.) From Nádraží Holešovice Station, take Metro red line (Line C) to Muzeum Station, then change to the green line (Line A) and continue toward Skalka to Jiřího z Poděbrad Station. Get off the escalators and take the right-hand exit to Slavíkova Street; walk 300 yards and turn right at the bottom of Ježkova. Continue to Bořivojova.

By plane: Take #119 bus to last stop (Dejvicka). Walk downstairs to green Metro line (line A) and follow directions above.

Czech Inn

76 Francouzská, Prague 2

>   **Phone:** 267-267600 or 267-267612
>   **Fax:** 283-870636
>   **E-mail:** info@czech-inn.com
>   **Website:** czech-inn.com
>   **Rates:** 285–990 Kč (about $15–$50 US) per person; doubles 1,320–1,650 Kč (about $66–$85 US)
>   **Credit cards:** Yes
>   **Beds:** Number varies
>   **Private/family rooms:** Yes
>   **Kitchen available:** Yes
>   **Season:** Open year-round
>   **Office hours:** 24 hours
>   **Affiliation:** None
>   **Extras:** Free internet access, cafe, bar, luggage storage

---

*T*he *Washington Post* once said that this place is "almost too hip to be a hostel," or something to that effect. Well, guys, deal with it.

It is, in design at least. Dorm rooms are clean, efficiently designed, and slightly modern-artish, even if the bunks themselves are just your basic everyday bunks. (There are some 1-, 2-, and even 3-room apartments both on and off the premises costing substantially more, and these are obviously nicer.)

The big hit here is the cafe-slash-bar, which serves meals and 4 different Czech beers from early morning (well, don't drink then) until late at night. There's Sky TV beaming in Euro-sports and news. Security is good, and there's free WiFi throughout, as well as terminals in the lobby. Bathrooms are nice; they have live music, trivia nights, and the like, too. What the heck else do you want for 15 bucks?

Best bet for a bite:
Right here
What hostellers say:
"Cool . . . for a hostel."
Gestalt:
Czech mates
Safety: ◣
Hospitality: ◣
Cleanliness: ◣
Party index: 🎉🎉🎉🎉

How To Get There:

By bus: From Flörenc bus station, take Metro C line (red line) toward Haje to I.P. Pavlova station (3 stops). Walk upstairs to street level and walk 15 minutes along Francouska Street to hostel. Or take #4, #22, or #23 streetcar to Krymska (3 stops) and walk 50 yards uphill to hostel on left.

By car: Contact hostel for directions.

By train: From Hlavní Nádraží station, take Metro C line (red line) toward Haje to I.P. Pavlova station (2 stops); walk upstairs to street level and walk 15 minutes along Francouska Street to hostel, or take #4, #22, or #23 streetcar to Krymska (3 stops) and walk 50 yards uphill to hostel on left. From Holešovice station, take Metro C line (red line) toward Haje to I.P. Pavlova station (5 stops) and follow the same directions.

Elf Hostel ◣

Husitská 11, Praha 3

Phone: 222-540963

E-mail: info@hostelelf.com

Website: hostelelf.com

Rates: 240–1,250 Kč (about $12–$63 US) per person; doubles 1100–1,520 Kč (about $55–$76 US)

Credit cards: No

Beds: 110

Private/family rooms: Yes

Kitchen available: Yes

Season: Open year-round

Office hours: 24 hours
Affiliation: None
Extras: Free tea, laundry ($), city tours, garden, patio, store, grill, garden
Neighborhood: Žižkov

![icons]

*T*his whole place has been painted by art students, friends of the owners—three women who wanted to try something new and started this hostel in the summer of 2000. Some of them may or may not have been connected to the musical *Hair*, because the whole place is very hippie-like.

No wonder long-termers like the Elf; they like the eccentric hostel as well as the area. And the prices are something to be considered, too—it's simply cheaper than most. There are a lot of guitars at this hostel, people grilling in the small garden terrace, trains coming by with waving engineers, and the like. The hostel shop sells everything from condoms to soda.

Attention has been paid to details: There's a nice historical pattern from the early 1900s painted underneath the ceiling at the reception. A small kitchen allows basic meals to be cooked. There's free tea all day and a laundry service. The heating in winter is among the best in town, too.

Unfortunately, there are no lockers or a safe.

One thing we've noticed: This place seems to be on the upswing. Bathrooms and upkeep are better than they were in past seasons, though security still would seem to be lax. At least there's always somebody at the reception—one night shift even brought a very alert (though otherwise quiet) watchdog! All in all, the Elf is hippy-dippy, but also iffy-iffy.

Don't miss the atmospheric local bar, the U Vystřeleného Voka, around the corner. The whole area, while a little rough around the edges, is just full of places like this: characteristic Czech rock clubs, discos, coffee and tea houses, skate shops, a sex shop . . . quite crazy, all in all. Come now, though, for the times they are a-changing—it might be scrubbed and polished up in a few years.

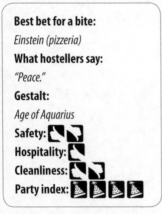

Best bet for a bite:
Einstein (pizzeria)
What hostellers say:
"Peace."
Gestalt:
Age of Aquarius
Safety:
Hospitality:
Cleanliness:
Party index:

How To Get There:

By bus: From Flörenc bus station, walk ¼ mile to hostel or take #133 or #207 bus 1 stop.

By car: Contact hostel for directions.

By train: From Hlavní Nádraží Station, take Metro Line C or walk ½ mile to Flörenc station, then continue ¼ mile to hostel or take #133 or #207 bus 1 stop.

From Nádraží Holešovice Station, take Metro Line C to Flörenc station, then follow directions above.

Faculty Guest House

Protestant Theological Faculty, Univerzita Karlova

Cerná 9, Praha 1

Phone: 221-988214

Fax: 221-988215

E-mail: majordomus@etf.cuni.cz

Website: etf.cuni.cz/ubyt

Rates: 750–1,200 Kč (about $38–$60 US) per person; doubles 1,560 Kč (about $78 US)

Credit cards: No

Beds: 25 (winter), 35 (summer)

Private/family rooms: Yes

Kitchen available: Yes

Season: Open year-round

Office hours: 24 hours

Affiliation: None

Extras: Breakfast ($), in-room phones, computer room, Bibles

Neighborhood: Suburbs

---

*T*he interesting thing about this Charles University student dorm is that it offers beds to traveleres all year long—even during the academic year—making it a great pick for families, older travelers, and those who want more amenities. You still share kitchens, bathrooms, and showers, but at least there's a sink in each room and the place was specially designed to be wheelchair-accessible.

Best bet for a bite:
Tesco supermarket on Vocelova

What hostellers say:
"Will there be a pop quiz on this?"

Gestalt:
Seminary vesicle

Safety:

Hospitality:

Cleanliness:

Party index:

The location of the place is very central. Close by is the National Theater; opposite this is the cafe Slavia. In the early 1900s, this was very popular among the local cafe society, including artists, politicians, and other celebrities; it recently reopened.

Sure, it's a bit institutional (and pretty expensive for Prague), but this place definitely fills the bill in every other way except being a place to socialize. But there's just one little detail you need to know: Charles U, despite the friendly name, is a seminary. That's right; we said seminary. Don't run away screaming. You can basically ignore the church ties—they don't proselytize, so far as we could tell—and they do provide a cheap, safe sleep without serving up a heavy side of religious dogma. Which always gets run over by your karma anyway, right?

How To Get There:

By bus: Contact hostel for transit route.

By car: Contact hostel for directions.

By streetcar: At night take #51, #52, #53, #55, #56, #57, or #58 night tram.

By train: From either Hlavní Nádraží or Nádraží Holešovice Station, take Metro Line C (red line) to Flörenc Station, then change to Line B (yellow line). Get off at Národní třída and walk along Ostrovní, keeping left and continuing to Cerná.

Hostel Advantage

Sokolská 11, Praha 2

Phone: 224-914062

Fax: 220-806912

E-mail: advantage@jsc.cz

Website: jsc.cz/advantage

Rates: 470–1880 Kč (about $24–$94 US) per person; doubles 1,400–1,880 Kč (about $70–$94 US)

Credit cards: Yes

Beds: 118
Private/family rooms: Yes
Kitchen available: Yes
Season: Open year-round
Office hours: 24 hours
Affiliation: HI-CKM
Extras: Luggage storage, shop, TV, breakfast, free WiFi, restaurant ($)
Neighborhood: Nové Město (New Town)

---

*S*o what's this big "advantage" you speak of? This one is close to town and small enough to be reasonably friendly. It's also cheap and central. And the sheets are perfectly clean. What's more, it has improved dramatically in recent years—enough so that we now feel good giving it the coveted "thumb up." Nice work, guys.

The hostel's located on a major street, which brings both access to the city and noise. Some of the dorm rooms inside have newer furniture, but others of them are quite spartan. Still, rooms are pretty spacious—one quirk of this place is that all rooms can be locked, though sometimes you must walk through another dorm room to reach your own digs.

Staff are friendly, for Prague—give 'em credit for that—and they'll never hassle you about things like lockouts or curfews. The little on-site store is well enough maintained, the small television lounge–slash–common space right next to the reception is hopping. A kitchenette has been added, and free Internet is nice. Breakfasts, showers, and towels are all included in your price (you'd be surprised how often that isn't the case in Europe). And there's an actually good restaurant in the basement. It's not often we see a place rise quickly, but this one has.

Best bet for a bite:
Radost FX (vegetarian)
What hostellers say:
"So-so."
Gestalt:
Dissed advantage
Safety:
Hospitality:
Cleanliness:
Party index:

How To Get There:
By bus: Contact hostel for transit route.
By car: Contact hostel for directions.
By streetcar: At night take #57 tram from the National Theater.

By subway: From Hlavní Nádraží or Nádraží Holešovice Station, take Metro Line C (red line) to I.P. Pavlova Station and take the stairs to the left side. Walk to Ječná Street and turn left into Sokolská. Hostel is on right.

By plane: Take #119 bus to Dejvicka Station, then Metro Line A to I.P. Pavlova Station and follow directions above.

Miss Sophie's Hostel 🔻🔻

Melounova 3, Prague 2

> **Phone:** 296-303530
> **Fax:** 267-267601
> **E-mail:** reservation@miss-sophies.com
> **Rates:** 420–575 Kč (about $21–$29 US) per person; doubles 1,150–1,390 Kč (about $58–$70 US)
> **Credit cards:** Yes
> **Beds:** Number varies
> **Kitchen available:** Yes
> **Season:** Open year-round
> **Office hours:** 24 hours
> **Private/family rooms:** Yes
> **Affiliation:** None
> **Extras:** Terrace, free WiFi access, breakfast ($), terrace, lounge, TV

👪📋✖️🛏️

---

*T*hey tout "the real Prague" at this place . . . and hostellers agree. It does deliver a true experience, and much, much more. Hell, this looks more like a boutique hotel (Reception staff are dressed up! Furniture is mod!) than a centrally located, clean, and safe hostel (which it most definitely is).

Leather couches, modern art, glass coffee tables, a sleek kitchen, hotel-quality apartment beds . . . not to mention a brick lounge in the basement with a flat-screen TV, that cool kitchen for hostellers' use, and a blanket no-smoking policy (is this still Europe?)—it all adds up to family friendly fun.

They offer dorms with 3, 4, or 5 beds, plus single and private/family rooms with 1 to 3 beds each, and then some nicer (if somewhat pricier) apartments with private bathrooms and full kitchens. Some are air-conditioned (ask when you book). There are storage rooms and luggage boxes under the beds—bring your own padlock for those. They'll even lend you, and we quote, "a hair dryer, iron, alarm clock, or [an] adapter" for no charge whatsoever (just a refundable deposit). Movies, too. Sweet!

For years Miss Sophie's suffered for lack of a true restaurant, cafe, or bar in-house. But they have gone the extra kilometer and recently added a breakfast of coffee and pastries. This is an amazingly nice place, and you'd never go hungry or thirsty in Prague anyway, so we don't mind the lack of a bar. Excellent choice, and a cool name to boot. Book it if you can.

> **Best bet for a bite:**
> *New Town*
> **What hostellers say:**
> *"Arty and luxe."*
> **Gestalt:**
> *Art attack*
> **Safety:** ◣
> **Hospitality:** ◣
> **Cleanliness:** ◣
> **Party index:** ◣ ◣ ◣

How To Get There:

By bus: From Flörenc bus station, take Metro C line (red line) toward Haje 3 stops to I.P. Pavlova station; exit to left and upstairs. Cross over to Katerinska Street, passing Pricewaterhousecoopers and Novotel, then take first right onto Melounova Street and continue to hostel on left.

By car: Contact hostel for directions.

By train: From Hlavní Nádraží station, take Metro C line (red line) toward Haje 2 stops to I.P. Pavlova station; exit to left and upstairs. Cross over to Katerinska Street, passing Pricewaterhousecoopers and Novotel, then take first right onto Melounova Street and continue to hostel on left. From Holešovice station, take Metro C line (red line) in direction of Haje 5 stops to I.P. Pavlova station and follow same directions.

PLUS Prague Hostel ◣

Přívozní 1, 7000 Praha
>   **Phone:** 220-510046
>   **Website:** plushostels.com
>   **Rates:** 270–410 CZK (about $14–$21 US) per person
>   **Credit cards:** No
>   **Beds:** Number varies

Private/family rooms: No
Kitchen available: No
Season: Open year-round
Office hours: 24 hours
Affiliation: None
Extras: TV, laundry, free WiFi, bar, restaurant, swimming pool, sauna

*M*ore distant from Prague's lovely old quarters than most other hostels reviewed here, this one is nevertheless worth a look for its amazing facilities, which include both a swimming pool and a sauna that are open 'til late at night (well, 'til 10 p.m.—is that late?).

Dorms are in configurations of 6 and 8 beds apiece; there are no single, doubles, or family rooms. The bar sometimes features DJs (this is Europe—what did you expect?).

Note that the restaurant on site does not serve lunch, only breakfast and dinner, and that there's no kitchen to speak of.

Best bet for a bite:
Try along U Uranie
What hostellers say:
"Pretty far from the action."
Gestalt:
Pool cues
Safety:
Hospitality:
Cleanliness
Party index:

How To Get There:

By car: Contact hostel for directions.
By bus: Contact hostel for transit route.
By train: Contact hostel for transit route.

Sir Toby's Hostel
Delnická 24, Praha 7
   Phone: 246-032610
   E-mail: info@sirtobys.com
   Website: sirtobys.com
   Rates: 207–380 Kč (about $11–$19 US) per person; doubles 855–872 Kč (about $43–$44 US)

Credit cards: No
Beds: 90
Private/family rooms: Yes
Kitchen available: Yes
Season: Open year-round
Office hours: 8 a.m.–6 p.m.
Affiliation: None
Extras: Free coffee, grill, laundry, free WiFi, backyard, library, bar, restaurant
Neighborhood: Holešovice

We don't know who this Toby fellow is, but he's doing something right. Because there are very few hostels in this world one might actually plan out a trip to return to one day. And Sir Toby's definitely could be one of them—everybody who comes into its orbit loves the place. But how the heck do they charge so little for a hostel this good?

The hostel is inside a historic building in the Holešovice area of Prague, very close to the city's secondary train station (and many incoming trains stop here first, so check with a conductor). This neighborhood is shifting from a mixed business and residential center to a predominantly residential area, and there are several big parks nearby, as well as the Pražská Trznice (Prague Market)—a huge place to buy in quantity at low prices. As befits this interesting area, the people who come to stay here seem both offbeat and sophisticated. Neat trick.

It's a fairly quiet place, though the kitchen "can be pretty crazy." If you have been staying at a party place and need some days to relax, you might do well to sleep here for a night or two. The dorms are relatively small, each room with its own design—one has its own piano, and even though it's out of tune a lot, it's kinda fun. Everybody hangs out in the first-floor kitchen anyway, with a tape player and tapes—many of the guests bring their own recordings—plus dining table, chairs, and lots of sofas. Always you'll find tea and coffee for free.

Best bet for a bite:
Rustika
What hostellers say:
"Small is beautiful!"
Gestalt:
Toby, or not Toby
Safety:
Hospitality:
Cleanliness:
Party index:

Despite the so-so 'hood, security is tops. Bedroom and bathroom facilities here are very good; there's even a tub and very nice, hot water, plus comfortable beds. And the area seems safe. If you want to make sure your bed has a locker underneath it, just ask when reserving; usually there are enough. (They do require padlocks, however.)

The subterranean bar is where the action is, and conviviality reigns supreme (as do Czech pilsners). Highly recommended. Sir Toby's also has a phone, a small library, a meditation and prayer room, a small backyard where barbecues are held at least once a week during the summer, laundry service, an Internet terminal, and a small supply of event tickets. Don't be surprised when the same person who checked you in during the afternoon suddenly appears on stage that night. Families get a 25 percent discount—a nice incentive to stay here—and everyone gets a handout at check-in with house picks of the local sights and hot spots.

The Art Nouveau building has gotten a facelift, uncovering some of its former beauty. Management also added 60 more beds in the renovation.

Staff couldn't be better, either. They like their jobs, and they are big fans of Prague. After a stay here, you will be, too.

How To Get There:

By bus: Contact hostel for transit route.

By car: Contact hostel for directions.

By train: From Hlavní Nádraží, take Metro Line C (red line) 2 stops to Vltavska. From outside the station, take any streetcar departing to the left. Get off at the Delnická tram stop (second stop), walk to the corner of Delnická Street, and turn left. From Nádraží Holešovice train station, take Metro to Vltavska and follow directions above.

Key to Icons

Attractive natural setting

Ecologically aware hostel

Superior kitchen facilities or cafe

Offbeat or eccentric place

Superior bathroom facilities

Romantic private rooms

Comfortable beds

A particularly good value

Wheelchair-accessible

Good for business travelers

Especially well-suited for families

Good for active travelers

Visual arts at hostel or nearby

Music at hostel or nearby

Great hostel for skiers

Bar or pub at hostel or nearby

Editors' choice: Among our very favorite hostels

Sokolska Hostel

52 Sokolska St., Prague 2

Phone: 252-546181

Website: hostel52.com

E-mail: hostel52@gmail.com

Rates: 160–500 Kč (about $8–$25 US) per person; doubles 800–1,000 Kč (about $40–$50 US)

Credit cards: Yes

Beds: 50

Private/family rooms: No

Kitchen available: No

Season: Open year-round

Office hours: 24 hours

Affiliation: None

Extras: Free Internet access, laundry, airport pickups, travel information desk, breakfast ($)

Neighborhood: Staré Město (Old Town)

*W*hile other hostels in town just keep getting better, the Sokolska is barely treading water. And that just ain't good enough.

Oh, you'll like the "no's" about this place. No curfew. No lockout. No hidden charges. No smoking.

It may look like a "no way" on the outside, but so far Sokolska has been mostly a "yes, and it was a nice surprise" on the inside. Cleanliness is OK (not perfect; it varies by the day and week), and the bunks could be airier; but this is not a bad place to set up for the night. You choose from 12-bed, 5-bed, and 4-bed coed (not single-sex) dorms; be aware of that if you're on the shy side. The bunks are a bit flimsy but seem clean enough.

Best of all is the location: The famous Staré Město (Old Town) section of Prague is quite close, and so is Vaclavske Square, with its shopping, eats, and National Museum (the city's oldest).

> **What hostellers say:**
> *"No personality, great location."*
> **Gestalt:**
> *Central perks*
> **Safety:**
> **Hospitality:**
> **Cleanliness:**
> **Party index:**

How To Get There:

By car: Contact hostel for directions.

By plane: From Ruzyne Airport, take bus N 119 to the Dejvicka subway station; this takes 20 minutes. Take Metro Line A (green line) from Dejvicka to Muzeum Station, then change to Line C (red line) and continue 1 stop to I.P. Pavlova station. Exit here, cross the road to Sokolska Street, and walk to #52.

Travellers' Dlouhá Hostel
Dlouhá Pension and Hostel

Dlouhá 33, Praha 1

> **Phone:** 224-826662 or 224-826663
>
> **Fax:** 224-826665
>
> **E-mail:** hostel@travellers.cz
>
> **Website:** travellers.cz
>
> **Rates:** 270–850 Kč (about $14–$43 US) per person; doubles 800–1,000 Kč (about $40–$50 US)
>
> **Credit cards:** No
>
> **Beds:** 157
>
> **Private/family rooms:** Yes
>
> **Kitchen available:** Yes
>
> **Season:** Open year-round
>
> **Office hours:** 24 hours
>
> **Affiliation:** HI-CKM
>
> **Extras:** Bars, disco, TV, store, bicycle rental, in-line skate rental, free Wi-Fi access, laundry service, city tour, breakfast, jukebox, club
>
> **Neighborhood:** Staré Město (Old Town)

Y ou will feel the pulse at this place—literally. The pulse of techno, that is: The Roxy dance club is located directly underneath it. And when you factor in the upkeep, this place is just OK, not great. In a city of many far better choices, it's worth a miss—unless you crave techno. Then this place is your daddy.

Headquarters for the Prague hostel chain called Travellers, this year-round place attracts a young crowd that's here to party—and they won't stop until 5 a.m. Maybe. Only then do the 4 bars in the Roxy close down, and the international crowd (including plenty of Brits) crawls/staggers home.

The location of the hostel—between the Old Town and the Josefov (Jewish neighborhood)—is as central as can be. The style of the rooms is a mixture of Empire and Bavarian, with carpeting every-

Best bet for a bite:
Apetit (buffet)
What hostellers say:
"Do a little dance . . . get down tonight."
Gestalt:
HQ to the rescue
Safety:
Hospitality:
Cleanliness:
Party index:

where except in the really attractive bar, where it would soon be destroyed. All in all, the place is loads of fun, though not all that quiet—did we mention the club? So if you want to have a good time in Prague and stay quite centrally, without spending much time in your actual hostel, this is one of your best choices in town. If you want peace and quiet with the kids, move along, cowboy.

The downside? Showers aren't exactly numerous, and cleanliness is sliding downhill fast. Couple that with staff who can seem indifferent, even rude at times, and you've got the makings of a less than perfect stay.

At least the free included breakfast, served from 8 to 10:30 a.m., is one of the best in town: more buffet than continental. And there's a ton to do within these walls. The third-floor bar also serves as a breakfast room in the morning; then, about 7 at night, it changes personality and dons shades. The bar serves draft beer and hot snacks and has cable TV, and the view over the Old Town is great from up there. Reception also sells beer, soda, sandwiches, and more. You can rent bicycles and in-line skates at the desk, they've got 2 fast Internet terminals in the lounge, and laundry service is available.

Worried about safety at night? There's a police station right around the corner, and the centrality means there's plenty of foot traffic even at night. So you're probably safe getting to and from the hostel. In fact, your biggest threat might be from fellow travelers: We heard several reports of intra-hostel theft. Keep a sharp eye on your stuff, and if humanly possible, take your valuables with you when you go out.

How To Get There:

By bus: Take Metro Line B 1 stop to Namesti Republiky station. Exit onto Revolucni Street and walk along streetcar tracks toward river; take second left (Dlouha Street). Walk 150 yards to hostel on right, beside Roxy nightclub.

By car: Contact hostel for directions.

By train: From either train station, take Metro Line C to Flörenc station; change to Line B, and continue 1 stop to Namesti Republiky station. Exit onto Revolucni Street and walk along streetcar tracks toward river; take 2nd left (Dlouha Street). Walk 150 yards to hostel on right, beside Roxy nightclub.

U Melounu Hostel

Ke Karlovu 7/457, Praha 2

> **Phone:** 249-19330
> **Fax:** 249-18322
> **Rates:** 450–990 Kč (about $24–$50 US) per person; doubles 1,000–1,400 Kč (about $50–$70 US)
> **Credit cards:** Yes
> **Beds:** 53
> **Private/family rooms:** Yes
> **Kitchen available:** Yes
> **Season:** Open year-round
> **Office hours:** 24 hours
> **Affiliation:** None
> **Extras:** Breakfast, food shop, phone cards, parking, Internet access ($), grill, garden, laundry ($)
> **Neighborhood:** Nové Město (New Town)

---

*T*he self-proclaimed "Rolls Royce" of Prague's hostels (although its name translates as the Czech for "watermelon"; make of that what you will), this place is right next to a maternity hospital—and just about as quiet. Don't come for a party or centrality to the action, but do come if you're with a family or if you treasure space and relaxation. Oh—and it's hardly the cream of the city's crop. Good, but not great.

In the midst of a green area in New Town, the building has only one floor, and right in the middle is a beautiful garden. Dorms are 6-bedded, which is nice, and the double rooms all have private baths—even nicer, especially for couples. There's a small kitchen with a stove and a fridge on the first floor, plus a common room in which the free included breakfast is served; you can even specify a vegetarian breakfast if you order a day in advance. (Prices are a little high, thus the free sheets, towels, and breakfast.)

The good hostel shop sells sandwiches,

Best bet for a bite:
Train Station Cafe at Hlavní Nádraží Station
What hostellers say:
"It's a palace!"
Gestalt:
Green acres
Safety:
Hospitality:
Cleanliness:
Party index:

cookies, and soda as well as phone cards, beer, and more. They'll even do wake-up and taxi calls for you and arrange a group barbecue if enough people ask for one. Still, staff here prefer the place to be almost mouse-quiet, so be prepared to head to town and hit a pub if you really want to get rowdy.

This hostel is particularly interesting for people with dogs—they're accepted for free, and they'll love the surroundings—as well as those with cars: There's actually a garage on-premises.

How To Get There:
By bus: Take #504 night bus. From Flörenc bus station, take red line (Metro Line C) to I.P. Pavlova Station, then follow directions below.
By car: Contact hostel for directions.
By train: From Hlavní Nádraží Station, take Metro Line C 2 stops to I.P. Pavlova Station. Use main escalator and take exit on left; cross the street and turn left into Sokolská, then make an immediate right onto Na Bojišti and continue to end. Turn left and walk down Ke Karlovu to hostel on right.

From Nádraží Holešovice Station, take Metro 5 stops to I.P. Pavlova Station. Take main escalator and exit on left; cross street and turn left into Sokolská, make an immediate right onto Na Bojišti and continue to end. Turn left and walk down Ke Karlovu to hostel on the right.

Denmark

*O*f all the countries in Europe, we're casting a vote for Denmark as having the best system of hostels. Oh, Ireland is in the mix with a great network, and so is Switzerland. But Denmark's hostels, most of them affiliated with Hostelling International, are absolutely wonderful: clean, friendly, efficient, and—in a country where everything is expensive (an American soda can cost the equivalent of 4 bucks, a sandwich around 10, and don't ask about hotels)—these hostels are a godsend.

The rural hostels are awesome, among Europe's best. This book deals only with urban hostels, however, and in Denmark you'll really save money at these places—despite the fact that they're not as quiet or green as the ones out in the sticks.

Practical Details

Denmark's national rail service, known as DSB, is extremely efficient—and also very popular among the Danes. As a result, during high summer season it can be difficult or impossible to reserve a spot on certain international or city-to-city trains, which you're often required to do. This is a country where you need to plan in advance, rather than try to wing it.

The unit of currency in Denmark is the Danish krone or crown (DKK). There are about 5 ½ Danish kroner to 1 US dollar at this writing—so that 90 DKK dorm room costs about $16 US and that 65 DKK sandwich cost you . . . 12 bucks?! Yikes! Things are expensive here, so plan accordingly; you'll spend more than you ever believed possible. Believe it.

Denmark's country code is 45. When calling from within Denmark, dial the numbers AS PRINTED. When calling from outside of Denmark, dial 45 and DROP THE FIRST ZERO from the numbers printed in this book. Remember: A phone card is very useful here, and directory assistance is expensive.

ÅRHUS

You might not think of Århus (pronounced *oar'-hoos*) as a destination at first, but we're here to tell you it belongs in your travel itinerary of Denmark. This is a university town—comparable to, say, Madison or Chapel Hill—with the resulting concentration of cool bars, clubs, and restaurants. Plus there's a set of beaches right in the city limits, and historical attractions including a folk museum. Interestingly, the two hostels in this city have very different feels and are located in vastly different neighborhoods. It just depends on what you want: sun, fun, and relaxation, or the buzz of the city and a cheap bed.

The city's train station is small enough to figure out with a minimum of trouble. Public transit here consists of a set of fairly efficient bus routes (although one of the hostels is quite far out of town, so you'll ride for a while). If you're staying in town, you're lucky: You can simply stroll through some of the city's oldest streets and get a feel for the place en route to the hostel.

ÅRHUS HOSTELS AT A GLANCE

	RATING	PRICE	IN A WORD	PAGE
Århus Pavillonen Hostel	⚑⚑	160–650 DKK	beachy	p. 103
Sleep-In Hostel	⚑	180–210 DKK	central	p. 104

Århus Pavillonen Hostel ⚑⚑

Marienlundsvej 10, Århus

Phone: 086-212-120

Fax: 086-105-560

E-mail: info@aarhus-danhostel.dk

Website: aarhus-danhostel.dk

Rates: 160–650 DKK (about $28–$118 US) per HI member; doubles 385–650 DKK (about $70–$118 US)

Credit cards: No

Beds: 151

Private/family rooms: Yes

Kitchen available: Yes

Season: January 9–December 16

Office hours: 7–11 a.m.; 4–10 p.m.

Affiliation: HI-Danhostel

Extras: Laundry, breakfast ($), store, parking, playground, kitchen, beach access, TV lounge

_T_his former motel has been converted into a very good hostel. The only disadvantage is its remote position about 2.5 miles out from the center, but that's actually a plus if you need a break from cities.

Dorms can get tight in summer, but about a dozen double rooms are simply old motel units and thus better than the usual dorm room. Trouble is, Danish families have booked up most of these well in advance of you.

Even so, there are grills outdoors and a very simple kitchen for cooking—you need to bring your own utensils and plates—which will keep you in the social mix. You'll find lots of families and cyclists here beside you, not partiers, and that can be a welcome switch. Staff are incredibly friendly here, too (the manager is a cycling nut). They'll help you out with directions, pack your breakfast in a sack to eat as a picnic lunch at the beach, and point out bike routes.

Best bet for a bite:
Riverside, along the Vadestedet

Insiders' tip:
Beach is a five-minute walk away

What hostellers say:
"Nice and quiet out here."

Gestalt:
Beach ball

Safety:

Hospitality:

Cleanliness:

Party index:

How To Get There:

By bus: Take #1, #6, or #9 bus from downtown to Marienlund stop and walk 300 yards to hostel.

By car: Contact hostel for directions.

By train: From train station, catch #1, #6, or #9 bus to Marienlund stop and walk 300 yards to hostel.

Sleep-In Hostel

Havnegade 20, Århus

> **Phone:** 086-192-055
>
> **Fax:** 086-191-811
>
> **E-mail:** sleep-in@citysleep-in.dk
>
> **Website:** citysleep-in.dk
>
> **Rates:** 180–210 DKK (about $33–$38 US) per person; doubles 450–500 DKK (about $82–$91 US)

Credit cards: Yes
Beds: 127
Private/family rooms: Yes
Kitchen available: Yes
Season: January 11–December 19
Office hours: 24 hours
Affiliation: None
Extras: Bike rentals, cafe, game room, laundry, Internet access, TV lounge, grill, breakfast ($)

M ost of Europe's so-called Sleep-Ins are nothing more than a bunch of mattresses on the floor of a gym—about what you'd expect in a Salvation Army or a disaster relief center—and this one, lately, is sliding down into that same category. It's not a better choice than the official hostel in any sense except one: If you want to spend most of your time pub-hopping and clubbing, it's a few miles closer to the center of the city. In fact, it is the center. This place is steps away from nightspots, unlike the other hostel, which requires some transit waits and rides to get in and out of the central city.

Dorms and bathrooms are adequate at best, not kept very clean, but at least staff keep the activities rolling. There's a cafe with a good notice board, they rent bikes, and the double rooms are dirt-cheap and very acceptable given the high, high price of sleeping in a hotel bed in this town. Internet access is free. Breakfast consists of a spread of organic foods (cool!), though it's quite expensive (about $12 US per person), as usual in Denmark.

Just don't expect the peace and quiet of the other hostel—you are smack-dab in the center, and there may be occasional traffic noises, drunks passing by, or what-have-you. Also note that this hostel tends to ding you for extra charges, everything from sheets to towels to food. And bathrooms aren't spic-and-span, either.

Best bet for a bite:
Swing Cafe
Insiders' tip:
Some trains stop at Europaplads
What hostellers say:
"Great place."
Gestalt:
Sleep tight
Safety:
Hospitality:
Cleanliness:
Party index:

For fun, there's plenty of walking to do—including an authentic folk museum and several old, old churches and squares—but we'd hit the Åboulevarden, a twin strip of lanes that bookend the city canal. These streets are incredibly hip, packed with restaurants, pubs, jazz bars, and clubs—some of which rock until late at night. Just make sure you're looking sharp: These Danes sure know how to dress.

How To Get There:

By bus: From train station, take #3, #7, or #14 bus two stops to Europaplads. Cross street to hostel.

By car: Contact hostel for directions.

By train: From train station, walk north 3⁄4 mile to Europaplads platform; cross street to hostel.

COPENHAGEN

Copenhagen is, to put it simply, one of the coolest cities in Europe. A decade or two ago it wasn't really even on the radar; now new buildings, restaurants, and clubs are going up fast, as the Danes enjoy a long-overdue renaissance. The hostel situation here is pretty good, too—more than a half dozen to pick from, none of them bad at all.

You'll arrive at Copenhagen's Central Station, a massive all-inclusive complex that can be a bit confusing with all the fast-food joints and shops competing for your attention here. Plus, there are two separate ticket offices and a travel agency that also happens to sell tickets. How to make sense of it all? Hit the grocery store near the ticket offices for sustenance, then go for the ticket machines. You need to take a number and get in long lines for the ticket windows; it can take nearly an hour just to get served.

If you're hard up for info on what to do in town, exit the station and walk a block up the street to the city's main tourist office, which is wonderfully named: Wonderful Copenhagen (WoCo for short). Consult WoCo's website at visitcopenhagen.com to learn more about the city.

There's so much to see that you'll need a strategy. Want to focus on people-watching? Head for Nyhavn (pronounced *New' howen,* or something like that), a harborside area with bobbing boats and glamorous Danes drinking beer, eating great food, or just generally hanging out with one another. Or get up to Nørrebrø, on both sides of the river, a very hip district with enough hostels, eateries, clubs, and bars to keep you going. Whatever you do, though, don't miss Tivoli, a sprawling amusement park very close to Copenhagen's train station. Come at night, when it's lit up and especially pretty. Great for a date, though it's not cheap at all.

The Copenhagen Card (cphcard.com) can help ease the pain of the high admission price of this city's attractions, too. Buy the card and you get all local transit rides and most museum entry included, plus Tivoli entrance (which normally costs $17 US all by itself). The card costs from about $50 US for one day's use for adults (half price for kids), up to about $130 for five days' fun (again, half price for kiddies). You also get 10–25 percent discounts on various bike and auto rentals, restaurant and cafe bills, tours, and other museums (like the Museum of Erotica, wink-wink) that aren't fully covered by the pass.

COPENHAGEN HOSTELS AT A GLANCE

	RATING	PRICE	IN A WORD	PAGE
Downtown Copenhagen Hostel	👍	100-1200 DKK	newish	p. 116
Generator Copenhagen	👍	127-205 DKK	hoppin'	p. 117
Amager Hostel	👍	160–490 DKK	big	p. 110
Sleep-In Heaven Hostel	👍👎	140 DKK	poor	p. 119
Copenhagen City Hostel	👍👎	195–225 DKK	enormous	p. 114
Sleep-In Green Hostel	👍👎	120 DKK	crunchy	p. 118
Bellahøj Hostel	👍👎	145–510 DKK	efficient	p. 111
City Public Hostel Vesterbrø	👎	130–170 DKK	crowded	p. 113

Copenhagen

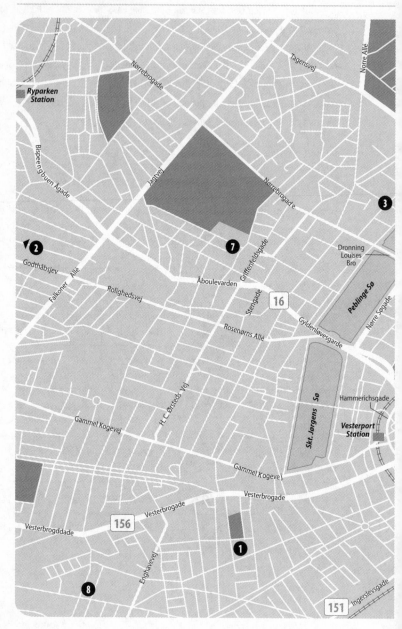

Ryparken
Station

Nørrebrogade

Tagensvej

Norre Allé

Bispeengbuen Ågade

Jagtvej

Nørrebrogade

3

Godthåbsjev

Falkoner Allé

Rolighedsvej

Åboulevarden

7

Griffenfeldsgade

Dronning
Louises
Bro

Peblinge Sø

Norre Søgade

2

Stengade

16

Gyldenløvesgarde

Rosenørns Allé

H.C.Ørsteds Vej

Skt. Jørgens Sø

Hammerichsgade

Vesterport
Station

Gammel Kogevej

Gammel Kogevej

Vesterbrogade

Vesterbrogade

156

Vesterbrogade

Vesterbrogddade

Enghavevej

1

8

Ingerslevsgade

151

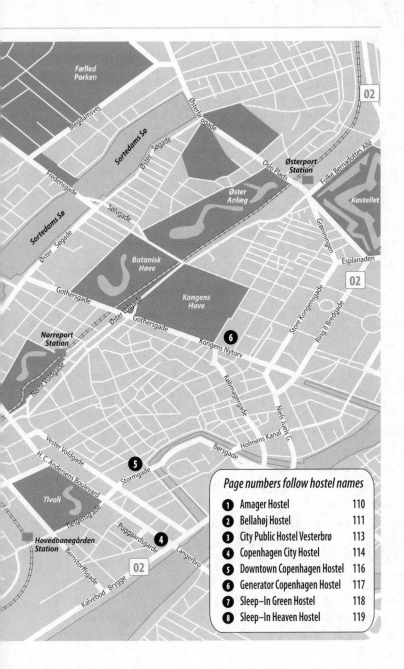

Amager Hostel

Vejlands Allé 200, 2300 Copenhagen S

Phone: 032-522-908

Fax: 032-522-708

E-mail: copenhagen@danhostel.dk

Website: copenhagenyouthhostel.dk

Rates: 160–490 DKK (about $26–$93 US) per HI member; doubles 430–530 DKK (about $76–$93 US)

Credit cards: Yes

Beds: 512

Private/family rooms: Yes

Kitchen available: Yes

Season: January 2–December 16

Office hours: 24 hours

Affiliation: HI-Danhostel

Extras: Laundry, meeting rooms, parking, TV, currency exchange, free WiFi

*T*his monster, family-oriented hostel named for its surrounding neighborhood (Amager; say *"ah-MAR"*) south of the city center is pretty good, with transit connections to the downtown areas where the action is. A big glass atrium and the obligatory Danish flag welcome you to this property, where all the dorms are 2-, 4-, or 5-bed rooms, and they're more than acceptable, not to mention far less expensive than comparable hotel rooms in Copenhagen.

On the other hand, it sometimes feels like you're in Siberia here—which will be a problem if you've come to soak up Copenhagen nightlife. (If you've brought a car—I doubt you have, but still—then you'll be fine.)

As one of two "official" Danhostel properties in Copenhagen, standards of cleanliness and order are higher than they are at simpler places elsewhere in town. And interestingly, there are no dorm rooms. You either sleep in a family room (2 to 5 beds) with a group of your buddies or loved ones or a sweetie, or else rent a single room—pretty cheap for what you get, actually. No 12-bed sardine jobs here. (Hallways are really long, though.)

Just don't expect a party at the hostel itself: This is among the biggest hostels (some say the biggest) in all Europe, and size naturally subtracts from the intimacy of the place.

Still, staff are professional and upbeat and keep the hostel running very smoothly indeed. And, being Danish and official, it's about as spic-and-span as a hostel can be. Other good things here include a laundry, kitchen, television lounge, and a lack of backbreaking rules such as lockouts and curfews. The playground outside is good for kids.

The place does receive a lot of school groups debarking from buses here, so we can't guarantee peace and quiet in the hallways. There's also one other curious quirk: The walls are surprisingly thin. So you might hear noise seeping into your room from other conversations (including those of the school groups). Trying to locate at the end of a bunkroom, rather than in the middle, is about all you can do about this issue.

One other caveat. Like many "official" Danish hostels, they charge you for everything: an obligatory hostel membership (which is, like, 25 bucks), the sheets, the towels, the breakfast. The surrounding neighborhood isn't too interesting, either, so you'll want to get into town to see Tivoli, the clubs, and all the rest. It takes a little fiddling with the public transit schedules to do that, but you're rewarded with a very comfortable sleep once you get back at night—especially for the price.

How To Get There:
By bus or train: From main train station, take either the #46 bus or S-train Line C to the Sjælør stop, then change to a #37 bus and continue to the Holmens Bro stop.
By car: Contact hostel for directions.

Bellahøj Hostel
Herbergvejen 8, 2700 Brønshøj (Copenhagen)
> **Phone:** 038-289-715
> **Fax:** 038-890-210
> **Website:** copenhagenhostel.dk
> **E-mail:** bellahoej@danhostel.dk
> **Rates:** 145–510 DKK (about $26–$93 US) per HI member; doubles 410 DKK (about $75 US)

Best bet for a bite:
Pølse wagons
What hostellers say:
"Clean and modern."
Gestalt:
Amagervelous
Safety:
Hospitality:
Cleanliness:
Party index:

Credit cards: No
Beds: 248
Private/family rooms: Sometimes (off-season only)
Kitchen available: Yes
Season: February 1–December 2
Office hours: 24 hours
Affiliation: HI-Danhostel
Extras: Parking, TV lounge, free WiFi, luggage storage, laundry, grill, snacks

*A*ways out in the northern suburbs, about 3 miles from downtown, this hostel used to be a primo pick despite its remoteness, thanks to its cleanliness and relatively quiet facilities. But frankly, it has slipped all the way off our "recommended" list.

The reception floor is the most popular area, with a good little TV lounge, plenty of chairs, and very popular Internet access. Staff will sort you out, get you your sheets, sell you an ice-cream bar, then send you off into the building, which holds more beds than at first appears. There are 7 quad rooms, 31 six-bed rooms, and then 3 larger dorms of more than six beds all told. A few double rooms are especially nice but quite limited in supply, so don't plan on snagging one of them. The regular dorms, frankly, are too cramped and the beds are not the most comfortable we've slept on. You'll be charged for sheets and towels no matter what. Deal.

The basement's the place to find the kitchen, which gets heavy use—since the hostel is nowhere near any restaurants—and is very well organized, if not always cleaned up. Note: They charge you for silverware! The laundry's also down here. Breakfast is served in a big main-floor dining room that opens onto a surprisingly green backyard, which borders a little bog and field area. And are those goats next door?

Best bet for a bite:
Better eat here
What hostellers say:
"Fun place."
Gestalt:
Danes cook
Safety:
Hospitality:
Cleanliness:
Party index:

The breakfast is worth missing. Upsides? There's a Wi-Fi in the lounge. OK. And the place is always busy with Europeans of all stripes coming and going, so this is a good place to meet fellow travelers, at least. Find one with a car and you're set for wheels.

But that's about it.

How To Get There:
By bus: Catch #2 bus from train station or #11 bus to from Rådhus to Bellahøj or Brønshøj stop, then walk 200 yards to hostel. At night catch #82N bus.

By car: Contact hostel for directions.

By train: Catch #2 bus from train station to Bellahøj or Brønshøj stop and walk 200 yards to hostel. At night catch #82N bus.

City Public Hostel Vesterbro ⚑
Absalonsgade 8, 1658 Copenhagen V

Phone: 036-981-166
Fax: 036-980-081
Website: citypublichostel.dk
E-mail: info@citypublichostel.dk
Rates: 130–170 DKK (about $24–$31 US) per person
Credit cards: No
Beds: 205
Private/family rooms: No
Kitchen available: Yes
Season: May 24–August 29
Office hours: 24 hours
Affiliation: None
Extras: Lockers, breakfast ($)

You're not far from most of Copenhagen's top sights and Central Station in this short-season, summer-only hostel run by the Vesterbro Youth Center. For the surprisingly expensive price of a bed, though, you trade in privacy, comfort, cleanliness, and everything else. The biggest dorm on the bottom floor tops out at 66 beds and is quite irritatingly loud, though you might get lucky and score a "smaller" (i.e., hotter and smellier) room of just 20 beds, or even—pray that you do—a more bite-size room of 4 as you go up the stairs.

Best bet for a bite:
Farmers' market on Israelsplads
Insiders' tip:
Free Internet at Use It
What hostellers say:
"Hej, hej, hej."
Gestalt:
Close to the Vesterbrø
Safety:
Hospitality:
Cleanliness:
Party index:

Beds are flimsy, squeaky, pillow-less, and a bit unclean. Just plain uncomfortable. Get our drift? At these prices, you expect a lot more, but the City Public doesn't deliver. And they charge for lots of niggling extras, too.

The (only) good news is that a kitchen is available for hosteller use: Stock up on fresh veggies from the farmers' market at Israelsplads, or try one of the small grocery store chains like Irma, Netto, or Brugsen. Staff were decently friendly (too bad security is nonexistent). Still staying here for its price and centrality? Fine. Hang out in the hostel lounge or lawn in front and be thankful there's no curfew or lockout; you're not gonna want to spend much time here, or in the seedy surrounding area.

Bottom line? They should be ashamed of charging you this much money. Heck, they should be paying us.

How To Get There:
By bus: Take #6 or #16 bus to Vesterbrø Station.
By car: Contact hostel for directions.
By train: From Central Station, take S-train to Vesterbrø Station.

Copenhagen City Hostel

H. C. Andersens Boulevard 50, 1553 Copenhagen V
  Phone: 033-118-585
  Fax: 033-118-588
  Website: dgi-byen.com/hotels
  E-mail: cphcitybooking@danhostel.dk
  Rates: 195–225 DKK (about $35–$41 US) per HI member
  Credit cards: Yes
  Beds: 1,020
  Private/family rooms: Yes
  Kitchen available: Yes

Season: January 4–December 21

Office hours: 24 hours

Affiliation: HI-Danhostel

Extras: Laundry, kitchen, television, free WiFi, cafe, breakfast ($), playroom, foosball, currency exchange, bicycle rental

This hostel is the best-positioned in the city, if you're interested in 2 key tourist attractions: Tivoli (a cool combination amusement park/dining area) and Christiansborg, the hippie enclave to end all hippie enclaves. Unbelievably, it's steps away from both, and also only 3 blocks from the back side of the city's busy central train station.

But it's also the biggest, by far. Not in Copenhagen. Not in Denmark. In all of freakin' Europe! Now that renovations are complete (it's actually owned by a local hotel chain), this hostel is filled with more than 1,000 bunks. You've just gotta love the modern design scheme, which is so Copenhagen to a "T": stylish little beds slung low on scando-blonde wood floors you could eat off of (so far); scarlet pillow covers; and oh-so-Danish little night lamps. The dining room looks like an IKEA cafeteria outtake, for heaven's sake. By Copenhagen standards this is a tall building, so upper floors come with great views of the city, Opera House, and islands.

But all this luxury and location comes at a price. This is among the most expensive bunks in C-town, and there's a steep, steep surcharge (about $10 US) for linens. Breakfast isn't free, and the kitchen's pretty minuscule. So it's far from perfect.

Still, we can't complain too much, other than commenting on the impersonal, swept-clean element to it all. This almost isn't hostelling. It's hotelling.

What hostellers say:
"Like a hotel."

Gestalt:
On the (Den)mark

Safety:

Hospitality:

Cleanliness:

Party index:

How To Get There:

By car: Contact hostel for directions.

By train: Contact hostel for transit details.

By bus: Contact hostel for transit details.

By plane: Contact hostel for transit details.

Downtown Copenhagen Hostel

Vandkunsten 5

København K

> **Phone:** 070-232-110
>
> **Fax:** 069-802-005
>
> **E-mail:** info@copenhagendowntown.com
>
> **Rates:** 100–1,200 DKK (about $18–$218 US); doubles 300–1,200 DKK (about $55–$218)
>
> **Credit cards:** Yes
>
> **Beds:** Number varies
>
> **Kitchen available:** Yes
>
> **Private/family rooms:** Yes
>
> **Season:** January 1–December 1
>
> **Affiliation:** HI-Danhostel
>
> **Extras:** Bar

---

*J*ust 2½ blocks from Tivoli Gardens, this newish Danhostel-affiliated hostel does actually live up to its billing as a true "downtown" hostel. (And you'd be surprised how many places don't.)

It features a bar, a so-so kitchen, and a great central location (though it can get a bit noisy in the street at night). They loan (not rent) iPads here—let's see how long that lasts—and will store your stuff for a price. The hostel is pervaded by a young-ish vibe, and there are tons of activities, such as local tours. We wouldn't peg this one as ideal for families, though it does offer smallish private rooms. (None of them come with private bathrooms.) Note that while the hostel closes for all of December, the hostel bar remains open year-round. Curious.

What hostellers say:
"Lookin' good."

Gestalt:
Downtown train

Safety:

Hospitality:

Cleanliness:

Party index:

How To Get There:

By car: Contact hostel for directions.

By bus/train: From main train station, walk south on Reventlowsgade 1 block to Tietgensgade; turn left and continue 4 blocks. Turn left on Vester Voldgade, walk 1 block, take next right, and walk 1½ blocks to hostel on right.

Generator Copenhagen Hostel

Adelgade 5-7
København 1304

Phone: 078-775-400
Rates: 127–205 DKK (about $23–$37 US); doubles 410 DKK ($75 US)
Beds: Number varies
Kitchen available: Yes
Private/family rooms: Yes
Season: Year-round
Office hours: 24 hours
Affiliation: None
Extras: Bar, free WiFi, breakfast ($)

*N*oisy, convivial, not cheap, with a peppy young-people vibe, this newish entry on the Cope scene is a winner . . . so far. And you can't knock the centrality: It's just off Kongens Nytorv—also known as "the biggest square in the city."

On the outside it looks like a modern-art light exhibit (from 20 years ago). Inside, the hostel's surprisingly clean and well-run in the early going, with a bar, which surprised us because the Generator chain has an up-and-down record around Europe (see: London, etc.). Dorms range in size from 3 to 8 beds apiece—and yes, they do have single and double rooms, too, for an extra charge. Those private rooms have mirrors, lockers, USB plugs, and (let's face it, here's why you really want these) private bathrooms.

Yep, there's a bar. Just bring earplugs. You know, in case.

What hostellers say:
"Fun"
Gestalt:
Generation Why
Safety:
Hospitality:
Cleanliness:
Party index:

How To Get There:
By car: Contact hostel for directions.

By bus/train: From Norreport station, turn right on Gothersgade, follow street for 2 blocks, and turn left on Adelgade. Hostel is beside fitness center.

Sleep-In Green Hostel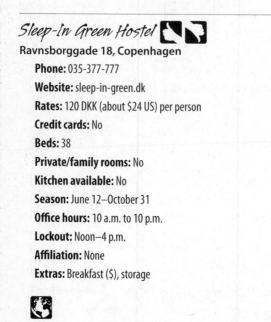
Ravnsborggade 18, Copenhagen

> **Phone:** 035-377-777
> **Website:** sleep-in-green.dk
> **Rates:** 120 DKK (about $24 US) per person
> **Credit cards:** No
> **Beds:** 38
> **Private/family rooms:** No
> **Kitchen available:** No
> **Season:** June 12–October 31
> **Office hours:** 10 a.m. to 10 p.m.
> **Lockout:** Noon–4 p.m.
> **Affiliation:** None
> **Extras:** Breakfast ($), storage

---

*D*enmark has always been a leader in world environmental issues, and it stands to reason that Copenhagen would proudly sport its own earth-friendly hostel. This is it. Of Copenhagen's seasonal hostels, Sleep-In Green is open the longest and is situated—in our opinion—in the hippest neighborhood of them all: Nørrebro, a 5- to 10-minute bus ride from Central Station.

Too bad the hostel has some serious flaws.

Yes, you'll find low-flow showers and toilets, nontoxic paint, recycling facilities, healthy, untouched-by-chemicals food, and so on. The dorms (one with 6 beds, another with upward of 30!) are nicely painted, if rather noisy; there aren't any private rooms here. Expect to get to know your neighbors, who'll quite possibly be European students with leftish political stands. And don't expect clean rooms and bathrooms—the earthy ethos seems to extend to the accumulation of dirt and muck in the wrong places. Note that the formerly low bed price has been jacked up and is somewhat offset by the a la carte charges for lots of little extras like breakfast and sheets; what seemed like a good deal at 11 bucks a night suddenly becomes 15 or 20. Bottom line? Bring your own sheets and food to save money.

Still, some of the staff are cool, there's a nice view of the backyard (no, you can't use it), we applaud the green-friendly message, and this is the best-located hostel in town along with its cousin Sleep-In Heaven (see next entry). If you don't mind huge crowds of non-deodorant-wearing young hippies and a lack of cleanliness and security, this could be your pick.

We do mind, and we can't recommend it. At all.

Best bet for a bite:
Here in Nørrebrø
Insiders' tip:
Free bikes in the city
What hostellers say:
"It's not easy bein' green."
Gestalt:
Green achers
Safety:
Hospitality:
Cleanliness:
Party index:

How To Get There:

By bus or train: Take Nørrebrø bus #5 or #16 or night bus #81N or #84N. Or contact hostel for transit route.

By car: Contact hostel for directions.

Sleep-In Heaven Hostel

Struenseegade 7 (Seventh floor), 2200 Copenhagen N

Phone: 035-354-648

E-mail: morefun@sleepinheaven.com

Website: sleepinheaven.com

Rates: 140 DKK (about $25 US) per person; doubles 360 DKK (about $65 US)

Credit cards: No

Beds: 100

Private/family rooms: Yes

Kitchen available: No

Season: Open year-round

Office hours: 24 hours

Affiliation: None

Extras: Lockers, free Internet access, breakfast ($), bar, pool table, earplugs

*T*he motto here is "It's more fun." Well . . . we wouldn't go that far.

This place is more popular with backpackers than with family types, and it's run by a couple of Danish guys who provide loads of bunks at a low price. You're in hip and trendy Nørrebrø, where there are scads of great restaurants, bars, and nightclubs, as well as being in the thick of the university area, so the vibe is very young.

However, the place itself has its limitations. For one thing, there's a stench that sometimes pervades the dorm rooms and seems to have done so from time immemorial. It's way too noisy, too; security is lax; guests tend to be a bit obnoxious; and cleanliness remains an issue.

The dorms are large rooms divided into compartments (rickety triple bunks, in many cases), but you'll still feel like a sardine. There are also 2 coveted private rooms. You'll have to pay for sheets and breakfast, which might dent your budget slightly, but outside the hostel there's a private garden in which you can chill out and strike up conversations with other hostellers.

Key to Icons

Attractive natural setting

Ecologically aware hostel

Superior kitchen facilities or cafe

Offbeat or eccentric place

Superior bathroom facilities

Romantic private rooms

Comfortable beds

A particularly good value

Wheelchair-accessible

Good for business travelers

Especially well-suited for families

Good for active travelers

Visual arts at hostel or nearby

Music at hostel or nearby

Great hostel for skiers

Bar or pub at hostel or nearby

Editors' choice: Among our very favorite hostels

The place is huge, too huge, and feels desolate and impersonal at times. And there's no kitchen, which is weird.

One positive: The joint is open year-round, a blessing for those searching for accommodations in the dead of the Danish winter, when nearly all hostels are closed down. And at least you're in Nørrebro, a great hipster area for exploring (which is not central, by the way).

Yeah, staff are friendly, and they dispense good beer. So it's not all bad. Just somewhat bad. And overcrowded. Give it a pass unless you have a high tolerance for those things.

How To Get There:
By bus or train: Contact hostel for transit details.
By car: Contact hostel for directions.

Best bet for a bite:
Community House nearby
Insiders' tip:
Playtime magazine for listings
What hostellers say:
"Great place!"
Gestalt:
Heaven 17
Safety:
Hospitality:
Cleanliness:
Party index:

France

*I*t's easy to get to France from the US directly, and is often cheaper than flying to London first and taking the train. From elsewhere in Europe, Eurolines France (28, avenue du Général-de-Gaulle, Paris; telephone 08-9289-9091, which is NOT a free call) runs buses to Paris and other points.

Practical Details

Once you're here, France's train system is among the world's best—especially the TGV super-fast bullet trains that blast you from Paris out into the countryside at upward of 100 miles an hour. TGV trains always cost a little extra, however, and you must reserve your ticket at least 10 minutes before your departure at the French stations; it costs about $15 US per reservation to complete the transaction, even packing that Eurail pass.

For short hops in France, you buy one-way *simple* (pronounced "sample") or round-trip *retour* ("ray-tour") tickets at train stations. Always remember to punch your ticket before you get on the train. There will be an orange machine in every station that stamps the current date and time on the ticket's magnetic strip, giving you 24 hours to use it or lose it. France no longer has its own individual country pass; RIP, France Railpass. You now have to buy a bundled France-Spain, France-Italy, France-Germany, or France-Switzerland pass; prices vary widely, so check with Eurail (eurail.com) for pricing and advice. Remember that trains don't run as frequently on weekends. Saturday is usually the worst day to travel within France. International trains and sleeper cars usually run seven days a week, while Friday and Sunday are variable. If you want to go to the south of France, for example, lots of trains will be running from the cities to the country on Friday afternoon. Sunday, everyone's either going to the beach/ski slopes or going home.

To take the bus in France, you buy short-hop bus tickets from drivers or long-distance tickets at bus stations. Again, always remember to punch your ticket; there will be a machine on every bus that stamps the current date and time on the ticket's magnetic strip. Most are good for one hour.

Dealing with French pay phones can be a pain. Instead, buy France Telecom phone cards at tobacco shops or other small markets and stick 'em into the phones. (Push the card in lightly, with the little computer chip facing up.) Local calls won't eat up much of these cards, but long-distance calls within a country will; figure about 10 to 15 minutes per card at most.

France's phone code is 33. To call French hostels from North America, dial 011-33 and DROP THE FIRST ZERO from all numbers in this book. To call French hostels from within France, dial them AS WRITTEN. And to dial a hostel from within its home city, DROP THE CITY CODE (the part beginning with zero).

France's unit of currency is the euro.

LYON

Lyon doesn't get much press, but the French—and foodies everywhere—love it anyway. (After all, this is the town that invented mayonnaise!) Restaurants are excellent, the architecture isn't bad, and it's more manageable than Paris in a day, if a lot less beautiful. Use this city as a hub for Provence and the south of France; you can get anywhere from the train station.

There's one hostel here now (there used to be two), but it's decent. To get around town, use the one-line subway ("whoa! these trains don't have drivers!"). The only problem is finding the stations, which are sometimes hidden behind stores or surprisingly ornate (and small) Metro signs. Ask the hostel staff to draw you a map, if necessary—they probably will.

Auberge de Jeunesse du Vieux Lyon

41–45 Montée du chemin neuf, 69005 Lyon

> **Phone:** 0478-150550
> **Fax:** 0478-150551
> **E-mail:** lyon@fuaj.org
> **Rates:** €23.30–€24.70 (about $29–$31 US) per HI member
> **Credit cards:** Yes
> **Beds:** 164
> **Private/family rooms:** Yes
> **Kitchen available:** Yes
> **Season:** Open year-round
> **Office hours:** 7 a.m.–noon; 2 p.m.–1 a.m.
> **Affiliation:** HI-FUAJ
> **Extras:** Garden, patio, bar, e-mail, tourist information, bike storage, laundry, breakfast

---

Insiders' tip:
Metro is great
What hostellers say:
"This place rocks and rolls."
Gestalt:
Lyon sleeps tonight
Safety:
Hospitality:
Cleanliness:
Party index:

Lyon's central Hostelling International hostel is pretty good. Amazing, especially since this city really isn't a big destination; visitors are usually rushing through on their way to somewhere else.

Breakfast is included, and you can send or receive e-mail. There's a laundry, kitchen, patio, extremely popular bar, and garden. Views of downtown Lyon from the upper floors are absolutely awesome, and the building has been completely renovated in recent years, so it's in pretty good shape.

The beds consist of doubles, quads, and about 20 bigger bunkrooms with an average 9 beds each—definitely a little too big, the only drawback here. There are also 4 wheelchair-accessible rooms and a wing of family rooms that can be delightfully cool or dreadfully chilly, depending on time of year.

Social life is the real draw here, though. The happy-go-lucky staff keep the fun (and booze) flowing and serve a free and popular breakfast of juice, cereal, bread, and coffee. Lyon as a town is also surprisingly fun—packed with eateries and clubs and other fun stuff, plus a gorgeous church right beneath your window. Come on, check it out—it's only 2 hours by fast train from Paris, after all.

How To Get There:

By bus or train: From Part Dieu Station, take #99 bus; from Perrache Station, take #31 bus.
By car: From Paris, take A6 to Lyon; from Marseille, take A7 to Lyon; call hostel for directions.
By subway: From downtown, take D subway line to St-Jean stop, then take cable car up to top of hill.

MARSEILLE

Marseille is one of the most exotic—and dangerous—places in France. This old, old port city has long been the meeting place for sailors from Africa and points beyond, and you'll find it to be a sensory assault: crazy traffic, barking market vendors, dingy streets, and the beautiful sea. There are two hostels here, but neither of them is either central or recommendable. In fact, they're awful. Use an inexpensive hotel somewhere safe instead.

MARSEILLE HOSTELS AT A GLANCE				
	RATING	**PRICE**	**IN A WORD**	**PAGE**
Auberge Bonneveine		€22–€23.40	poor	p. 125
Chateau de Bois-Luzy		€18.90–€20.40	unfriendly	p. 126

Auberge Bonneveine

47, avenue Joseph-Vidal (Impasse du Dr. Bonfils), 13008 Marseille

Phone: 0491-176330

Fax: 0491-739723

E-mail: marseille-bonneveine@fuaj.org

Rates: €22–€23.40 (about $28–$29 US) per HI member

Credit cards: Yes

Beds: 150

Private/family rooms: Yes

Kitchen available: No

Season: January 19–December 18

Office hours: 6 a.m.–1 a.m.

Curfew: 1 a.m.

Affiliation: HI-FUAJ

Extras: Meals ($), breakfast, laundry, lockers, bar, bike rentals

What hostellers say:
"NO, no, no."
Gestalt:
Marseille what?
Safety:
Hospitality:
Cleanliness:
Party index:

*A*s it's almost on the beach, this hostel is the first pick in town of the Euro-beach bums. You know the type: wraparound shades, Jetsons-era rave clothes, cigarettes perpetually dangling from their mouths, and attitudes out to here.

But there's no way you'd want to come here. The place is poorly kept, not friendly . . . just a disappointment. Breakfast is included with your bed here, they serve other meals, and there's a laundry for washing your bathing suit afterward (when it's working, that is). Those are about the only positives.

Crime is a problem in the area—and at the hostel as well. Even the hostel's storage lockers reportedly aren't crook-proof. In fact, since you're in the heart of the Marseille waterfront, some extra caution is definitely in order. This work about area is as diverse as any you'll find in France—a sweltering melting pot of cultures and economic classes all scrabbling to wheel and deal themselves into a better (if not exactly straight-arrow) life.

This might be the town where the expression "thick as thieves" was invented, so be very, very careful at night. Heck, even during the daytime, try to travel with a group.

How To Get There:
By bus: Take #44 bus to Place Bonnefons stop or #583 bus to Bourse Square.
By car: Call hostel for directions.
By subway: Take #2 Metro (subway) line to Prado stop.
By train: Marseille/St-Charles Station is 3 miles; from station take #2 Metro (subway) line to Rond Point du Prado stop.

Chateau de Bois-Luzy Hostel
Allée des Primevères, 13012 Marseille
> **Phone:** 0491-490618
> **Fax:** 0491-490618
> **Rates:** €18.90–€20.40 (about $24–$25 US) per HI member
> **Credit cards:** No
> **Beds:** 90

Private/family rooms: Yes
Kitchen available: Yes
Season: January 5–December 20
Office hours: 7:30 a.m.–noon; 5–10:30 p.m.
Lockout: 10 a.m.–5 p.m.
Curfew: 10:30 p.m.
Affiliation: HI-FUAJ
Extras: Meals ($), laundry, TV, bike storage

*T*hough beautiful on the outside, this place is a bit like a supermodel: not necessarily so pretty once it opens its mouth.

Let's put it another way. This place is just plain weird. And unfriendly. And haughty. And remote. And most definitely not a chateau. And . . . well, we give up. Don't come. There are plenty of other options (not hostel options, but options) in the area.

This 19th-century mansion with a knockout view of the city far below looks good from the out-

What hostellers say:
"What is this guy's problem?"
Gestalt:
Mansion on the hill
Safety:
Hospitality:
Cleanliness:
Party index:

side . . . once you get here. It's pretty darned far out of town. Try almost 5 miles from the smoggy city center. Then, once you've negotiated the public transit and strapped on your walking shoes—or somehow have brought a car to this coast (pretty difficult, given the parking and tiny streets and odd directions)—this is not the place you expected: pretty at first glance, but ultimately too simple, too unwelcoming, and carrying too many rules to ensure a good stay. (They lock you out almost a full day, for example. Thanks, guys.)

Rooms come in a variety of shapes, sizes, and colors. You've got your basic double rooms, your triples, and your quads. Finally, there are a few larger dorm rooms—but none has more than 8 beds, and most have about 6. There's a kitchen and a television lounge. And that's it. What are you supposed to do with yourself, way out here, without a car or a hostel activities director? Don't have a clue.

As we've mentioned, the management doesn't impart a lot of warmth, they don't plow their profits back into upgrades, and they don't allow you the freedom to hang out in the city late at night. Strikes one, two, and three. Go ahead and complain. The owner won't care. He'll probably just laugh.

The facility is surrounded by green fields, some of which are used for sports contests. That's a plus? Guess so. Plenty of shops and restaurants are nearby, too, though they won't be anywhere as cheap or gritty as the stuff you could find right in the heart of Marseille.

Two words: SKIP. IT.

How To Get There:
By bus: Take #6 or #8 bus to J. Thierry or Marius-Richard stop.
By car: Call hostel for directions.
By train: Marseille/St-Charles Station is 3 miles away; call hostel for transit route.

PARIS

Paris, City of Lights. Practically every other European traveler begins or ends a European adventure here, so it's not really surprising that there are more hostels concentrated in the greater Paris area than in just about any other city on the Continent. Some are OK; some are dingy; some are central; some are miles out in the suburbs. We've done our level best to separate the wheat from the chaff here.

Getting into town is no problemo. A ring of train stations surrounds Paris, shuttling travelers to and from all points in Europe; all the city's train stations are on the subway.

From the airport, use the bus (Roissybus from Charles de Gaulle airport, Orlybus from Orly)—at €7–€10 (about $9–$13 US) it's far cheaper than a taxi for a solo traveler, and practically as quick.

Once you're downtown, parking is atrocious. Chances are you're not hauling a car into the city, but if you are—well, just don't. Get rid of it at a parking garage or lot or rental drop-off area in the burbs, or just don't rent one until you leave town. Besides the fact that driving in Paris can needlessly consume hours of vital sightseeing time, you won't need a car anyway. Instead, rely on that Metro subway system—one of the world's best—and the buses that race all over the city. Taxis are expensive and scarce except at the train stations, but they're quite useful when you need to make a desperate dash.

Before doing anything else, take time to figure out the Metro map—which can be quite confusing at first glance—and orient yourself according to line number (*ligne* in French). You need to know what stop is at the END of the line you're traveling in order to figure out which side of the platform to get on. Got it? Let's say you wanna take Line #5 away from town to the north. That line ends at Bobigny Station. OK! Now, in the station look for a sign with a 5 in a circle that says "Direction Bobigny." Presto, that's your line.

You can buy books of 10 tickets (way cheaper than the €1.70/$2 US single tickets) at any station; ask for a *carnet*—say "un carnay"—and fork over about €13 (about $16 US), or half that much for children age 4 to 11. As you enter the subway, place the skinny ticket into the slot in the gate and take it out again when it pops up. You'll have a few seconds to get through the gate, so be speedy, and don't push your luggage ahead of you to avoid getting it caught in the doors. (If it doesn't work, go to the ticket window and try to explain, using sign language.) That's it: In seconds you'll be elsewhere in town. Hang onto the ticket 'til you get off, too, since conductors will occasionally demand to see it.

PARIS HOSTELS AT A GLANCE

	RATING	PRICE	IN A WORD	PAGE
FIAP Jean-Monnet		€29–€63	educational	p. 144
CISP Maurice Ravel		€20–€40	clean	p. 143
Le Village Hostel		€40–€55	convivial	p. 145
Pajol Hostel		€29.50	new	p. 147
AJ le D'Artagnan		€28.60	lively	p. 140
AJ Cité des Sciences		€26.50	distant	p. 134
AJ Jules Ferry		€26.50	fey	p. 138
Woodstock Hostel		€22–€28	hoppin'	p. 150
AJ Leo Lagrange		€25.20	quiet	p. 141
AJ des Jeunes		€14–€20	chaotic	p. 136
Aloha		€30–€32	poor	p. 133
Young & Happy Hostel		€24–€35	iffy	p. 151
Three Ducks Travelers Hostel		€18–€25	dirty	p. 148

Paris

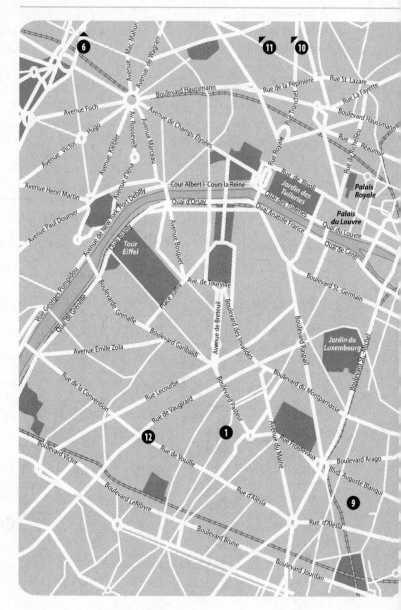

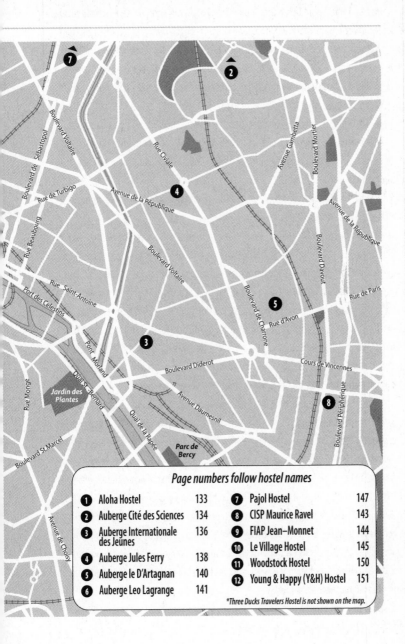

Three Ducks Travelers Hostel is not shown on the map.

Page numbers follow hostel names

*Three Ducks Travelers Hostel is not shown on the map.

The RER (suburban railway) is a related system, even more efficient (there are lots fewer stops), and your Metro ticket gets you on board at no extra cost unless you need to go outside city limits to the airports or Disneyland Paris. Check the map; you can often zip from a station to the action much faster using the RER. Each station also has helpful boards posting the next incoming train and where it'll be stopping—one advantage over the Metro.

"Paris Visite" passes give you much the same access as the *carnets,* for longer periods of time. Passes for one to five days cost about €10–€31 (about $13–$39 US), half price for children 4–11. You must buy these online, from a travel agent, or from a person in a station—not a machine—and you must write your full name on them, write the range of dates of use on the card, and copy the number from the card to the actual magnetic ticket. A lot of work, but you do save a little.

We'd avoid most Parisian buses except as a cheap sightseeing tour. To get to the airport, use Air France buses because they have luggage compartments.

Once you're here, act like a local. Don't stand in those huge aboveground lines to get into the Louvre; go late in the day, and take the underground mall stairway instead of the aboveground cattle call. Score cheap clothes at flea markets. Buy food at farmers' markets. Watch yourself at night in dimly lit alleys like in Saint-Germain or around the train stations.

As for the hostels: Not a one of them really knocks your socks off. We'd guess that Paris is so popular you could rent out a paper bag and charge 10 bucks for it, and maybe that's why. For what it's worth, the HI-affiliated hostels are a little cleaner and better run than almost all the independent ones—but they're much worse located, and more boring and institutional. You've got to fight hard to find a good bed in this town. Choose carefully.

The independents tended to be more relaxed. Too relaxed, actually. Most of them are run by the same group, called C.H.E.A.P. These hostels vary wildly in quality from pretty nice to funky/yucky; definitely check our reviews before booking into these places. All are in great locations, at least, so if you can stand the beds, you'll probably love the surroundings.

In case all the good hostels are full, there are two other sets of accommodations you might want to know about: MIJE and BVJ. (Their French names are too long to deal with just now.) We haven't included them in this book because they discriminate based on age: You can't get in unless you're under a certain age. Since that would exclude some of our readers, we're not giving up the goods on those guys. But there's a fantastic BVJ almost under the nose of the Louvre and another in the heart of Paris's Latin Quarter; contact the organization to learn more about these and other BVJs.

Also call to learn about MIJE's network, which in Paris consists of three fine hostels for young people only in the Marais neighborhood.

Aloha Hostel

1, rue Borromée, 75015 Paris

15th Arrondisement

Phone: 0142-730303

Fax: 0142-731414

E-mail: friends@aloha.fr

Website: aloha.fr

Rates: €30–€32 (about $39–$40 US) per person; doubles €68 (about $85 US)

Credit Cards: No

Beds: 130

Private/family rooms: Yes

Kitchen available: Yes

Season: Open year-round

Office hours: Contact hostel for hours

Lockout: 11 a.m.–5 p.m.

Curfew: 2 a.m.

Affiliation: None

Extras: TV, breakfast, bar

*O*nce in the lower tier of the pack of Parisian hostels, the Aloha had long been steadily descending toward the bottom of the pile. That's too bad, because location-wise it's got many of the rest of them beat hands-down. So it's worth a look for that reason, but that reason only: We still cannot recommend a stay here, though it has "risen" above several other bottom-feeding joints in the past few years.

This was never the lap of luxury to begin with, though. The place, despite a high bed number, is small (and feels small). Dorms contain 2 to 6 beds each, and although they're in somewhat good condition, they're also kinda tight. There's 1 humongous dorm, too. The upper-floor bunk beds are atmospheric, beneath a sloping roof and giving views down onto the hopping streets. They also have a very few double rooms, which would be the beds of choice if this were actually a halfway decent place.

As for bathrooms . . . well, they're teensie-weensie, not much space at all. We're talking just one little shower—it's in a closet that opens into a hall—and just a couple of toilets for the whole darned place.

Best bet for a bite:
Rue Cler

What hostellers say:
"Tight quarters."

Gestalt:
Hawaii five-oh

Safety:

Hospitality:

Cleanliness:

Party index:

Worst of all, it's just extremely dirty here, worse every year. So resign yourself to waiting in line and bumping into people constantly. You might never get that shower, but at least your dorm room likely has a sink; it could be sponge-bath city. The outdoor kitchen is minuscule, and common space consists of a couple tables in the lobby.

Staff will sell you beer and wine from the check-in desk sometimes, which oils conversation considerably. But that's about all they'll do; they're not friendly and helpful, generally speaking. We like the bright-red gas pumps in the bar area, but points off for the official hostel motto: "Fun . . . that's the point, isn't it?" Boy, is that lame. And inaccurate.

The real draw here, anyway, isn't the hostel but rather the neighborhood. Everyone who stays here remembers one thing about it: The Eiffel Tower is around the corner, and when you turn that corner—well, it's almost a religious experience. You've arrived in Paris. And nearby are those quintessential Parisian cafes, produce markets, student fast-food eateries, and even a laundry and a post office. Not a bad place at all to base yourself.

Annoyingly, though, lots of Americans and Brits stay here, possibly detracting a bit from that purely French experience you wanted.

How To Get There:

By bus or train: Call hostel for transit route.

By Metro: Take Metro to Volontaires stop, then walk west on rue de Vaugirard; turn right at rue Borromée and continue to hostel.

By plane: Two large airports outside Paris; call hostel for transit route.

Auberge Cité des Sciences

24, rue des Sept Arpents, Le Pré Saint-Gervais, 93310 Seine St. Denis Paris
Just outside 19th Arrondisement

Phone: 0148-432411

Fax: 0148-432682

E-mail: paris.cite-des-sciences@fuaj.org

Rates: €26.50 (about $33 US) per HI member
Credit cards: Yes
Beds: 185
Private/family rooms: Yes
Kitchen available: Yes
Season: January 1–November 9; December 1–31
Office hours: Midnight–11 a.m.; 4 p.m.–midnight
Affiliation: HI-FUAJ
Extras: Breakfast, laundry, lockers, bike rentals

$\mathcal{S}$uffering from the usual "official" hostel curses (roving gangs of schoolkids, a gulag-like architecture, and running-down or already run-down infrastructure), this place is also pretty far out from central Paris. In fact, it's technically not in the city but in the suburb called Le Pré Saint-Gervais. Still, you might get stuck here simply because the rest of the city's hostels are filled up. At least it's on a Metro line and quite handy to several northern Parisian rail stations. But that cuts both ways; train station neighborhoods tend not to be the greatest, and this is no exception.

Beds here come 2 to 6 to a room, and things can get a little tight. On the plus side, they keep the common room open all day during the room lockout and maintain a laundry and an ironically itsy-bitsy kitchen. For the laundry, you need a few euros' worth of coins—but, frustratingly, reception doesn't always have enough change on hand.

Accommodations are a little sterile, and not clean enough. Rooms in the newer of the 2 buildings have big, big windows with absolutely no awnings or curtains. (Don't come bopping out of the shower au naturel, if you know what we mean.) The 4-bed private rooms for families and other folk come with their own washing facilities—a sink that shoots cold water for about two seconds. The shower, also push-button, shoots hot water—but there's

Best bet for a bite:
Bakery at Metro exit
Insiders' tip:
Sidewalks too narrow for luggage
What hostellers say:
"Your French stinks."
Gestalt:
Blinded by science
Safety:
Hospitality:
Cleanliness:
Party index:

no curtain. Toilets are not included; you have to clomp down the hallway and pray the WC is free. The newer building is more crowded but also more congenial, a lot more conducive to the sort of social mixing you came here to do.

The scene here consists of people gathering in the big common room to write post-cards, practice their French, and listen to live music performed by locals who tend to dress in drag. You can also make calls with phone cards purchased from the vending machine. Laundry facilities are located in the basement, along with the gigantic storage area.

Unfortunately, there's virtually nothing to do at or around the hostel except sit at one of the outdoor tables watching the street. Pinch us. Since the neighborhood's so blah and distant and potentially dodgy, you'll need to whip out your Metro pass and ride the rails to see anything of note. At least the crowd here at the hostel tends to be lively and friendly, and staff—those who will deign to speak English with you, anyway—are OK.

Oh, and if you're into high-tech museums, the Cité des Sciences nearby does a great job of letting you touch, feel, and even smell science and nature up close and personal. Not too Parisian, but it's a cool rainy-day trip.

How To Get There:
By car: Contact hostel for directions.
By bus: Take PC or #170 bus to Port de Pantin stop, then walk 200 yards to hostel.
By Metro: Take #5 Line (toward Bobigny) to Hoche station; walk to hostel

---

Auberge Internationale des Jeunes
10, rue Trousseau, 75011 Paris
11th Arrondisement
> **Phone:** 0147-006200
> **Fax:** 0147-003316
> **Website:** aijparis.com
> **Rates:** €14–€20 (about $18–$25 US) per person; doubles €32–€40 (about $40–$50 US)
> **Credit cards:** Yes
> **Beds:** 40
> **Private/family rooms:** Yes
> **Kitchen available:** No
> **Season:** Open year-round

Office hours: 24 hours
Lockout: 10 a.m.–3 p.m.
Curfew: 1 a.m.
Affiliation: None
Extras: Laundry, breakfast, Internet access
Note: Must be 35 or younger to stay.

*C*haos.

That's a good word to describe this hostel, Paris's cheapest—and possibly among its best located—but also one of the most crowded.

Most dorms contain 2 to 4 beds, and it's a bit cramped here. The bigger the room, paradoxically, the worse it gets. The bathrooms have also seen better days. At least all the quad rooms have their own, er, facilities. Sure, they give you free breakfast—but nobody liked it. The daytime lockout is annoying, too, though

Best bet for a bite:
Monoprix
What hostellers say:
"Another night? Umm . . . no."
Gestalt:
French fried
Safety:
Hospitality:
Cleanliness:
Party index:

this is far from the only Paris hostel to indulge in that practice.

But the location's good, near La Bastille—once a famous French jail. But now the jail is gone and it's a hip, edgy neighborhood of bars, immigrants, and shops. (You can't hear the action from your bunk, which is a plus.) You can mail letters, stock up on grub at one of 4 supermarkets, and take care of other errands all within a block or two. A number of cool clubs are located here, too, though they tend to specialize in bad imitation soul music.

Yes, it's cheap. No, it's still not worth staying here.

How To Get There:

By bus: Call hostel for transit route.
By Metro: Take #8 Line to Ledru-Rollin stop; walk east on rue du Faubourg St-Antoine 1 block to rue Trousseau; turn left.
By train: From Gare du Lyon, walk to Ledru-Rollin; turn and walk east on rue du Faubourg St-Antoine 1 block to rue Trousseau; turn left.

Auberge Jules Ferry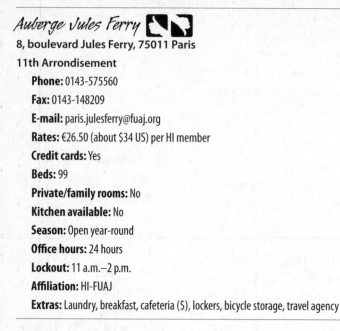

8, boulevard Jules Ferry, 75011 Paris

11th Arrondisement

Phone: 0143-575560

Fax: 0143-148209

E-mail: paris.julesferry@fuaj.org

Rates: €26.50 (about $34 US) per HI member

Credit cards: Yes

Beds: 99

Private/family rooms: No

Kitchen available: No

Season: Open year-round

Office hours: 24 hours

Lockout: 11 a.m.–2 p.m.

Affiliation: HI-FUAJ

Extras: Laundry, breakfast, cafeteria ($), lockers, bicycle storage, travel agency

---

*A*n extremely light breakfast is included at this big (but not warehouse-huge) Paris hostel, which strives to be as efficient the rest of the Hostelling International joints in and around town—but isn't. It's more hoppin' than you'd expect. This one's placed in an excellent location near two cool neighborhoods, La Bastille and the Marais, and is definitely one of the better hostels in the city.

However, expect slightly cramped rooms, a sorry excuse for a kitchen, and variable cleanliness. Yeah, this place is definitely not perfect, even if it's better than some of the other dives in town. Consider that.

Staff are pretty strict about curfew-busting, the 3-hour lockout (boo!), food-snatching, or using too much water in the showers, but you can probably deal with it because it's still one of the best deals you'll find in town, and they're not bad once you get to know them. The atmosphere, in particular, is surprisingly

Best bet for a bite:
Brasseries around République
What hostellers say:
"Wheee!"
Gestalt:
Fairy tail
Safety:
Hospitality:
Cleanliness:
Party index:

laid-back once you return after the lockout. Yes, people actually have fun here. The Hostelling International office nearby serves as an information depot, travel agency, and more.

Arrive early at the trim 6-story building, though, for two simple reasons: First, they don't ever take advance reservations by phone. Second, this is always one of the first places to fill up in the morning.

How To Get There:

By car: Contact hostel for directions. No parking on site.

By bus: Take #46, #54, #56, #65, #75, #96, N1, or N2 bus to République or Jules Ferry stop and walk 200 yards to hostel.

By Metro: Take Metro to République stop; walk east along rue du Faubourg du Temple to boulevard Jules Ferry; turn right.

By plane: From airport, take #350 bus to hostel.

By train: Gare du Nord and Gare de l'Est, ¼ mile away. Call hostel for transit route.

Attractive natural setting	Comfortable beds	Visual arts at hostel or nearby
Ecologically aware hostel	A particularly good value	Music at hostel or nearby
Superior kitchen facilities or cafe	Wheelchair-accessible	Great hostel for skiers
Offbeat or eccentric place	Good for business travelers	Bar or pub at hostel or nearby
Superior bathroom facilities	Especially well-suited for families	Editors' choice: Among our very favorite hostels
Romantic private rooms	Good for active travelers	

Key to Icons

Auberge le D'Artagnan

80, rue Vitruve, 75020 Paris
20th Arrondisement

> **Phone:** 0140-323456
> **Fax:** 0140-323455
> **E-mail:** paris.le-dartagnan@fuaj.org
> **Rates:** €23.50 (about $30 US) per HI member
> **Credit cards:** Yes
> **Beds:** 412
> **Private/family rooms:** Yes
> **Kitchen available:** No
> **Season:** Open year-round
> **Office hours:** 8 a.m.–1 a.m.
> **Lockout:** Noon–3 p.m.
> **Affiliation:** HI-FUAJ
> **Extras:** Laundry, meals ($), breakfast, bar, disco, movies, lockers, concerts, piano,
> climbing wall, Internet access ($), shop

This is about the only "official" Paris hostel we can even halfheartedly recommend. It's a huge edifice in kind of a weird area for a hostel, in a drab neighborhood that's really only close to a train station and giant Père-Lachaise Cemetery (where Jim Morrison and others now rest). So if you've come to lay flowers at the Lizard King's feet, well, this is the hostel for you. Otherwise it's just too far from the action. But, on the upside, this is among the best hostels in town. (That's not saying much, because most of the hostels here frankly suck.)

There are tons of activities here. They show free movies every week, host concerts, and run a bar in the basement. Did we mention the discotheque? (Nobody dances, but that's beside the point.) All that, plus a laundry, family and private rooms, and meals. Free breakfast is included with your bed, and it was pretty good, though it wasn't as sumptuous as the staff-only lunch spread that's off-limits to hostellers. There should be a kitchen, but there isn't. It's reasonably clean and boring as all get-out.

Drawbacks? Try the attitude sometimes displayed by a hipper-than-you'll-ever-be staff, who'd rather watch you fumble for hours with unresponsive pay phones than explain that they don't work. The in-house cafe attempts cowboy cooking with a Tex-Mex menu that just doesn't quite cut it, and plumbing is outdated and not always in good repair. Most annoying, groups of French schoolkids tend to book the place and make a lot of noise in the halls at night. Also don't be surprised by the thinnish sheets, bare-bones rooms, and (in summer) big groups of European teenies roaming the halls.

Still, it's a good place compared with its Paris brethren. Dorms are generally 3- to 4-bed affairs (though there are also some 8-bed dorms), kept fairly clean. They're a welcome change from the gargantuan dorms we'd feared when we laid eyes on the place. All the activity from below does occasionally filter upward; try to get a top-floor bunk if you don't want noise or the omnipresent cigarette smoke hovering about.

The real trade-off here, as we said, is location; you need to hoof it to the Metro, then ride awhile, to get to most places you want to be. Otherwise, this isn't a bad hostel at all.

Best bet for a bite:
Bastille area
What hostellers say:
"Got a light?"
Gestalt:
Lachaise lounge
Safety:
Hospitality:
Cleanliness:
Party index:

How To Get There:
By bus: Eurolines terminal is ½ mile from hostel.
By Metro: Take #3 Metro line to Porte de Bagnolet stop; walk ⅓ mile to hostel.
By plane: From airport, take #351 bus to hostel.
By train: From Gare de Lyon, walk ½ mile to hostel or take #57 bus.

Auberge Leo Lagrange

107, rue Martre, 92110 Clichy (Paris)
Just outside 17th Arrondisement
  Phone: 0141-272690
  Fax: 0142-705263
  E-mail: paris.clichy@fuaj.org
  Rates: €25.20 (about $32 US) per HI member
  Credit cards: No
  Beds: 329
  Private/family rooms: Yes

Kitchen available: Yes
Season: Open year-round
Office hours: 24 hours
Affiliation: HI-FUAJ
Extras: Breakfast, lockers, bar

*B*reakfast is included, and so are free sheets, at this grim-looking hostel on the outskirts of Paris—which is actually, technically speaking, a couple blocks outside Paris in the suburb of Clichy, if you're gonna get picky about things.

Bunkrooms are small—just 2 to 4 beds in all of 'em—and FUAJ has provided free breakfast, a bar, and lockers for hostellers' enjoyment. Don't forget to hang out with your new buds in the balcony chairs, either. All in all, a place removed from the frenzy of most other Parisian hostels. But the rude staff, poorly maintained bathrooms, and noise should make you think twice.

This is fairly close to both Montmartre and the Champs-Elysées, although you'll need to do a little fancy footwork to get there. And, as with FUAJ's other hostels, you'll need to hop Le Metro to get to downtown's chief attractions. Can't imagine wanting to stay here in burb-land unless every other decent place on your list is already booked up, though. Since it's so super-basic, not well cleaned, and in need of repairs, we say: Avoid if you can.

Given the extremely remote locale, we're sure you can.

Best bet for a bite:
Try Montmartre
What hostellers say:
"Far out. Literally."
Gestalt:
Lagrange hall
Safety:
Hospitality:
Cleanliness:
Party index:

How To Get There:

By bus: Take #54, #154, or #174 bus to Mairie de Clichy.
By car: Call hostel for directions. Street parking available ($).
By Metro: Take #13 Metro line (toward Asnières Gennevilliers) to Mairie de Clichy station; walk 150 yards to hostel.
By train: St-Lazare Station, ½ mile away; call hostel for transit route.

Cisp Maurice Ravel

6, avenue Maurice Ravel, Paris 75012

12th Arrondisement

Phone: 0144-756000 or 0144-756006

Website: cisp.fr

Rates: €20–€40 (about $23–$42 US) per person; doubles €50 (about $62 US)

Credit cards: Yes

Beds: 600

Private/family rooms: Yes

Kitchen available: No

Season: Open year-round

Office hours: 6:30 a.m.–1:30 a.m.

Affiliation: CISP

Extras: Restaurant ($)

![fork and knife icon]

This place is so cheap, and so clean, it's a wonder more hostellers haven't discovered it yet.

Well, OK, not so fast. Like a lot of Paris hostels, it is located a half hour out from the center of town in a fairly dodgy suburb where you'll want to be careful at night. And it's kinda spartan on the furnishings. Still, rooms this clean and airy ought to be commanding hotel rates. And the big breakfast is positively energizing. Note that it's pretty hard to make friends here at the hostel itself, owing to the layout—and the fact that everybody's headed into town anyway. But if you can put up with that, and the remote location, this might be one of the better picks in town.

Note: There's a great annex, known locally as Kellerman, in the 13th Arrondisement; ask about it when booking or checking in.

What hostellers say:
"Great breakfast"

Gestalt:
Ravel rouser

Safety: [icon]

Hospitality: [icon]

Cleanliness: [icon]

Party index: [icons]

How To Get There:

By bus: Contact hostel for transit details.

By car: Contact hostel for directions.

By train: Contact hostel for transit details.

FIAP Jean-Monnet

30, rue Cabanis, 75014 Paris

14th Arrondisement

Phone: 0143-131717 or 0143-131700

Fax: 0145-816391

Website: fiap-paris.org

Rates: €29–€63 (about $36–$79 US) per person, doubles €84 (about $105 US)

Credit cards: Yes

Beds: 500

Private/family rooms: Yes

Kitchen available: No

Season: Open year-round

Office hours: 24 hours

Lockout: 9 a.m.–2:30 p.m.

Curfew: 2 a.m.

Affiliation: UCRIF

Extras: Cafeteria ($), laundry, club, conference rooms, game room, classes, tourist
information, breakfast, Internet access

f tour groups didn't get first dibs on the beds in this FIAP (a French acronym that nobody at the hostel could explain), it would be darned near perfect. As it is, this great hostel might not have any space when you call—especially in summer—for individual hostellers. But we're including it because if they do have room, it's a great place to hang.

Clean and educational, that's what this place is. How educational? Try French classes taught right in the hostel! Plus concerts and shows in the hostel's lounge and a tourist info desk to point you the right way in the city of lights. On the practical side, there's a laundry and cafeteria plus a game room for idle pursuits. Your rate includes a self-serve, missable continental breakfast; you can pay a few euros extra per day for a "restaurant" breakfast.

What hostellers say:
"Huge but fun."

Gestalt:
Monnet, Monnet

Safety:

Hospitality:

Cleanliness:

Party index:

And the rooms—well, they're every bit as clean and nice as you'd expect, in configurations of 2 to 8 beds each; en-suite bathrooms are often present, too. Rooms in the back section are bigger—ask about one when booking.

Only problem is, if it's summertime you're probably not going to get a bunk. That doesn't seem fair. There's a brutal 9 a.m. checkout . . . no exceptions. But that's the way it is. Try to come off-season if you can. It can also get stuffy in summer.

This place is far from luxurious, but it's just about your best bunk bet in Paris.

How To Get There:

By bus or train: Call hostel for transit route.

By Metro: Take Metro to Glacière stop, then walk down boulevard St-Jacques to rue Ferrus; make a left, then immediate right onto rue Cabanis.

By plane: Two large airports outside Paris; from Charles de Gaulle, take RER Line B to Denfert Rochereau; from Orly take Orlybus to Denfert Rochereau.

Le Village Hostel

20, rue d'Orsel, 75018 Paris

18th Arrondisement

Phone: 0142-642202

Fax: 0142-642204

Website: villagehostel.fr

Rates: Rates: €40–€55 (about $50–$66 US) per person; doubles €110 (about $138 US)

Credit cards: No

Beds: 95

Private/family rooms: Yes

Kitchen available: Yes

Season: Open year-round

Office hours: 7:30 a.m.–2:30 a.m.

Lockout: 11 a.m.–4 p.m.

Curfew: 2 a.m.

Affiliation: None

Extras: Breakfast, bar, Internet access, fax, terrace, TV room

S o you're walking downhill off Sacre Coeur, still blown away by the church (and hordes of Americans snapping pics of it), and you turn a corner; there it is, a big blue neon hostel sign. You've found one of the newer hostels in Paris, already a darling of certain cheapie guidebooks even if it is one that still has kinks to work out. Still, overall, this place gets good marks—it seems to be standing the test of time, even improving, which is rare in this business. Trust us.

What hostellers say:
"Montmartre rocks!"
Gestalt:
Village people
Safety:
Hospitality:
Cleanliness:
Party index:

The beds are good, so far, though the mostly Aussie and American crowds do beat up the furniture fast. Bunks come in rooms with from 2 to 4 beds (in summer they add more to reduce your privacy, but the price is also less); some coveted doubles are available. This place has the best views and terrace in Paris, so that's definitely worth something. Management and staffing are decent, while the small bar appears to be where the socializing gets done. Cleanliness is better than you'd expect at an independent hostel, which is a very welcome change. But while rooms are pristine, some are still a bit itchy and scratchy. (Also, we really hate the push-button showers here. Fix this.)

All in all? It's not perfect and certainly not one of the very best places in town, but in a sea of has-beens and never-weres, the Village does deliver decent value and a truly Parisian experience. It's pretty basic, but pretty quiet. And it's got personality, something far too many Euro-hostels lack. Put it on your short list; we have to consider it one of the better options in a river of mediocrity.

How To Get There:

By bus and train: Contact hostel for transit route.
By Metro: Take Metro to Anvers stop; walk up rue Steinkerque to rue d'Orsel and turn right; walk ½ block. Hostel is on left.
By car: Contact hostel for directions.

Auberge de Jeunesse Pajol (Pajol Hostel) ⬉

Rue Pajol, 75018 Paris

18th Arrondisement

   Phone: 0144-898727

   E-mail: paris.pajol@hifrance.org

   Rates: €29.50 (about $37 US) per HI member; doubles €59 (about $64 US)

   Credit cards: Yes

   Beds: TK

   Private/family rooms: Yes

   Kitchen available: Yes

   Season: Open year-round

   Office hours: 7:30 a.m.–1 a.m.

   Affiliation: HI-FUAJ

   Extras: Breakfast, bar, Internet access, fax, terrace, TV room

This new FUAJ/Hostelling International–run hostel opened just as this edition was going to press. It looks great, and—given the incredibly weak array of hostels in the city—it might soon rocket to the top of our list, if the advance word bears out. For now, we can only tell you what we've heard, not what we've seen.

As the staff will helpfully tell you time and again, the hostel was carved out of a former warehouse that belonged to the French railway system. The solar panels on top tip you off right away that something is different. There's a definite "green" vibe throughout . . . literally. The hostel was designed with gardens, grounds, and even ponds. (Monet would approve.)

There's also a bar, a laundry for dishing up the dirt (er, something like that), and a kitchen.

How To Get There:

By bus: Take #48, #60, or #65 bus to hostel.

By subway: Take Metro line #2 to La Chapelle station or line #12 to Marx Dormoy station.

Three Ducks Travelers Hostel 🦆

6, place Etienne Pernet, 75015 Paris

15th Arrondisement

>**Phone:** 0148-420405
>
>**Fax:** 0148-429999
>
>**Website:** 3ducks.fr
>
>**Rates:** €18–€25 (about $23–$31 US) per person; doubles €46–€52 (about $58–$65 US)
>
>**Credit cards:** Yes
>
>**Beds:** 95
>
>**Private/family rooms:** No
>
>**Kitchen available:** Yes
>
>**Season:** Open year-round
>
>**Office hours:** 8 a.m.–2 a.m.
>
>**Lockout:** 10 a.m.–5 p.m.
>
>**Curfew:** 2 a.m.
>
>**Affiliation:** None
>
>**Extras:** Storage, lockers, courtyard, breakfast, sheets ($)

🗑️

Beaten-down and packed with beer-guzzling North Americans, Aussies, and Europeans, this place is Party Central—and that's about all it's got going for it. This is a contender for Paris's very worst hostel in every way but one: If you're absolutely intent on getting bombed off your butt and then hitting on some other soused hosteller in the process, then you'll love it.

But first things first. The rooms here—which contain 2 to 8 beds apiece—are cold, cramped, and dirty. There's not enough heat in winter, and some beds don't have pillows. That's right. No pillows. (It's BYOP, apparently? Whatever, dudes.) Bathrooms are even worse, not even approaching cleanliness or hotness of water—this is what happens when scrungy hosteller after hosteller kneels before the porcelain god at the end of a long drunk, maybe. Management somehow gets away with locking you out of the place all day long, too (outrageous!), though they don't appear to use that free time to do cleaning or upkeep.

Some hostellers told us that the staff here were tough to deal with, while others claim staff are helpful; it probably depends on what you're wanting. If it's a party, then they'll help you out. Got a complaint? Tough luck. Breakfast is free but not terribly nutritious; when we stopped in, it was weak hot chocolate and a cheapo baguette. They also ding you with extra charges for sheets, towels, everything.

The bar—the only reason people could possibly want to stay here—throbs all night long with bad music, making sleep all but impossible. The atmosphere resembles a 24-hour hookah party, with hostellers traipsing in and out, smoking, drinking, and becoming ill from dusk till dawn.

Our call? This is about the equivalent of lying down and sleeping in the middle of the Champs Elyseés, we'd say—and sleeping in the street is about 20 bucks cheaper!

What hostellers say:
"Partyyyy!"
Gestalt:
Daffy ducks
Safety:
Hospitality:
Cleanliness:
Party index:

How To Get There:
By bus or train: Call hostel for transit route.
By Metro: Take Metro to Commerce stop. Walk south on rue du Commerce toward church; hostel is on right.
By plane: Two large airports outside Paris; call hostel for transit route.

Attractive natural setting	Comfortable beds	Visual arts at hostel or nearby
Ecologically aware hostel	A particularly good value	Music at hostel or nearby
Superior kitchen facilities or cafe	Wheelchair-accessible	Great hostel for skiers
Offbeat or eccentric place	Good for business travelers	Bar or pub at hostel or nearby
Superior bathroom facilities	Especially well-suited for families	Editors' choice: Among our very favorite hostels
Romantic private rooms	Good for active travelers	

Key to Icons

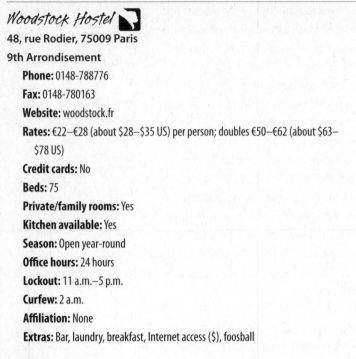

Woodstock Hostel 🦅

48, rue Rodier, 75009 Paris

9th Arrondisement

Phone: 0148-788776

Fax: 0148-780163

Website: woodstock.fr

Rates: €22–€28 (about $28–$35 US) per person; doubles €50–€62 (about $63–$78 US)

Credit cards: No

Beds: 75

Private/family rooms: Yes

Kitchen available: Yes

Season: Open year-round

Office hours: 24 hours

Lockout: 11 a.m.–5 p.m.

Curfew: 2 a.m.

Affiliation: None

Extras: Bar, laundry, breakfast, Internet access ($), foosball

S

*B*y the time we got to Woodstock . . . ah, never mind. This hostel dubs itself "The American Youth Embassy in Paris," and—as the name implies—the place is partly staffed by folks from the US of A. So it feels very American. If you're looking for the quintessential French hostel experience, you've come to the wrong place—but every so often it's comforting to bunk with those who know where you're coming from.

The bar on the ground level is the nerve center of the place, and the music blaring 24 hours a day creates an exciting social atmosphere (if you like rock music). Luckily, walls in the bunkrooms are thick enough to block out most of the sound waves. So the party ends when you want it to. There's a nice mix of doubles, triples, and dormitory-style rooms, all within a very fair price range for Paris. Another room is available to store your packs for the day, suitable as long as you trust your roomies.

A breakfast is included with your overnight stay, itself not very American. But the hostel baguettes, jelly, coffee, and hot chocolate should give you the French jump start necessary to get through that first museum after a late night. As a bonus, the hostel's just 2 blocks from the Metro, close to the famous Sacre Coeur church, and also just a short walk from Paris's pulsing red-light district.

Drawback? Prices are rising here, and cleanliness and upkeep are declining. Never a welcome combo. Basically, it's a reasonably fun and happy place most of the time, but never all that clean. All in all, this place just doesn't cut it . . . too dirty and poorly kept. It's not the worst hostel in town and it is very well located, so it will do in a pinch. But we wouldn't stay more than a night or two, max.

Best bet for a bite:
Grocery store on corner
What hostellers say:
"Which state are you from?"
Gestalt:
Back to the garden
Safety:
Hospitality:
Cleanliness:
Party index:

How To Get There:

By bus or train: Call hostel for transit route.

By Metro: Take Metro to Anvers stop, then walk across street to park with gazebo; walk through park and make a right on avenue Trudaine, then turn left on Rodier. Hostel is on left.

By plane: Two large airports outside Paris; call hostel for transit route.

Young & Happy Hostel

80, rue de Mouffetard, 75005 Paris
5th Arrondisement

Phone: 0147-074707
Fax: 0147-072224
Website: youngandhappy.fr
Rates: €24–€35 (about $30–$44 US) per person; doubles €80 (about $100 US)
Credit cards: Yes
Beds: 75
Private/family rooms: Sometimes
Kitchen available: Yes
Season: Open year-round

Office hours: Call hostel for hours
Lockout: 11 a.m.–4 p.m.
Curfew: 2 a.m.
Affiliation: None
Extras: Breakfast, fax, Internet access, bar, kitchen

t IS young, but we're NOT happy.

This Paris hostel tries to be good to you, but its small space and odd management practices don't quite mesh with ideal hostelling.

It's somewhat unclean (yet inexplicably popular with Japanese visitors), and packs in the meat: The watchword here is tiny. Rooms (2 to 6 beds apiece) are close quarters, hallways are narrow, and there's little common or eating space. A small breakfast and showers are free.

Safety:	◣
Hospitality:	◣ ◣
Cleanliness:	◣
Party index:	🎉 🎉 🎉 🎉

The real draw here is the surrounding area, which is fairly cool—if a bit distant from the central city. It's yet another Parisian neighborhood of shops, bars, and student hangouts where real Parisians live. Come to the Mouffetard market, the city's oldest, where farmers and others hawk their goods. It's not the best market in the city, not by far, but if you want a quickie introduction to the market phenomenon (and you like fresh fruit), check it out.

How To Get There:
By bus or train: Call hostel for transit route.
By Metro: Take Metro to Monge stop; follow rue Ortolan to rue Mouffetard.

Germany

*T*his is it: the land that inspired Walt Disney World—for real—a land of great rivers, tasty wines, oompa-loompa sounds, and some of the best damn beer in the world. If only Germany's "official" hostels reflected this spirit. Unfortunately, they reflect another side of Germany—the cold, efficiently planned one. The independent hostels of Germany, however, are another story altogether: There's lots of variety and craziness in both Berlin and Munich, and you'll find picking through the options fun.

Practical Details

Deutsche Bahn (DB), the national train company, is incredibly efficient; their trains are fast (sometimes very fast), clean, comfortable, and—obviously—quite punctual. Ticket agents all speak English and have access to DB's lightning-fast trip-planning software, which can get you where you want to go faster than you can. Trust us. While these rail systems cross an incredible variety of landscape, even the iron horse can't get everywhere. It's likely, at some point, that you will need to supplement your train travel with some form of gondola, lift, bus, cog railway, or steam train.

Germany no longer has its own rail pass. Instead, you have to pay more for a combined pass with an adjacent country such as France, Austria, Denmark, or the Czech Republic. Of course, Germany's excellent rail system is covered by all Eurail "Global" and "Select" passes, too.

A Eurail pass also saves you money in Germany on some bus tours and routes (such as the bus from Nurnberg to Prague, and along the so-called Romantic Road); on Lake Konstanz and Danube River ferries; on Berlin's S-Bahn light rail system (free); on the overnight Berlin-to-Sweden train; and on various other German ferries. Best of all, it gets you a free ride on the KD Rhine Line's scenic Rhine River ferries.

If you're gonna be around for a really long time, you can buy a BahnCard in German train stations for around $75 US. The card gets you a 25 percent discount on second-class tickets for a whole year, and the savings can really add up.

A few other things to keep in mind:

- The EurAide offices in the Munich and Berlin train stations are an absolute godsend for trip planning. They'll set up your train reservations, reserve sleeper-train beds, give tours, whatever you need—at little cost, and in clear English.

- Germany is a big country. Going from Berlin to anywhere else is gonna take you half a day, at least, maybe all day. The superfast InterCity Express (ICE) trains blast along at top speeds, and they can save you time, but they also cost a little extra—reservations are required, too. Definitely go for second-class tickets on these babies unless you're loaded.
- Big-city German train stations and their neighborhoods can get a little rough late at night. Ever heard of skinheads? Germany invented them, and they're still actively circulating the streets and stations of East Berlin, among other places. Stay away from those guys with the jackets and white-laced boots. You don't need the trouble.

German's country code is 49. To call German hostels from North America, dial 011-49 and DROP THE FIRST ZERO from the numbers printed in this book; to call from within Germany, dial the numbers AS PRINTED. To call the US, Canada, or wherever else you might hail from, dial 001 and then the number you are calling. (Remember: It's cheaper to make coin calls at night, and directory assistance—dial 11810—can get expensive.)

Germany's unit of currency is the euro.

BERLIN

Population 3.5 million and growing, Berlin's one crazy place these days. Flush with its position as capital of a reunified Germany (let's face it, you never realized Bonn was the old capital anyway), construction projects are sprouting like mad. There's a palpable energy as entrepreneurs, artists, clubbers, and just about everyone else tries to carve out an exciting new direction. It's probably the most exciting city in Europe right now.

That's not to say it's a physically attractive place, though. Years of Iron Curtain life have turned chunks of the city into run-down quarters and fascist-architecture hotels and housing projects. You come here for the culture and the fascinating history, not pretty buildings and quaint alleyways. Fortunately, some parks provide a bit of green relief from the concrete, and some are quite close to the central sightseeing districts.

Getting Oriented

Zoologischer Garten Station—almost always called Zoo Station (thanks, U2) or Bahnof Zoo—is big and confusing, but it will probably be your introduction to Berlin and it's the best place to orient yourself and get ready for the party. Want a big hint? The place to get all your local tourist tips—not to mention make onward train reservations—is the American-run

EurAide office at Zoo Station. Also at the train station you'll find tour companies such as Berlin Walks, a very good one (try the Third Reich tour).

For purposes of organizing your visit to this sprawling city, we've divided Berlin into a few areas. Going from west to east, the huge downtown area is composed of the western districts known as Charlottenberg, Tiergarten, and Schöneberg; two central areas near the old Berlin wall, Mitte ("middle") and Kreuzberg; and two eastern neighborhoods, Prenzlauer Berg and Friedrichshain. Each of these areas has its own individual character, and collectively they are chock-full of hostels. Any hostel that's outside these five areas is probably gonna take some time to get to.

In each write-up we've indicated where the hostel is located. If a hostel's not in one of these areas, we've labeled it as being in the Outer Districts.

Getting Around

Berlin's so big that it had to gradually build a tremendous transport network to get everyone around—and it did. What's amazing is that when East and West Berlin joined hands in 1989, the two networks were seamlessly joined. Today tons of buses, streetcars, subways, and commuter trains ensure that things keep moving.

Subways (the U-Bahn) are marked by a "U." Aboveground trains (the S-Bahn, free with Eurail passes) are marked by an "S." Bus and streetcar stops are marked with an "H" by the side of the road, and night buses (those with an "N" in the number) run all night long, though less frequently than day buses do.

Buy a transit pass each day (or every couple days), then use it—a lot—to sightsee and get around. You might pay a little bit extra, but if you're gonna be hopping around a lot, it works out as a better deal than individual tickets. And it's really worth the time you'll save not having to stand in line or trying to decipher ticket machines.

Transit passes come in several levels. The Tageskarte, the daily transit pass, costs roughly $9 to $10 US per day; up to five people doing all their traveling together can save by buying a remarkable German innovation called the *Gruppenkarten* (group card) for about $20 US per day. The system also sometimes offers one- and three-day "Welcome Cards," as well as a weekly pass for those staying a little longer. Check with EurAide at the Berlin station when you arrive, do the math, and see whether you can save money with one.

By the way, if you're driving into the city—and some do this—you'll need a special sticker certifying your rental car is emissions-checked. It's cheap, less than 10 bucks, but you have to get the sticker from city hall or selected gas stations. What a pain.

Berlin

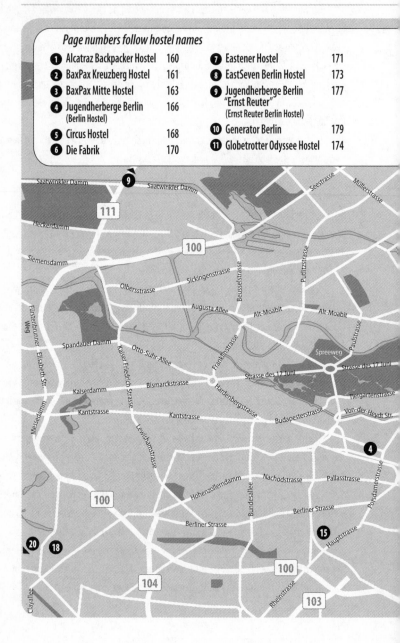

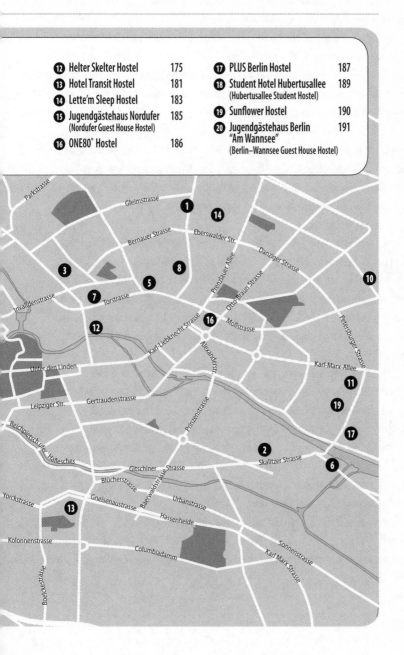

What to See

You could spend days and days in Berlin, alternating between Cold War sightseeing and bar-hopping among the city's hundreds of enjoyable *kneipen* (pubs).

To see the sights, we'd possibly begin with a quick walk or ride. From Zoo Station, you might take a public transit ride over to Charlottenburg Palace. It's every bit as impressive as you'd expect; there are spacious grounds, plus museum after museum filled with regal items. A closer site to the station would be the Kaiser-Wilhelm-Gedächtniskirche memorial church, about a block away.

In the other direction, toward the Wall, you might try a get-acquainted stroll along famous Kurfurstendamm Boulevard (Berliners-in-the-know just call it Ku-damm), a long, wide, and drab—but oh-so-Berlin—collection of department stores, restaurants, and bars.

After getting that first taste of the city, we'd hop a bus for the Mitte district, where the sights come fast and furious near the former border checkpoint that divided East and West known as the Checkpoint Charlie House.

The Brandenburg Gate, built in the late 1700s, is the usual starting point on a walking tour from west to east and a point of pride for Berliners, who now consider it the heart of their city. The huge radio tower—with its 1,200 feet of steel and antenna right in the center of town—is the next obvious point on a tour. You can ascend to a platform halfway up and check out the new German capital from high in the air. From there, head east along wide Unter den Linden ("Under the Lime Trees") Boulevard for a really grand look at Berlin's pre-Nazi glories.

Or make a short hop over to Museumsinsel, a small island in the Spree River stocked with enormous and impressive museums; look for such landmarks as the huge cupola of the Berliner Dom (cathedral). Some of the offerings include the Altes Museum (Old Museum), Alte Nationalgalerie (Old National Gallery), Bode Museum, and Pergamon Museum.

Nearby you'll find a number of churches that testify to the atrocities of World War II, including the Nikolaikirche (first begun in the 13th century). Also close by, the Nikolaiviertel section is the city's most ancient. Begin at the Nikolai church and filter through alleys and squares, stopping for a bite or a beer when you get the urge.

Most of the same key sights, in roughly the same order, can be seen by jumping onto the city's #100 bus at Zoo Station and riding from west to east. That's the cheap way. For a more romantic look at things, find out about one of the city boat tours running along the Spree River.

BERLIN HOSTELS AT A GLANCE

	RATING	PRICE	IN A WORD	PAGE
Circus Hostel	👍👍	€19–€60	cool	p. 168
Globetrotter Odyssee Hostel	👍👍	€9–€48.50	rockin'	p. 174
PLUS Berlin Hostel	👍👍	€14–€24	wonderful	p. 187
Eastener Hostel	👍👍	€15–€27	tiny	p. 171
EastSeven Hostel	👍👍	€18–€23	hotshot	p. 173
One80° Hostel	👍	€15–€29.50	relaxing	p. 186
Die Fabrik Hostel	👍	€18–€38	fun	p. 170
Hotel Transit Hostel	👍	€21–€49	great	p. 181
Sunflower Hostel	👍	€14.50–€38	improving	p. 190
BaxPax Mitte Hostel	👍	€14–€26	arty	p. 163
Lette 'm Sleep Hostel	👍	€12–€21	relaxed	p. 183
Generator Berlin	👍	€14–€45	popular	p. 179
Nordufer Guest House Hostel	👍	€19.90	OK	p. 185
Ernst Reuter Berlin Hostel	👍	€24	quiet	p. 177
Alcatraz Hostel	👍	€18–€48	remote	p. 160
Berlin-Wannsee Guest House Hostel	👍	€15	distant	p. 191
Student Hotel Hubertusallee	👍	€18–€48	far-out	p. 189
BaxPax Kreuzberg Hostel	👍	€12–€22	OK	p. 161
Jugendherberge Berlin	👍	€27	blah	p. 166
Helter Skelter Hostel	👍👎	€11–€18	clubby	p. 175

The Hostel Scene

Predictably enough, the hostels in Berlin range from near-dumps to boring warehouse-style places to near-pristine palaces. (We did note that an amazing number of the places here, no matter what they're like, charge you extra dough just to get sheets. Sheets. Boo to that!)

We've found that the backpacker-style joints here are about as groovy as any in Europe—there's a very laid-back feel to them, which is at odds with the normal hostels-in-Germany way of doing things. In other words, the difference between an "official" hostel and an "independent" one in this city is huge in terms of atmosphere.

Alcatraz Backpacker Hostel

Schönhauser Allee 133a, 10437 Berlin

Phone: 030-4849-6815

E-mail: ok@alcatraz-backpacker.de

Website: alcatraz-backpacker.de

Rates: €18–€48 (about $23–$60 US) per person; doubles €50–€55 (about $63–$66 US)

Credit cards: No

Beds: Number varies

Private/family rooms: Yes

Kitchen available: Yes

Season: Open year-round

Office hours: 24 hours

Affiliation: None

Extras: Free Internet access, breakfast ($), bike rentals, safe, luggage storage, library, yard, television, kitchen, foosball

---

*L*ocated in Prenzlauer Berg.

Don't know why they named this place for a prison, because there's nothing wrong with this hostel at all. It's a good choice.

The big coed dorm here is cheapest, of course, but they also have double, triple, and quad rooms, and they will try to give you a single-sex room if you ask and they're not full up. Beds and bunks were a bit skinny, yet everything—including bathrooms—is funkily decorated, and nicely clean. The modern kitchen alcove was also well kept, and certainly adequate for the task of preparing nosh. The friendly staff serves breakfast, points you to

Internet access, rents bikes very cheaply, and will store your valuables or luggage. Other nice features included trippy murals and a nice back garden with picnic tables covered by umbrellas. Great place to hang out.

However, the hostel felt a bit sterile—no party action at all. They charge for sheets. (Boo.) And while it's technically located in the fun Prenzlauer Berg 'hood, there's actually little to do in the surrounding area either. You're a little bit marooned. (No wonder they call it Alcatraz! Now we get it.) That means you've got to use public transit and get away from here to have any fun, then get back later.

What hostellers say:
"Um, where's Berlin?"
Gestalt:
Escape from Alcatraz
Safety:
Hospitality:
Cleanliness:
Party index:

We did like the pretty unique late checkout feature; for just a few extra bucks it's worth gold, in our opinion, when you're stuck with a late flight or train departure.

Our consensus: This hostel is fine. Better than fine. Management seems to be doing a commendable job, and they've earned our thumbs-up. However, Berlin is such a fantastic city that you need to be in the action to sample and enjoy it, and that simply isn't possible at this location. So we can't recommend it as a top-three pick. Still, worth a hard look when other, more central joints are booked up.

How To Get There:

By bus or train: Take U-Bahn line U2 toward Pankow to Eberswalderstrasse Station. Exit station to Allee and continue to hostel on left at number 133a.

By car: Contact hostel for directions.

BaxPax Kreuzberg Hostel

Skalitzer Strasse 104, 10997 Berlin-Kreuzberg

> **Phone:** 030-695-18322
> **Fax:** 030-695-18372
> **E-mail:** info@baxpax.de
> **Website:** baxpax.de
> **Rates:** €12–€22 (about $16–$28 US) per person; doubles €52–€66 (about $65–$83 US)
> **Credit cards:** Yes

Beds: 65
Private/family rooms: No
Kitchen available: Yes
Season: Open year-round
Office hours: 24 hours
Affiliation: None
Extras: Bike rentals, tours, free WiFi, pool table, movie theater, laundry

ocated in Friedrichshain/Kreuzberg.

Simple, clean, nicely designed, and just plain fun, this hostel is housed in an old factory that once produced men's bowler hats. Keying into the hip Oranienstrasse neighborhood, it caters to hostellers who need little privacy. Most contain between 4 and 10 beds—real beds, not bunks—though there's also a massive section known as the "K-Studio," where they jam 50 bunks into 2 rooms. Bathroom facilities are shared and rooms are coed, although there is also 1 dorm just for women, and the quality of the showers leaves something to be desired.

Although it's located in a high-traffic area, the sleeping rooms face the back of the building, providing some quiet. The hostel sets aside a place behind the desk for backpacks and other luggage—we'd rather see lockers—and there's a safety box for smaller valuables like passports and nose rings. You'll have to shell out extra dough for sheets and towels, though. The public phone here only takes change, no phone cards. Sheesh! Staff will sell you various transport tickets, including long-distance bus tickets for one of the new intra-Europe coach companies.

The place is quite roomy—it was a factory, after all—and has plenty of common areas. Management claims you can drive a car (maybe a Trabi) through the extra-wide hallways, though we're not saying you should actually try.

Best bet for a bite:
Kaiser's Markt
Insiders' tip:
See last paragraph
What hostellers say:
"Gettin' better."
Gestalt:
Pax a punch
Safety:
Hospitality:
Cleanliness:
Party index:

For food, the Kottbusser Tor area is just a subway stop away. This neighborhood is populated by Turkish immigrants, and there are good and cheap markets supplying fresh fruits and veggies, which is great since there is a well-equipped kitchen to play chef in. German supermarkets also abound. If you're into other people's unwanted junk, flea markets here should keep you occupied. During the summer there's a pool at Görlitzer park to dunk your toes in.

How To Get There:
By bus: Contact hostel for transit details.
By car: Contact hostel for directions.
By train: From Zoo Station, take U-Bahn line U2 one stop to Wittenberg Platz, then change to U1 and continue to Görlitzer Bahnhof. Hostel is 10 yards from station.

BaxPax Mitte Hostel
Chausseestrasse 102, 10115 Berlin
> **Phone:** 030-283-90965
> **Fax:** 030-283-90955
> **E-mail:** mitte@baxpax.de
> **Website:** baxpax.de
> **Rates:** €14–€26 (about $19–$33 US) per person; doubles €54–€70 (about $67–
> $82 US)
> **Credit cards:** Yes
> **Beds:** 60
> **Private/family rooms:** Yes
> **Kitchen available:** Yes
> **Season:** Open year-round
> **Office hours:** 7 a.m.–10 p.m.
> **Affiliation:** None
> **Extras:** Bike rentals, laundry, tours, Internet access, linens ($), television

---

*L*ocated in Mitte.

Now under the control of the BaxPax mini–hostel chain, this place (formerly known as the Backpacker Mitte) is super-friendly, arty, and gets big points for being a hoppin' hang-out in the heart of the Mitte neighborhood and all its pleasures. The character isn't so much Berlin, however, as a get-together of dudes and dudettes from California and Jersey and Australia, places like that. You'll hear lots of sentences beginning with grating constructions like "Like, you know, it was, like, so, like, cool, when we, like, threw up on the bartender."

If that sets your heart to racing with joy, by all means head for this place. If it doesn't, enjoy the rooms at night, and spare yourself the lame conversations when your roommates approach.

OK, sorry; let's talk more about the hostel, not the hostellers. We noted several different kinds of decor in the rooms, which are surprisingly fancy and decorated in a typical Mitte-'90s design (you'll have to see it to see what we mean; for example, the color orange is prevalent, and one room has an underwater theme). Other rooms are a little more sedate, with flowery motifs, but all are a welcome change from the depressing or institutional walls of your usual hostel. This one almost feels homey. The dorms contain 2 to 6 beds each. (One big room way up on the top floor, euphemistically called "the Penthouse," has a lot more beds; avoid it if you can.)

Sheets do cost extra, but there's a laundry on the premises. They offer all the usual services, too, renting bicycles and even giving advice on work and work visas and stuff like that. All in all, this is a very hosteller-friendly sort of place—and staff speak fluent English and stay friendly, which really helps things.

The self-serve kitchen, unusual for a Berlin hostel, is handy and extremely well equipped—especially since there's a market just around the corner for groceries in case you want to whip up a creative feast. If you abhor the thought of cooking, though, the hostel has an arrangement with a restaurant downstairs that offers significant discounts on meals to its guests. The restaurant also serves breakfast for a few bucks.

Wanna see the city with a bunch of other hostellers? No problem. The hostel has also made an arrangement with a tour company, Berlin Walks; you can meet tour guides at the

Best bet for a bite:
Humboldt University Mensa (cafeteria)
What hostellers say:
"Like, you know . . ."
Gestalt:
Mitte you there
Safety:
Hospitality:
Cleanliness:
Party index:

reception desk for a walk around town. (Yes, it costs money.) Ask at reception for more details. Future plans include a cool backyard where you can chill and grill to your heart's content. And if you're tripping through Berlin during November through February, you'll be rewarded with an ample discount on the cost of your bed. If you're part of a foursome or more, one of you may receive a free night. Unfortunately, those discounts don't carry over into the peak season.

As we've said, there is really nothing special about the atmosphere here; you'll likely spend a lot of your free time hanging around drinking beer with fellow English-speakers. Fun, we suppose, but you're here to see Berlin—and fortunately this place is very near the center of Berlin's active, almost crazed nightlife.

The nighttime action in Mitte is intense, as it has been since the days of playwright Bertolt Brecht and the cabaret scene of the 1920s. Think Liza Minnelli belting "Life is a ca-bah-ray old chum" in pseudo-S&M gear—except with more piercings, tattoos, and multicolored hair—and you've more or less got the picture.

While a little skimpy in the bathroom department, overall this is an OK place to crash.

How To Get There:
By bus: Contact hostel for transit details.
By car: Contact hostel for directions.
By train: From Zoo Station, take U-Bahn line U6 to Zinnowitzer Strasse stop; walk to hostel.

Attractive natural setting	Comfortable beds	Visual arts at hostel or nearby
Ecologically aware hostel	A particularly good value	Music at hostel or nearby
Superior kitchen facilities or cafe	Wheelchair-accessible	Great hostel for skiers
Offbeat or eccentric place	Good for business travelers	Bar or pub at hostel or nearby
Superior bathroom facilities	Especially well-suited for families	Editors' choice: Among our very favorite hostels
Romantic private rooms	Good for active travelers	

Key to Icons

Jugendherberge Berlin (Berlin International Youth Hostel)

Kluckstrasse 3, 10785 Berlin

Phone: 030-747-687910

Fax: 030-747-687911

E-mail: jh-berlin@jugendherberge.de

Rates: €27 (about $34 US) per HI member

Credit cards: No

Beds: 341

Private/family rooms: Yes

Kitchen available: No

Season: Open year-round

Office hours: 24 hours

Curfew: 3 a.m.

Affiliation: DJH-HI

Regional office: Berlin-Brandenburg

Extras: Cafeteria ($), Internet access ($), computer room, table tennis, VCR, TV room, parking, breakfast, information desk, meeting rooms, garden, luggage storage, laundry ($)

Note: Must be a Hostelling International member to stay.

Located in Schöneberg.

Huge, German, and perfect in every way—except in terms of being offbeat, or humorous—this place is the DJH's showpiece, a contemporary design that warehouses you without making you feel like a piece of meat. Most of the time.

It's a big, bland building with a somewhat interesting postmodern sculpture on the front lawn. Inside, they've got more than 300 beds in a tremendous variety of shapes and sizes. Breakfast is included in the price, no matter what sort of room you get, and the auxiliary services they offer are incredible. Try Internet access, a computer workroom, a game room with table tennis, meeting rooms, and meals, for starters. Three lounges—including one with a television—provide areas for hanging out. Everything is cleaner than clean, for once.

Remember that there are stairs here, which are a pain in the keister (i.e., the lower back) if you're hauling serious nonemotional baggage. It's also a bit of a hike from the nearest subway station (which itself requires a transfer from the main train station). Again, we caution: Travel lightly.

But the draw here is that it's in the Schöneberg neighborhood, known as Berlin's quiet place to hang in a cafe without the crush of city noise and traffic. (It's also the center of gay Berlin, but that's another story.) This hostel is very central, close to both the Potsdamer Platz and the world-famous Brandenburg Gate, where Berliners celebrated—and continue to celebrate—the smashing of the Wall.

While in the area, you might head over to the Topographie des Terrors museum for a brutal history lesson of war-crimes exhibits. Appropriately (and chillingly) enough, it's on the same spot where the Gestapo and SS ran their operations for a dozen years, up to and through World War II. Find it by walking over (or taking the S-Bahn) to Anhalter Bahnhof Station.

One tip for the wise: Call ahead if you will arrive at the hostel after 6 p.m., or you might not be able to check in at all. Bummer, but that's the way they run it. And don't try arguing. You can't argue with Germans.

Best bet for a bite:
Merz Schöneberger
Insiders' tip:
Market on Wednesday to Saturday mornings
What hostellers say:
"Kinda sterile."
Gestalt:
In the warehouse district
Safety:
Hospitality:
Cleanliness:
Party index:

How To Get There:
By bus: Take #129 bus to Gedenkstätte.
By car: Take autobahn to Berlin, exiting at signs for Innsbrucker Platz; turn left at Hauptstrasse and continue to Potsdamer Strasse. Make a left onto Lützowstrasse, then make a right onto Kluckstrasse and continue to hostel.
By train: From Zoo Station, take U-Bahn line U2 toward Vinetastrasse to Wittenbergplatz stop, then take U-Bahn line U1 or U15 to Kurfürstenstrasse Station. Walk ¼ mile up Potsdamer Strasse; make a left onto Lützowstrasse, then make a right onto Kluckstrasse and continue to hostel.

Circus Hostel

Weinbergsweg 1a, 10119 Berlin

Phone: 030-2000-3939

Fax: 030-2000-393-699

E-mail: info@circus-berlin.de

Website: circus-berlin.de

Rates: €19–€60 (about $24–$75 US) per person; doubles €58–€100 (about $70–$125 US)

Credit cards: No

Beds: 180

Private/family rooms: Yes

Kitchen available: No

Season: Open year-round

Office hours: 24 hours

Affiliation: None

Extras: Internet access, bar, travel office, breakfast, restaurants ($), TV room, laundry, museum tickets, city tours

Located in Mitte.

Remember that TV show *Everybody Loves Raymond*? Well, maybe so—but everybody also loves the Circus. This place has more fanboys and -girls than just about any other hostel we've ever reported on in Europe.

Already close to the action in the historic center of Berlin, the hostel (which was formerly a trading house) had been serving up terrifically clean and stylish rooms at surprisingly low prices for as long as we could remember. And then, in 2010, the owners closed the place for 3 months so that they could make it even better, acting on suggestions from hostellers like you.

That's right. We're talking modern showers with better water pressure; locking storage boxes in the dorm rooms (with charging sockets); new furniture; and a bigger, better lobby. There's also a touch-screen guide to the city to prep you for your adventuring.

What remains from before? The laid-back atmosphere, happy and flexible staff, a lack of rules, and Internet access. The spiffy, modern building began life as an annex to the original Circus building at Rosenthaler Platz Station, better for families and couples perhaps than single travelers. But now everyone likes it. There's even an elevator.

Dorms consist of single, double, triple, quad, five-bed, and six-bed rooms. Of the 7 double rooms, 4 have a standard double bed and 3 have 2 single beds, which can be pushed together to simulate a double. Duvets cover beds. Only the apartments—doubles and quads—have their own kitchens and bathrooms; other showers and bathrooms are located in hallways, and there are no communal kitchens besides those in the apartments. Luckily, supermarkets and cheap, good restaurants abound in the surrounding area. Note that these private rooms and apartments with en-suite bathrooms cost a lot more than those without; go for one with shared facilities if you can handle that.

The services here are fantastic, all administered by cool staff. They include 3 Internet terminals; a bar; a booking service selling cut-rate train, bus, and museum tickets; and free breakfast (provided by one of the restaurants) with your bunk—it includes rolls, salami, croissants, and hot beverages. They've also got bicycles for rent and washers and dryers for the grungy hosteller. The television lounge gets international satellite TV, and they lay out newspapers for you to read as well. You can even book an onward bed at certain other European hostels.

Put this one on your short list of places to stay.

Best bet for a bite:
Trattoria
Insiders' tip:
Oranienburger Strasse for Indian
What hostellers say:
"I like it!"
Gestalt:
Big top
Safety:
Hospitality:
Cleanliness:
Party index:

How To Get There:
By bus: Contact hostel for transit details.
By car: Contact hostel for directions.
By train: Take U8 Subway line to Rosenthaler Platz Station. Hostel is yellow building on corner.

Die Fabrik

Schlesische Strasse 18, 10997 Berlin

Phone: 030-611-7116 or 030-617-5104

Fax: 030-618-2972

E-mail: info@diefabrik.com

Website: diefabrik.com

Rates: €18–€38 (about $23–$48 US) per person; doubles €52–€58 (about $65–$73 US)

Credit cards: No

Beds: 120

Private/family rooms: Yes

Kitchen available: No

Season: Open year-round

Office hours: 24 hours

Affiliation: None

Extras: Bike rentals, breakfast ($), meals ($)

Located in Kreuzberg.

Once an industrial building (hey, that describes pretty much every pre–Curtain Down building in Berlin), this hostel has been well renovated into a very good hostel-cum-bed-and-breakfast near the river that divides Berlin right in half. It has sustained its excellence for a while now.

It's cheapest in the cavernous 15-bed bunkroom at the bottom, also known in Europe as a "sleep-in," but it's actually not too bad. You'll get more exercise and pay more for the privacy of smaller quad, triple, double, and single rooms as you ascend. All rooms are roomy and airy with plenty of windows. The double rooms are best—legitimately groovy hostel doubles.

Best bet for a bite:
Fried chicken at Kleine Markthalle on Legiendamm

Insiders' tip:
Exercise caution after dark

What hostellers say:
"Lots a fun."

Gestalt:
Fabrik of society

Safety:

Hospitality:

Cleanliness:

Party index:

They rent bicycles, offer breakfast—though you've gotta pay extra for that—and serve meals in a cafe. Unfortunately, there's no breakfast, but that's a minor quibble in this case. Because the location, in too-hip-to-be-true Kreuzberg, is ideal. This is the neighborhood to hit for Berlin's best Turkish food, not to mention oodles of punkers, longhairs, and other not-conforming-to-society folk.

How To Get There:

By bus: Take #265 or N65 bus to Taborstrasse stop; walk to hostel.
By car: Contact hostel for directions.
By train: From Zoo Station, take U-Bahn line U1 or U15 to Schlesisches Tor stop; walk to hostel.

Eastener Hostel

Novalisstrasse 14, 10115 Berlin

> **Phone:** 0175-11-23-515
> **E-mail:** contact@eastener-hostel.de
> **Website:** eastener-hostel.de
> **Rates:** €15–€27 (about $20–$34) per person; doubles €50–€76 (about $63–$95 US)
> **Credit cards:** No
> **Beds:** 17
> **Private/family rooms:** Yes
> **Kitchen available:** Yes
> **Season:** Open year-round
> **Office hours:** 10 a.m.–noon; 6–9 p.m.
> **Affiliation:** None
> **Extras:** Free internet access, free coffee

Located in Mitte.

A tiny hostel in a stone apartment building near many of the coolest things in East Berlin, the Eastener consists of a grand total of 17 beds tucked into 5 rooms; though some of these rooms are a bit narrow, all in all this place is immaculately clean and faultlessly friendly. The place isn't big enough to offer tons of amenities, so it makes up for it with the little things: newspapers, tea, good bunks, a partial kitchen, and free walking tours (in English!) that depart right from the front door each morning. All rooms have sinks, too.

The location is aces, a few minutes' walk from hip and hoppin' Oranienburger Strasse and about 20 to 30 minutes' walk from the Brandenburg Gate and Checkpoint Charlie.

The owner deserves kudos for his no-smoking policy (the lack of which has ruined many a cashmere sweater in, say, a hostel in Paris).

Small, friendly, clean, reasonably quiet . . . this place is a serious anomaly in this chaotic town. As the hostel's own site clearly states: "THIS HOSTEL IS DEFINATELY NOT A PARTY HOSTEL. SMOKING IS NOT ALLOWED IN THE HOSTEL ANYWHERE."*

Best bet for a bite:
Cafe across the way
What hostellers say:
"Perfect!"
Gestalt:
Star in the East
Safety:
Hospitality:
Cleanliness:
Party index:

(*Exact wording and capitalization included. No revisions have been made. Subject to credit approval. Not responsible for misprints. Do not attempt. See dealer for details.)

There are free daily morning tours in English and Spanish of the area, too. All things considered, it's hard not to like this place, and we do. Like it. This is one of your best picks in the city—if you can score one of those precious beds. Just be prepared for a place that's mouse-quiet (and thus boring if you're coming for a party).

How To Get There:

By car: Contact hostel for directions.

By bus: Contact hostel for transit details.

By train: From Zoo Station, take any S-Bahn on track 5 to Friedrichstrasse. Change to U6 (toward Alt-Tegel) and continue 1 stop to Oranienburger Tor station. Exit station in same direction as the departing train, then walk 100 yards (passing Oranienburger Strasse); take second right onto Torstrasse, continue 100 yards, then make first left onto Novalisstrasse. From Ostbahnof, take any S-Bahn four stops to Friedrichstrasse. Change to U6 (toward Alt-Tegel) and continue one stop to Oranienburger Tor station. Follow directions above.

By plane: From airport, take #128 bus to Kurt-Schumacher-Platz U-Bahn station, then take U6 line to Oranienburger Tor. Exit station in same direction as the departing train, then walk 100 yards (passing Oranienburger Strasse); take second right onto Torstrasse, continue 100 yards, then make first left onto Novalisstrasse.

EastSeven Berlin Hostel

Schwedter Strasse 7, 10119 Berlin

Phone: 030-936-22240

Fax: 030-936-22240

E-mail: info@eastseven.de

Website: eastseven.de

Rates: €18–€23 (about $23–$29 US)

Credit cards: Yes

Beds: Number varies

Private/family rooms: No

Kitchen available: Yes

Season: Open year-round

Office hours: 24 hours

Affiliation: None

Extras: laundry ($), breakfast ($)

Located in Prenzlauer Berg.

This newish, orange-facaded winner in so-hip Prenzlauer Berg rules, so far. It's full of 4- and 8-bedded dorms that exude friendliness and service. It's clean, hip, accommodating, and well thought-out and decorated. The kitchen and lounge are even set off from the main hostel in a sort of carriage house, which actually is a good thing. Sort of like a hostelling separation of church and state. There's a laundry (you pay, but they do the work). Heck, they reportedly will even lend you cribs if you've brought a wee one. We can count on one hand the hostels that will go that extra kilometer.

So far, so good.

What hostellers say:
"Even Rick Steves liked it?"
Gestalt:
Lucky Seven
Safety:
Hospitality:
Cleanliness:
Party index:

How To Get There:

By car: Drive to Alexanderplatz, the central city square with the large television tower, then north along Schönhauser Allee; turn off onto Schwedter Strasse at the Senefelder Platz U-Bahn station. Hostel is on right.

By bus: Take U2 subway line toward Pankow to Senefelder Platz. Walk along Schwedter Strasse about 80 yards to hostel on right.

By train: Take S-Bahn to Alexanderplatz; change to U2 subway line and continue toward Pankow 2 stops to "Senefelder Platz." Walk down Schwedter Strasse about 80 yards to hostel on right.

Globetrotter Odyssee Hostel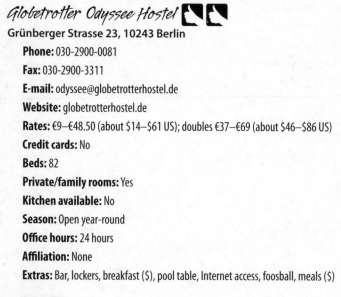

Grünberger Strasse 23, 10243 Berlin

> **Phone:** 030-2900-0081
> **Fax:** 030-2900-3311
> **E-mail:** odyssee@globetrotterhostel.de
> **Website:** globetrotterhostel.de
> **Rates:** €9–€48.50 (about $14–$61 US); doubles €37–€69 (about $46–$86 US)
> **Credit cards:** No
> **Beds:** 82
> **Private/family rooms:** Yes
> **Kitchen available:** No
> **Season:** Open year-round
> **Office hours:** 24 hours
> **Affiliation:** None
> **Extras:** Bar, lockers, breakfast ($), pool table, Internet access, foosball, meals ($)

---

*L*ocated in Friedrichshain.

This is it: Berlin's most party-hearty hostel (and that's saying something in a town where almost every hostel must have a bar to survive). Even when you're not partying, you'll be socializing. Yet it's fun, fun, fun—from the nautical theme to the conviviality that pervades all.

The rooms? They've got double cabins (er, rooms), quads, 6-bed dorms, and 8-bed ones, too; per usual, the cost of your bunk drops with each incremental drop in privacy. They've got lockers, a pool table, and e-mail access, and the bar's open till dawn. (No, silly, there's no curfew here.) In fact, someone at the hostel told us that it never closes! Overall, there's a young and funky vibe, great for 21-year-olds and not too ideal for traveling families or older folks.

You can shoot some stick in the pool room and store stuff in lockers. Even the absence of a laundry is somewhat mitigated by the fact that there's one right around the corner—ask the staff for details.

If you can't believe such a happening place could be clean and safe, well, think again. This place breaks the rules and redefines hostelling excellence in a city that never sleeps.

What to do in the nabe? The Odyssee is located in Friedrichshain, Berlin's drab-looking yet quickly developing nightspot-of-the-moment. It's actually starting to get a little expensive to live around here, which must seem incredible to the old-timers in the neighborhood; nevertheless, you'll find adequate night-crawling options. Consult with the front desk for options and opinions, and ask a local hanging out in the streets.

Best bet for a bite:
Dachkamer
Insiders' tip:
Pentascop's a freaky bar
What hostellers say:
"Wilde."
Gestalt:
Space Odyssee
Safety:
Hospitality:
Cleanliness:
Party index:

How To Get There:

By bus: From Ost Station take #147 or #250 bus to hostel.

By car: Contact hostel for directions.

By train: From Zoo Station take any S-Bahn train east to Warschauer Strasse stop, then walk north up Warschauer Strasse; turn left at Grünberger Strasse. Hostel is on right.

Helter Skelter Hostel

Kalkscheunenstrasse 4–5, 10117 Berlin

    Phone: 030-2809-7979

    E-mail: info@helterskelterhostel.com

    Website: helterskelterhostel.com

    Rates: €11–€18 (about $14–$23 US) per person; doubles €54 (about $65 US)

    Credit cards: No

    Beds: 58

    Private/family rooms: Yes

Kitchen available: No
Season: Open year-round
Office hours: 24 hours
Affiliation: None
Extras: Breakfast, free WiFi, bar

Note: Hostel was temporarily closed at press time.

---

ocated in Mitte.

Charles Manson would be proud of the recent name change here. Formerly the Club-house Hostel, the Helter Skelter boasts a superior location—close to a hopping area with a serious nightlife factor—and friendly staff (some of them from English-speaking countries) push it into the "thumbs-up" category. Even better, school groups are not accepted here.

As you'd expect from the name, the vibe is noisy and slightly Goth. The dorms are colorfully painted and clean, with an IKEA feeling. (You know—the cheapie Swedish home store heavy on blond woods and minimalist, black and steel-gray fixtures? You know, right?) These rooms are divided into triples, doubles, and singles with no bunks. Sleep sacks are not allowed, so you'll have to fork over about 2 bucks for sheets; at least this is a fee you have to pay only once during the course of your stay. They have no kitchen and don't offer the services of some of the city's other backpacker-style joints. But there is something like a lounge, where you can hang around on fluffy sofas and drink beer, coffee, tea, or juices. (Most go with the beer. Cheap beer. Lots of the cheap beer.) Free WiFi is available for couch-surfers, and late sleepers will rejoice over the gracious noon checkout time. The all-you-can-eat (and drink) breakfast is yet another positive.

Remember that this place books up very early, however. Staff advise you to make a firm booking 2 to 3 weeks in advance between Apr and Oct if you want a double room, a week in advance during that time for dorms.

Why so popular? It's near one of the best parts of Mitte, that's why—right in the heart of Berlin's nightly party. There are so many sights, bars, and restaurants here you'll be tripping over yourself. Staff told us that the hottest techno club in Berlin is steps away from the hostel and that Oranienburger Strasse and Tor are notorious for their shiny, happy club scene. Guests come from every corner of the globe to be part of it; during high season you'll encounter Americans, Brits, Japanese, Koreans, and, of course, Europeans. (In January and February, for some reason, the hostel is inundated with folks from South America living it up during their school breaks.) Staff are multilingual, obviously.

This hostel goes out of its way to provide local tours given by the owner, who worked in Berlin for the British embassy when the city was still divided and can give hostellers an in-depth overview of the city's complicated political history. He illuminates even the drabbest, most insignificant-looking building (which other people would simply ignore). The tour lasts 5 hours, so wear those comfy walking shoes. If you'd rather see the city on your own schedule, the hostel staff sell transit passes. They can also make reservations and book round-Europe bus tickets for you.

How To Get There:

By bus: Contact hostel for transit details.
By car: Contact hostel for directions.
By train: Take S-Bahn line S1 or S25 to Oranienburger Strasse stop or U-Bahn line U6 to the Oranienburger Tor stop; walk to hostel.

Jugendherberge Berlin "Ernst Reuter" (Ernst Reuter Berlin Hostel)

Hermsdorfer Damm 48–50, 13467 Berlin

> **Phone:** 030-404-1610
> **Fax:** 030-404-5972
> **E-mail:** jh-ernst-reuter@jugendherberge.de
> **Rates:** €24 (about $30 US) per HI member
> **Credit cards:** No
> **Beds:** 111
> **Private/family rooms:** Yes
> **Kitchen available:** No
> **Season:** Closed December 6–January 6
> **Office hours:** 24 hours
> **Curfew:** 1 a.m.
> **Affiliation:** DJH-HI
> **Regional office:** Berlin-Brandenburg
> **Extras:** TV, table tennis, foosball, breakfast, meals ($), laundry, lockers, luggage storage, information desk

Note: Must be a Hostelling International member to stay.

*L*ocated in Outer Districts.

This hostel is located in the suburbs of Berlin, with excellent connections into the city center by public transport (night and day), despite the long haul out here. If everything else is full, it's not a bad choice.

The series of connected buildings making up the hostel were constructed of stone, then nicely decorated and painted. A green lawn, lush overhanging trees, and picnic tables out front dress up the outside—too bad it's some 9 miles outside the city, making a stay here next to impossible unless you've got either wheels or a lot of fortitude for using the public transit system.

Some rooms and sections are newer and better lit than others. The dorms inside are mostly 5- or 6-bed affairs (16 of those); there are 4 family rooms as well. Bathrooms and showers are in the hallways; in some cases you have to walk downstairs a floor to use 'em. Ugh!

Anyway, they have plenty of hosteller services to distract you, including Internet access, a guest laundry, a television lounge for couch potatoes, a game room with 2 table tennis tables, and an information desk dispensing crucial info about the city. They serve a big breakfast buffet throughout the day, then at night often serve a hot dinner for about 4 bucks. (There's no kitchen for hostellers to cook in.)

Jogging trails and woods surround the hostel, yet you can buy food just a couple hundred yards away when hunger pangs strike. You can also hit the nearby Alt-Tegel subway station's shops for other vital goods, often at lower prices than in the city.

Best bet for a bite:
U-Bahn for grub
Insiders' tip:
Tip magazine for listings
What hostellers say:
"Um, where's Berlin?"
Gestalt:
Mellow yellow
Safety:
Hospitality:
Cleanliness:
Party index:

And here's one final tip: Rather than endure the complicated transit route to get into town, inquire about taking the local sightseeing boat from here into central Berlin; it leaves from the Tegel Greenwich promenade. Neat.

Note: Call ahead if arriving after 6 p.m. or you might not be able to check in. Yeah. Again.

How To Get There:

By bus: From Zoo Station, take U-Bahn line U9 to Leopoldplatz stop, then change to U-Bahn line U6 and continue to Alt-Tegel stop; change to #125 bus and continue to Jugendherberge (hostel) stop.

By car: From the north take Highway 111 to Berliner Ring, exiting at signs for Hermsdorfer Damm. From the south take Highway 115 and Highway 111 to Stadtring Nord, exiting at signs for Hermsdorfer Damm.

By train: From Zoo Station take U-Bahn line U9 to Leopoldplatz stop, then change to U-Bahn line U6 and continue to Alt-Tegel stop; change to #125 bus and continue to Jugendherberge (hostel) stop. From Ost Station take S-Bahn train to Friedrichstrasse stop, then change to U-Bahn line U6 or S-Bahn line S25 and continue to Tegel Station.

Generator Berlin

Storkower Strasse 160, 10407 Berlin

Phone number: 030-417-2400

Fax: 030-417-24080

E-mail: generatorhostels reservations@generatorhostels.com

Website: generatorhostels.com/en/berlin

Rates: €14–€45 (about $18–$56 US); doubles €47–€52 (about $60–$65 US)

Credit cards: Yes

Beds: 900

Private/family rooms: Yes

Kitchen available: No

Season: Open year-round

Office hours: 24 hours

Affiliation: None

Extras: Bar, TV room, breakfast, lockers, laundry, shop, meals, Internet access, courtyard, foosball, walking tours

---

Located in Friedrichshain.

Modeled after the huge and strange Generator Hostel in London, this Generator may not, er, generate quite the same buzz; that's partly because it's stuck way out by a suburban train station, partly because it attracts a school-group-type crowd, and partly because we still don't get the overall sci-fi strangeness of the decor. Still, this place is good and improving. Too bad the location sucks.

Anyhoo, there are tons of beds—more than 900, at last count!—divided into many, many rooms of 14, 8, 7, 6, 5, 4, 3, and 2 beds; there are also some single rooms. Only the

Best bet for a bite:
Nord Sud
What hostellers say:
"Um . . ."
Gestalt:
Generation Z
Safety:
Hospitality:
Cleanliness:
Party index:

singles, doubles, and triples can potentially have their own private bathrooms, though obviously you pay more for that privilege. All are clean.

Kudos for the other amenities, too, such as a bar/beer garden (that means it's outdoors), a television room with satellite TV, an included free breakfast, lockers in each dorm, a small laundry room, meals, and the all-important Internet access. A small free breakfast is fine, and you can pay a bit more for a heartier one. We liked the always-open, fun bar and the opportunity to take a walking tour of the city. There's also a game room and a small shop dealing in books, essential supplies, and the like. (The food's not much good here, though; try to pack some in from a store near the station.) It's even surprisingly clean. Food, drink, cleanliness . . . what's not to like?

One thing, maybe: It all feels a bit clinical. This remote nabe just doesn't have it happening, and despite the beer garden action—your best bet for fun here—you might as well have checked into a barracks for the size. Anyway, one good thing is this: The presence of a nearby station means you can potentially party late-night in the city and whisk back via S-Bahn anytime. However, check on schedules at the desk before you foray out. And take care late at night in East Berlin.

How To Get There:

By bus: Contact hostel for transit route.

By car: From the west, take A2 or A9 or A10 (Berliner Ring) going toward Frankfurt; continue to Dreieck Nuthetal, join A115, continue toward Berlin Zentrum to Dreieck Funkturm. Merge onto A100 going toward Hamburg. Take first turnoff (Kaiserdamm) and then B2/5 going toward Zentrum and Unter den Linden. Continue 4 miles to Alexanderplatz; cross under train overpass and take second left onto Mollstrasse, which becomes Landsberger Allee, for 2 miles. Hostel is on left.

From the northwest, take A24 to A10 (Berliner Ring) going toward Frankfurt, then merge onto A114 at Dreieck Pankow, which becomes B109; continue 1 mile, turn left onto B96a, then make a left again onto Landsberger Allee. Continue to hostel on left.

From the northeast, take A11 to A10 (Berliner Ring) going toward Hamburg, then merge onto A114 at Dreieck Pankow, which becomes B109; continue 1 mile, turn left onto B96a, then make a left again onto Landsberger Allee. Continue to hostel on left.

From the east or southeast, take A113 or follow A14 to A113; continue to end of A113, then continue along B96a into Friedrichshain. Turn left into Warschauer Strasse and continue along Petersburger Strasse; turn left into Landsberger Allee, and continue to hostel on left.

By train: From Zoo Station or Ostbahnhof, take S-Bahn eastbound to Ostkreuz; change to Ring S-Bahn train northbound and continue to Landsberger Allee. Hostel is big blue-and-white structure beside station; walk up steps toward Syringenstrasse, turn right after wire fence, and enter hostel at right.

Hotel Transit Hostel

Hagelberger Strasse 53–54, 10965 Berlin

> **Phone:** 030-789-0470
> **Fax:** 030-789-04777
> **E-mail:** welcome@hotel-transit.de
> **Website:** hotel-transit.de
> **Rates:** €21–€49 (about $26–$61 US) per person; doubles €59–€72 (about $74–$90 US)
> **Credit cards:** Yes
> **Beds:** 290
> **Private/family rooms:** Yes
> **Kitchen available:** No
> **Season:** Open year-round
> **Office hours:** 24 hours
> **Affiliation:** None
> **Extras:** TV room, bar, breakfast, courtyard

*L*ocated in Kreuzberg.

This hotel with the fun, cool design touches also doubles as a hostel, and it offers considerable goodies—a nice courtyard, roomy dorms, a good location, and friendly, English-speaking staff—that come with the hotel. You might forgive the simplistic feel and lack of common socializing in the place, because it's a clean and safe joint in which to rest.

The cool furnishings in the loft-style dorms and doubles give you a happy feeling right away. Attempt to watch television in the room shared with the hoppin' bar, or hang in the

Best bet for a bite:
Chandra Kumari (Sri Lankan)
Insiders' tip:
Bike rentals nearby
What hostellers say:
"More fun than I thought possible."
Gestalt:
Transition abroad
Safety:
Hospitality:
Cleanliness:
Party index:

courtyard; we don't care. Sleep in if you want, 'cause there's no lockout and a free breakfast buffet is included with your bunk. Be warned, though, that this place attracts its fair share of school groups. When we checked the place out on a Monday night (a night not known for being raucous), the bar was teeming with garrulous kids, making it apparent that the hostel succeeds at bringing folk together. Staff assure us that was a fluke . . . but you'll have to go yourself to find out for sure.

The rooms have no more than 6 beds each, ensuring a (relative) modicum of privacy—much appreciated when you've done time in the notorious *mehrbettzimmer* (dormitories, literally "many-bedded room") in lots of other hostels. If you and your traveling companion require even more privacy, there are doubles at a slight extra cost, still well within reach of the budget hosteller.

Breakfast is offered at no extra cost—a buffet that includes cheese, sausage, bread, cereal, and choice of coffee, tea, or hot chocolate. You can eat as much as you want, so you might make it through till dinner if you're lucky. As an additional service, the hostel works with two local tour companies to help you understand the intricate political and cultural history of this sprawling metropolis. Note that these tours do cost extra.

This a great neighborhood, as we've said before, and—as befits it—there's a great travel store called Outdoor on Bergmannstrasse. Head there to stock up on guidebooks and maps, some of them actually in English. For some nice green space in which to toss around a Frisbee, head to nearby Viktoria Park.

An equally (or perhaps even increasingly) cool annex called the Transit Loft opened in 2001 in a renovated factory in the hip Prenzlauer Berg neighborhood. Sporting 47 rooms of one to five beds each, it's slightly more expensive than the Kreuzberg location if you get a private room; dorms cost the same in both locations.

How To Get There:
By bus: Contact hostel for transit details.
By car: Contact hostel for directions.
By train: From train station take U-Bahn line U6 or U7 to Mehringdamm stop; walk to hostel.

Lette 'm Sleep Hostel

Lettestrasse 7, 10437 Berlin

> **Phone:** 030-4473-3623
> **Fax:** 030-4473-3625
> **E-mail:** info@backpackers.de
> **Website:** backpackers.de
> **Rates:** €12–€21 (about $16–$26 US) per person; doubles €44–€75 (about $55–$94 US)
> **Credit cards:** Yes
> **Beds:** 45
> **Private/family rooms:** Yes
> **Kitchen available:** Yes
> **Season:** Open year-round
> **Office hours:** 24 hours
> **Affiliation:** None
> **Extras:** Free Internet access, TV, information desk, garden, snacks, free coffee, summer beer garden

Located in Prenzlauer Berg.

This place is pretty good for the money. The clean-enough dorms are 3- to 7-bedded. Each room has only a sink, not a bathroom, but there are plenty of other extras—a television lounge, Internet access for checking that e-mail, a hosteller kitchen, and a beer-gardeny backyard. Some of the double rooms have kitchens, a great bonus, but there's also a main kitchen for everybody to use. Staff are very helpful and friendly, speak multiple languages, and will point you toward the best sights, bars, and discount transit deals. We've heard increasing complaints about local residents and long-term hostellers contaminating the place's happy atmosphere, though, so be alert.

Best bet for a bite:
Offenbach Stuben

Insiders' tip:
Nosthalgia bar for good vodka

What hostellers say:
"But I don't wanna sleep."

Gestalt:
Prenz charming

Safety:

Hospitality:

Cleanliness:

Party index:

Though the area looks like grunge central, there are actually quite a few rock clubs, pubs, and cafes nearby, so you can't possibly get bored in the surrounds. Ignore the postapocalyptic look of the area and the half-finished buildings, and head out for a beer or a coffee. There's also a convenient Spar market (a sort of German take on a 7-Eleven) close at hand. Note that although it's usually a reasonably quiet and safe neighborhood, there are occasional security lapses; keep an eye on your stuff just in case. By the way, if you want to send out signals to the Germans that you're hip and with the scene, refer to the surrounding 'hood as "Prenzle Berg." That's what the locals do.

This hostel is extremely popular in July and August, so much so that reservations are not accepted. Staff advise that you either call and be placed on a rather lengthy waiting list or just stay the night elsewhere and show up at the hostel around midday after most folk have checked out.

How To Get There:

By bus: Contact hostel for transit details.

By car: Contact hostel for directions.

By train: Take U-Bahn line U2 to Eberswalder Strasse stop, then walk down Danziger Strasse 1 block to Lychener Strasse. Turn left and continue to Lettestrasse, then turn right and walk to hostel.

Key to Icons

 Attractive natural setting

Ecologically aware hostel

Superior kitchen facilities or cafe

Offbeat or eccentric place

Superior bathroom facilities

Romantic private rooms

 Comfortable beds

A particularly good value

Wheelchair-accessible

Good for business travelers

Especially well-suited for families

Good for active travelers

 Visual arts at hostel or nearby

Music at hostel or nearby

Great hostel for skiers

Bar or pub at hostel or nearby

Editors' choice: Among our very favorite hostels

Jugendgästehaus Nordufer
(Nordufer Guest House Hostel)

Nordufer Strasse 28, 13351 Berlin

> **Phone:** 030-4519-9112
> **Fax:** 030-452-4100
> **E-mail:** Nordufer@t-online.de
> **Website:** jugendgaestehaus-nordufer.de
> **Rates:** €19.90 (about $25 US) per person
> **Credit cards:** No
> **Beds:** 130
> **Private/family rooms:** Yes
> **Kitchen available:** No
> **Season:** Open year-round
> **Office hours:** 7 a.m.–5 p.m. (sometimes later)
> **Affiliation:** None
> **Extras:** Pool access ($), breakfast, meals ($)

Note: Must be under age 27 to stay unless traveling as a family.

*L*ocated in Outer Districts.

This place is definitely off the beaten track, outside the city's central sightseeing zone—though actually very well equipped if you don't mind the commute.

They've got everything from singles to doubles to larger dormitories. It's all quiet enough and well managed, and staff are relaxed enough to lay back on what rules there are here. Breakfast is included with your bed, by the way, and it's very good and plentiful. You can also pay a bit extra for access to a swimming pool next door, or head for the lake instead.

Best bet for a bite:
Schleusenkrug beer garden/cafe (by the canal)
Insiders' tip:
#100 bus great for cheap sightseeing
What hostellers say:
"I feel so relaxed!"
Gestalt:
Pool party
Safety:
Hospitality:
Cleanliness:
Party index:

Of all the Outer District hostels in town, this one is the closest; it's just across the canal from Tiergarten. You won't find tons and tons of nightlife around here, but strap on your walking shoes and you'll find parks aplenty.

How To Get There:
By bus: From Zoo Station, take U-Bahn line U9 to Leopoldplatz stop; change to line U6 and continue to Seestrasse stop, then take #126 bus to hostel.

By car: Contact hostel for directions.

By train: From Zoo Station take U-Bahn line U9 to Westhafen stop, then cross bridge and continue to Nordufer Strasse. Or take U-Bahn line U9 to Leopoldplatz stop; change to U6 line and continue to Seestrasse stop, then take #126 bus to hostel.

One80° Hostel

Otto-Braun-Strasse 65, 10178 Berlin

Phone: 030-3641-2590
Fax: 030-3641-25919
E-mail: reservation@one80hostels.com
Website: one80hostels.com
Rates: €15–€29.50 (about $19–$37 US) per person
Credit cards: Yes
Beds: Number varies
Private/family rooms: No
Kitchen available: No
Season: Open year-round
Office hours: 24 hours
Affiliation: None
Extras: breakfast ($), bar, bike rental, free WiFi, photo booth, laundry

---

*L*ocated in Mitte.

Placed right in the thick of the hip Alexanderplatz 'hood, the One80 boasts an extremely hip vibe and the added benefit of having opened relatively recently; the place isn't nearly as beat-up as competing digs.

The hostel is packed with 4-, 6-, and 8-bedded dorms that are fairly standard as these things go. Tasty breakfasts can be bought for about €5 (about $6 US). It's at night, though, that the hostel really comes to life—odd in a city this rich in nightlife—in the form of a bar and a club. Use the photo booth to snap a memorable shot of you doing shots on someone's belly (what?) and retrieve 'em later, back home, from the hostel's server. Also don't miss the wacky circular sofas (you'll see what we mean) and the ultra-clean-and-new laundry room. Good pick.

Best bet for a bite:
Hotel bars nearby
What hostellers say:
"Great new addition."
Gestalt:
Alexanderplatz the great
Safety:
Hospitality:
Cleanliness
Party index:

If you're coming around the U.S. Labor Day, don't miss Berlin Music Week, an annual event saturating the area with club music, DJs, and world beats.

How To Get There:

By bus: Contact hostel for transit route.
By train: Take S-Bahn line S5, S7, or S75 toward Wartenberg, Ahrensfelde, or Strausfeld to Alexanderplatz station. Exit at Alexanderplatz/Dircksenstrasse. Cross Alexanderplatz and stay right. Follow streetcar tracks to Theanolte-Baehnisch-Strasse; pass Holiday Inn. Turn left onto Otto-Braun-Strasse. Continue to hostel.
By car: Contact hostel for directions.

PLUS Berlin Hostel

Warschauer Platz 6, 10245 Berlin

Phone: 030-2123-8501
Fax: 030-2936-0476
Website: plushostels.com
Rates: €14–€24 (about $17–$30 US); doubles €48–€64 (about $60–$80 US)
Credit cards: Yes
Beds: Number varies
Private/family rooms: Yes
Kitchen available: No
Season: Open year-round

Office hours: 24 hours

Affiliation: None

Extras: breakfast ($), free WiFi, free Internet access, swimming pool, sauna

_L_ocated in Friedrichshain.

An indoor swimming pool and a sauna? What the HECK?

Yes, ladybugs, this hostel does indeed offer both of the aforementioned amenities. No, we can't believe it, either. And they don't suck—they're well maintained. Come view this amazing eighth wonder of the hostel world before it dries up and blows away.

Inside the handsome brick building, dorms range from doubles to quads and 6-bedded rooms; they're very good. The all-you-can-eat (AUCE, if you will) breakfast buffet every morning is huge, though, regrettably, not free. At least the dining room is beautiful

Best bet for a bite:
Burgermeister across the Ober-baum bridge

Insiders' tip:
Pack swim togs & flipflops

What hostellers say:
"Awesomeness."

Gestalt:
Pool party

Safety:

Hospitality:

Cleanliness

Party index:

and modern. The bar is popular and hip at night, just as you'd imagined it would be. There's art everywhere, too—can't say we were surprised by that—and the common space is something to behold. (Say hi to the bear.)

People seem to have actual fun here, as opposed to the manufactured fun some hostels reach for (or the potential fun other hostels suck out of you with a litany of regulations and totally drab facilities). No wonder it books full wayyyy ahead in the primo summer months; be forewarned, and book early.

Half a block from the river and a quick walk from the Warschauer Strasse S-Bathn station, this hostel is handy to whatever you wanna do. For that, we give 'em a big thumb up or two.

In four words: It's a great place.

How To Get There:

By car: Contact hostel for directions
By bus: Contact hostel for transit route.
By train: Contact hostel for transit route.

Student Hotel Hubertusallee

Delbrückstrasse 24, Berlin

   Phone: 030-891-9718
   Fax: 030-892-8698
   Rates: €18–€48 (about $23–$60 US) per person; doubles €44–€66 (about $55–$82 US)
   Credit cards: No
   Beds: Number varies
   Private/family rooms: Yes
   Kitchen available: No
   Season: Open year-round, but students only Oct to Feb
   Office hours: 24 hours
   Affiliation: None
   Extras: Breakfast

---

ocated in Outer Districts.

Situated a couple miles southwest of the city center, near a small lake, this one's hardly worth mentioning—it's neither easy to get to nor super attractive. You can only rent singles or entire doubles, triples, or quads—bring friends. And they charge you for sheets, besides.

On the other hand, let's give them credit for this: Every room in the joint has a bathroom and shower in it, and that's saying something.

Best bet for a bite: *U-Bahn stop*
Insiders' tip: *Buy a transit pass*
What hostellers say: *"Nice bathrooms."*
Gestalt: *Shower power*
Safety:
Hospitality:
Cleanliness:
Party index:

Consider it a good desperation pick if you happen to have a car (yeah, right). Otherwise it's probably best to cross it off your list.

How To Get There:

By bus: Take #119 or #129 bus to hostel, or contact hostel for transit details.
By car: Contact hostel for directions.
By train: Contact hostel for transit details.

Sunflower Hostel

Helsingforser Strasse 17, 10243 Berlin

> **Phone:** 030-4404-4250
> **Fax:** 030-5779-6550
> **E-mail:** hostel@sunflower-hostel.de
> **Website:** sunflower-hostel.de
> **Rates:** €14.50–€38 (about $18–$48 US) per person; doubles €48–€68.50 (about $60–$86 US)
> **Credit cards:** Yes
> **Beds:** 100
> **Private/family rooms:** Yes
> **Kitchen available:** No
> **Season:** Open year-round
> **Office hours:** 10 a.m.–6 p.m. weekdays, 11 a.m.–4 p.m. weekends
> **Affiliation:** None
> **Extras:** Breakfast ($), bar, Internet access, foosball

Located in Friedrichshain.

This place out in the far reaches of East Berlin is getting excellent buzz from happy hostellers, but the drawback to this goodness is that it's quite far from the center—you might even need to call a cab.

They operate a coin laundry and serve cheap beer. It's clean and well-run enough, though hardly the most rocking place in the world—the distant location could account for this. On the other hand, you can actually buy a beer right out on the street out front (don't you love Germany?). So there is that. On the other hand, the street we're speaking of is drab and unfriendly-looking. Not a hangout place at all. So there is that.

Bedding consists of 1 big dorm, plus a supply of double, triple, and quad rooms at slightly higher prices per person. Some rooms have balconies, and the kitchen is airy.

Gestalt:
Sunflower children
Safety:
Hospitality:
Cleanliness:
Party index:

A good place, with an attitude that veers between cool and preachy. How so? Check these statements about what the hostel will and won't do for you:

"We are not your parents, and those who are looking for a parental substitute away from home in order to be educated or stuffed with maternal care and support, then we recommend for you to look elsewhere. Thank you!"

Reax: Chillax. We agree . . . but did you really need to spell it out?

"We are not a couch-surfing-substitute. We pay tax and give people jobs. No pay, no stay—simple!"

Reax: Sing it, sister!

"We do love and adore Johnny Cash, John Wayne and Clint Eastwood, but if you pretend to be anyone or even all of them, that is a reason why we would recommend you to stay elsewhere. 'CAUSE YOU ARE NOT!'"*

Reax: We SO love this place! Swooon!

*Best paragraph ever written by any hostel in the world, anywhere, ever.

We think it's worth staying, and our hostel pals agree.

How To Get There:

By bus: Contact hostel for transit route.

By car: Contact hostel for directions.

By train: Take S-Bahn train to Warschauer Strasse Station and walk to hostel.

Jugendgästehaus Berlin "Am Wannsee"
(Berlin-Wannsee Guest House Hostel)

Badeweg 1, 14129 Berlin

  Phone: 030-803-2034

  Fax: 030-803-5908

E-mail: jh-wannsee@jugendherberge.de
Website: jh-wannsee.de
Rates: €15 (about $19 US) per HI member
Credit cards: No
Beds: 288
Private/family rooms: Yes
Kitchen available: No
Season: Open year-round
Office hours: 24 hours
Curfew: 1 a.m.
Affiliation: DJH-HI
Regional office: Berlin-Brandenburg
Extras: Lake, disco, garden, table tennis, parking, laundry, TV room, luggage storage, volleyball, chess, pool table

Note: Must be a Hostelling International member to stay.

Located in Outer Districts.

To get here you make a very long trip out to what turns out to be a peaceful, sleepy neighborhood that comes with its own lake. That's correct: It's set right on Berlin's biggest lake.

It's a depressing building once you arrive, however, with an exceptionally plain postindustrial design even for a German hostel. Think a concrete structure with multicolored flags. On second thought, think "bomb shelter." A few bright splotches of paint here and there do help a bit. All 72 rooms here are four-bedded, and the staff have decked the place out with everything modern you'd need. There's a disco of sorts, a game room with table tennis, a television lounge, a luggage room, and a guest laundry. It's all adequate if a bit boring. Caution, however, before booking your bunk: Schoolkids often book this big place

Best bet for a bite:
Better eat here
Insiders' tip:
Peacocks on Pfaueninsel
What hostellers say:
"Nice lake!"
Gestalt:
See side
Safety:
Hospitality:
Cleanliness:
Party index:

absolutely full, meaning this peaceful, quiet neighborhood is occasionally overrun with the pitter-patter of restless German youths. But the big, good breakfast and campfires by the lake might still entice you.

To escape you might head for the lake and walk, swim, or boat. There's also the Wannsee Museum on the lake, memorializing the infamous place where the Nazis met in 1938 and decided to carry out a mass extermination of Jews. Pretty much a buzzkill, it has to be said, though this history's obviously very important—just be prepared to be bummed out and occupied with dark, serious thoughts for the remainder of your stay if you wander into it.

Note: Call ahead if you want to check in after 6 p.m. They'll all too happily refuse to check you in otherwise.

How To Get There:
By bus: Take #118 bus to Badewag stop and walk 30 yards to hostel.

By car: From Berliner Ring take Highway A 115, following signs toward Mitte to exit for Spanische Allee; make a left onto Kronprinzessinnenweg and another left onto Badeweg.

By train: From Zoo Station take S-Bahn line S1 or S7 to Nikolassee Station. Exit station at Strandbad sign and make a left onto Fußgängerbrücke; cross bridge and make a left onto Kronprinzessinnenweg. Hostel is on right.

MUNICH (MÜNCHEN)

Ah, Munich, city of monks. That's what the name means. Honestly. Of course you'd never know it—it's the least German of German cities. In other words, it's easygoing, fun-loving, and (relatively) sunny compared to the rest of 'em. This ain't fast-paced Berlin; it's the kind of place where people sit around for three hours in the midday sun drinking beer. And those are people with jobs.

Still, it's a little hard at times to reconcile all this merrymaking with a recent past as the nerve center of Nazi activity during the dark years of World War II.

Orientation
You'll most likely start your visit at the big and confusing Munich Hauptbahnhof, one of the busiest train stations in Europe. Getting off the train, you're confronted with a jumble of tracks, each bunch earmarked for a specific type of travel: Slow local trains, slick intercity trains, speedy international trains, and ultramodern overnight trains all have their own areas, all helpfully noted by little signs.

Munich (München)

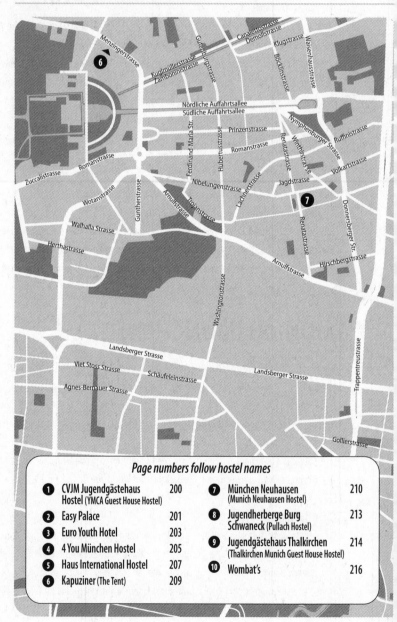

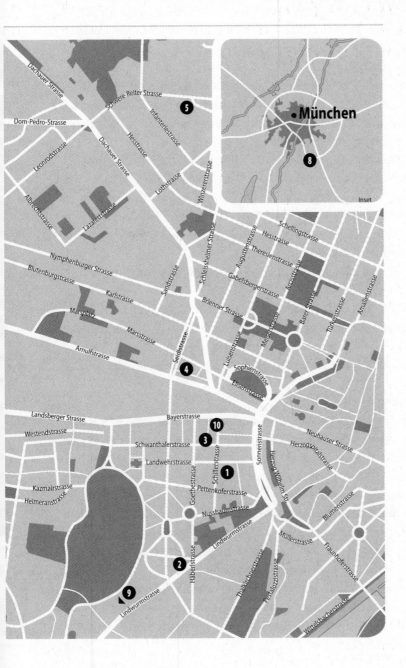

In German.

Before you leave the station, make your first stop the EurAide office, on the quiet side of the station beside track #11. The staff at this American-run office (funded by the Germans) speak perfect English and help you find your way through train schedules, make train reservations for a small charge (it's worth it, trust us), or book a tour. The station itself contains any services you need under one roof—a travel agency, 24-hour lockers and luggage storage, restaurants, a currency exchange, a cool Internet cafe (upstairs near the exit), a newsstand, a tourist office, and bike rentals. There are public phones everywhere that accept German phone cards (buy 'em at the post office or newsstand).

Surprisingly, the immediate area surrounding the train station is not as shabby as it could be. But there's not much to see here if your hostel is elsewhere; you'll probably be making a beeline for the U-Bahn or S-Bahn station to check into your hostel. Wanna get an immediate taste of the city? Head straight out of the station and follow the crowds to Marienplatz through a no-car pedestrian zone. This is where most of the tourist action can be found (see What to See, later in this section).

Of the in-town neighborhoods, Schwabing is by far the coolest. It's the heart and soul of Munich, located between the enormous and lively English Garden and even bigger Olympic Park. The "Jugendstil" of art was born here, and many beautiful buildings survived World War II bombings. Though Schwabing has gotten a little too hip for its own good—there are suits and cell phones all over the place now—the area still has Munich's best cafes, pubs, good-value restaurants, and cinemas. Bottom line? This is as laid-back as Germany ever gets. Visit here.

Getting Around

Getting around Munich should be no trouble, as the city maintains a top-flight transit network of buses, commuter trains (S-Bahn), and subway cars (U-Bahn) called the MVV. The system is efficient, fairly clean, and always busy. Look for an "S" on a green circle for commuter rail stations and a "U" on a blue square for subway stations. Bus stops are marked by street signs with an "H" on them.

You can purchase single tickets for this system starting at about $3.25 US or—to save time and money while hopping around—a transit pass such as the following:

The one-day pass (Single-Tageskarte) costs about $7 US for one or about $13 US for two adults traveling together (called a Partner-Tageskarte).

The three-day pass goes for about $18 US for one adult, about $30 US for two.

It's probably better to buy one of these passes than to go for the complicated Streifenkarte ("strip ticket") book of 10 tickets, which can work out cheaper but is also a pain to use if you're not a local. Also note that two people traveling together can buy "partner" tickets for a discount and that the rates above apply to inner-city trips. Rides to outlying hostels cost more; you pay extra for longer trips on the Munich system.

Remember to validate (punch) your ticket at the blue box as soon as you board your streetcar, bus, or subway car. Don't forget to do this. Secret transit police may be riding alongside you, dressed like normal Munichers, and they'll fine you big if you "forgot" to stamp your ticket.

There are two things you need to keep in mind when using the subways and commuter trains.

Number one: This is one of those rare cities where the S-Bahn's aboveground trains are actually handier for getting to most of the sights and hostels than the subway, so when in doubt, go for the S-Bahn signs instead of the U-Bahn signs.

Number two: If you've got a Eurail pass, you can cruise the S-Bahns for free—yes, free!—as long as you have penciled the current date in the box. This is not a good idea normally, because it wastes a day of your expensive pass. However, if you have already used the pass to get into town or you're almost at the end of your trip, pencil in that date.

Feeling flush? In a hurry? Taxis troll for passengers at the exit near track #11. They are beige, clean, and fairly inexpensive.

What to See, Drink & Eat

The main tourism information office is located just outside the train station (follow the signs). It's open most days until 8 p.m., though it closes a bit earlier on Sunday. The tourist officers there are among the friendliest and most helpful we've ever met.

After picking up maps and getting their advice, begin in the Altstadt ("old town"), where the Marienplatz is the focal point for the worthwhile sights and beer. Even without much time, you can taste the mood of the city within a few minutes in this sunshine-filled pedestrian zone containing the majestically twin-towered Frauenkirche, St. Michael's Kirche, the Rathaus, and the royal Residenz.

A little southeast and you'll be walking through the Isartor—a gate built in the early 14th century, the last remaining piece of the ring that formerly closed Munich—toward the Viktualienmarkt. You've gotta see this place: an open market teeming with foodies in search of plump olives, freshly squeezed carrot juice, shaded beer gardens, and tons of small restaurants. Eat here now!

Culture vultures might head in the other direction, to art museums such as the Alte and Neue Pinakotheks and the modern Haus der Kunst. You'd also do well to entertain yourself at the huge and fun Deutsches Museum (on the other side of the Isar River) or the informative BMW and Siemens museums.

If the weather's good, skip the museums and head instead for the Englischer Garten (English Garden), Europe's oldest public park, with several great beer gardens, fields, and sunbathers—basically one of the best places to discover Munich in a nutshell.

Note that almost all the Munich museums and sights are closed on Monday, so do something else.

The beer, of course, flows in a never-ending river through this town. This is arguably the best beer in the world—if you like dark beers, it is the best in the world—so suck it up and suck some down. You can get a draft or bottle or keg of the stuff anytime anywhere, but it's especially obvious during beery festivals in March (March Beer Festival), May (Maibock), and September (Oktoberfest). Beer garden listings are included in some of the hostel write-ups that follow.

Finally, know that Munich's restaurants are pricey—even more so in crowded areas, such as around the station, as there are loads of tourists to rip off there. A better choice might be the many pizza and falafel take-out joints, the Wienerwald fast-food chain, or the Mickey D's outlets in the station, if you can stand them.

The Hostels

Munich's hostels are, for the most part, clean and safe. Some even manage to be fun and interesting. Despite the huge annual beer fest, they don't have the same fluctuations in standards that similar party-oriented cities like Amsterdam do.

There's a big difference between DJH hostels and the rest here. Travelers older than 26 will be turned away from the "official" DJH-affiliated hostels but not from most independently operated hostels. The DJH joints here also tend to have inconvenient locations, harsher rules, and loads of noisy (sometimes bratty) schoolchildren. On the other hand, the independent places tend to slide a bit in terms of quietness and cleanliness. You make the choice.

Be aware, too, that during Oktoberfest—which actually takes place the last two weeks of September, strangely enough—all hostel prices listed in this section jump at least 10 percent but often as much as 100 percent, depending on the greed of the hostel managers involved. (We're kidding. But think about it: Some places don't raise the rate at all, while others double it. Anyway, they could charge the moon and you'd still pay it, wouldn't you?)

Note that an unusually high percentage of Munich's hostels are located close to its main train station. There's lots of red-light business to be found here, as well as the usual suspects hanging out in the station, so be a little cautious at night—though Munich is, generally speaking, a very safe place.

MUNICH HOSTELS AT A GLANCE

	RATING	COST	IN A WORD	PAGE
Wombat's	⬛⬛	€12–€27	fun	p. 216
Pullach Hostel	⬛	€24–€41	regal	p. 213
Euro Youth Hotel	⬛	€13.50–€80	beery	p. 203
Kapuziner (The Tent)	⬛	€7.50–€10.50	groovy	p. 209
Haus International Hostel	⬛	€21–€49	big	p. 207
CVJM	⬛	€27.50–€42.50	Catholic	p. 200
Munich Thalkirchen Park Hostel	⬛	€31	strict	p. 214
Munich Neuhausen City Hostel	⬛	€29.80–€31.90	institutional	p. 210
4 You München	⬛⬛	€22–€55	green	p. 205
Easy Palace	⬛⬛	€19–€59	declining	p. 201

Attractive natural setting

Ecologically aware hostel

Superior kitchen facilities or cafe

Offbeat or eccentric place

Superior bathroom facilities

Romantic private rooms

Comfortable beds

A particularly good value

Wheelchair-accessible

Good for business travelers

Especially well-suited for families

Good for active travelers

Visual arts at hostel or nearby

Music at hostel or nearby

Great hostel for skiers

Bar or pub at hostel or nearby

Editors' choice: Among our very favorite hostels

Key to icons

CVJM Jugendgästehaus Hostel (YMCA Guest House Hostel)

Landwehrstrasse 13, 80336 Munich

Phone: 089-552-1410

Fax: 089-550-4282

E-mail: hotel@cvjm-muenchen.org

Website: cvjm-muenchen.org/en/youthhostel/youthhostel

Rates: €27.50–€42.50 (about $35–$31 US) per person; doubles €61 (about $73–$80 US)

Credit cards: Yes

Beds: 85

Private/family rooms: Yes

Kitchen available: No

Season: Closed November 1–March 30

Office hours: 7 a.m.–midnight

Curfew: 12:30 a.m.

Affiliation: None

Extras: Restaurant ($), breakfast

S

N ote: 10 percent surcharge for guests over 26. Unmarried couples not allowed to share double rooms.

Y ou might think about packing rosary beads if you plan to stay at this hostel, since it's run by the local Catholics. But don't worry—it's not really a crash course in New Testament 101. On the contrary, it's a good hostel. But: Their policy about having to be married to share a double room might turn you way off.

After a complete renovation, the place looks more like a bank than a hostel. Staff are surprisingly friendly and keep everything looking pretty fresh and clean. There are only single rooms, doubles, and triples here, none of them very large and all sporting furniture of a fairly recent vintage. They almost resemble decent hotel rooms, rather than the barnyard floors that a couple other places in town resemble. Ask for an off-the-street room, though (some of which face a courtyard) because they're pleasantly quieter than street-facing rooms. The hostel maintains its own restaurant, bar, and common room, all of which provide some opportunity for mixing and mingling, though you'll never confuse this place with a party joint, obviously.

Downsides? Not many. There are only a few bathrooms per floor (with the sinks in the rooms, which always strikes us a little bit odd), which can lead to a wait. And while even many HI-affiliated hostels have trashed ridiculously outdated edicts, the folks here are still Catholic enough to hold the line. You'll have to deal with rules, rules, rules— among them: curfews, no unmarried couples sharing a room, no smoking, single male travelers discouraged, no booze, and you get locked in just past midnight. If you're a night person, this could put a serious crimp on your appreciation of Munich's charms. All these rules do give the place a bit of the air of a Catholic school; you half expect nuns to bring out the rulers and begin whacking your knuckles.

Best bet for a bite:
La Vecchia Masseria for pizza
Insiders' tip:
Head for the Augustinerkeller beer garden
What hostellers say:
"Jeez ... I mean, gosh ... too many rules."
Gestalt:
Church chat
Safety:
Hospitality:
Cleanliness:
Party index:

But it's not the staff's fault—they're just (wink, wink) following orders and actually are reasonably friendly. Sheets and breakfast are included with the cost of your bed. Everything's kept spic-and-span, just as you'd expect, and it is very central, just steps from the huge Munich train station where you're undoubtedly going to be arriving.

Party? You'll have to pray for one. But Ned Flanders would be in heaven.

How To Get There:

By bus: Contact hostel for transit details.
By car: Contact hostel for directions.
By train: From the main train station, turn right and walk down Schillerstrasse; take the second street on the left.

Easy Palace
Mozartstrasse 4, 80336 Munich
Phone: 089-558-7970
E-mail: info@easypalace.de
Website: easypalace.com

Rates: €14.0–€59 (about $19–$74 US); doubles €89 (about $111 US)
Credit cards: No
Beds: 300
Private/family rooms: Yes
Season: Open year-round
Kitchen available: Yes
Office hours: 24 hours
Affiliation: None
Extras: Meals ($), laundry, kitchen, lockers, Internet access

[S] [trash can icon]

---

*O*nce a top bunk in town, the Easy Palace no longer is. One of the managers of the Euro Youth Hotel (see below) opened this hostel in the summer of 2003. The building was built in the '50s as a low-end hotel, then later converted into a drinking hall. When the old lads weren't exploring the bottom of their glasses, they obviously did all they could to wear down the "palace."

After the latest transfer of ownership, each of the rooms was equipped with a toilet, shower, and smallish kitchen—but some of those facilities were later torn out to add more bunks. A few of the bunkrooms here have just 2 beds and a bathroom (some of them even have kitchens, and those are great for families), but most now have 4 to 6 beds and share bathroom facilities with other bunkrooms' denizens. The big 8-bed dorms are among Munich's best deals, price-wise. Unfortunately, things have slipped here since the place (please, not "palace") opened. It's just not clean or well-kept enough.

In addition, if you intend to mingle with fellow backpackers, this hostel doesn't create too many opportunities. There's space for common rooms or even a bar downstairs, but no dice so far. At least the staffers do all they can to compensate, with a friendliness and efficiency we appreciate. The additions of a kitchen and hostel laundry, as well as Internet, were welcome. And breakfast is served in the restaurant next door (hostellers get discounts on

Best bet for a bite:
Resto next door
Insiders' tip:
Oktoberfest just 2 blocks away
What hostellers say:
"Ain't no palace."
Gestalt:
Million-dollar hotel
Safety: [icon]
Hospitality: [icon]
Cleanliness: [icon]
Party index: [icon] [icon]

the meals); no wonder many of 'em end up hanging out there later on, in the evening, over a few glasses of Hofbräu. Still, we can no longer flag this as a recommended pick. Walk on by.

Adding it all up, this place has its flaws. The price is nice, and even the location—a bit away from the shady around-the-station area where several other hostels are located—is decent. But we can't recommend it—only go here if better places are full up.!

How To Get There:

By bus: Contact hostel for transit route.

By car: Contact hostel for directions.

By train: From Hauptbahnhof, take U-Bahn U1 or U2 line 1 stop to Sendlinger Tor Station, then change to U3 or U6 line and continue 1 stop to Goetheplatz station. From Goetheplatz, walk to Mozartstrasse; hostel is on right. Or, from Hauptbahnhof, simply walk 1 mile along Goethestrasse and turn right onto Mozartstrasse at Goetheplatz.

Euro Youth Hotel

Senefelderstrasse 5, 80336 Munich

Phone: 089-5990-8811

Fax: 089-5990-8877

E-mail: info@euro-youth-hotel.de

Website: euro-youth-hotel.de

Rates: €13.50–€85 (about $17–$106 US) per person; doubles €48–€195 (about $60–$219 US)

Credit cards: No

Beds: Number varies

Private/family rooms: Yes

Kitchen available: No

Season: Open year-round

Office hours: 24 hours

Affiliation: None

Extras: Bar, breakfast ($), laundry, information

N ote: Must be 35 or younger to sleep in largest dormitory.

We had always heard very good reports of this place, but when we finally got there for the first time, we were greeted by a receptionist who too busy playing video games to notice us. That's OK, we have since forgiven her—because this is now your best choice in Munich, so long as you don't mind a little noise and a little (OK, potentially a lot of) beer. Our recent visits have even noted some improvements in the dorms and showers, which came as a bit of a surprise.

Housed inside a once-fancy hotel right next to Munich's big main train station, the place opened in 1999. They've got everything from a cheap, monster-like 30-bed dormitory to more expensive quad and double room digs (with shared bathrooms, of course; this ain't the Ritz, but they do give all private roomers free breakfast). Upstairs rooms are small yet quite decent, despite a somewhat short supply of showers. The ground-floor big dorms aren't as worth your money—right behind the bar, they're a little cramped and noisy. There's also little hard-core security here, and you have to trek to the basement to use showers and bathrooms. So it's not a perfect place. But it's good enough.

The best thing of all here isn't the bed or the company—it's the beer. The place is owned lock, stock, and barrel by one of Munich's (and Germany's) finest breweries, Augustiner. Needless to say, there's a constant flow of the suds, and the price isn't bad: a few bucks for a half-liter draft of this most excellent brew is less than you'll pay just about anywhere else in town. And you can crawl/stagger/wander back to your bunk later, no designated driving or weird subway station changes required.

Best bet for a bite:
Somewhere in Karlsplatz
Insiders' tip:
Beer gardens in the Viktualienmarkt
What hostellers say:
"Pour me another!"
Gestalt:
Beer guardian
Safety:
Hospitality:
Cleanliness:
Party index:

Friendly? Central? Absolutely yes, on both counts. The laundry is a huge bonus after traveling on the train or scrounging around Europe for a few weeks, and you can also pay extra for a breakfast (though it's a little expensive by Munich standards). This place fills the bill if you know what to expect.

How To Get There:

By bus or train: Contact hostel for transit details. Or from main train station, exit right-hand side and turn down Bayerstrasse; continue to Senefelderstrasse.

By car: Contact hostel for directions.

---

4 You München Hostel

Hirtenstrasse 18, 80335 Munich

Phone: 089-552-1660

Fax: 089-552-16666

E-mail: info@the4you.de

Website: the4you.de

Rates: €22–€55 (about $28–$66 US) per person; doubles €84 (about $105 US)

Credit cards: Yes

Beds: 212

Private/family rooms: Yes

Kitchen available: No

Season: Open year-round

Office hours: 24 hours

Affiliation: None

Extras: Cafeteria ($), breakfast ($), tours, luggage storage, kindergarten, lockers

---

N ote: 10 percent surcharge for guests over 26.

A group of enthusiasts once took over a run-down 5-story 1950s-era hotel with a mission: start up Munich's first independent hostel. But they focused so much on ecology, on making it a green hostel—they even added wooden light switches—that they forgot to use a little business sense. And "green" didn't always equal "clean."

The project flopped. The place changed hands, passing to newer, savvier (if less idealistic) management. Bottom line? Things are straightening out, though there's still a ways to go.

The building, located on a quiet little street just a few feet from the train station's craziness, has seen better days, and the somewhat beat-up dorm rooms (which have large lockers, by the way) are a little too used-looking. Bunk beds are decent but hardly superior-quality,

Best bet for a bite:
*Buxs on Frauenstrasse
(near Viktualienmarkt) for veggies*

Insiders' tip:
Sussman's has newspapers in English

What hostellers say:
"Duuuuude."

Gestalt:
2 cool 2 be 4gotten

Safety:

Hospitality:

Cleanliness:

Party index:

and a little too tightly packed in. The showers range from abysmal to frustrating. At least things are kept cleaner than they used to be here (the showers, though, are sometimes an unwelcome exception). If you're an eco-hog, check out the walls, floors, beds, and everything else while you're here: they've almost certainly been reused and/or recycled, depesticided, defumigated, detoxified, and unpainted.

Prices are cheapest for the youngest hostellers, more expensive as you age (or as the quality of your room improves). Breakfast and other meals—which cost extra—are tasty, organic, and healthful, possibly as an antidote to all the beer and city fumes you'll be swilling the rest of the time. The addition of free WiFi is a plus, as are the lockers, city walking tours, and luggage storage room.

The place is still very politically and ecologically correct. Smoking is allowed only in a "smoker room," and a hostel kindergarten takes care of kiddies during the daytime. Nevertheless, we've gotta admit one thing: This is already one of Munich's best hostels in which to meet fellow travelers, though school groups occasionally take over the place and render the hallways noisy and smoky.

Note that the hostel also includes a pricier "hotel" section upstairs, part of the same complex but with better-equipped single and double rooms (they're more expensive, of course); these rooms all come with private bathrooms, and breakfast is included.

All things considered, this is one to consider since it's very close to the city's central train station.

How To Get There:

By bus or train: Contact hostel for transit route. Or from main train station, exit left-hand side to Arnulfstrasse; take an immediate right onto Pfeffenstrasse, then another quick right onto Hirtenstrasse.

By car: Contact hostel for directions.

Haus International Hostel

Elisabethstrasse 87, 80797 Munich

Phone: 089-1200-60

Fax: 089-1200-6630

E-mail: info@haus-international.de

Website: haus-international.de

Rates: €21–€49 (about $27–$61 US) per person; doubles €58–€78 (about $73–$98 US)

Credit cards: Yes

Beds: 545

Private/family rooms: Yes

Kitchen available: No

Season: Open year-round

Office hours: 24 hours

Affiliation: None

Extras: Restaurant ($), swimming pool, TV room, disco, bar, garden, patio, table tennis, breakfast ($)

I n one word, this hostel is big—and not so conveniently located, either. Wait, that's more than one word. But despite these shortcomings, it has improved in recent years to the point that it's among the best bunks in town. Simple but warm and friendly enough. Tour groups even occasionally book into it, so you know it isn't absolutely terrible. You can't believe how huge the '70s-style building is—it's one of two hostels in town that have 500-odd beds—yet, remarkably, it's often quite full due to the unending parade of school kiddies who provide the hostel with its bread-and-butter clientele.

The common area on the ground floor looks practically Soviet, though, and the rooms and floors have taken lots of abuse. Double rooms are in acceptable condition, though the bigger ones are overpriced for what you get: worn carpets, beat-up closets, perhaps a smidgen of graffiti. There's a disco in the basement, where you can also improve your skills in '80s video games (think Pac-Man, Ms. Pac-Man, Frogger, Super Mario). Euro-teenyboppers congregate there, so you should head downtown instead.

Decor mostly consists of bland and worn fixtures and rooms, though they're trying to spruce up the place. Unfortunately, the U-Bahn doesn't come anywhere near this joint, so

Best bet for a bite:
*Pizzeria da Tanino on
Theo-Prosel-Weg*
Insiders' tip:
BMW museum near Olympic park
What hostellers say:
"Big but bland."
Gestalt:
Haus, broken
Safety:
Hospitality:
Cleanliness:
Party index:

you've gotta hoof it quite a ways or take a bus (#33 bus from Rotkreuzplatz) that doesn't run at night. The Old Town is about a 40-minute walk, perhaps more. Advice? You might have to split a taxi, kiddies, so factor that into your budget. At least some rooms have nice views of the city.

Good things? There are some. A swimming pool, beer garden, cafeteria serving meals, and television lounge. Perhaps most important, though, the hostel's in approximately—and we stress approximately, not exactly—the same part of town as the Schwabing neighborhood, which some have compared with New York's Greenwich Village, it's so cool (though it's a lot cleaner and safer). OK, Schwabing actually stretches from the city center to Munich's northern border, and the Haus International is even quite a bit north of this hoppin' district, but you could conceivably see Schwabing on the same journey you're making out to the hostel.

This hostel is also exceptionally close to the city's Olympic Stadium, with its awe-inspiring tinted-glass suspended roof. You could take a dip in the stadium swimming pool, which is open to the public; in winter, you can rent skates and take to the ice. Other highlights of that park include tours of the grounds and a speedy lift to the top of the Olympic Tower.

Not up for all that? Head for the Old Town.

How To Get There:

By bus or train: Take U-Bahn line U2 toward Feldmoching to Hohenzollernplatz stop, then walk to hostel; or change to #12 tram or #33 bus and continue to Barbara Strasse stop. Hostel is next to gas station.
By car: From any highway into the city, take Mittlerer Ring to Schwabing exit and continue to hostel.

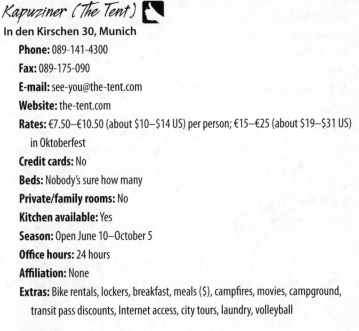

Kapuziner (The Tent)

In den Kirschen 30, Munich

- **Phone:** 089-141-4300
- **Fax:** 089-175-090
- **E-mail:** see-you@the-tent.com
- **Website:** the-tent.com
- **Rates:** €7.50–€10.50 (about $10–$14 US) per person; €15–€25 (about $19–$31 US) in Oktoberfest
- **Credit cards:** No
- **Beds:** Nobody's sure how many
- **Private/family rooms:** No
- **Kitchen available:** Yes
- **Season:** Open June 10–October 5
- **Office hours:** 24 hours
- **Affiliation:** None
- **Extras:** Bike rentals, lockers, breakfast, meals ($), campfires, movies, campground, transit pass discounts, Internet access, city tours, laundry, volleyball

*N*ote: Must be under age 27 to stay.

This place, simply put, remains a three-ring circus—figuratively and literally—minus the animals. (Unless you count that hosteller who spilled ground beef all over your bunk as a pig.) Very appropriate, given that it is located beneath, yes, a gigantic tent. Only in Europe.

You read that correctly. A bed here isn't really a bed, but rather a mattress on the floor of the tent—talk about urban camping—with a skimpy blanket. On warm nights you might not mind, though you're obviously sacrificing tons of privacy and amenities and security. Oh, they've got some plain bunk beds, too, marginally more like home but not much more. (They cost a bit extra but are worth it if you're a light sleeper who is unused to sleeping on the ground.) Still, it's all in good fun and the skank factor isn't too high. This is also super-cheap, among the cheapest "beds" in all of urban Europe (not hard to see why).

Plumbing facilities consist of camp-style showers and toilets. They show movies, sell cheap city transit passes (that city ownership really comes in handy), offer free breakfast, rent bikes, have an Internet terminal, and maintain lockers for your stuff. The real draw, though, is

Best bet for a bite:
HL Markt for picnic supplies
Insiders' tip:
Bring earplugs
What hostellers say:
"Roll another one!"
Gestalt:
Big top
Safety:
Hospitality:
Cleanliness:
Party index:

the ambience, which is as groovy as they come. They light bonfires at night, grill stuff, bring out the guitars and the red wine . . . what a great feeling developing under the stars.

It's in a bit of an inconvenient location, but there's always space, and the enthusiastic staff are great. They are soooo laid-back here, it's scary. Age limit? Yes, they've got one, but the odds are, like, 50-50 on a given night that the folks manning the store won't even care. There's a 3-night maximum stay rule, too, but we imagine that's equally flexible, depending on the mood of the receptionist. Who knows?

Note that this hostel is sponsored by the City of Munich and kept on a tight budgetary leash, so its future is not secure. It could be gone by the time you crack this book, or it could be around forever.

How To Get There:

By bus or train: From main train station take #17 tram to Botanischer Garden stop, then walk up Franz-Schrank-Strasse to In den Kirschen; hostel is on right. Or take U-Bahn line U1 to Rotkreuzplatz stop, then change to the #12 tram to Botanischer Garden stop; walk up Franz-Schrank-Strasse to In den Kirschen.

By car: Contact hostel for directions.

Jugendherberge München–Neuhausen (Munich Neuhausen City Hostel)

Wendl-Dietrich-Strasse 20, 80634 Munich

> **Phone:** 089-202-44490
> **Fax:** 089-202-444913
> **E-mail:** muenchen-city@jugendherberge.de
> **Rates:** €29.80–€31.90 (about $38–$40 US) per HI member; doubles €67.60–€71.60 (about $85–$90 US)
> **Credit cards:** Yes

Beds: 335
Private/family rooms: Yes
Kitchen available: Yes
Season: Closed December 1–31
Office hours: 24 hours
Affiliation: HI-DJH
Regional office: Bavaria
Extras: TV room, bike rentals, bistro ($), meeting rooms, foosball, patio, garden, breakfast, luggage storage, laundry, lockers, information desk, bar, games, bike tours ($)

*N*ote: Must be under age 27 to stay unless traveling as a family.

As more and more competitors enter the crowded Munich hostelling market, things have improved, even at the city's Hostelling International–affiliated hostels—especially at this one. Built and opened all the way back in 1927, between the wars, this was Hostelling International's very first city hostel and Europe's biggest until the 1990s, when a trend toward building huge, warehouse-like spaces exploded. So this place had obviously aged past its prime. But now, minus the curfew and lockout that once made it a bad choice, and with a few tweaks, it's finally starting to meet backpackers' needs. Though the furniture doesn't seem to have changed too much since, well, 1927, things are being kept in one piece and acceptably clean. It's kinda boring, but we'll give it a nod anyway, especially if you don't mind staying a bit outside the center of Munich.

The hostel is located 2 miles west of the central train station but reachable by public transit. Once there, you'll find the hostel compound is actually made up of several linked stone buildings with a nice garden and bar between them. Three big stone arches frame the front doors; behind, you'll find a few double rooms and mostly six-bed dorms.

Best bet for a bite:
Santa Fe on Balanstrasse
Insiders' tip:
Sheets are free here
What hostellers say:
"Getting better."
Gestalt:
Institutionalized
Safety:
Hospitality:
Cleanliness:
Party index:

However, take heed: There's one giant 30-bed dormitory they call the "stable," with stinking socks and snorers all around; if you end up here you'll want to lock your stuff up fast. (Thankfully, lockers in the rooms are big enough for backpacks.) This huge room must be a real treat around Oktoberfest, what with the various scents of beer, sweat, urine, and other fluids wafting through the air.

There are also 17 double rooms, 24 quads, and 36 six-bed rooms in addition to the monster dorm, if that gives you some sense of the size of this place. Bathrooms and showers are in the hallways, not in the rooms.

There are good and bad things about the place. On the downside of the ledger, rooms on the street can be noisy, and the showers are closed down at 10 p.m. The neighborhood is not great at all. They have a kitchen, sure, but it comes without pots, plates, or other helpful items—you've gotta bring your own. None of the private rooms come with private bathrooms, which is too bad. Finally, it's likely to be packed with annoying school groups from April through October, when Europe's summer holidays occur.

But the staff are fairly friendly, and they certainly offer plenty of services: You can arrange bike tours for a fee at the front desk, for example. There's a television lounge and tourist information desk. And check out the rather unusual on-premises restaurant, too—it's set in a streetcar. Yep. You heard us. Kinda cool, plus there's a patio for chilling as well. You have the option of paying for a half-board or full-board plan that includes meals, and vegetarian food can be ordered as long as you tell 'em in advance. As for party potential, this is a good place to meet people, if not exactly to rock hard.

The hostel's located in Neuhausen, the neighborhood most commonly associated with the Schloss Nymphenburg palace, and some say it's got a snooty attitude to match. It shouldn't be too proud, though, since most of the buildings here were completely destroyed during World War II, and the ones that still stand reflect a monotonous architectural conformity. There are a few cheap restaurants around—ask the receptionist—plus an Internet cafe nearby on Nymphenburger Strasse; access is free, but you have to eat or drink to use it. Our tip? You might do best to contemplate life in the Hirschgarten, one of the nicer beer gardens in the city.

Just remember that this place is always popular; you'll want to book ahead or arrive before noon to stay the night.

How To Get There:

By bus: Take #12 or #17 streetcar and walk ¼ mile. Or, from main train station, take U-Bahn line U1 to Rotkreuzplatz Station; walk along Wendl-Dietrich-Strasse ½ mile to hostel.

By car: Entering city, follow signs for Olympiapark, then make a right onto Nymphenburger Strasse. (If coming from Lindau, make a left.)

By train: From main train station take U-Bahn line U1 to Rotkreuzplatz Station; walk along Wendl-Dietrich-Strasse ¼ mile to hostel.

Jugendherberge Burg Schwaneck 🏠 *(Pullach Hostel)*

Burgweg 4–10, 82049 Pullach im Isartal (Munich)

Phone: 089-744-86670

Fax: 089-744-86680

Website: burgschwaneck.de

Rates: €24–€41 (about $30–$51 US) per HI member; doubles €68 (about $85 US)

Credit cards: Yes

Beds: 130

Private/family rooms: Yes

Kitchen available: No

Season: Closed December 21–January 15

Office hours: 7:30 a.m.–12:45 p.m. and 1:30–5:30 p.m.

Curfew: 11:30 p.m.

Affiliation: HI-DJH

Regional office: Bavaria

Extras: Meeting room, grill, pool table, meals ($), terrace, breakfast, bowling, sports facilities, patio

🍁 ✖ ♥ 🐕 Ⓢ 🎱 🚲

---

*N*ote: Must be under age 27 to stay unless traveling as a family.

If you're staying here, you're in for some amazing castle (yeah, castle) hostelling. But you're so distant from the action that once you check in you might never get into Munich at all—at the very least you'll have to work to get in and out of town via the S-Bahn (commuter train) in time for the brutal curfew. If you're wanting a country break between cities, though, this is just ideal.

Situated in a park, in a real-life castle with some history to match (ask the staff about the parties that were thrown here back in the 19th century), it's full of 4- to 8-bed dorms. Good breakfasts are included with your bunk, which is probably gonna be more comfortable than you expected. The views from the patio are stupendous, and they've decked the place out with some nice touches: bowling, some sports facilities, a game room, stuff like that.

How To Get There:

By bus: Contact hostel for transit details.
By car: Head south from Munich on Highway B11 to Pullach.
By train: From Munich take S-Bahn line S7 to Pullach Station, then walk along Margarethenstrasse to Heilmannstrasse; turn right on Charlottenweg and continue to hostel, about ½ mile total.

Best bet for a bite:
Meals on site
Insiders' tip:
Prinz for entertainment listings
What hostellers say:
"Fit for a king!"
Gestalt:
Royal flush
Safety:
Hospitality:
Cleanliness:
Party index:

Jugendgästehaus Thalkirchen (Munich Thalkirchen Park Hostel)

Miesingstrasse 4, 81379 Munich

Phone: 089-7857677-0
Fax: 089-7857677-66
E-mail: muenchen-park@jugendherberge.de
Website: muenchen-park.jugendherberge.de
Rates: €31 (about $39 US) per HI member; doubles €75 (about $94 US)
Credit cards: No
Beds: 366
Private/family rooms: Yes
Kitchen available: No
Season: Open year-round
Office hours: 24 hours
Lockout: 9:30 a.m.–2 p.m.
Curfew: 1 a.m.
Affiliation: HI-DJH

Regional office: Bavaria

Extras: TV room, playground nearby, foosball, pool table, parking, luggage storage, table tennis, garden, cafeteria ($), laundry, lockers, breakfast, bike rentals, meeting rooms

---

*F*ar out of town and not exactly full of warm fuzzies, this shouldn't be your first choice in Munich in spite of its modern look—all elevated walkways and glassy rooms admitting more light and sunshine (well, when there is sunshine) than most other German hostels combined.

Dorms contain from 2 to 15 beds. They've got 62 twin rooms—that means two single beds, not one double bed—plus 53 rooms with three or four beds each, and a half-dozen six-bed dormitories. Some are even adapted to be wheelchair-accessible, and these dorms are all segregated by sex (as is usual in an HI-affiliated joint). All bathrooms and showers are in the hallways, but at least breakfast is included with your bunk. There are some family rooms, too, but you've

Best bet for a bite:
Cafeteria here
Insiders' tip:
Stay in town instead
What hostellers say:
"Better but marginal."
Gestalt:
Tough as nails
Safety:
Hospitality:
Cleanliness:
Party index:

got to actually prove you're traveling with your family to rent one of 'em.

The pluses include a television lounge with a DVD player, game room with table tennis and a pool table, meeting room, bikes for rent, and a cafeteria serving meals and selling bag lunches. There's a locker in your dormitory room, which costs a few euros to use (and you get the money back later), then another bigger luggage room in the basement of the hostel for your big stuff; it's free. Get a key at the front desk. Generally speaking, this place is charmless, but it does seem to have improved a bit.

Beware, however: Staff are Germanly trained, and some managers have actually been known to ask for marriage certificates when couples want to share a room. (Hopefully that practice will be discontinued one day . . . but this is conservative Bavaria.) And, as we mentioned, it's a pain in the keister to get here. The hostel's situated in Thalkirchen, southwest of the city and some distance. Although it's close to the zoo, the Isar River, and woods and parks, you'll need wheels or some major public-transit time to even think about it as an option.

Given the staff's nitpicking nature, we'd think about skipping it.

How To Get There:

By bus: Take #3 streetcar to Thalkirchen stop and walk ¼ mile to hostel. Or take U-Bahn line U1 to Sendlinger Tor Station, change to U-Bahn line U3, and continue to Thalkirchen Station and walk ¼ mile to hostel. Or take line U3 to Thalkirchen and walk ¼ mile to hostel.

By car: Follow signs to Mittlerer Ring, then to Zoo; from Thalkirchen follow signs to hostel.

By train: From main train station take U-Bahn line U1 to Sendlinger Tor Station, then change to U-Bahn line U3 and continue to Thalkirchen Station. Or take line U3 directly from Marienplatz toward Furstenried West to Thalkirchen; from Thalkirchen walk ¼ mile to hostel.

Wombat's Backpackers Munich

Senefelderstrasse 1, D-80336 Munich

> **Phone:** 089-5998-9180
> **Fax:** 089-5998-91810
> **E-mail:** office@wombats-munich.de
> **Website:** wombats-hostels.com/munich
> **Rates:** €12–€29 (about $16–$34 US) per person; doubles €70–€80 (about $87–$100 US)
> **Credit cards:** No
> **Beds:** 300
> **Private/family rooms:** Yes
> **Kitchen available:** No
> **Season:** Open year-round
> **Office hours:** 24 hours
> **Affiliation:** None
> **Extras:** Internet access, laundry, pool table, bar, patio, breakfast ($)

---

*U*nless hostellers abuse the heck out of this place and reduce it to rubble (or chaos), this Munich entry will be the top pick in town for a long time. Brought to you by the same folks who started up the great Wombat's hostel in Vienna, this place has an equally chill vibe: a party, yes, but not one that's raging out of control.

It's an amazingly modern-looking place from the outside. Inside, in a big yellow lobby with a parquet floor fronting a glassed-in atrium with potted trees, you get a free welcome drink, free sheets for your bed, and city maps. Bunkrooms are clean and airy enough, fresh-painted if functional. At least you're not crammed in like a sardine.

Safety:
Hospitality:
Cleanliness:
Party index: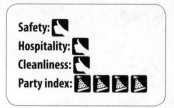

All rooms have en-suite bathrooms. And dig this: Most of the double rooms here have real live balconies! That is not a misprint, and you'll really appreciate it after you've been stuffed in windowless warehouses for a few days elsewhere. The bar on the ground level is where almost everyone seems to end up sooner or later. (But head elsewhere anyway; Munich is full of great beer gardens, the best in the world.) The patio is the star of the show here, a place for convivial hanging out and getting to know your fellow hostellers.

Fun staff, a good time, a short walk from Oktoberfest? Score on all counts. And they don't jack up prices year-to-year like many other places; you will still have money left over for dining out. This one's a winner and it's only getting better.

How To Get There:

By car: Contact hostel for directions.

By train: From the platforms, take the right-most exit out of the building onto Bayerstrasse. Cross the road, turn left, then turn down the first street on the right (Senefelderstrasse); the hostel is on the left.

By plane: Take S-Bahn lines S1 or S8 to the main railway station, Hauptbahnhof (approximately 45 minutes). At the station, you will find yourself in a maze of underground passages. Look for the exit to Bayerstrasse Ost. After you come up the escalator, make a U-turn, walk up Bayerstrasse, and take the first street to the left (Senefelderstrasse). Wombat's is the second house on the left.

Attractive natural setting	Comfortable beds	Visual arts at hostel or nearby
Ecologically aware hostel	A particularly good value	Music at hostel or nearby
Superior kitchen facilities or cafe	Wheelchair-accessible	Great hostel for skiers
Offbeat or eccentric place	Good for business travelers	Bar or pub at hostel or nearby
Superior bathroom facilities	Especially well-suited for families	Editors' choice: Among our very favorite hostels
Romantic private rooms	Good for active travelers	

Key to Icons

Greece

*G*reece is well known for sun-washed and whitewashed islands, floating in deep-blue seas, and—more ignominiously—for a huge debt load and a creaky hold on its membership in the euro monetary group. But it's also becoming increasingly known for the hedonism that descends upon it, summer or winter, in the form of British, Swedish, and American tourists (among others) seeking sun, sand, ruins, clubs, olives, ouzo, and feta cheese. That all adds up to one of the most interesting countries in Europe—a little disorganized, a little bit chauvinist, a lot hot in summer, but nevertheless one of those places that draws travelers back time and again.

Practical Details

As might be expected, Athens shifted into overdrive for the 2004 Olympics; among the city's improvements were a greatly expanded Athens Metro (subway) and a new airport. The Metro's three modern lines are slowly being expanded to the suburbs, but the city center is already decently serviced. Check at the train station or your hostel for a map. A single ride on the subway costs about €1 (about $1.25 US), while a one-day city transit pass—which includes access to all buses and streetcars—costs €3 (about $4 US). If you're really pinched for cash, note that buses cost only half as much as the subway but are far less efficient—and often require some serious local knowledge to figure out routes, schedules, and stops.

The modern airport is located about 20 miles southeast of the city center and is served by all the usual international carriers; log onto aia.gr for more info. A direct train link to downtown Athens opened in 2004. Express buses also connect the city with the airport 24/7/365; the X95 runs farthest into the center of town, stopping at Syntagma Square and its Metro stop (serving lines 2 and 3), while the X93 runs to the bus station and the X97 connects with a Metro stop. These buses are dirt-cheap, too. (There's also a new six-lane highway if you're brave enough to rent a car and attempt driving in Athens. Tip: Don't.)

Eurail passes cover certain ferry lines from Bari and Brindisi, Italy, to Patras, a ferry port three and a half to five hours' train ride from Athens. Find out which lines are accepting the pass—the lineup sometimes changes—and don't be swayed by whatever the ticket-sellers in Italy tell you; there are plenty of crooked outfits trying to cash in on your ignorance. READ YOUR EURAIL GUIDE CAREFULLY FIRST. Also note that the pass covers only your ticket; you'll have to pay a little extra for an actual seat, and quite a bit extra for a sleeping cabin.

The unit of currency in Greece is the euro. Prices for food and drink are generally low in Greece, but higher in Athens.

Greece's country code is 30 and Athens's city code is 210. To call Athens hostels from the US, dial 011-30 plus the numbers printed in each listing. To call Athens hostels from Greece, dial numbers EXACTLY AS PRINTED.

ATHENS

Smoggy, crowded, and historic, Athens is a sensory blitz and not to be lingered in. It's best to catch it on your way into Greece, soak up the amazing concentration of sights and humanity, then get the heck out of town before it drives you nuts—and get to one of those sunny islands you've heard so much about. There's a rudimentary subway system that the city plans to update eventually, but many travelers end up having to cope with the crowded city buses. Athens isn't really walkable, and in summer it's too hot to think about walking anyway.

ATHENS HOSTELS AT A GLANCE

	RATING	PRICE	IN A WORD	PAGE
Student & Traveller's Inn		€15–€20	good	p. 226
Athens International		€8–€10	busy	p. 219
Hostel Aphrodite		€9–€30	fun	p. 223
Pella Inn Hostel		€13–€17	marginal	p. 224

Athens International Hostel

Viktoros Hugo Str. 16, Athens 10438

> **Phone:** 210-523-2540
> **Fax:** 210-523-2540
> **Website:** athens-international.com
> **E-mail:** info@aiyh-victorhugo.com
> **Rates:** €8–€10 (about $10–$13 US) per person; doubles €25 (about $31 US)

Athens

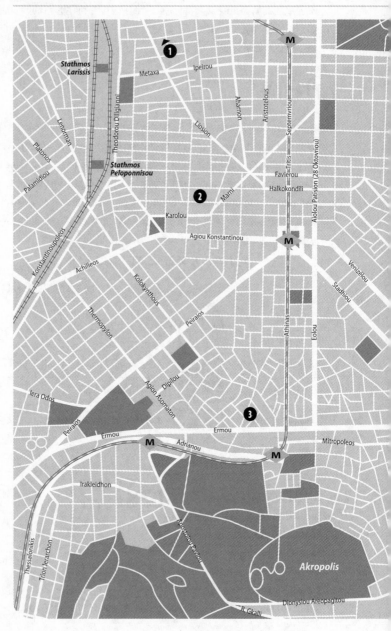

Leoforos Alexandras

Lofos
Strefi

C.Trikoupi

Ippokratous

Likavitos

Koniari

Solonos

Akadimias

Vasilissis   Sofias

Vasileos Alexandrou

Filelimon

Ethnikos
Kipos

Iradou

Attilou

Vasileos Konstantinou

Vasilissis Leoforos Amalias

Eratosthenous

Eftychidou

Panathinaiko
stadio

Diakou

Arxhitou

Imitou

Credit cards: No
Beds: 142
Private/family rooms: Yes
Kitchen available: Yes
Season: Open year-round
Office hours: 24 hours
Affiliation: HI
Extras: Laundry, breakfast, luggage storage, Internet access, information desk, lunch
($), kitchen

C heap? Yes. Great? Um, no.

The only "official" hostel in Greece, the Athens hostel is pretty far from the hub of the city's activity (the Plaka), though it does offer certain amenities. The place is very busy and popular, due to the cheapness factor. Therefore, you'll need to reserve waaay ahead of time. This, despite the so-so nature of the place. Some dorms are downright scuzzy (but some private rooms are nicer).Rooms here are small and rather (OK, very) basic. There are about 11 doubles and 29 quads, eliminating that crowded feeling so common in hostels that feature huge dormitories. However, there's a drawback: Once you leave the confines of the hostel and venture into chaotic Omonia Square, you'll get nothin' but noise—from cars, buses,

Best bet for a bite:
Metaxourgeio
Insiders' tip:
Pnyx Hill (near Acropolis) for peace and quiet
What hostellers say:
"No, I'm not looking for a 'good time,' OK?"
Gestalt:
Greece-y
Safety:
Hospitality:
Cleanliness:
Party index:

and people. Little coffee shops line the square, but they mostly seem patronized by (again, loud) elderly folk. There's not much peace or quiet in these parts, sorry to say. And be wary at night; prostitutes can overtake the area, drawing a seedy element to the neighborhood. Not the best place to stick a hostel, even if the staff are extremely friendly and helpful.

How To Get There:

By bus: Take A7 or B7 bus to Kanigos Square, then walk 400 yards to hostel.
By car: Contact hostel for directions.

By subway: Take Metro line #2 to Metaxourhio Station, then walk 150 yards to hostel.

By train: From train station, walk ⅓ mile; or take #1 or #12 streetcar to Agiou Konstantinou and walk 300 yards to hostel.

Hostel Aphrodite

Einardou Str. 12 (at Michail Voda St.), Athens 10440

Phone: 210-8810-589 or 210-8839-249

Fax: 210-8816-574

E-mail: info@hostelaphrodite.com

Website: hostelaphrodite.com

Rates: €9–€30 (about $12–$36 US) per person

Beds: 80

Credit cards: Yes

Private/family rooms: Yes

Kitchen available: No

Season: March 1–November 1

Office hours: 24 hours

Affiliation: HI

Extras: Currency exchange, laundry, meals ($), luggage storage, safe, sunroof, breakfast, bar, travel information desk

---

*T*his whitewashed tenement block—on a neighborhood corner close to Athens's main train stations—is very close to some prime attractions and fairly maintained, so it's worth a look. Unfortunately, we can no longer recommend this place. They've got a supply of singles, doubles, triples, and quads—nothing spectacular, but some do have private bathrooms. Among the local attractions are the Acropolis (just half a mile away!), the National Arch Museum, and tons of little eateries and locals-only haunts. Buses to the beach pick up just a couple blocks away.

They run a bar, too, which is obviously the most popular room in the house, and you can hang out on a sunroof overlooking the city. The luggage room is sketchy but is an option; a hosteller laundry and meal service are more like it.

However—cleanliness suffers. Staff aren't friendly or knowledgable enough. Things break and they don't get fixed. This place has promise, but it isn't delivering on it yet. At all.

How To Get There:

By bus: Contact hostel for transit details.

By car: Contact hostel for directions.

By plane: From airport, take #090 or #091 bus to Syndagma Square stop, then change to #1 trolley bus and continue to Proussis stop. Walk north along Mikhail Voda to hostel on left.

By subway: Take Metro to Victoria Station and walk to hostel.

By train: From Larissis Station, cross street and walk straight out along Philadeleias Loulianou to Mikhail Voda and turn left. Continue down Mikhail Voda to hostel on left.

From Pelopennes Station, cross footbridge to Larissis Station. Cross street and walk straight out along Philadeleias Loulianou to Mikhail Voda and turn left. Continue down Mikhail Voda to hostel on left.

Best bet for a bite:
Market next door

What hostellers say:
"Somebody's been taking happy pills."

Gestalt:
Aphrodisiac

Safety: 🎉🎉

Hospitality: 🎉🎉

Cleanliness: 🎉🎉

Party index: 🎉🎉🎉🎉

Pella Inn Hostel 🎉🎉

Ermou Str. 104, Athens 10554

Phone: 210-3212-229 or 210-3250-598

Fax: 210-3212-229 or 210-3250-598

E-mail: info@pellainn.gr

Website: pellainn.gr

Rates: €13–€17 (about $17–$21 US) per person; doubles €36–€48 (about $45–$60 US)

Credit cards: No

Beds: Number varies

Private/family rooms: Yes

Kitchen available: No

Season: Open year-round

Office hours: 24 hours

Affiliation: None

Extras: Fax service, sundeck, garden, meals ($), laundry service, phones, air-conditioning, luggage storage, currency exchange, Internet access, car rentals, book exchange, breakfast

*L*ocation, location, location: This joint has got it in spades. It doesn't have much more to offer you, though—hostel here at your peril.

The place is really more a hotel than a hostel, which usually means that staff are probably more interested in making a buck than in fostering international peace and understanding—or in distributing warm fuzzies or keeping rates low, for that matter. That said, however, they do offer a lot of amenities here thanks to the presence of the aforementioned hotel.

Rooms are either singles, doubles, triples, or quads—many with private bathrooms, which cost more, of course. Like most other hostels in Athens, you aren't forced to share your sleeping space with more than three souls at a time, so that's one good thing.

You won't believe the great view of the Acropolis from the rooftop garden, either, although it's often tainted by smog (insert frown emoticon here). If you want to get away from that smog and head to the more desirable islands, staff will rent you a car for cheap. They'll also change your currency, hook you up with Internet access, do your laundry, and cook you a meal (all for a fee). Other amenities include a fax service, breakfast, a luggage storage area, and a free book exchange.

But we haven't gotten to the core issue here: The hostel portion is simply not well enough maintained. It's not clean enough, not airy enough, not air-conditioned well enough, not anything well enough. Sorry, guys. Maybe you're trying to push business over to the hotel side? But we wouldn't book into a hotel room based on what we've seen of the hostel. Damn, if only they didn't have that siren-like view. . . .

> **Best bet for a bite:**
> *Souvlaki stands around Syndagma*
> **Insiders' tip:**
> *Drop off used guidebooks at book exchange*
> **What hostellers say:**
> *"Um, no."*
> **Gestalt:**
> *Pella-grrr*
> **Safety:**
> **Hospitality:**
> **Cleanliness:**
> **Party index:**

How To Get There:
By bus: From city bus terminals A and B, take city bus to Omonia Square, then change to Metro and continue one stop to Monastiraki Station. Walk 50 yards along Ermou Str. to hostel at #104.
By car: Contact hostel for directions.

By plane: From airport, take Express Bus #091 to Syntagma Square, then walk along Ermou Str. to hostel at #104.

By subway: From port area, take subway seven stops to Monastiraki and walk 50 yards along Ermou Str. to hostel at #104.

By train: From train station, take #1 trolley bus to Syntagma Square, then walk along Ermou Str. to hostel at #104.

Student & Traveller's Inn 🗿

Kydathineon 16, Athens 10558

>**Phone:** 210-324-4808 or 210-324-8802
>
>**Fax:** 210-321-0065
>
>**Website:** studenttravellersinn.com
>
>**Rates:** €15–€20 (about $18–$24 US) per person; doubles €45–€50 (about $50–$62 US)
>
>**Credit cards:** Yes
>
>**Beds:** Number varies
>
>**Private/family rooms:** Yes
>
>**Kitchen available:** No
>
>**Season:** Open year-round
>
>**Office hours:** 24 hours
>
>**Affiliation:** HI
>
>**Extras:** Laundry, safe, currency exchange, meals ($), travel agency, courtyard, bar

🗑

---

*T*his is it: head-and-shoulders-above-the-crowd the best hostel in Athens, which suffers from a serious lack of decent beds.

Students, travelers, and everyone else would be all too happy to find decent accommodations near the Plaka—and the Student & Traveller's Inn, sister hostel to the Aphrodite (see p. 223), offers a much better location with many of the same amenities. Just remember: You stay here for the amazing location, not the facility, because if you're hunting for perfectly clean rooms, smooth customer service, or perfect upkeep, you won't find them here.

The bunkrooms are fairly bright, with wooden floors, real beds (instead of bunks), and windows that open to all the sensory experiences (good and bad) that are Athens.

These rooms could be kept a lot cleaner, however—our snoops were disappointed. A patio festooned with grapevines and tables makes a good place to schmooze with your newfound friends, partaking of meals offered as well as the occasional ouzo. Staff are sometimes Aussies or Brits, so English is not normally a problem; they can help you negotiate your way around this big and confusing city. You're also positioned near the Acropolis, which helps when making your sightseeing plans for the day.

If you want to book online, it's pretty easy to do—unless you're not very good at math. One time when we tried, up popped this challenge to differentiate human hosteller from computer robot spammer: "We are sorry but we need to verify you are human. Please type the total of 13 + 4 to the box on the right."

Got it! (Don't we?) Made you think for a second, didn't they?

Best bet for a bite:
Tavernas near the Plaka
Insiders' tip:
Greek folk museum is nearby
What hostellers say:
"G'day, mate."
Gestalt:
Inn-Sync
Safety:
Hospitality:
Cleanliness:
Party index:

How To Get There:
By bus or train: Contact hostel for transit details.
By car: Contact hostel for directions.

Attractive natural setting	Comfortable beds	Visual arts at hostel or nearby
Ecologically aware hostel	A particularly good value	Music at hostel or nearby
Superior kitchen facilities or cafe	Wheelchair-accessible	Great hostel for skiers
Offbeat or eccentric place	Good for business travelers	Bar or pub at hostel or nearby
Superior bathroom facilities	Especially well-suited for families	Editors' choice: Among our very favorite hostels
Romantic private rooms	Good for active travelers	

Key to Icons

Hungary

H ungry for a little Hungary? The former Eastern Bloc-er is experiencing new life as a tourist destination, and Budapest is by far the prime attraction. It's even inexpensive to reach and travel in, if a little remote. That's because, unlike the Czech Republic's system, Hungary's train network is covered by Eurail passes. That means you won't need to buy extra tickets from your departure station, usually Vienna (three to four hours away), Prague (six hours), or Paris or Berlin (overnight trains)—though reservations are required on many of these long-distance trains, and those do cost a few bucks.

Practical Details

Hungary's unit of currency is the Forint (abbreviated Ft.). At press time, 1,000 Ft. equaled a little more than 4 bucks in cold, hard US cash.

The bills come in the following denominations:

200 Ft.	=	approximately 85 cents US
500 Ft.	=	approximately $2 US
1,000 Ft.	=	approximately $4 US
2,000 Ft.	=	approximately $8 US
5,000 Ft.	=	approximately $20 US
10,000 Ft.	=	approximately $40 US

The coins come in pieces worth:

1 Ft.	=	approximately ½ cent US
2 Ft.	=	approximately 1 cent US
5 Ft.	=	approximately 2 cents US
10 Ft.	=	approximately 4 cents US
50 Ft.	=	approximately 20 cents US
100 Ft.	=	approximately 40 cents US

Hungary's country code is 36, and the Budapest city code is 1. To dial Budapest hostels from the US, dial 011-36, then the numbers listed below. To dial Budapest hostels from within Hungary but outside the city, dial 06, pause, and then the numbers listed below EXACTLY AS PRINTED.

To dial Budapest hostels from within Budapest, just dial the number's seven digits AS PRINTED HERE.

BUDAPEST

Thermal baths, bridges across the Danube, a castle on a hill . . . Budapest is simply a wonderful city to wander through, tasting goulash and checking out the relics of the Communist era. (It's actually two cities—Buda and Pest—divided by the river.)

There are dozens of places in Budapest calling themselves hostels, and you'll be accosted at Keleti Station by mobs of hustlers touting them. Avoid these. Many are low-end hotels, others are open for only a very short summer season, and the lineup changes each year as new fly-by-night places open and others close down. Stick with the picks in this book.

If you simply can't resist the lure of these guys, don't let yourself be pressured into a quick decision. Observe two rules if you're thinking about an independent hostel. First, make them show you the location on a city map, and be sure the hostel is right in the central city—you might decide not to stay, and you don't want to be lost or stranded when they get ticked off by your refusal. Second, hand over no cash until after you've seen a room. If they won't agree to these two conditions, they're probably dishonest; move it along.

Note that almost all of Budapest's hostels have kitchens and Internet access, and all provide sheets, but not all of them take credit cards. Also remember that many smaller hostels here link their rates to the US dollar, meaning that if the dollar is strong, they'll raise prices. That means the prices listed in this chapter (unlike those in every other chapter) aren't written in stone. They may change on the fly.

BUDAPEST HOSTELS AT A GLANCE				
	RATING	PRICE	IN A WORD	PAGE
Backpack Guesthouse		2,800–4,500 Ft.	tops	p. 232
Red Bus Hostel		3,000–11,000 Ft.	great	p. 236
Caterina Hostel		7,000–8,000 Ft.	clean	p. 234

Budapest

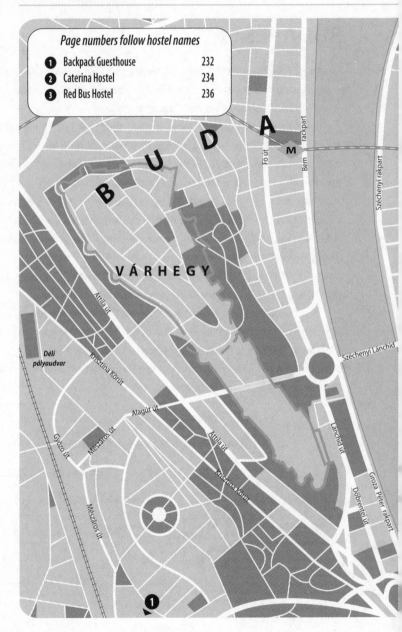

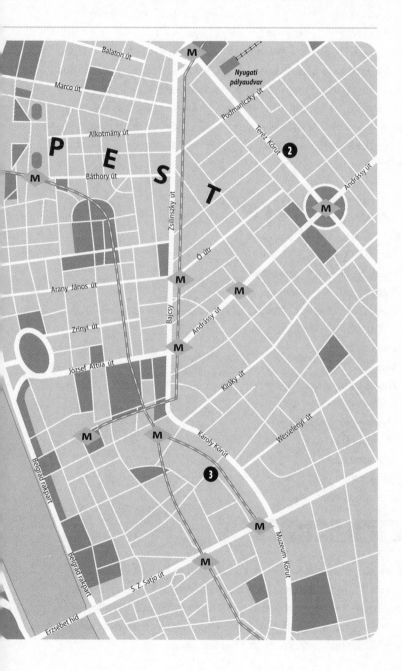

City tours and car rentals are often available from a Budapest hostel, though the hostels get commissions for these—so they're not unbiased recommendations. Finally, smaller hostels tend to be run by just one or two staffers, so don't plan on checking in at 3 in the morning or checking out very early without letting them know ahead of time.

One more thing you need to know: If you use the city's public transit system, you must re-punch a new ticket anytime you change transit methods—even if that's just to a different subway line. Yes, your ticket's good for half an hour, but only on that line. You cannot transfer it; you need to punch a new ticket during the transfer. This system is policed by roving inspectors—quite a few of them—so make sure you've bought an extra ticket if our directions indicate you need to change lines.

Backpack Guesthouse

Takacs Menyhért út. 33, Budapest

Phone: 1-385-8946 or 1-209-8406

E-mail: backpackguest@hotmail.com

Website: backpackbudapest.hu

Rates: 2,800 Ft.–4,500 Ft. (about $11–$18 US) per person; doubles 9,000 Ft.–11,000 Ft. (about $36–$44 US)

Credit cards: No

Beds: 50

Private/family rooms: Yes

Kitchen available: Yes

Season: Open year-round

Office hours: 24 hours

Affiliation: None

Extras: Kitchen, TV room, bar, city tours, laundry ($), free Internet access, outdoor excursions, lockers, camping

*T*aa-daa! Best hostel in Budapest, here you are. Congrats, Backpack Guesthouse. You've earned it. Unfortunately, it's a loooooong way to Tipperary. But once you've done the bumpy bus ride out here—they claim it's only 12 minutes, believe it or not, but you'll find otherwise—you know this is where you belong. Forget downtown Budapest for one night and simply have a good time with the other hostellers who've somehow stumbled into this amazing place, which is small, cheap, clean, and personable all at the same time.

Truckloads of paint went into and onto Attila (yes, really) and Bori's house, making it look like nothing else on earth and certainly no other hostel in Europe. No two rooms are alike; there are two cozy doubles (neither with private bathroom, however) and a few dorm rooms with 6 or 8 beds—and fans—each. There's a mellow kitchen scene, a comfy combination bar-and-TV room (which, we noticed, is stocked with 300 class-A videos in English), and the reception produces both good mood and groovy tunes all day and night long. There's a laundry (4 bucks per load), Internet access a small garden in front of the house, and another, bigger one behind it. It's summer? Sleep in the tree house! (Yes, Virginia, they have hammocks.)

Best bet for a bite:
Ask about free goulash on Sundays
Insiders' tip:
Bring your crampons
What hostellers say:
"This is heaven!"
Gestalt:
Leader of the (back)pack
Safety: 🏔
Hospitality: 🏔
Cleanliness: 🏔
Party index: 🎉 🎉 🎉 🎉

Oh, and in case you're still interested in far-off Budapest, there's an information-packed board next to the reception. You can also book a tour with one of the helpful staffers, well worth a few extra bucks to have a local guide. Food? If it's not Sunday night—when they dole out stew—order a pizza. Daily orders go out around 6 p.m., just before the big group "where to go out today" conference, so you don't have to find the way back alone at night. Don't forget to drink a cheap beer and use the free Internet service, either.

All this good feeling, spirit, and general cleanliness make for a good hostel. However, the buzz about this place is spreading, so advance reservations are now absolutely essential. Even harder than snagging a spot here is checking out. Some hostellers, in fact, never made it out: Many of the reception crew are former guests who just couldn't say good-bye.

Now, if only this house were closer to the city center.

How To Get There:

By train: From Keleti pu. Station, walk across street to Pizza Hut and catch #7 or #73 bus to Tetenyi út. (fifth stop after crossing river). Walk back underneath railway overpass, turn left, and continue to third right.

By bus: Take Metro line no. 3 (toward ÚJPEST-KÖZPONT) 5 stops to FERENCIEK TERE. Take bus to Tetenyi út. (fifth stop after crossing river). Walk back underneath railway overpass, turn left, and continue to third right.

By car: Contact hostel for directions.

Caterina Hostel

Terèz krt. 30 III-28 (door code #48), Budapest

Phone: 1269-5990

E-mail: info@caterinahostel.hu

Website: caterinahostel.com

Rates: 7,000–8,000 Ft. (about $28–$32 US) per person; doubles 22,000–26,000 Ft. (about $88–$104 US)

Credit cards: No

Beds: 38

Private/family rooms: Yes

Kitchen available: Yes

Season: Open year-round

Office hours: 8 a.m.–10 p.m.

Affiliation: None

Extras: TVs, free Internet access and Wi-Fi (most units), laundry ($), city tours

*B*asically a ramshackle, third-floor apartment that is really difficult to find, this is the kind of hostel you really only find in Central Europe. It's operated by the owner and a mother-daughter tag team, each named, yes, Caterina, and it's conveniently located just off central Oktogon Square with its Metro, trolley, and bus stops all almost right in front of the hostel entrance. "Caterina always cleaning, yes, much cleaning!" they told us once. Unfortunately, that isn't the case any longer —cleanliness has slipped of late. There are 2 apartments on both sides of the Oktogon, one with 18 beds, the other with 20 more. And then there are another 2 apartments to rent for small groups (up to 4 people on a per person basis). The bright and spacious dorm rooms come with 4, 6, or 8 beds apiece. There are no lockers, but considering the hostel's small size, safety shouldn't be an issue. Three of the rooms have their own televisions.

There are 2 cozy double rooms as well—along with the apartments, these are an incredible bargain, but they're weirdly constructed. The floors are a little tall, maybe 10 ½ feet high, so they've gone and wedged in an extra step-up "floor" above the bunks—a double with a curtain instead of a door. You have to climb up steps to get there, kind of like climbing to a tree house, and once there you can hardly stand upright or scramble back down during middle-of-the-night emergencies. Not the most comfortable setup, more like a tiny train compartment. Anyhow, Internet access is now free, while the laundry runs you about 3 bucks per load.

This place remains a serviceable choice in town but the lack of upkeep now trumps the warm hospitality. Iffy at best.

How To Get There:

By bus: From main bus station, walk to Deák tér Station. Take Metro M1 line in direction of Mexicói út 3 stops to Oktogon stop.

By car: Contact hostel for directions.

By train: From Keleti pu. Station, take Metro Line #2 (red line) 3 stops toward Déli pu. to Deák tér Station, then change to orange line (#1) and continue to Oktogon Station. The hostel is right on the corner of Andrassy út. and Oktogon Square.

From Nyugati Station, take Metro M3 line toward city center (in the direction of Köbánya-Kispest) 2 stops to Deák tér Station. Change to M1 line and continue in direction of Mexicói út. 3 more stops to Oktogon stop.

Best bet for a bite:
Cactus Juice (tapas bar; good tunes)
What hostellers say:
"Used to be better."
Gestalt:
Mama mia
Safety:
Hospitality:
Cleanliness:
Party index:

![] Attractive natural setting	![] Comfortable beds	![] Visual arts at hostel or nearby
![] Ecologically aware hostel	![] A particularly good value	![] Music at hostel or nearby
![] Superior kitchen facilities or cafe	![] Wheelchair-accessible	![] Great hostel for skiers
![] Offbeat or eccentric place	![] Good for business travelers	![] Bar or pub at hostel or nearby
![] Superior bathroom facilities	![] Especially well-suited for families	![] Editors' choice: Among our very favorite hostels
![] Romantic private rooms	![] Good for active travelers	

Key to Icons

Red Bus Hostel
Semmelweis utca 14, Budapest

> **Phone:** 1-266-0136
> **Fax:** 1-266-0136
> **E-mail:** redbusbudapest@hotmail.com
> **Website:** redbusbudapest.hu
> **Rates:** 3,000–11,000 Ft. (about $15–$55 US) per person; doubles 10,500 Ft.–11,000
> Ft. (about $53–$55 US)
> **Credit cards:** Yes
> **Beds:** 50
> **Private/family rooms:** Yes
> **Kitchen available:** Yes
> **Season:** Open year-round
> **Office hours:** 24 hours
> **Affiliation:** None
> **Extras:** Free breakfast, Internet access, tours, kitchen

The Red Bus Hostel actually consists of two places in the city center of Budapest—neither one is in a bus, however (huh?), so don't start trolling the streets looking for one. They are set in typical old Hungarian buildings; booking and check-in are handled at the office listed above.

Both facilities are a little hard to find. The rooms are attractive if not always spotlessly clean, with nicely high ceilings; dorms hold 6 to 8 beds each, and there's a supply of doubles and triples as well. Because of its downtown location, this is an ideal base from which to do all of your Budapest sightseeing and partying. (The hostel itself is very quiet, a dead zone nightlife-wise. That isn't necessarily a bad thing.)

There's Internet access to keep in touch with fellow road mates, the hostel's open 24 hours for night owls, the kitchen is huge, and management maintains (and actually tries to enforce) a friendly no-smoking policy—good if you're sensitive to the smoke that often pervades independent European hostels. (There is a small smoking area, separate from dorms and most of the common areas.)

All in all, it's an OK addition to the Budapest lineup. However, don't expect to have fun here. We quote here from the hostel rules: "Please no playing of musical instruments!" We've got two problems with that statement. One: Why not? Two: Was the exclamation point really necessary? One other quibble: We have heard complaints that this hostel routinely loses advance reservations. Double- and triple-confirm before arriving, and have a backup plan just in case.

How To Get There:
By bus or train: Take Metro to Astoria Station. Exit station and follow exit sign for Kossuth Lajos út. Walk along Kossuth Lajos út. just 15 yards and take first right onto Semmelweis utca. Hostel is at end of street, on the left.
By car: Contact hostel for directions.

Best bet for a bite:
Cafe Eklektika near Astoria station
Insiders' tip:
Stroll west to the river
What hostellers say:
"Slept like a baby."
Gestalt:
This Old Hostel
Safety: 🗦
Hospitality: 🗦🗧
Cleanliness: 🗦🗧
Party index: 🎉

Ireland

I t's green, rainy, and musical, and there's lots of Guinness, right? Well, yes, but there's more to Ireland than just all that. Hostels, for one thing, amazingly thick on the ground around the country—and most of them are darned good. Call the independent IHH-affiliated joints first; though laid-back, they offer the best mixture of socializing and comfy beds.

To see the best of Ireland, begin in Dublin and make a counterclockwise trip to the Southeast, the gorgeous Southwest, the West, the Northwest, and Northern Ireland—which of course is a different country, part of the United Kingdom—and finally circle back to Dublin again. There are tons of budget flights to the east and west from London and elsewhere in England. Or try taking a ferry from Wales, France (covered by Eurail), or England.

Practical Details

Students can get a good deal on Irish transportation by buying a Travelsave Stamp from the USIT student travel network or at Ireland's larger transit stations. You've got to be a student or under a certain age, but if you are, this stamp saves you half off each long-distance bus or train ride you take while holding it.

Ireland's national rail company, Irish Rail, is part of the CIE government transport network that helps get you around the country. Contact Irish Rail (irishrail.ie) for schedule and fare information. You can generally get anywhere the train serves—which isn't everywhere, unfortunately—for less than €35 (about $50 US) one-way. In the Dublin area, the DART (Dublin Area Rapid Transit) suburban train calls at 25 stations within a good-size radius of the city.

Consider getting a railpass such as the Irish Explorer—which gives you five days of riding on Ireland's (but not Northern Ireland's) rail network for €160 (about $200 US) within a 15-day window. (There's a bus-and-train version of the pass, too.) Remember to buy any railpass before you get to Ireland. Not traveling so much? Buy short-distance tickets one by one at Irish train stations instead; it'll cost less.

Buses are cheaper than trains in Ireland, and they go many more places; as a result, you're probably going to spend some time riding them. (For a bus trip of, say, Dublin to Cork and back, you'd pay about half the train fare.) The buses are reasonably on time and scenic, with lots of locals riding alongside you happy to give advice, opinions, or soccer scores. You might have to wait around for one, but eventually there'll be a bus going wherever you're going; just remember that on Sunday and certain Mondays, some lines run less frequently.

Irish Bus is the country's national bus carrier (also known by its Gaelic name, Bus

Eireann). For rates, schedules, bus station information, and other stuff, peruse their comprehensive Website—buseireann.ie. Local buses fill the rest of the gaps, and these can range from incredibly efficient lines to laughable ones.

Bicycling is one of the very best ways of all to see Ireland; though challenging at times, the terrain rewards cyclists with view after splendiferous view. Rental agencies are everywhere—and many hostels within this book rent two-wheelers out, as well—or you could try one of the many tour outfitters that run country-road tours of various regions. The national clearinghouse for cycling information and tours is in Dublin and is known as Walking Cycling (irelandwalkingcycling.com). Also check the website dublincitycycling.ie for more info on cycling in the Dublin area; you can find cycle tour outfits covering all of Ireland at the city's cycling website, dublin.ie/transport/cycling-walking.htm.

The unit of currency in Ireland is the euro.

All phone and fax numbers in this book are listed as you dial them from Ireland or Northern Ireland. To call Irish hostels from within Ireland, dial them EXACTLY AS PRINTED. To call Irish hostels from the US, dial 011-353 and then DROP THE ZERO from the number printed.

DUBLIN

This is probably why you've come to Ireland: to experience Dublin in all its hectic glory—the bookshops, rain, pubs, clubs, university students, pictures of U2 and James Joyce plastered all over town, and much, much more. After weeks running around the Irish countryside, coming here can be a bit overwhelming—but it's sure to inject a bit of cosmopolitan culture in any trip that has started to degenerate into a string of rainy days or dull meals. And once you've landed in Dublin, it's not far to the surrounding counties—some, in fact, can even be reached with the DART bus and train system that serves the greater Dublin area.

Many of these smallish villages are popular with local tourists, and for good reason: They often come with their own castles, some of which have been transformed into arts centers, recording studios, or other strange (yet strangely appropriate) uses.

Getting around Dublin isn't too hard at all. The central city is very compact, based along both sides of the River Liffey, so much of it's walkable. Buses run seemingly everywhere else you want to go, too. Dublin Bus (01-873-4222, or dublinbus.ie) offers everything from one-day to one-month passes on its extensive network of services in both the urban and suburban areas. You can buy tickets from drivers, at more than 200 offices in the greater Dublin region, or at the central Upper O'Connell Street Station. (Bear in mind that not all bus drivers are able to give change.)

Dublin

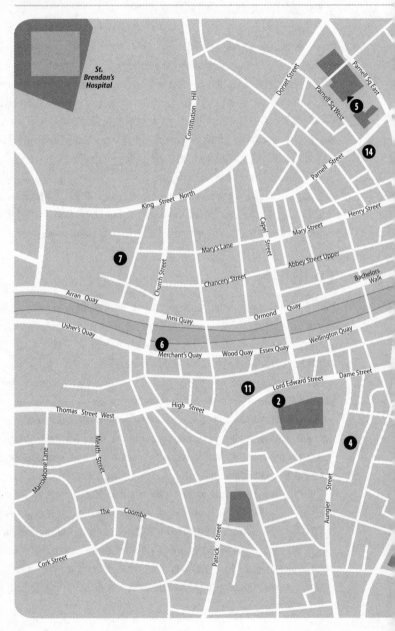

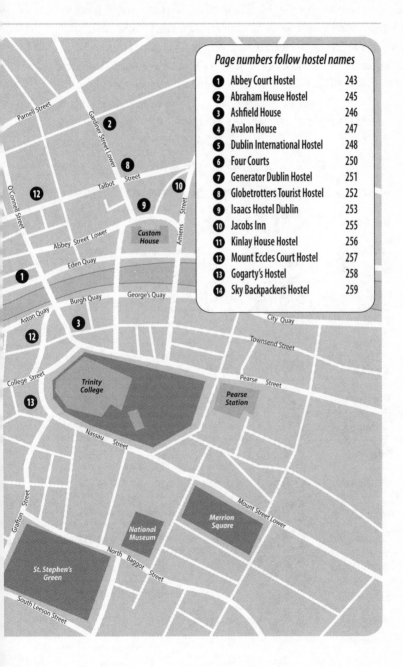

If you'll be using only buses while in town, get a Dublin Rambler ticket—basically a pass. You can travel for one, three, or five hassle-free days around town on the Dublin Bus (Bus Eireann) system and also use the Airlink service to and from the airport. It costs from €6.50 (about $8 US) to €23 (about $29 US), depending on how long you need it for.

You can reach some hostels just outside the city using the DART suburban trains that chug north and south from the city center to such quaint-sounding places as Howth and Dun Laoghaire. The city's bus and municipal transit systems sell various passes for frequent train or train and bus users; one popular all-inclusive pass, known as the Short Hop, will run about

DUBLIN HOSTELS AT A GLANCE

	RATING	PRICE	IN A WORD	PAGE
Generator Dublin Hostel	◖◖	€13–€93	excellent	p. 251
Globetrotters	◖	€12–€49	impressive	p. 252
Four Courts	◖	€12–€19	improving	p. 250
Dublin International Hostel	◖	€13–€33	institutional	p. 248
Jacobs Inn	◖	€14–€45	good	p. 255
Abbey Court	◖	€12–€26	friendly	p. 243
Abraham House	◖	€9–€30	OK	p. 245
Kinlay House	◖	€15–€30	central	p. 256
Avalon House	◖◗	€15–€25	tight	p. 247
Ashfield House	◖◗	€9–€30	middling	p. 246
Isaacs Hostel Dublin	◖◗	€12–€35	noisy	p. 253
Gogarty's Hostel	◖◗	€14–€24	happy	p. 258
Sky Backpackers	◖◗	€12–€26	historic	p. 259
Mount Eccles Court Hostel	◖◗	€10–€19.50	poor	p. 257

€12 (about $15 US) per day (discounts for longer periods) or about €18 (about $23 US) for a family of two adults and up to four children. It's valid on almost everything except the city's special night buses and airport transit.

Around town, besides the obvious Big Three draws—St. Stephen's Green, Trinity College, and the hip Temple Bar neighborhood—an amazing number of old castles, buildings, and parks are scattered within the city limits. Dublin Castle is the most central, but there's also Rathfarnham Castle (built in 1583 and pretty impressive), the National Botanic Gardens (more than 20,000 species of things growing here), the Pearse Museum, and the spooky Kilmainham Gaol. All have small admission charges and daytime open hours, and they can be reached by public buses.

At night? We love to hit the pubs, what else? You can't walk 10 feet without stumbling into another one. O'Shea's Merchant on Bridge Street is typical: The walls are plastered with photos and old knickknacks that give a real sense of continuity and history to the place. Locals file in to play the real Irish music, not the stuff you get on package tours. There's a tinge of sadness—always the sadness—but a sense, too, that people come here to acknowledge life.

That's the best of Dublin: life pressing forward in defiant, even jubilant, celebration.

Abbey Court Hostel

29 Bachelor's Walk, O'Connell Bridge, Dublin

> **Phone:** 01-878-0700
>
> **Fax:** 01-878-0719
>
> **Website:** abbey-court.com
>
> **E-mail:** info@abbey-court.com
>
> **Rates:** €12–€26 (about $15–$33 US) per person; doubles €59–€79 (about $79–$99 US)
>
> **Credit cards:** Yes
>
> **Beds:** 228
>
> **Private/family rooms:** Yes
>
> **Kitchen available:** No
>
> **Season:** Open year-round
>
> **Office hours:** 24 hours
>
> **Affiliation:** IHH
>
> **Extras:** Meals, free Wifi and Internet access, free breakfast, laundry, lockers, TV

*Y*ou can't get any closer to the famous O'Connell Bridge than this hostel; it's practically right on top of the thing.

They've got quite nice dorms here, family rooms with twin beds and en-suite bathrooms (which cost a bit more), free Internet terminals and WiFi, and a laundry, and they serve meals. Breakfast is free. It's really, really well run—a testament to ownership that, for once, actually cares. This is a clean, secure bunk with a very good breakfast included—though you should try to avoid the very largest (read: tightest) dormitories if you can.

And here's another reason to think about booking: Prices are on the way down. How many places can you say that about? Yet it's true: A bunk here is about a third cheaper than it was just three years ago. We like where this is going.

Gestalt:
Abbey Road
Safety:
Hospitality:
Cleanliness:
Party index:

When you stay here, you're just across the river from the hip Temple Bar area, where everybody wants to be, and famously wise Trinity College. Yep—this is the number-one hostel in Dublin for location, and one of the top five overall.

How To Get There:
By bus: From Busarus station, walk ¼ mile along Abbey Street or along river to O'Connell Bridge; hostel is just past bridge, on right.
By car: Contact hostel for directions.
By train: From Connolly Station, walk 300 yards to river, turn right, and continue about ⅓ mile to O'Connell Bridge. Hostel is just past bridge, on right.

Key to Icons

Attractive natural setting	Comfortable beds	Visual arts at hostel or nearby
Ecologically aware hostel	A particularly good value	Music at hostel or nearby
Superior kitchen facilities or cafe	Wheelchair-accessible	Great hostel for skiers
Offbeat or eccentric place	Good for business travelers	Bar or pub at hostel or nearby
Superior bathroom facilities	Especially well-suited for families	Editors' choice: Among our very favorite hostels
Romantic private rooms	Good for active travelers	

Abraham House Hostel

82-83 Lower Gardiner St., Dublin 1

Phone: 01-855-0600
Fax: 01-855-0598 .
E-mail: stay@abraham-house.ie
Rates: €9–€30 (about $11–$38 US) per person; doubles €48–€50 (about $60–$63 US)
Credit cards: Yes
Beds: 191
Private/family rooms: Yes
Kitchen available: Yes
Season: Open year-round
Office hours: 24 hours
Affiliation: IHH
Extras: Bureau de change, breakfast, laundry, TV, pool table, restaurant ($), Internet, towels

*N*ot exactly central, this place might be a good bet if you're getting in late or getting out early—it's on the way to Dublin's out-of-town airport. But they skimp on the cleaning, and that's reason enough to give it a pass in a town packed with better bunks.

Dorms come in rooms of 4 to 10 beds, and they also do private rooms. They change currency, serve breakfast, and maintain the usual TV room and pool table combo. Overall, the place is OK—wearing out a bit from heavy use through the years, as it's always been a very popular pick. (Take note and book ahead if you're intent on staying here.)

Staff and management do a good job here of making you feel at home; the facilities aren't always up to snuff. Sometimes they're adequate, sometimes better than you expected, and sometimes things are beat up. Getting one of the 20 private rooms could improve the experience a bit.

This is a solid, middle-of-the-road Dublin pack: unspectacular, but certainly not the pits. That distant location, though, makes it an unlikely pick.

What hostellers say:
"So-so."
Gestalt:
Abraham sandwich
Safety:
Hospitality:
Cleanliness:
Party index:

How To Get There:

By bus: Bus station in Dublin; call hostel for transit route.
By car: Call hostel for directions.
By train: Train station in Dublin; call hostel for transit route.

Ashfield House

19-20 D'Olier St., Dublin 2

> **Phone:** 01-679-7734
> **Fax:** 01-679-0852
> **E-mail:** ashfield@indigo.ie
> **Website:** ashfieldhouse.ie
> **Rates:** €9–€30 (about $11–$38 US) per person; doubles €48–€50 (about $60–$63 US)
> **Credit cards:** Yes
> **Beds:** 104
> **Private/family rooms:** Yes
> **Kitchen available:** Yes
> **Season:** Open year-round
> **Office hours:** 24 hours
> **Affiliation:** IHH
> **Extras:** Breakfast, meals ($), laundry, bike rentals, currency exchange, laundry, cafe

---

*T*here's a pretty mixed bag of opinion about this Dublin hostel, which boasts a really excellent position near that awesome Temple Bar nabe we keep telling you so much about. (Watch for U2 sightings, just in case Ireland's favorite stands-the-test-of-time band decides to show up at a pub near the hostel steps for a beer.)

This hostel's not terrible, but it's not good, either—furnishings are showing the hands of time, so the positive vibe is dampened, and cleanliness ranges from kinda clean to occasionally grimy.

What hostellers say:
"So-so."

Gestalt:
Kiss my Ashfield

Safety:

Hospitality:

Cleanliness:

Party index:

Most dorms contain the usual number of beds—in this case, 4 to 12 apiece, though there's also a monster 18-bedded bunkroom—and the beds themselves are decent. The hostel also maintains a kitchen for fixing meals, changes currency, serves a minimal free breakfast, offers a laundry service (for a fee), and serves meals in a cafe if you're feeling lazy. The staff will rent you a bike, too, although we'd recommend seeing this hustle-bustle town on foot.

It's not enough to compensate for the cleanliness issue. The location is outtasight, though.

How To Get There:

By bus or train: Call hostel for transit route.
By car: Call hostel for directions.

Avalon House

55 Aungier St., Dublin 2

Phone: 01-475-0001
Fax: 01-475-0303
E-mail: info@avalon-house.ie
Website: avalon-house.ie
Rates: €15–€25 (about $20–$30 US) per person; doubles €50–€60 (about $63–$75 US)
Credit cards: Yes
Beds: 281
Private/family rooms: Yes
Kitchen available: No
Season: Open year-round
Office hours: 24 hours
Affiliation: IHH
Extras: Cafe ($), bureau de change, breakfast, laundry, TV, fireplace, lockers, Internet

*W*e'd like to give our highest marks to Avalon House, universally checked off in previous years by our hostellers as one of Dublin's better hostels. We'd like to, but we can't; it wants to be home away from home, but it too often turns out to be more like a warehouse. The likeable staff are friendly, no question—but the facilities are aging.

A brick building that once housed a medical school, it's quite close to wonderful Trinity College and St. Stephen's Green, the hub of Dublin. (Wouldn't that make it Hublin? Just wondering.) The entire first floor here is a cafe with cheap, good food. This restaurant and coffee shop are two good bets in the city's sometimes bleak eating scene. Dorms here, in a separate area, generally contain 4 to 10 beds, and they're OK—but can get quite crowded and loud, as they're just too small to handle the load. Some have en-suite bathrooms, which is good, but they're not as sweet and clean as they could be.

At least you can book one of the private rooms, change money, hang with fellow hostellers in the common area, and get accustomed to the coed hall bathrooms.

Oh, and one more big bonus if you're starting your Irish sojourn here: Stay a night and you can book all your future IHH nights from here to save the hassle of doing it later.

What hostellers say:
"It's OK, I guess."
Gestalt:
Halfalon
Safety:
Hospitality:
Cleanliness:
Party index:

How To Get There:

By bus: Call hostel for transit route.
By car: Call hostel for directions.
By ferry: Take 46A bus to downtown.
By train: From DART, take train to Pearse Station.

Dublin International Hostel

61 Mountjoy St., Dublin 7

> **Phone:** 01-830-1766
> **Fax:** 01-830-5808
> **Website:** anoige.ie
> **Rates:** €13–€33 (about $16–$41 US) per HI member, doubles €48–€50 (about $60–$63 US)
> **Credit cards:** Yes
> **Beds:** 297
> **Private/family rooms:** Yes
> **Kitchen available:** Yes

Season: Open year-round
Office hours: 24 hours
Affiliation: HI-AO
Extras: Breakfast, meals ($), laundry, conference room, bureau de change, tours, Internet access, bike rentals, parking, TV, shuttle service, luggage storage ($), sheets ($)

*O*K, it's time to revise our opinions about this place. Once a warehouse-like structure with strict rules, few smiles, and iffy facilities, Dublin's "official" hostel has become a pretty good option in the city—and it's not all that far from the historic center, somewhat surprisingly. We can now wholeheartedly recommend it, especially for families or travelers beyond college age. (Heavy drinkers may want to look elsewhere, though.)

Gestalt:
Nun of the above
Safety:
Hospitality:
Cleanliness:
Party index:

A former convent packed with almost 300 beds—the actual number depends on whom you ask, on which day, at which time of year—the place is huge and uninspiring at first glance, with all the charm of a nun's habit. It's not in the greatest neighborhood, either—a bit of a sketchy area up on the city's workabout north side. Just to be safe, we wouldn't go strolling around outside alone at night.

Dorms are not exactly bleak but not exactly beautiful—big, and packed with basic beds that are sometimes comfy and sometimes less so—but the cafe and kitchen partially redeem the place. Also, some rooms have their own bathrooms, so you don't always have to fumble your way to distant facilities at 3 in the morning, and the double rooms are a real bargain in Dublin—nice rooms at lower-than-hotel prices. Also, there are now fewer rules here than in many other HI-affiliated joints, and it's kept obsessively clean. Can't knock that.

They also kick in plenty of services like decent food, free big breakfasts, and a currency exchange. Yes, it's still kind of sterile. But if you can afford to pay a bit extra for a smaller, 2- to 6-bed dorm, you might enjoy it.

How To Get There:
By bus: From downtown, take #10 bus 1 mile to hostel.

By ferry: Ferry from Holyhead, Wales, to Dublin dock (2½ miles away), then catch Stena bus to Central Station, 1 mile from hostel. From Dun Laoghaire (7½ miles), catch Stena bus to Central Station.

By foot: From O'Connell Street bridge, walk north to Parnell Street; make a left, then right on Parnell Square. Go 4 blocks to Mountjoy.

By plane: From airport, take #41A bus to near hostel.

By train: Connolly Station is 1 mile; Heuston Station is 2 miles.

Four Courts Hostel

15-17 Merchants Quay, Dublin 8

> **Phone:** 01-672-5839
>
> **Fax:** 01-672-5862
>
> **E-mail:** info@fourcourtshostel.com
>
> **Website:** fourcourtshostel.com
>
> **Rates:** €12–€19 (about $15–$24 US) per person; doubles €48 (about $60 US)
>
> **Credit cards:** Yes
>
> **Beds:** 230
>
> **Private/family rooms:** Yes
>
> **Kitchen available:** Yes
>
> **Season:** Open year-round
>
> **Office hours:** 24 hours
>
> **Affiliation:** None
>
> **Extras:** Free WiFi and Internet access, laundry, currency exchange, lounge, game room, pool tables, tour desk, breakfast

---

*T*his huge, independent hostel has a riverside location (right on the Liffey), a little bit of a hike to Trinity, Grafton Street, and everything else you wanna see. It's also a rising star on the Dublin scene and now one of your very best bets in town—not to mention a highly convenient base hostel for exploring this cool city (just so long as you don't mind wearing out a little shoe leather).

The hostel is made up of 3 connected Georgian mansions, fitted out with dorms containing anywhere from 4 to 10 beds apiece. There is also a selection of double rooms for couples and families. Laundry? Parking? Front-desk security? Big-screen TVs? Kitchen? Free continental breakfast? Natch. There's even an elevator, for crying out loud.

Gestalt:
Courts and spark
Safety: ◣
Hospitality: ◣
Cleanliness: ◣
Party index: ▲ ▲ ▲

Staff and management do seem to genuinely care about hosteler comfort and will honor special requests if reasonable. The kitchen is a plus. Sure, there are some problems here—it's a bit cramped. Still, they get major points for trying and for responding to hosteller complaints.

How To Get There:

By bus: From Busarus station, take #90 bus to hostel.
By car: Contact hostel for directions.
By ferry: Take #53 or #53A bus to hostel.
By train: From Heuston or Connolly Station, take #90 bus to hostel.
By plane: From Dublin airport, take #748 bus to hostel.

Generator Dublin Hostel ◣ ◣

Smithfield Square, Dublin 7

> **Phone:** 01-9010-222
> **E-mail:** dublin@generatorhostels.com
> **Website:** generatorhostels.com
> **Rates:** €13–€93 (about $16–$116 US) per person; doubles €93 (about $116 US)
> **Credit cards:** Yes
> **Beds:** 500
> **Private/family rooms:** Yes
> **Kitchen available:** Yes
> **Season:** Open year-round
> **Office hours:** 24 hours
> **Affiliation:** None
> **Extras:** Kitchen, free WiFi, laundry, cafe

B eds are comfy, times are fun. The 6-floor Dublin outpost of the Generator hostel chain is one of the better facilities in the group (see: London, et al.). However, it's mighty distant from most of what you'd want to do in Dublin; consider that a small pinch of reality in an otherwise ideal hostel universe.

They operate a kitchen. They use key cards here (good for security). Furniture is IKEA-like in its clean lines. Some dorms are a bit tight (they really wedge the beds into those babies), but overall this is hostelling better than it is most anywhere else in the UK and Ireland.

Gestalt:
Generation Xcellent
Safety:
Hospitality:
Cleanliness:
Party index:

Special shout-out to the ladies' Jacuzzi rooms (that's really what they're called): hotel-quality small dorms with en-suite bathrooms and . . . Jacuzzis. Ladies only. Sorry, Charlie.

How To Get There:
By car: Contact hostel for directions.
By bus/train: Contact hostel for transit details.
By plane: Take Airlink 747 bus to Usher's Quay; cross bridge to Smithfield Square and hostel.

Globetrotters Tourist Hostel
46-48 Lower Gardiner St., Dublin 1
   Phone: 01-873-5893
   Fax: 01-878-8787
   E-mail: gtrotter@indigo.ie
   Website: globetrottersdublin.com
   Rates: €12–€49 (about $15–$61 US) per person; doubles €49–€55 (about $61–$66 US)
   Credit cards: Yes
   Beds: 250
   Private/family rooms: No
   Kitchen available: Yes
   Season: Open year-round
   Office hours: 24 hours
   Affiliation: IHH
   Extras: Breakfast, meals, laundry ($),luggage storage, TV, free Wifi

---

*S*urprisingly, the venerable Globetrotter has slipped back a notch in recent years. For years it was, simply put, the king of the hill in Dublin, and it probably remains so, years after we first visited. But there are chinks in the armor now, too.

"Globetrotters" is a word we've seen hostels around the world slap onto their front doors— often with dire consequences—but this place is for real. Memo to managers: Just calling yerself a globetrotter doesn't mean you've accomplished it. Too often, it's the bedbugs doing the trotting.

Gestalt:
World party
Safety:
Hospitality:
Cleanliness:
Party index:

The nifty courtyard Japanese garden is the place hostellers congregate in peaceful bliss in the middle of one of Europe's most intriguing cities. Granted, some of the dorms back inside are 10-bed affairs, and the doubles cost a little extra. But if you've snagged one of the 38 private B&B–style rooms, you know this is pretty cool anyway: B&B, plus hostelling companions, all in one shot. Even the dorms (with 6, 8, 10, or 12 beds each) are relatively comfy.

What else can we say? OK, how about this: This hostel is just a block from Dublin's main bus station, maybe 2 blocks from its train station, and the neighborhood actually doesn't suffer too badly. Just in case, though, security here is tight.

How To Get There:

By bus: From bus station, walk 1 block to hostel.
By car: Call hostel for directions.
By train: From train station, walk 2 blocks to hostel.

Isaacs Hostel Dublin

2-5 Frenchmans Ln., Dublin 1
   Phone: 01-855-6215
   Fax: 01-855-6574
   E-mail: hostel@isaacs.ie
   Website: isaacs.ie
   Rates: €12–€35 (about $15–$42 US) per person; doubles €55–€69 (about $53–$63 US)
   Credit cards: Yes
   Beds: 235
   Private/family rooms: Yes

Kitchen available: Yes
Season: Open year-round
Office hours: 24 hours
Lockout: 11 a.m.–5 p.m.
Affiliation: IHH
Extras: Cafe ($), bike rentals, lockers, bureau de change, music, meals ($), sauna

*T*his 18th-century building was once a warehouse for a wine merchant. Now it's a rockin' hostel, almost legendary among the droves of hostellers who descend on Dublin each summer.

The place consists of singles, big but fun dorms, lots of private rooms, decent food, some bathrooms right in the rooms, and regular live-music nights to initiate you into the Irish way as soon as you've arrived.

Gestalt:
Train a-comin'
Safety:
Hospitality:
Cleanliness:
Party index:

However—and it's a big however—this place definitely isn't for light sleepers, and things have declined quite a bit here over the past few years. You couldn't sleep any closer to the train tracks if you wanted to (not that you do): They literally run right over the place. It reminded us of the scene in *The Blues Brothers* where Jake and Elwood Blues nap in Elwood's apartment, right underneath Chicago's elevated train.

Bathrooms and showers are grungy much of the time. Also, there's an annoying 6-hour lockout during the heart of the day. Given that the place isn't all that clean and that the staff's attitude at times sucks, it's probably a miss, though a few travelers do seem to love it for the way it mashes together hostellers from different countries in spite of the upkeep issues.

How To Get There:
By bus: From Busarus bus station, walk around corner to hostel.
By car: Call hostel for directions.
By train: Take DART to Connolly Station, then walk along Talbot Street to Frenchmans Lane and turn left to hostel.

Jacobs Inn Hostel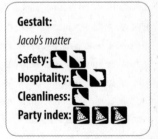

21 Talbot Place, Dublin 1

   Phone: 01-855-5660
   Fax: 01-855-5664
   E-mail: jacobs@isaacs.ie
   Website: isaacs.ie
   Rates: €14–€45 (about $18–$56 US) per person; doubles €70–€80 (about $88–$100 US)
   Credit cards: Yes
   Beds: 295
   Private/family rooms: Yes
   Kitchen available: Yes
   Season: Open year-round
   Office hours: 24 hours
   Lockout: 11 a.m.–3 p.m.
   Affiliation: IHH
   Extras: Meals ($), TV, pool table, bureau de change, laundry, lockers

Incredibly close to Dublin's main bus and train stations (you can see them from the hostel), this big hostel manages to be reasonably friendly and well-kept. It sports good-size dorm rooms—with usually around 6 beds apiece—but also a good supply of doubles, triples, and quads for couples and families. Security could be better, but the location is ace.

Plus there are other amenities, like a little restaurant that stays open all day long, good en-suite bathrooms in the dorms (news flash: showers seem to work), a currency exchange, a television room, free WiFi, and more. The breakfast is no big deal, but that's OK.

Another bonus here? There's live Irish music, Irish dancing, and movies—not all at the same time, thankfully.

But like we said, the negative point here is the size—it's big, and that can mean noise, lines for facilities, and so forth. They do a pretty good job running the place; its own popularity may be its downfall one day. But so far Jacob's remains a good pick.

Gestalt:
Jacob's matter
Safety:
Hospitality:
Cleanliness:
Party index:

How To Get There:

By bus: 2 blocks behind Busarus bus station; ask at station for directions.

By car: Call hostel for directions.

By train: Take DART to Connolly Station, then walk along Talbot Street to Talbot Place; turn left to hostel.

Kinlay House Hostel

2-12 Lord Edward St., Dublin 2

Phone: 01-679-6644

Fax: 01-679-7437

E-mail: info@kinlaydublin.ie

Rates: €15–€30 (about $18–$38 US) per person; doubles €50–€60 (about $63–$75 US)

Credit cards: Yes

Beds: 149

Private/family rooms: Yes

Kitchen available: Yes

Season: Open year-round

Office hours: 24 hours

Affiliation: IHH

Extras: Breakfast, cafe ($), laundry, bike rentals, bureau de change, lockers, TV

S o this is it: the southern Dublin Temple Bar neighborhood you've heard so much about—and Irish rock stars.

And Kinlay House's brick Victorian supplies some of the best-positioned, if not the most comfortable, bunks in town. Beds come packed 4 to 6 to a room, usually, unless you grab one of a dozen or so private rooms (some with en-suite bathrooms, thank goodness). There are also 3 "XC" dorms with 16 to 24 bunks each—lots of camaraderie, sure, but avoid this if you like privacy.

Gestalt:
Kin-do
Safety:
Hospitality:
Cleanliness:
Party index:

Overall, it's a nice building, with great views of town. You'll like the laid-back atmosphere, the laundry, and the continental breakfast they throw in with your bed price. You might love or hate the mostly coed nature of the dorms, though. Cleanliness could be much better, too—it used to be better, in fact. Why?

We'll keep the thumbs up in place for now, but Kinlay House is dangerously close to losing that thumb up.

Be afraid, Kinlay House. Be very afraid.

How To Get There:

By bus: Call hostel for transit route.
By car: Call hostel for directions.
By train: Train station in Dublin; call hostel for transit route.

Mount Eccles Court Hostel

42 North Great Georges St., Dublin 1

Phone: 01-873-0826
Fax: 01-878-3497
E-mail: reservations@eccleshostel.com
Website: eccleshostel.com
Rates: €10–€19.50 (about $13–$25 US) per person, doubles €50–€57 (about $63–$71 US)
Credit cards: Yes
Beds: 115
Private/family rooms: Yes
Kitchen available: Yes
Season: January 3–December 24
Office hours: 24 hours
Affiliation: IHH
Extras: Free Internet access and WiFi, breakfast ($), free parking, TV, garden, pool table

---

This 18th-century Georgian convent is sorta central, sorta not, and the ownership tried to outfit it with the right stuff—a mixture of various sizes of dorms and private and double rooms. Unfortunately, things don't live up to the promise. Dorms are too big—go for a double or quad—and the place isn't well-cleaned or -maintained, a situation that has continued for several years running. Note that the apartments rented out by the hostel are much better than the dorms, hotel-quality. Oh, and here's another reason you might slightly consider staying: The James Joyce Center is practically right next door, so if you're totally gaga over the *Dubliners* author, you might consider the place for a night (not more, please). But you're going to need to hoof it to get to the rest of the city's sights, pubs, and so forth. Repeat: Pass.

Gestalt:
Nun too soon
Safety: ↘
Hospitality: ↘↘
Cleanliness: ↘↘
Party index: 🍸🍸

How To Get There:

By bus or train: Contact hostel for transit route.
By car: Contact hostel for directions.

Oliver St. John Gogarty's Temple Bar Hostel ↘↘

18-21 Anglesea Street (at Fleet), Dublin 2
>   **Phone:** 01-671-1822
>   **E-mail:** info@gogartys.ie
>   **Website:** gogartys.ie/hostel
>   **Rates:** €14–€24 (about $18–$30 US) per person; doubles €50–€62 (about $63–$78 US)
>   **Credit cards:** Yes
>   **Beds:** Number varies
>   **Private/family rooms:** Yes
>   **Kitchen available:** Yes
>   **Season:** Open year-round
>   **Office hours:** 24 hours
>   **Affiliation:** IHH
>   **Extras:** Restaurant, bar, live music, free welcome drink, TV, free WiFi, luggage storage, laundry ($)

🗑

*T*he single reason for staying at this hostel is the super location, a double whammy of good luck: One, it's in Temple Bar. Two, it's next to a pub with the same name as the hostel. Live music abounds. So you can drown your sorrows and sing along to a tune even if you don't like the bunks.

And frankly, you might not. They come packed 6 or 8 or more to a room and are only so-so at best. At least dorms have their own bathrooms. The vibe? Something of a party, not surprising given the locale. Upkeep is about what you'd expect: something between nonexistent and slight.

Gestalt:
Beer and now
Safety:
Hospitality:
Cleanliness:
Party index:

The private apartments here aren't really part of the hostel and cost a lot more—upward of €100 ($125 US) for a quad—but they offer more amenities. However, don't book the "penthouse" section expecting a "penthouse" experience. It's far from that. Skip this upgrade and sleep cheaper in a double room in one of our higher-rated Dublin hostels.

How To Get There:

By bus or train: From Connolly station, take Luas (Light Rail) Red Line to Abbey Street stop and turn left; walk to Ha'penny Bridge, cross bridge through Merchants Arch into Temple Bar, make an immediate left, then take second right. Hostel is at corner. From Heuston Station, take Luas (Light Rail) Red Line to Abbey Street stop; turn right and walk to Quays, cross Ha'penny Bridge, and continue through Merchants Arch into Temple Bar. Make an immediate left, then take second right. Hostel is at corner.

By car: Call hostel for directions.

Sky Backpackers Hostel

2–4 Litton Ln., Dublin 1

> **Phone:** 01-872-8389
> **Fax:** 01-872-0039
> **Website:** littonlane.hostel.com
> **Rates:** €12–€26 (about $15–$33 US) per person; doubles €45–€70 (about $94–$125 US)
> **Credit cards:** Yes
> **Beds:** 96
> **Private/family rooms:** Yes
> **Kitchen available:** Yes
> **Season:** Open year-round
> **Office hours:** 24 hours

Affiliation: IHH

Extras: TV lounge, laundry, free WiFi, luggage storage, breakfast

---

W haaaaat the heck happened here? Talk about location—and history: Sky Backpackers (formerly known as the Litton Lane Hostel) has it in spades. This hostel sits right on the River Liffey, in the thick of Dublin, a short stroll from almost any part of downtown Dublin you're interested in seeing. Hell, this very property used to be a recording studio where freakin' U2

Gestalt:

Litton shame

Safety:

Hospitality:

Cleanliness:

Party index:

themselves laid down tracks (back before they went all techno, we mean). So did Vanmo—excuse us, Van Morrison—who's practically a god in his native land.

But somewhere between there and here, this hostel went from being a pretty good place to a sour-milk dive. They offer the usual bunkrooms (breakfast is included with your rate), plus apartments and private rooms. (The apartments cost in the $100-a-night range, but they're better than the skanky dorms here—partly because they gain you access to special family-friendly amenities like a laundry and kitchen.)

How To Get There:

By bus: From Busarus station, walk ¼ mile along Abbey Street or along river to O'Connell Bridge; hostel is just past bridge, on right, down Litton Lane.

By car: Contact hostel for directions.

By train: From Connolly Station, walk 300 yards to river, turn right, and continue about ⅓ mile to O'Connell Bridge. Hostel is just past bridge, on right, down Litton Lane.

Key to Icons

Attractive natural setting	Comfortable beds	Visual arts at hostel or nearby
Ecologically aware hostel	A particularly good value	Music at hostel or nearby
Superior kitchen facilities or cafe	Wheelchair-accessible	Great hostel for skiers
Offbeat or eccentric place	Good for business travelers	Bar or pub at hostel or nearby
Superior bathroom facilities	Especially well-suited for families	Editors' choice: Among our very favorite hostels
Romantic private rooms	Good for active travelers	

Italy

There's no other place like Italy in the world. Here culture, landscape, food, fashion, and *amore* (that's love) blend together in an intoxicating mixture. You might be a little apprehensive about going off to Italy, what with tales of *mafiosi* and thieves and long lines and such, but after you've been there a week I guarantee you'll never want to leave. Italy is the reason it's always a good idea to ask your airline about the penalties for changing your return date to a later one—a much later one.

Most hostellers will want to hit the big cities first, and we've described them below. But by all means save some time for the Italian countryside, too: Places like Tuscany, Umbria, and Liguria possess some of the most amazing scenery in the world (and some good hostels, too). It'll bring out the artist in you.

Practical Details

Alitalia is Italy's largest airline, but its fares are often higher than those of competitors. Shop around carefully, or take a train from London, Paris, Brussels, or elsewhere; you can catch an overnight train to Italy from just about everywhere in continental Europe. If you want to save money, Eurolines is a good company running comfortable long-distance buses around Europe for very competitive rates—including England to Italy and points between. In Italy, contact Eurolines Italia; their website is eurolines.it.

Once you're here, trains are the best way to get around Italy—just don't count on superefficiency. Sure, it's dirt-cheap to ride by rail, even long-distance (you pay according to distance, with an extra charge on the fastest trains even if you have a Eurail pass). But as for schedules, stations, arrival times? They're all are subject to potential change, so plan ahead to avoid missing connections—and always have a backup plan in case things go wrong or all the train employees go on strike. They often do. (This being Italy, they sometimes actually prepublish the strike dates, just to be courteous.)

Tickets are so cheap here that passes are useful only if you'll be traveling a lot, staying only one or two nights in each place. Italy's Railpass is available in many different permutations, similar to the Eurail pass. Or get a flexible pass.

Remember that trains don't run as frequently on weekends; Saturday is usually the worst day to travel within Italy. International trains and sleeper cars usually run seven days a week. If you want to go to the Italian beaches, for example, lots of trains will be running from the cities to the country on Friday afternoon. Sunday, everyone's either going to the beach or returning home.

Buses are a cheaper, slower ride, useful in parts of Italy where trains simply don't go—reasonably on time, scenic, with lots of locals riding alongside you happy to give advice or opinions or soccer scores. Buy tickets for long-distance buses at the local bus station; buy tickets for city buses at tobacco shops called *tabbachi* ("tabacky"), not from the drivers. Punch your ticket on the bus.

Italy's country code is 39. To call Italian hostels from North America, dial 011-139 and then the numbers AS PRINTED IN THIS BOOK. To call Italian hostels from within Italy, simply dial the numbers AS PRINTED. Don't use loose change or your calling card; instead, rent a cell or buy Telecom Italia phone cards at tobacco shops and other small markets and stick 'em into the slots in the phones. (Push the card all the way in—hard—with the magnetic strip facing up.) Local calls won't eat up much of these cards, but long-distance calls within a country definitely will; figure about 10 or 15 minutes per card at most.

Italy's unit of currency is the euro.

FLORENCE (FIRENZE)

Firenze's wonders can't be overstated, and although you're going to have to wait in line to experience them, the place is really something. The art hanging indoors and the architecture standing outdoors rival anything else in the world. A few words here can't possibly do it all justice, so just go see it. Parts of the city are gorgeous; parts are somewhat dirty and noisy, but you probably won't care. Simply dive in and try to ignore the press of the crowds.

Getting to Florence is easy; walking downtown is, too. Streets radiate outward from the extremely convenient train and bus stations—which, for once, are actually located near the action, across from a great church and just ten minutes' walk from some of the most amazing buildings and paintings in Italy. Get a really good map and use it; the streets can be a bit maddening here. Also watch yourself late at night in dim alleys, and take advantage of lots of American-geared services around town: stores, Internet places, cafes, and the like.

The hostel situation is very good here. This city has five decent hostels, with not a really horrible one in the bunch, and we can honestly say this came as a surprise. Most of the joints aren't very central, but a 15-minute walk will usually get you right into town. Usually.

In short, Firenze's one of a kind. A bit of a madhouse, but we love it.

Ostello Di Archi Rossi

Via Faenza 94r, Firenze 50123

Phone: 055-290-804

Fax: 055-230-2601

E-mail: info@hostelarchirossi.com

Rates: €21–€60 (about $26–$75 US) per person; doubles €50–€90 (about $63–$113 US)

Credit cards: No

Beds: 87

Private/family rooms: Yes

Kitchen available: No

Season: Open year-round

Office hours: 6:30 a.m-2 a.m.

Lockout: 11 a.m.–2:30 p.m.

Curfew: 1 a.m.

Affiliation: None

Extras: Movies, patio, meals ($), free breakfast, lockers, laundry ($), free WiFi and Internet access, kitchenette

Florence (Firenze)

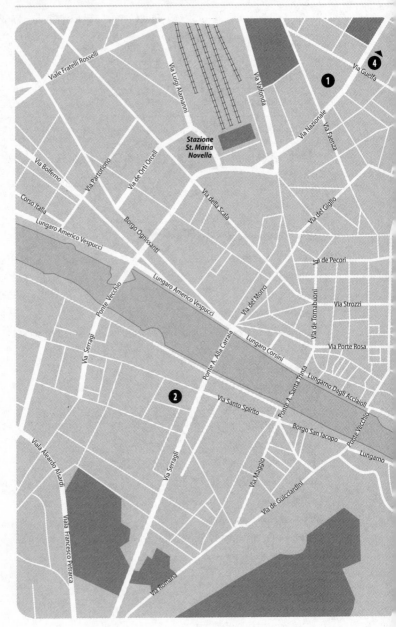

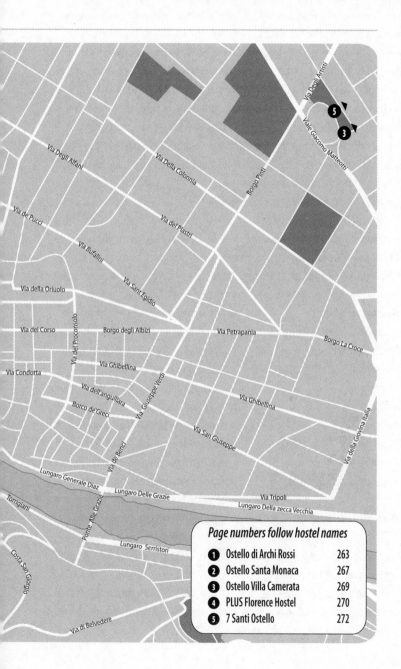

Via Degli Artisti

Via Giacomo Matteotti

5 ◄

3 ◄

Via Degli Alfani

Via Della Colonnia

Via de Pucci

Borgo Pinti

Via del Piastri

Via Bufalini

Via Sant'Egidio

Via della Oriuolo

Via del Corso

Via del Proconsolo

Borgo degli Albizi

Via Petrapania

Borgo La Croce

Via Ghibellina

Via Condotta

Via dell'anguillara

Via Giuseppe Verdi

Via Ghibellina

Via della Giovina Italia

Borco de' Greci

Via San Giuseppe

Via de Benci

Lungaro Generale Diaz

Lungaro Delle Grazie

Via Tripoli

Torrigiani

Lungaro Della zecca Vecchia

Ponte Alle Grazie

Lungaro Serristori

Costa San Giorgio

Via di Belvedere

The Archi Rossi—named for red arches, not for some dude named Archie Rossi—is the kind of place where guests draw their own masterpieces on the walls with hostel-supplied crayons. And it has made quite an impression on hostellers, no longer "merely good" but instead "legitimately great," especially in a town that's a bit hurting for good hostel beds. It isn't grungy like other backpacker-type places in Europe, and it isn't a 24-hour party. In other words, one of the best options in Italy; we can't find anything to complain about here.

The entranceway could easily pass for that of a museum or nice hotel. Inside, it's just as nice: Bunks often come with en-suite bathroom, though they say you should get here by 9 a.m. if you want any hope of getting a bed. We'd take it one step further and advise you to get your butt over there as early as possible. Don't count on calling; they don't take reservations. The 10 private rooms with en-suite bathrooms are especially in demand. Singles, triples, quads, and 5-, 6-, and 9-bed dorms are also available.

The hostel provides a huge and free breakfast buffet (you read those words correctly), free Internet and WiFi access, hot showers, sheets, and blankets; a towel rental will cost you all of half a euro. Guests have access to a microwave and refrigerator—not a full kitchen, but hey, it's something and still appreciated. The hostel cafe serves pizza and pasta dinners 6 nights a week. Showering and other stuff you do in the bathrooms (don't get too fresh) will be enhanced by the very clean facilities. And people love the nice outdoor terrace as a gathering place.

Best bet for a bite:

Il Giardino di Barbano for pizza

What hostellers say:

"Really nice."

Gestalt:

Archi's bunkers

Safety:

Hospitality:

Cleanliness:

Party index:

The staff are very nice and do speak some English. The best thing about this hostel is its location: It's only 5 minutes from the train station and 10 or 15 minutes by foot to such sites as San Lorenzo, Il Duomo, and some nice shopping areas. There's easy access to both the local orange buses that zip (OK, crawl) around Florence and the blue SITA buses, which go off to day trips in the surrounding countryside.

Just bring earplugs to block out those delightful Italian street sounds at night—this is just 2 blocks from Florence's main train station, so it ain't super-quiet even if it is super-convenient for arrivals and departures.

One more bonus? Prices are not rising—they're holding steady despite the crush of visitors and popular press. All in all, a pretty good—heck, make that outstanding—retreat from the hectic hustle and bustle of Florence.

How To Get There:

By bus: From bus station, walk left around corner to train station and cross through station onto via Nazionale. Walk to via Faenza; turn left. Hostel sign is neon blue. Or take via Val Fonda, turn corner at via Cennini, and follow it to via Faenza; cross street. Hostel is on right, marked by blue sign.

By car: Call hostel for directions.

By train: From Firenze Station, exit left onto via Nazionale and walk to via Faenza; turn left. Hostel sign is neon blue. Or take via Val Fonda, turn corner at via Cennini and follow it to via Faenza; cross street. Hostel is on right, marked by blue sign.

By plane: Airport is outside Florence. From airport, take bus to train station stop and walk up via Val Fonda to via Cennini; turn corner and follow via Cennini to via Faenza, then cross street. Hostel is on right, marked by blue sign.

Ostello Santa Monaca (Santa Monaca Hostel)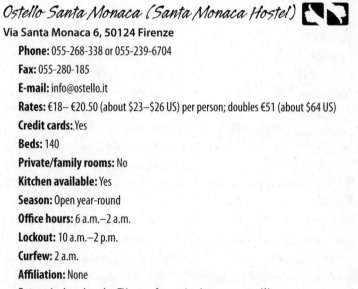

Via Santa Monaca 6, 50124 Firenze

- **Phone:** 055-268-338 or 055-239-6704
- **Fax:** 055-280-185
- **E-mail:** info@ostello.it
- **Rates:** €18– €20.50 (about $23–$26 US) per person; doubles €51 (about $64 US)
- **Credit cards:** Yes
- **Beds:** 140
- **Private/family rooms:** No
- **Kitchen available:** Yes
- **Season:** Open year-round
- **Office hours:** 6 a.m.–2 a.m.
- **Lockout:** 10 a.m.–2 p.m.
- **Curfew:** 2 a.m.
- **Affiliation:** None
- **Extras:** Lockers, laundry, TV room, fax service, Internet access ($)

---

*T*his hostel, located away from the madding crowds on the other side of the Arno (but it's a short walk to the Uffizi across a pretty bridge), provides quiet seclusion and clean bathrooms, to boot. It's OK but basic, and has one big drawback (we'll get to that in a second).

Though not affiliated with HI, it still has some rules, such as a 4-hour lockout starting at 10 a.m. (boo!) and a (more tolerable) 2 a.m. curfew. Neither of those are at all unusual in Florence—deal with it. Booked full? Put yourself on a waiting list during the morning office hours, then hang out in the area.

Dorms border on the claustrophobic, with a minimum of 8 bunks and a maximum of 20 bunks. Ouch! No lockers, either, so if you're sleeping by a door, you'd be smart to chain your stuff to something. However, there's a safe deposit box for small valuables like passports and traveler's checks. It's tight as a tick here, but at least it's kept clean. The kitchen can't be recommended.

Best bet for a bite:
Sugar Blues (organic deli)
Insiders' tip:
Internet cafe just down street
What hostellers say:
"Pretty social."
Gestalt:
Santa's little helper
Safety:
Hospitality:
Cleanliness:
Party index:

You're bound to run into people you've seen scrambling all over Europe in other hostels. You'll look at your traveling partner and say, "Hey, wasn't that the guy who put his foot in my face as he climbed to the top bunk at the Young & Happy in Paris?" or "Wasn't she the loud American who wouldn't shut up?" Yep, they might in fact be the ones, but they could also turn out to be someone you yukked it up with (or thought was cute but were afraid to say anything to).

The big negative here? It is stuffy. No A/C here, and if you're coming to Italy in the summer (many of you will be) you will suffer. Unless you grew up in the Outback, maybe.

Other hostellers object to noisy rooms and small dorms packed with too many bunks, and those concerns are legit. It's a barely passable place in which to rest your head in one of Europe's most culture-soaked towns, but you can do better.

How To Get There:
By bus or train: Call hostel for transit route.
By car: Call hostel for directions.
By plane: Airport outside Florence; call hostel for transit route.

Ostello Villa Camerata (Friendship Village Hostel)

Viale Augusto Righi 2/4, 50137 Firenze

> **Phone:** 055-601-451
> **Fax:** 055-610-300
> **E-mail:** firenze@aighostels.it
> **Rates:** €19–€21 (about $24–$26 US) per HI member; doubles €65 (about $81 US)
> **Credit cards:** No
> **Beds:** 322
> **Private/family rooms:** Yes (none in high season)
> **Kitchen available:** No
> **Season:** Open year-round
> **Office hours:** 24 hours
> **Lockout:** 10:30 a.m.–2 p.m.
> **Curfew:** Midnight
> **Affiliation:** HI-AIG
> **Extras:** Meals ($), bar, library, movies, laundry ($), Internet access, TV, campground, parking, breakfast

*T*his exceptionally popular, Hostelling International–run hostel asks that you reserve months in advance with a letter and credit card deposit, or several weeks ahead if you fax. Bottom line: Don't just show up expecting a bed. (To which we'd add: Don't show up expecting palatial greatness, despite the nifty grounds, greenery on all sides, and handsomeness of the villa.)

We have to say this about Villa Camerata: It's one of the more polarizing hostels in Europe. Some people like this huge hostel for its fabulous gardens and belly-busting pasta-and-salad meals, but underneath that glossy surface it's a pretty basic place. Dorm rooms are fairly standard and nothing special at all; a family wing supplies quad rooms with their own bathrooms—quad rooms that are not

Best bet for a bite:
Il Latini (in city center)
What hostellers say:
"Love it."
Gestalt:
Candid camerata
Safety:
Hospitality:
Cleanliness:
Party index:

available during the peak summer season, we should hasten to add (when you'd most want them if you were traveling with a family). The rooms are aging and far from luxe, but those private bathrooms do come in handy with the kids.

The dining room is a sociable place for exchanging addresses and stories, as are the handsome marble front porch, the Internet center, and most everywhere else here. (Aside: It also seems to be one of the best places in Italy to hook up with others for ride-sharing to future destinations.) And breakfast is included with your bunk, which is always nice.

The big minus here is the usual Hostelling International–in–Europe story: First, this is quite a jaunt from town. You have to ride a city bus for almost half an hour from the Duomo to get out here, and then—if it's late at night—walk a poorly lit half-mile driveway with woods on both sides. A bit creepy-feeling, although in summer things should be hopping enough in the nabe to make you feel safe. Hopefully. There's no kitchen, either, so pack in your food—buy it at the city's fantastic central market, back behind the train station (ask a local if you can't find it). There's a busy campground here, as well.

Oh, and keep in mind that you might occasionally be sharing bunkrooms with school-children who could seriously cramp your style—as will the great distance from town, the hot-and-cold staff, and a half-day lockout that boots you out to the curb for a while. At least wonderful Florence is a half hour away.

How To Get There:

By bus or train: From Firenze Station, exit track 5 and take #17A or #17B bus to hostel stop, walk through gates and follow signs ¼ mile to hostel.
By car: Call hostel for directions.
By plane: Call hostel for transit route.

PLUS Florence Hostel

15 Via Santa Caterina D'Alessandria, 50129 Florence
 Phone: 055-628-6347
 Website: plushostels.com
 Rates: €19–€30 (about $24–$38 US); doubles €80 (about $100 US)
 Credit cards: Yes
 Beds: Number varies
 Private/family rooms: Yes
 Kitchen available: Yes
 Season: Open year-round

Office hours: 24 hours
Affiliation: None
Extras: 2 swimming pools, sauna, bar, restaurant, free WiFi, terrace

"*M*ichelangelo did it in the 15th Century and now PLUS have done it in the 21st."
That's the boast this Florence hostel, one of the originals in the good PLUS Hostels mini-chain, lays down.

And do they live up? Yes and no. The place is good, even very good, and it sports 2 pools and a sauna, but it could be better—it's a bit loud for our taste, and staff varied in their helpfulness.

Anyway, back to those pools and that sauna: The indoor pool, sauna, and Turkish bath are open in winter only, and then an outdoor pool opens for summer only (while those other facilities close down seasonally). There's a base-ment bar called Opera, which almost makes sense in this town.

Dorms are 4-, 6-, and 8-bedded. All have bathrooms, and all beds come with reading lamps and fleece blankets (score). Two caveats here: First, the location is not great—sorta behind the train station, away from the river, the Duomo, the Uffizi, and everything else you've come to see. And sec-ond, the price goes way up in summer.

Still, how many hostels have pools and a sauna? In a town that's sometimes a little too uptight, give it a shot.

> **Best bet for a bite:**
> *Taverna del Bronzino nearby*
> **What hostellers say:**
> *"Pretty good."*
> **Gestalt:**
> *Adult swim*
> **Safety:**
> **Hospitality:**
> **Cleanliness**
> **Party index:**

How To Get There:

By train: From Santa Maria Novella station, exit by pharmacy to street. Cross street and turn right; turn left at McDonald's on Via Largo Fratelli Alinari and walk ¾ mile along Via Nazionale through Piazza Indipendenza to Via di Santa Caterina d'Alessandria. Hostel is on left.

By bus: Exit bus station, exit into Piazza della Stazione. Cross street to McDonald's and turn left onto Largo Fratelli Alinari. Continue ¾ mile along Via Nazionale through Piazza Indipen-denza to Via di Santa Caterina d'Alessandria. Hostel is on left.

By car: Contact hostel for directions.

7 Santi Ostello (7 Saints Hostel)

Viale dei Mille 11, 50131 Firenze

> **Phone:** 055-504-8452
>
> **E-mail:** info@7santi.com
>
> **Website:** 7santi.com
>
> **Rates:** €14–€24 (about $18–$30 US) per person; doubles €78 (about $98 US)
>
> **Credit cards:** No
>
> **Beds:** 180
>
> **Private/family rooms:** Yes
>
> **Kitchen available:** No
>
> **Season:** Open year-round
>
> **Office hours:** Vary; call for hours
>
> **Affiliation:** None
>
> **Extras:** Bar, TV, laundry, fax, free WiFi, meals ($)

*P*art of a convent beside the Church of the Sette Santi (Seven Saints), this relatively new hostel touts its central location near Campo di Marte and amenities as reasons to pay extra cash for a night's stay. To be sure, it's a big and attractive place, but not perfect despite the cost. (Curiously, annual infestations of mosquitoes are one of the negatives to watch out for.)

Singles, doubles, and bunks in quad to 6-bed dorm rooms are priced according to a fairly complicated structure based on size and bathroom availability. Positives include telephones on each floor (though you may have to search for one that works; they sometimes conk out), a sports field, a laundry, and fax service. They don't give you a free breakfast but do serve a pretty decent dinner (you have to pay, of course).

Downsides? A few. It isn't kept perfectly clean, which is a bit of a surprise, and it's not always comfortable inside the bunkrooms. We'll give it a marginal nod this time around—but we're watching you, 7 Santi.

Best best for a bite: Affrico

What hostellers say:
"Not very close to town."

Gestalt:
Santi clause

Safety:

Hospitality:

Cleanliness:

Party index:

How To Get There:

By car: From the northern A11 superhighway, follow signs to exit for Artemio Franchi (soccer stadium). Football Stadium; from the southern A11, follow signs to SP127 (local highway) and Artemio Franchi soccer stadium.

By bus: Take #17 bus to Chiesa dei Sette Santi stop; walk 1 block to hostel.

By train: From Santa Maria Novella Station, take #17 bus to Chiesa dei Sette Santi stop; walk 1 block to hostel.

MILAN (MILANO)

Milano, way up in the center of the flat northern part of the country, is Italy's style and power capital—a city defined by Gucci fashion shows, execs power-lunching with cell phones glued to their ears, and everyone looking just a little too perfect. It's also a place experiencing a surprising recent upswing in violent crime, so look sharp at night. There really isn't as much to see in Milan as you might think—the stock exchange is more symbolic of its current role in Italian society—but the *duomo* (cathedral) here is one of the country's finest and well worth finding, even if it is quite a hike from the main train station. Take the city subway to get there.

Attractive natural setting	Comfortable beds	Visual arts at hostel or nearby
Ecologically aware hostel	A particularly good value	Music at hostel or nearby
Superior kitchen facilities or cafe	Wheelchair-accessible	Great hostel for skiers
Offbeat or eccentric place	Good for business travelers	Bar or pub at hostel or nearby
Superior bathroom facilities	Especially well-suited for families	Editors' choice: Among our
Romantic private rooms	Good for active travelers	very favorite hostels

Key to Icons

Ostello Piera Rotta Milano (Piero Rotta Milan Hostel)

Via Salmoraghi 1 (at via Calliano), 20148 Milano

Phone: 02-392-67095

Fax: 02-330-00191

E-mail: milano@aighostels.ie

Rates: €20.50–€21.50 (about $26–$27 US) per HI member; doubles €46–€60 (about $58–$75 US)

Credit cards: Yes

Beds: 330

Private/family rooms: Yes

Kitchen available: No

Season: January 13–December 24 and December 27-December 31

Office hours: 24 hours

Lockout: 9:30 a.m.–3:30 p.m.

Curfew: 1 a.m.

Affiliation: HI-AIG

Extras: Internet access, gardens, TV, lockers, fax, bar

*T*his place obviously has little of the easygoing attitude pervasive at other northern Italian hostels; the no-exceptions lockout and strict lights-out policy could sour your experience. Definitely don't come here expecting lots of warm and fuzzy vibes. It's got some positives and negatives, but we can't give it a full recommendation.

We'll concede that the hostel's location can be serene, on the outskirts of town, but this could seriously cramp your partying style, since you have to return by the 1 a.m. curfew. But we've also heard that on some nights crowds of teens gather on the front lawn, talking and smoking. There's a 3-day-max stay, too.

Best bet for a bite:
La Nuova Tavernetta

What hostellers say:
"Are we anywhere near the downtown?"

Gestalt:
Milan-dollar hotel

Safety:

Hospitality:

Cleanliness:

Party index:

Your only consolation? Milano isn't really a destination. It's more of a business center, where fashion, design, and movie powerhouses operate and tourists find little to do. It's a mighty convenient transit hub, however, with lots of high-speed trains going all over Europe and lots of flights heading off to North America.

You are almost always guaranteed a room here, at least, so don't worry too much about being shut out. (You can always call ahead to be sure.) Beds are poor quality, though, and bathrooms are just short of a horror show. Bring your own T.P. We can't emphasize this enough.

One minor good point: They've recently restructured the layout a bit here, cutting down on total bed count, adding some much-needed private rooms and reducing (slightly) the number of huge dorms. There are currently 3 single rooms, 4 doubles, 5 triples, 22 quads, and (eek) 36 dorms of five or more beds. That's actually a bit of an improvement over the previous setup.

Remember that Milano empties out in August—completely—so that's the worst time to come here. Nothing is open. Nothing. DO NOT COME IN AUGUST. There. We warned you.

Still, this is the cheapest possible lodging option in one of Italy's most expensive cities. And it's certainly clean and well run (if you like Gestapo tactics), if a tad hospital-like. No, make that dentist-like—a dentist with more than 300 chairs.

How To Get There:

By bus: Take bus #68, #90, or #91 to hostel stop, then walk 200 yards to hostel.
By plane: Two airports. Milano Linate is 15 kilometers (about 10 miles) from hostel; Milano Malpensa is 40 kilometers (about 25 miles) from hostel. Call hostel for transit routes.
By subway: Contact hostel for transit route.
By train: Centrale Station, 5 miles from hostel; contact hostel for transit route.

ROME (ROMA)

Chances are, if you've come to Italy, you're going to end up in Rome sooner or later. We've just got two words to say before we leave you off here: Good luck.

Seriously, if you're flying into Rome, don't even try to deal with the chaos while jet-lagged. Instead, we'd recommend that you grab a train straight from the airport (which is south of the city) and head away to Naples, one of its associated islands, or the beautiful

Rome (Roma)

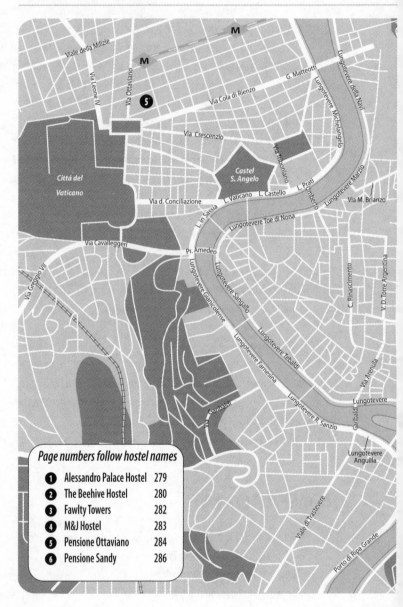

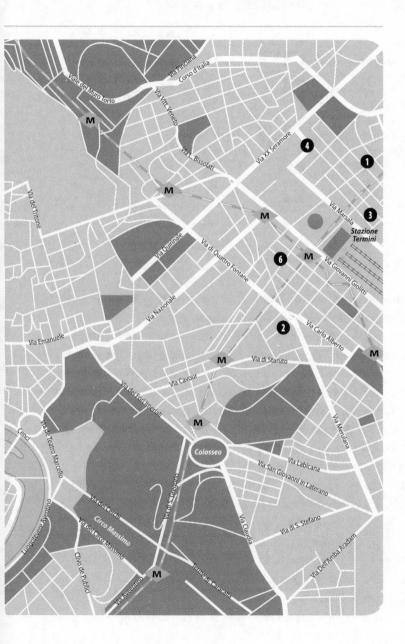

ROME HOSTELS AT A GLANCE

	RATING	PRICE	IN A WORD	PAGE
The Beehive		€25–€35	homey	p. 280
Alessandro Palace Hostel		€22–€35	fine	p. 279
Pensione Ottaviano		€25–€33	tiny	p. 284
Fawlty Towers		€25–€65	yikes	p. 282
Pensione Sandy		€21–€33	small	p. 286
M & J Hostel		€20–€30	mediocre	p. 283

Amalfi coast—somewhere south of Rome on the blue ocean where you could catch up on sleep and prepare mentally for the cauldron that is Rome.

Once there, you'd have to be nuts to rent or drive a car—and we're pretty crazy when it comes to driving. But this is one place where we threw our hands up and cried uncle. Use the bus system, which may be hard to understand at first but does the job. Taxi drivers appear to be insane but are actually pretty savvy. The Metropolitan (subway) can be quite useful.

Coming by train? Be extra careful around the Stazione Termini, the main train station where most Roman hostellers arrive. This area—as well as several of the busiest tourist areas in the city, such as the Spanish Steps—is notorious for thieves and pickpockets. Don't wear that expensive camera around your neck, don't flash too much cash, don't wear shorts that advertise your greenhorn status, don't walk alone down tiny alleys at night, and don't pay attention to the hordes of kids who'll do anything—even toss a baby in your face—to occupy you for just the moment it takes to snatch your wallet. Our advice: Wear a money belt.

As for the hostel scene: It's going downhill. To be honest, we can recommend only two of the seven hostels in the city, and one of them is so small that it's probably going to be full. This doesn't bode well for the discriminating hosteller, who may have to suck it up and stay in a divey joint for a night or two. (Our advice? Consider a cheap hotel if our top picks are full.)

Other advice? Well, when in Rome, do as the Romans do. Whatever that means.

Alessandro Palace Hostel

Via Vicenza 42, Roma 00185

   Phone: 064-461-958

   Fax: 064-938-0534

   E-mail: info@hostelsalessandro.com

   Website: hostelsalessandro.com

   Rates: €22–€35 (about $28–$44 US) per person; doubles €88–€120 (about $110–$150 US)

   Credit cards: Yes

   Beds: 53

   Private/family rooms: Yes

   Kitchen available: Yes

   Season: Open year-round

   Office hours: 24 hours

   Affiliation: None

   Extras: TV, coffee, bar, free WiFi, fridge (some units), lockers, safe (some units)

This hostel remains a very good choice in Rome. The young staff, pub, train-side position, and laid-back atmosphere at Alessandro's more than make up for a bit of a tight fit in some of the dorm rooms here and the slightly chaotic streetside location (but hey, this is Rome—everything's chaotic). You can avail yourself of cooking facilities as well as free-flowing coffee and pizza parties when they happen. The lack of a curfew could mean people traipsing in at later hours of the night and making your attempts at sleep futile. Caveat emptor.

Still, it's a pretty good pick. Management seems to encourage travelers to get to know one another over glasses of vino, and overall things have seemed to get incrementally better here year by year; give it a chance if you want a central bunk in Roma. And the newish annex to the Palace—only about a minute's

What hostellers say:
"Better than I expected."

Gestalt:
Alessandro in wonderland

Safety:

Hospitality:

Cleanliness:

Party index:

walk from the home base hostel—is even better. All rooms in that building are kitted out with televisions, small refrigerators, WiFi access, lockboxes or lockers, and air-conditioning. You can book rooms with or without private bathrooms in this annex; of course, the ones with privies cost a bit more, but we definitely would spring for those if traveling as a couple or a family.

This isn't the lap of luxury, but hey, this is Italy—you're going to spend most of your time outside anyway. And if you can accept that it's a bunk, it's actually a pretty good one.

How To Get There:

By bus: Call hostel for transit route.

By car: Call hostel for directions.

By train: From Termini station walk along via Marsala approximately 65 feet and turn left onto via Vicenza. Walk about 4 blocks to hostel.

The Beehive Hostel

Via Marghera 8, Roma 00185

>**Phone:** 064-470-4553
>
>**E-mail:** info@the-beehive.com
>
>**Website:** the-beehive.com
>
>**Rates:** €25–€35 (about $31–$44 US) per person; doubles €65–€115 (about $76–$144 US)
>
>**Credit cards:** Yes
>
>**Beds:** 23
>
>**Private/family rooms:** Yes
>
>**Kitchen available:** No
>
>**Season:** Open year-round
>
>**Office hours:** 24 hours
>
>**Affiliation:** None
>
>**Extras:** Alarm clocks, hair dryer, luggage storage, walking and biking tours, earplugs, safe, garden, free WiFi and Internet access, art gallery, yoga classes, cafe, bar

---

*I*t wasn't that long ago that Rome desperately needed a friendly and clean hostel—and then it got one! The owners of the Beehive, an American couple who chucked the prefab life of Los Angeles for the joy of running a small hostel in Rome, opened this place and, right from the outset, were clearly focused on keeping their guests happier than happy. The good location and a slew of additions ramped up the cool factor, and it quickly became apparent this small, homey joint was Rome's best hostel. It still is; it probably will be forever, at this rate. It's one of the best urban hostels in all of Europe, in fact.

Only one problem: It's small (which is not even really a problem). There's only a single dorm room here, with just 8 beds, plus 7 double private rooms (one of which can actually accommodate three travelers). So you're almost certainly going to be turned away just due to the awesome popularity of this awesome place. They do work with a local network to manage some off-site single and double rooms, too (with cooking facilities), so they're dealing with the popularity factor. Still, it's best if you can book into the original 'Hive simply to get the wonderful experience of being here.

The hostel is close to the action, in the hip and energetic neighborhood near one of the biggest train stations in Europe (Termini). Dorm rooms are bright and spacious, if slightly spartan. In traditional Italian fashion, there are no rugs covering the tiled floors, but these rooms are outfitted with modern furniture, and most of them are doubles—it's almost like a secret little hotel. There's also one coed dormitory containing 8 beds. Rates are reasonable for such a desirable location. Beds have reading lamps; some of the bathrooms have tubs. In all, you'll be well taken care of here, and you won't have to worry about dodgy accommodations in questionable pensiones. There is also a vegetarian cafe on the premises, which replaced the hostel kitchen and extends the green ethic. They serve great baked goods, coffee, homemade pancakes, and the like. At night you can buy and drink a glass of wine outdoors beneath fruit trees. How much more Roma can you get?

When the Beehive moved to its present, quieter location (it was originally elsewhere), the owners added a very popular garden—sometimes referred to as the "outdoor living room"—and eliminated their previous lockout rule, expanded office hours, hooked up free

Best bet for a bite:
Naschmarkt
Insiders' tip:
Knock on the correct door!
What hostellers say:
"Like sleeping with friends! Um, 10 friends."
Gestalt:
Believable
Safety:
Hospitality:
Cleanliness:
Party index:

Internet access, and created a mini-guidebook to Rome for guests to tote around town. Good? That's not all. They sometimes host yoga and shiatsu classes in the space, and rotating art exhibits have been known to showcase the work of local artists.

Could this place be any better? Honestly, we don't think so. It could only be bigger. But then it might not be better anymore. The chicken or the egg . . . Anyway, enjoy it if you can.

How To Get There:
By bus or train: From Termini station, exit to right (north side of station) past Cafe Trombetta and continue straight across via Marsala to via Marghera; continue 2 blocks to hostel on left.
By car: Contact hostel for directions.

Fawlty Towers
Via Magenta 39, Roma 00185
   Phone: 064-450-374 or 064-454-802
   Fax: 064-543-5942
   E-mail: info@fawltytowers.org
   Website: fawltytowers.org
   Rates: €25–€65 (about $31–$76 US) per person; doubles €75–€85 (about $94–$106 US)
   Credit cards: Yes
   Beds: 150
   Private/family rooms: Yes
   Kitchen available: Yes
   Season: Open year-round
   Office hours: 24 hours
   Affiliation: None
   Extras: Terrace, Internet access, TV room, air-conditioning

---

*N*o, there's no bumbling bellhop named Manuel here or owner Basil Fawlty finding himself constantly in compromising positions. This hostel just borrowed its name from a popular British comedy that starred ex–Monty Python funny guy John Cleese.

But that's the only funny thing about this hostel, and if you stay here, the joke's on you—because things have fallen right off a cliff. Unclean, overcrowded, poorly managed: check, check, check.

Rooms are too small, not well cleaned enough, and either chilly or too stuffy (temperature control seems to be a serious issue here, in both winter and summer). Don't expect anything like good customer service. Even the double private rooms are no relief.

The one positive is that hostellers seem to enjoy the social terrace that assists in bonding with fellow bunkmates. On second thought, maybe they're just trying to escape from those awful dorms.

Give it a pass.

What hostellers say:
"How could anyone recommend this?"
Gestalt:
Fawlty wiring
Safety:
Hospitality:
Cleanliness:
Party index:

How To Get There:

By bus: Hostel is within walking distance.
By car: Call hostel for directions.
By train: Train station adjacent to hostel.

M & J Hostel

Via Solferino 9, Roma

Phone: 064-462-802
Fax: 064-462-802
E-mail: info@mejplacehostel.com
Website: mejplacehostel.com
Rates: €20–€30 (about $25–$38 US) per person; doubles €80–€90 (about $100–$113 US)
Credit cards: No
Beds: 50
Private/family rooms: Yes
Kitchen available: Yes
Season: Open year-round
Office hours: 24 hours
Affiliation: None
Extras: Radio, TV, refrigerator, bar, ceiling fans

*T*his hostel has always been bad, but it just seems to be getting even worse over time; it remains one of your worst choices in Rome, even while it markets itself as a place that has it all for young backpackers who want "luxe" amenities like a hostel TV, in-house bar, fridge, and ceiling fans (huh? how about some A/C?). Note to hostel: These amenities mean next to nothing when you're staying in such a poorly run place, one that has the temerity to then ding you for extra charges for things good hostels don't charge anything for.

It's certainly a social place, but it gets too cramped during the summer high season. We can't understand why, because it's usually not clean enough. Sagging beds, grimy rooms, and even the possibility of creeping critters—things aren't getting any better over time, despite the complaints. In fact, they might be getting worse. This place almost merited our coveted "turkey" award.

No, no, no. Do not stay here.

Best bet for a bite:
Coffee bar across road from Termini station
What hostellers say:
"Is 'the worst' a rating?"
Safety: 🔪
Hospitality: 🔪
Cleanliness: 🔪
Party index: 🎉🎉🎉🎉

How To Get There:

By bus: From Termini station, exit through main exit to main road. Turn right and cross at to via Solferino. Or exit onto via Marsala and turn left; at traffic light, turn right onto via Solferino.

By car: Follow Centro signs to Termini station; via Solferino is nearby.

By train: From Termini station, exit through main exit to main road. Turn right and cross at to via Solferino. Or exit onto via Marsala and turn left; at traffic light, turn right onto via Solferino.

Pensione Ottaviano (Ottaviano Home Hostel)

Via Ottaviano 6, Roma 00192

> **Phone:** 063-973-8138
> **Fax:** 065-574-857
> **E-mail:** info@pensioneottaviano.com
> **Website:** pensioneottaviano.com
> **Rates:** €25–€33 (about $31–$41 US) per person, doubles €100 (about $120 US)

Credit cards: Yes
Beds: Number varies
Private/family rooms: Yes
Kitchen available: No
Season: Open year-round
Office hours: 7 a.m.–midnight
Lockout: 10 a.m.–2 p.m.
Affiliation: None
Extras: TV, lockers, Internet access

This independent hostel sits close to St. Peter's, a mere block from the Vatican. Yes. The Vatican.

But while it started out with so much promise, it has never really delivered since. Run by the same folks who own Pensione Sandy (see p. 286), it's close to the action, sure. Staff are helpful, and you're welcome to use the hostel's Internet access to keep in touch with your envious pals back home. But you need to bear in mind that this place is small, crowded, and somewhat beat-up: no comfy beds or new furniture here. It used to be kept spotless, but those days are long gone; now it's so-so at best, and sometimes downright grungy.

What hostellers say:
"Pass the rosary beads."
Gestalt:
Popeless
Safety:
Hospitality:
Cleanliness:
Party index:

Some of the rooms do have their own refrigerators, though. Access to all of Rome's wonders from the Metro stop is just a short stroll away. The ambience inside the place is rather bland, and common space is almost a nonentity (the lounge basically doubles/triples as the kitchen and reception area). Bathrooms are so-so at best. The crowd was almost 100 percent Aussie and American when we visited.

The place has seen better days, and it's hardly comfortable. But it is homey and relaxed. You make the call—if you're really intent on seeing the Vatican and don't expect perfection, stay a night. With the kids or not going Catholic? Skip it.

How To Get There:

By bus or train: Take metro line A (toward Battistini) to Ottaviano station; walk along Via Ottaviano to hostel at No. 6.

By car: Call hostel for directions.

By subway: Take metro line A (toward Battistini) to Ottaviano station; walk along via Ottaviano to hostel at No. 6.

Pensione Sandy (Sandy Hostel)

Via Cavour 136, Roma 00184

> **Phone:** 064-884-585
> **E-mail:** info@sandyhostel.com
> **Website:** sandyhostel.com
> **Rates:** €21–€33 (about $26–$41 US) per person; doubles €70–€100 (about $88–$120 US)
> **Credit cards:** Yes
> **Beds:** 30
> **Private/family rooms:** Sometimes
> **Kitchen available:** No
> **Season:** Open year-round
> **Office hours:** 7 a.m.–midnight
> **Affiliation:** None

The hostels in Rome are basically all just getting worse, except for the top two (consult our handy chart on p. xxx if you're confused). This one in particular has seen a real decline in cleanliness and comfort. Bring your Tiger Balm to soothe your back after you schlep your backpack up the 4 flights of stairs to reach this small hostel. But once here, you'll be welcomed into a fairly hoppin' scene. Beds are cots rather than bunks, but at least you'll be sharing your room with only two to four other folks.

It's really close to the Coliseum, just a couple blocks, but that's the only good thing we say about the place. (In fact, you're central to a lot of the sights that attracted you to the "mother of civilization" in the first place, like the Santa Maria Maggiore church.) However,

Best bet for a bite:
Pizza bars around the station

What hostellers say:
"Oh my God, no."

Safety:

Hospitality:

Cleanliness:

Party index:

you're also painfully close to the Stazione Termini—Rome's central train station—so you'll want to watch yourself after dark.

But it doesn't matter how close it is to anything or everything. The aging furnishings, bad smell, filth, and management that doesn't seem to care much add up to a big fail. This has gone from once being a serviceable option in the city we love to one we absolutely can't ever recommend to anyone in a million years.

Worst place in town? We think so. And in Rome, that is saying something.

How To Get There:
By car: Call hostel for directions.

By train: From Termini station, exit station near track #22 and walk 7 blocks along Via Cavour to hostel on left.

By subway: Take Metro line B toward Laurentina station to Cavour Colosseo station. Walk uphill along Via Cavour to hostel.

VENICE (VENEZIA)

You're gonna come here, and the only way to get around is by boat or on foot. So when you arrive at Santa Lucia train station, the first thing you want to do is grab a *vaporetto* (commuter boat) downtown. Take the #82 line to get to the center fast if you must, but we prefer the #1 boat—it's super-scenic and gets you right into the sights at once.

To walk around, get a great map and watch for little bridges and side canals; when you get lost (you will), ask locals to point you back toward San Marco plaza at the center of it all, or else just find signs and troop off again.

VENICE HOSTELS AT A GLANCE

	RATING	PRICE	IN A WORD	PAGE
Ostello Santa Fosca	◣	€10–€30	quiet	p. 291
Alloggi Gerotto Calderan	◣	€21–€27	decent	p. 290
Ostello Venezia	◣◥	€25	marginal	p. 292

Venice (Venezia)

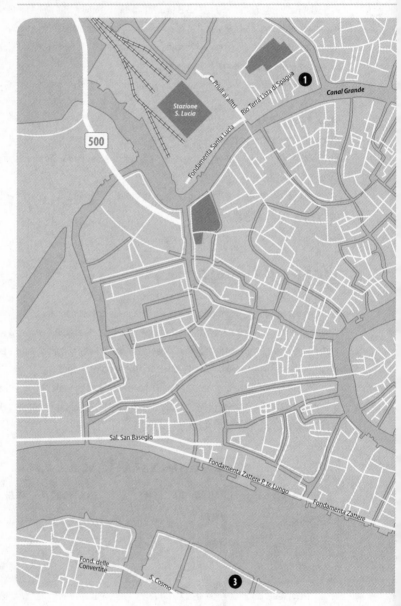

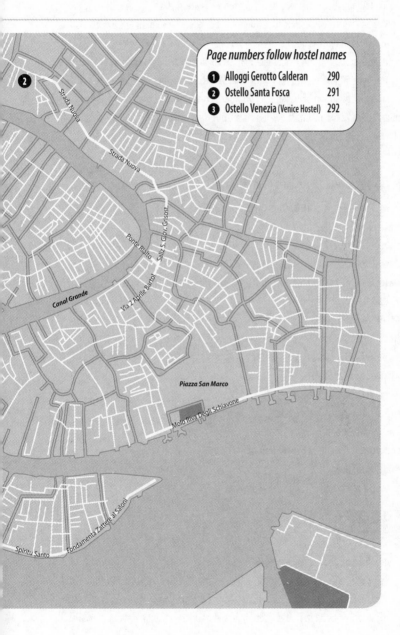

Quite convenient are the many smaller picturesque gondolas: They appear to have been built for tourists, but actually they ferry residents across the bigger canals all day long for a pittance. Avoid the rip-off gondola tours and buy a regular commuter ticket on a cross-city boat instead; it's just as good.

There's a surprising and serious lack of hostel beds here, though. The only big and legit one is the huge HI joint—and it's not even in Venice proper, but on another island. Two little places rent out dorm beds, but they only partly resemble true hostels. Lots of religious organizations in Venice maintain dorms as well, but their strict curfews and no-unmarried-couples rules kept 'em out of this book.

Alloggi Gerotto Calderan

Campo San Geremia 283, Cannaregio, Venezia 30121

Phone: 041-716-048
Fax: 041-275-9217
E-mail: info@casagerottocalderan.com
Rates: €21–€27 (about $26–$34 US) per person; doubles €46–€110 (about $59–$133 US)
Credit cards: No
Beds: 30
Private/family rooms: Yes
Kitchen available: No
Season: Open year-round
Office hours: Vary, contact hostel for current hours
Curfew: 12:30 a.m.
Lockout: 10:30 a.m.–2 p.m. (dorms only)
Affiliation: None
Extras: Internet access ($)

N ote: Must be age 35 or younger to book dormitories.

A passable place, decent enough as a pick though it definitely has its off nights. This little hostel, near the city's Santa Lucia train station (in other words, where land gives way to water), surprised us a bit. It offers both bunks in a variety of configurations as well as a bunch of nicer private rooms, giving hostellers the best of both worlds. And, bully for you, showers are included in the rate. They're pretty nice for hostel showers, that's for sure. The place is both kept clean and staffed by friendly folks. Some rooms look out onto the Campo St. Geremia square, with its eye-catching church and palace.

Gestalt:
Have Venice day
Safety:
Hospitality:
Cleanliness:
Party index:

Now for the downsides. (Get your pencil.) There are not a lot of extras, at all—even Internet access costs you. They don't take credit cards, which may or may not be an annoyance to you. An even bigger issue was the temperature control: They don't exactly have it mastered, if you know what we mean. Then there's the midday lockout, which is only administered to dormitories. How is that fair? The final negative thing to keep in mind is that this is a walk-up hostel . . . and it's 4 floors tall. Pack light.

As we said, this place still gets a passing grade . . . but not by a whole lot. Also remember that while it boasts that good location near Santa Lucia where you'll almost surely arrive from other Italian parts, this hostel is not central to the rest of the action for which Venice is justly famous. You'll need to take the *vaporetto* and gondola boats to get there, or hoof it.

You might enjoy the quiet Venetian suburb of Canaregio, though, if you will roll into town very late or need to get out on an early train.

How To Get There:
By boat: From Santa Lucia Station, contact hostel for transit route.

Ostello Santa Fosca
Fondamenta Canal, Cannaregio 2372, Venezia 30121
    Phone: 041-715-775
    Fax: 041-715-775
    Website: ostellosantafosca.it
    E-mail: ostello@santafosca.it
    Rates: €10–€30 (about $13–$38 US) per person; doubles €30–€70 (about $38–$88 US)
    Credit cards: Yes
    Beds: 140 (winter: 30)
    Private/family rooms: Yes
    Kitchen available: Yes (summer only)

Season: Open year-round
Office hours: 7:30–noon and 4 p.m.–12:30 a.m. (summer); 8 a.m.–noon and 5–8
p.m. (winter)
Lockout: 9:30 a.m.–noon
Curfew: 12:30 a.m.
Affiliation: None
Extras: Game room, courtyard, WiFi ($), lockers ($)

A former convent, this hostel feels a bit like one (curfews galore). But it's a good place to bunk for a night or two if you don't mind the stripped-downness. The Santa Fosca has both dorm rooms and doubles; thumbs down, though, as we said, to the half-day lockout that lasts from 9:30 in the morning till noon. Yes, Venice is one great town, but sometimes we-the-jet-lagged need to simply kick back for a few minutes and decompress.

What hostellers say:
"Um, foosball, anyone?"
Gestalt:
Convent-ional
Safety:
Hospitality:
Cleanliness:
Party index:

College kids will appreciate the hostel (which is open year-round, unlike some Euro-hostels) for its relaxed 'tude and diversions to keep things loose. You can't hang out inside the hostel here all day, due to the aforementioned all-morning lockout, but it's still a good place within walking distance of some sights. Unfortunately, you get nicked for almost everything, including WiFi access (whaaaa?) and even the lockers. Ah, well.

How To Get There:
By boat: From train station, walk left along the main street over 3 bridges. Turn left over bridge at the P. S. Fosca and left along canal.

Ostello Venezia (Venice Hostel)
Fondamenta Zitelle 86, Isola della Guidecca, 30133 Venezia
Phone: 342-576-7349
Fax: 041-523-5689
E-mail: info@ostellovenezia.it
Website: hostelvenice.org

Rates: €25 (about $31 US) per HI member
Credit cards: Yes
Beds: 243
Private/family rooms: No
Kitchen available: No
Season: Closed December 11–28
Office hours: 7 a.m.–midnight
Affiliation: HI-AIG
Extras: Breakfast, meals ($), bar

---

*T*his place is backsliding fast. Too bad, because it had potential (if not centrality). Located inside an optimally placed former warehouse with a view of San Marco—from across the canal on the island of Guidecca, you understand—this place really packs 'em in and always seems booked full. Venice is probably the biggest destination for tourists in Italy, more so in summer, so reserve way in advance if you want a bunk in this somewhat strict hostel.

Still, it's fairly friendly and—best of all—efficient. Just remember that you'll have to take a little boat out to a remote island from central Venice, then haul your carcass and your backpack up steep flights of stairs. (Some hostellers compared it to Alcatraz. We can see why: You'll never escape late at night.)

Other complaints have been lodged about the plumbing: specifically, the showers. They have a tendency to run on the lukewarm side. Of course, being that the hostel is located next to really prime real estate, it gets supercrowded, and with crowds comes a lot of noise. If you're still coming, bring your earplugs to drown out the cacophony of sounds made by those who are sleeping and those who aren't. (When you see the architecture, you'll get why noise bounces around the place.) Meals are served here, but for some reason wine and other spirits are banned. That definitely could be a bummer if you're looking to imbibe.

Best bet for a bite:
Back on the mainland?
What hostellers say:
"Has fallen so fast."
Gestalt:
LOST
Safety: 🌑
Hospitality: 🌑🌗
Cleanliness: 🌑🌗
Party index: 🎉🎉🎉

AIG has heard about but failed to address this hostel's significant number of defects. The sad verdict? This island-bound bunk is almost no longer an option; it's edging dangerously close to thumbs-down territory.

How To Get There:

By boat: From Venezia train station, take *vaporetto* #41, #42, or #82 (costs roughly €1, takes about half an hour) to Zitelle stop. Bear right and walk 150 yards to hostel.

Luxembourg

This is a pretty small country to work into your itinerary: tiny, hilly, terribly expensive, and schizophrenic. But then, what would you expect from a place surrounded by all those other countries? And it's true that you can hear strains of German, French, and Flemish here in one place. It's worth an overnight jump off the train if you're passing through (you might be), and the countryside is nice.

There's only one big city to speak of—the capital city, with the same name as the country—and the cost of living is prohibitively high. Yet there are surprising numbers of English-speakers here, possibly due to liberal banking laws that encourage foreign holding companies to place their assets here in lovely Luxy. The official tongue of this land is French, but most residents speak German and English, too, so you'll find your language pretty well understood.

Key to Icons

Attractive natural setting	Comfortable beds	Visual arts at hostel or nearby
Ecologically aware hostel	A particularly good value	Music at hostel or nearby
Superior kitchen facilities or cafe	Wheelchair-accessible	Great hostel for skiers
Offbeat or eccentric place	Good for business travelers	Bar or pub at hostel or nearby
Superior bathroom facilities	Especially well-suited for families	Editors' choice: Among our very favorite hostels
Romantic private rooms	Good for active travelers	

294

Interestingly, the tiny country has always played a major role in European politics, getting a number of high officials elected to European Union and European Commission posts. The so-called father of modern Europe, Robert Schumann, was a native, too.

The dozen or so hostels here are all generally good, geared to school groups, outdoorsy types, and families. If you're keen on seeing a number of them, you should definitely find out about the Sentiers des Auberges de Jeunesse—or Jugendherbergs Wanderfade in German—a series of hiking trails that connect some of the rural hostels here. They're marked with classy blue-and-white signs in the woods and proceed through stone steps and hills from hostel to hostel. We only cover the main "city" hostel here.

Practical Details

Getting here isn't easy and it isn't hard. By train, you will usually connect through Strasbourg, Paris, Köln (Cologne), or Brussels. Almost all trains coming to Luxembourg go right through the capital city.

By plane, many flights from the US on Icelandair land in Luxembourg after a quick stop in Iceland. European cities are pretty well connected to the tiny capital city, too, especially through the national carrier, Luxair (luxair.lu), and its direct flights from London, Paris, Nice, Rome, and other key places. British Airways also flies from London's Gatwick Airport, and SAS can get you here from Copenhagen.

There are few train lines in Luxembourg, so you might need to supplement your journey with a bus ticket unless you're staying in the capital. Train passes are a waste of time here unless you'll be touring Belgium and the Netherlands extensively, so just buy point-to-point tickets. (You can find regional pass details in the Belgium and Netherlands chapters.) Hostellers might be wise, however, to buy a Luxembourg Card, which sets you back €11 (about $14 US) per day—you get a small discount on the extra days for two- or three-day cards—and gives you free or discounted admission to lots of attractions plus free use of public transit throughout the duchy. You can get the card at many hostels, hotels, campgrounds, and tourist information offices.

Luxembourg's monetary unit is the euro, and you'll need plenty of cash here. This is a relatively expensive country.

Luxumbourg's phone code is 352. To dial Luxembourg's hostel from the US, dial 011-352, then the number AS PRINTED. Luxembourg is so small that there is no initial zero or city code, unlike most other European countries. From inside the country, dial the number EXACTLY AS IT'S PRINTED HERE. Mail runs efficiently, and you'll find some unusual stamps if you look for 'em; this isn't Liechtenstein, but they're still interesting enough.

LUXEMBOURG CITY

Luxembourg City is, quite simply, the capital of the country and its only true metropolis. It's a bit like Monaco: a city unto itself, where everyone seems to possess incredible wealth (and they do). Getting around is a snap: The place is compact enough that you can walk anywhere—with a little huffing and puffing due to the hills—and there's also a bus system for outlying areas, though you probably won't need to worry about those at all.

To communicate on the fly, look for the Internet-style info terminals downtown on rue du Curé or inside the city's train station.

Luxembourg City Hostel

2 rue du Fort Olisy, L-2261 Pfaffenthal (Luxembourg City)

> **Phone:** 2627-66-650
> **Fax:** 2627-66-680
> **E-mail:** luxembourg@youthhostels.lu
> **Rates:** €22.90 (about $29 US) per HI member
> **Credit cards:** Yes
> **Beds:** 240
> **Private/family rooms:** Yes
> **Kitchen available:** Yes
> **Season:** Open year-round
> **Office hours:** 24 hours
> **Lockout:** 10 a.m.–2 p.m.
> **Curfew:** 2 a.m.
> **Affiliation:** HI-AJL
> **Extras:** Breakfast, meals ($), bar, bike rentals, laundry

*T*his big hostel, Luxembourg's mothership hostel (mother to a very small brood), is a good news/bad news situation: It's in a great location, fairly central (though you'll need to walk uphill to reach the town's prime attractions), but it's also pretty institutional—"modern" in this case meaning "characterless."

Yet hostellers seem to whoop it up in one of the five common areas, and that isn't a bad thing at all; you might actually have a little fun here. They've also got 8 family rooms for couples or folk with kids.

There's a surprising amount to do in this rich little capital city if you've landed at the hostel for a day or two. Take a Wenzel Walk tour down the river valley for a look at the rock upon which the castle's built plus underground tunnels, moat ruins, and more; an elevator at walk's end carries walkers back up top.

Museums also abound. The National Museum of History and Art, on Fishmarket, contains new and old art, archaeological finds, medieval weapons associated with the fort, and lots more stuff relating to the history of this city and country. The National Museum of Natural History takes on—what else—nature topics; one feature is an "ecodatabase" that is collecting records of the country's plants and animals.

Best bet for a bite:
Fast food stands to save a buck
What hostellers say:
"Mom STOP. Need more money STOP."
Gestalt:
De-Lux
Safety:
Hospitality:
Cleanliness:
Party index:

Luxembourgian festivals include a peppy spring fete in early May, where townsfolk carry new tree branches in a parade through town; an April pilgrimage to the city cathedral; and Schueberfour, the huge late-summer carnival that started out as a market for shepherds but just kept growing.

Other Euro-institutions to check out while here include the Court of Justice, the Court of Auditors, the Secretariat of the European Parliament, and some offices of the European Commission, to name but a few.

How To Get There:
By bus: Take #9 bus to hostel, or walk uphill 1 mile from bus station to hostel.
By car: Call hostel for directions.
By train: From station, take #9 bus to hostel or walk uphill 1 mile to hostel.

The Netherlands

*F*irst things first. This nation is not called Holland; that's only the northern part of the country. If you're in Amsterdam—often called A'dam (pronounced "A"-dam, not Adam! think "the letter A"), you're smack in North Holland. But that's just one province (sort of like a US state) in the larger country. So call it the Netherlands everywhere else you go, even though you will sometimes hear A'dammers referring to their fair country as Holland.

This is a very densely populated country. That might come as a surprise—until you hit the streets and find yourself bumping into people. Take a train or streetcar, and you'll find it's a very short distance between populated areas. But hey, look at it this way: It's really hard to get lost with all those roads, signs, bike paths, and people in the way. Anyway, it's not New York or Tokyo crowded (except on those Amsterdam trams).

Where to go? Easy. Go to Amsterdam for canals and museums; hit The Hague to see the capital buildings; the northern Netherlands have all the beaches, dunes, islands, and major cities; and the southern Netherlands have, um, some hills.

The Dutch are a hospitable people by nature, and their hostels pretty much reflect this—they're uniformly clean, safe, and, well, uniform. One trend that we didn't find great is that most of the hostels are built for school groups; except for all those independent hostels in Amsterdam, almost all the rest have remote locations, conference rooms, and lots of noisy kids. Unfortunately. We have kept our descriptions of totally group-oriented hostels brief in these pages, because you're unlikely to find a bed here in high season—or to enjoy it if you do.

Practical Details

There are plenty of flights into Amsterdam, the hub of the country. The budget airline EasyJet uses Amsterdam as a hub, and therefore has plenty of hops around Europe from Schiphol airport. The airline KLM (sometimes teamed with US airline Northwest) is based in Amsterdam and has tons of international flights. Schiphol airport, an increasingly major hub for both international and European traffic, is well connected to the center of Amsterdam and its train station by clean, frequent (seven or more times per hour), quick (15 to 20 minutes) trains. It's a lot cheaper than a cab, and probably faster too; buy train tickets at the airport right from the arrivals level.

You can also get to the Netherlands by ferry, starting from Harwich (an hour east of London by train from Liverpool Street Station) and taking a Stena ferry to Hoek van Holland, the Netherlands. The ferry runs twice daily—but it takes all day (or all night). From there it's about a 90-minute train ride to Amsterdam.

Eurolines runs comfortable long-distance buses around Europe for very competitive rates; it goes from Amsterdam to London, Paris, Hamburg, Munich, and beyond, for instance.

Once you're here, there are two main ways to get around the Netherlands: bikes and trains. Buses and cars are secondary options, but bikes or trains are probably easiest in such a flat, compact, densely populated country.

To get around by train, either buy a pass at stations or buy inexpensive point-to-point tickets. There are several kinds of trains in the country: InterCity trains are the fastest, stopping only in major cities, and sometimes charge an extra fee. Sneltreins are more regional, stopping sometimes but not everywhere. Finally, the Stoptrein is just what it says—a poky, locals-only train you will use only when you need to get to small towns and avoid otherwise.

Note that the Dutch aren't very good about putting English on their signs, so you might need to ask for help, and punch your train ticket before you get on the train, showing the conductor that it has been "used up."

If you're traveling heavily, look into buying a Benelux Pass (there is no longer an inexpensive Holland-only pass, unfortunately). This pass costs $165 to $225 US per under-26 traveler for a pass you can use for three to five days in one month (the cheaper pass is per person, for two adults traveling together; first-class passes cost more). If you're over 26, you'll pay more: $250 to as much as $525 per person for a pass you can use for three to five days. (The higher-end prices in that range are for first-class passes, which you'll never need.)

You can rent bikes either from most of the country's railway stations—that's what the Dutch do, so don't be shy about it—or from private companies. We're talking about a country of 15 million people here, and they own 12 million bikes! As a result, there are miles of marked paths through the Netherlands, and the local VVVs (tourist offices, pronounced "Fay Fay Fay"—we kid you not) will sell or give you maps of them. To rent, bring a picture ID and some money or a credit card for a deposit; it shouldn't cost much. Round blue signs with white bikes point out the way to bike trails; squat white "mushroom" signs point the way to various surrounding towns and tell you the distances to them. You can also "park" your bike at train stations for a small fee (sometimes waived) or bring them on the trains themselves for about €5–€7 (about $6–$9 US).

Finally, buses can be a cheaper ride than the train or more expensive, depending on local whims. It might take you all day to make connections, but most bus drivers are helpful and knowledgeable. As a bonus, they'll sometimes let you off where you want to go even if there isn't an actual scheduled bus stop there.

The unit of currency in the Netherlands is the euro.

The Netherlands' country code is 31. To call Amsterdam hostels from North America, dial 011-31 and DROP THE ZERO from the phone numbers listed in this book. To call Amsterdam hostels from within the Netherlands but outside Amsterdam, dial the numbers just as they are printed in the book. And to dial Amsterdam hostels from within the city, drop the initial city code (such as 020) and then dial the rest of the number as printed. Phones are pretty easy to use—you buy a phone card, available at some hostels and most newsstands or tobacco shops, to access most phones these days.

AMSTERDAM

Everyone, it seems, makes it to Amsterdam sooner or later—at least where young backpackers are concerned. The place has taken on a legendary status as a haven of lawlessness (prostitution and marijuana both being basically legal), and thousands of college kids come each summer to blow Mommy and Daddy's money on intoxicating substances and pleasures of the flesh. As a result, it's become one of the single craziest places on earth, a collision of weirdness and vice.

These seedier aspects aside, the actual residential neighborhoods of Amsterdam—where most of the locals and some of the hostels are—remain attractive and quiet, laced with dozens of placid (if not exactly drinkable) canals, plenty of trees, and tall, attractive town houses. The museums are terrific, most of them concentrated within a small area.

So it makes a great journey stop even if you're not into getting wasted; just remember that all this drug and sex activity has brought some crime with it. Thefts are more common here than in many larger European cities, so you've got to look sharp.

As you might expect, there's tremendous choice and variety within the hostel offerings; this is one of the very few cities we've been where every single hostel has a distinctive personality, so much so that if you say, "I'm stayin' at Bob's or the Pig," others will instantly know exactly what groove you've plugged into. Of course, the quality of the digs also varies hugely. Some of these places are out-and-out dives, especially the cheapies down by the red-light district. Others around town are nicer, if sometimes a bit farther out—though nothing is really that far from the center. At the wildest ones (see write-ups), you'll smell pot and beer everywhere and find stoned hostellers sprawled on the floor while others swap bong hits.

Then again, at the two Hostelling International joints, you'll stumble across tons of school groups having good, clean fun, and facilities will be conspicuously cleaner.

There are even two "Christian hostels" here: obviously not the places to score dope or engage in an orgy, but quite nice places if you don't mind the persistent religious iconography and messages scattered throughout.

The write-ups here serve as a good guide to the party places, snoozes, and dives; heed their advice. Also note that all these places get booked up fully during summer, so you'd best reserve a month or more ahead (if the place takes reservations, and many don't). Failing that, show up in the morning before noon and put your name on a list. Once you're in, most hostels can book you into a local bike tour or other excursion if you like.

One final note: If you're staying at one of the two Hostelling International–affiliated hostels in Amsterdam, you reap an additional benefit—a staggering array of hefty discounts at museums and other attractions around the city. They might range from tickets for a boat trip through the Amsterdam canals to Rijksmuseum tix or even a break on Eurolines long-distance bus fares.

Arriving in the city's Centraal Station, you'll be confronted with complete, utter chaos—a seething mass of tourists, locals, hookers, transit employees, and others, some half-stoned and the rest completely so, moving in all directions without apparent order. Our advice? Try not to come late at night, and know your bearings before you step off that train. Most of what you need is on the main level; lockers and luggage deposit are at the far left of the station (if you're inside it facing out), near track 2b. There's a change machine, too, to give you quick coins. Two ATMs sit right near the front station entrance, under a brightly lit red sign but still easy to miss amid the crowds.

Outside it gets complicated again. Unless you're staying right downtown—which is very possible in this compact city—you'll need to figure out which streetcar (tram) line goes to your hostel and buy transit tickets. The trams come and go in haphazard fashion to and from the front of the station; there are some useful diagrams showing which trams stop where just at the edge of the train-station canal. Walk straight out the front door, dodge through all the tram lines, and bear a bit right; go to the water, and check out the maps.

You can buy tram tickets at many places: tobacco shops, train stations, machines (with Dutch-only instructions), or bus stops. Even some trams sell 'em, but that's the most expensive way to get them. We normally get a transit pass in European cities, but in Amsterdam you'll walk so much—and the pass costs enough—that single tickets are probably a better deal. Those are easy to buy, although a little hard to figure out; you punch out two "strips" in the machine on the tram for each in-town journey, three each time you travel to the burbs. Transfers to buses are free if you change immediately; show the tram driver your punched ticket right after you get on. Punch the tickets as soon as you get on the tram, inserting the correct end (it usually has an arrow) into the slot and waiting for the *ding!* sound. Sometimes the conductor will want to see it, too.

The city's subway consists of just one short line, but it could be useful if you're visiting the outskirts. Watch yourself, though, because sleazy characters hang out downstairs in the Nieuwmarkt and other stops. It's probably best to take a tram or taxi instead.

Amsterdam

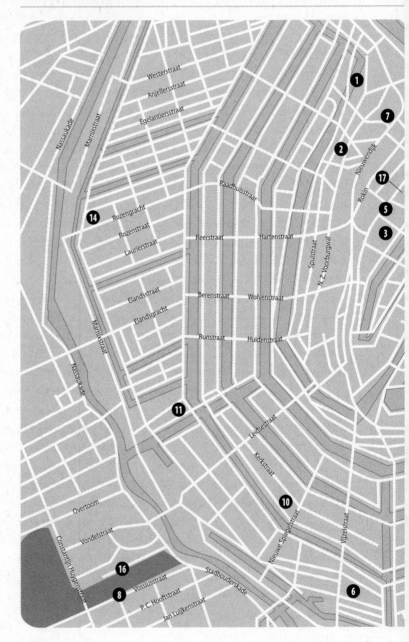

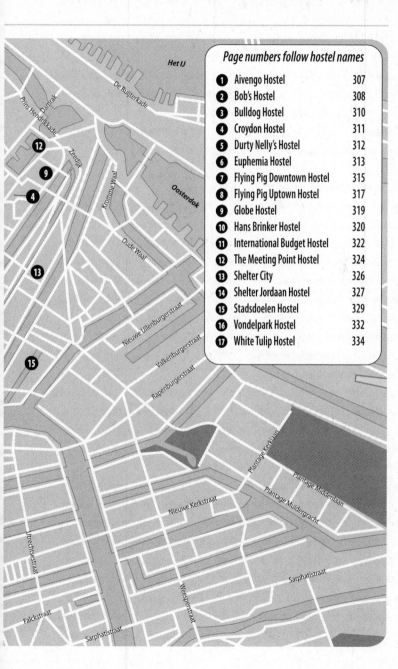

Het IJ

De Ruijterkade

Prins Hendrikkade

Damrak

Zeedijk

Krommme Waal

Oosterdok

Oude Waal

Nieuwe Uilenburgerstraat

Valkenburgerstraat

Rapenburgerstraat

Plantage Kerklaan

Plantage Middenlaan

Plantage Muldergracht

Nieuwe Kerkstraat

Utrechtsestraat

Weesperstraat

Sarphatistraat

Falckstraat

Sarphatistraat

Boat tours of the canals are quite popular, though not always worth the charge. A ton of operators are set up around town; head for a canal and you're sure to find one, especially down by Centraal Station. Tiny paddleboats are also popular, but we think they look silly and require a lot of pedaling for not a lot of distance gained.

Walking is the most attractive option, of course, but remember to walk on the black tar and not the red-painted lanes—or you'll risk decapitation by one of the zillions of bicycles zooming around town without regard for traffic laws.

Finally, if you can't beat 'em you could, of course, rent or borrow your own bike and join 'em; the city's network of bike lanes is one of the best in the world.

Nightlife & Attractions

Amsterdam is one of the world's great museum towns, and almost all the action is concentrated in the so-called Museumplein area—outside the central downtown but very close to three or four of the city's hostels. (Vondelpark and the Flying Pig Uptown are closest.) The big two are the Van Gogh Museum and the adjacent Rijksmuseum, which owns 20 Rembrandts as well as some of Vermeer's finest work and obviously puts on some great exhibits. The Van Gogh contains hundreds of the painter's drawings, paintings, and letters—everything from his early Dutch Brabant work (of peasants, miners, and potato eaters) to spectacular French canvases featuring his own self-portrait, still lifes of sunflowers, and some final paintings of cornfields and crows. Other exhibits feature contemporaries and influences such as Toulouse-Lautrec, Monet, and Gaugin.

And what else can we say about the famous Rijksmuseum that hasn't already been said? In addition to those 20 Rembrandts, four Vermeers, and plenty of other material documenting the history of Dutch painting, there are also collections of rare porcelain, Dutch tiles, old dollhouses, and Asian art complementing the paintings. Also note a good exhibit documenting the history of the far-reaching Dutch East India Company.

Nightlife, of course, is everywhere around town. The so-called Brown Cafes, little neighborhood bars dripping with character and great beer, are the primary draw as far as we're concerned. If you're looking for a different kind of high, there are some 200 "coffee shops" here where the Jamaican flag flies high—even though you're thousands of miles from the island. That can only mean one thing: It's not a place to get coffee; it's a place to get stoned. (There once were as many as 400 of these places, by the way, but the government has been cracking down on licenses under pressure from other countries.) The names are particularly amusing.

Now stop running down the street waving your money. You came here to sightsee, right? Didn't you? You didn't? Oh. Well, anyway, there are basically two kinds of sights here—the quaint and the decadent. If you're going for the former, hit the central city and then walk over to the Jordaan neighborhood (a mile or less due west of the train station by foot). Canals, cafes, and cute apartment buildings combine to evoke a Europe you thought existed only on postcards.

Want a different, more low-down kind of experience? The red-light district here is the world's most famous, and indeed you will see legalized prostitution very much in evidence. Well-endowed women fill every available window at night, it seems—and yes, they're for rent. A bit sad. Whatever you do, absolutely resist the temptation to snap a photograph of these gals. A bouncer will grab you before you can say "cheese."

Bar-wise, you can find an upscale concentration of places to eat and drink in Leidseplein, a nonsquare square just a block or two toward town from the museum complex; at night, it's a mishmash of fire jugglers, tourists, and pickpockets. Note that the bars here don't stay open all night—it's kinda like England or the States, where last call probably won't be past 2 a.m. As elsewhere in Europe, there is also a smattering of discos and late-night clubs.

For more information on all this and more, contact the ultra-well-run VVV, the official tourism office. They've got locations all over town, including booths at Centraal Station (upstairs near track 2), the airport, and on Leidseplein.

Finally, this is one of the most wired cities in Europe, so there are a number of cybercafes (avoid ones that require you to buy a drink or are full of pot smoke). The national phone company has installed many "Internet phone kiosks" around town, which look just like phone booths but contain tiny screens you activate with a phone card; it's hard to type, we found, but you can certainly do some quick Web cruising for info on the fly. Of course, with smartphones and netbooks and tablets and WiFi, you probably won't need to. But just in case.

Common Sense

Safety-wise, remember to carry your valuables in a money belt or front pocket whenever you're out and about: Pickpockets are all over the Amsterdam trams and streets, especially in broad daylight for some reason. If ever you should feel a sudden hard shove and/or a hand groping your back or backside, immediately check for your wallet—if it's gone, turn around fast, watching for anyone exiting your tram in a hurry. That's probably your thief.

Bring an umbrella and/or a raincoat, as it rains here practically every day at least for a few minutes. You thought England was bad? This is worse. Even bright, sunny days tend to cloud up by noon, dump some rain on the unsuspecting, then clear up again by sunset.

One final word of advice: If you're offended by porno shops or the presence of marijuana—the smell is everywhere, even on the street, and will probably get into your clothes at some point—steer clear of this town, since you won't be able to avoid them.

AMSTERDAM HOSTELS AT A GLANCE

	RATING	PRICE	IN A WORD	PAGE
Vondelpark Hostel		€19–€36.50	big	p. 332
Bulldog Hostel		€18–€105	smokin'	p. 310
Stadsdoelen Hostel		€18.50–€36	super	p. 329
Flying Pig Downtown		€14.90–€44.90	fun	p. 315
Flying Pig Uptown		€14.90–€42.90	mellow	p. 317
Shelter Jordaan		€12.50–€38.50	religious	p. 327
Euphemia Hostel		€15–€40	middling	p. 313
Durty Nelly's Hostel		€28–€50	beery	p. 312
Shelter City		€13.50–€38.50	crucified	p. 326
The Meeting Point Hostel		€14–€32	central	p. 324
Hans Brinker		€18–€35	raging	p. 320
Aivengo Hostel		€18–€20	basic	p. 307
International Budget		€17–€45	stoned	p. 322
Globe Hostel		€12–€36.50	iffy	p. 319
White Tulip Hostel		€11–€37	poor	p. 334
Bob's Hostel		€19–45	wasted	p. 308
Croydon Hostel		€13–€35	sucky	p. 311

Aivengo Hostel

Spuistraat 6, Amsterdam

Phone: 020-620-1155

Website: aivengoyouthhostel.com

Rates: €18–€20 (about $23–$25 US) per person

Credit cards: No

Beds: 40

Private/family rooms: No

Kitchen available: No

Season: Closed December–January

Office hours: 24 hours

Lockout: 1–5 p.m.

Curfew: 3 a.m.

Affiliation: None

Extras: Free internet access, TV room, lockers, kitchen, breakfast ($)

This smallish hostel touts itself as innovative, drug-free, and smoke-free. Dorms are actually pretty nice, almost artistic, especially the "sky room" up top. The Flying Pig chain apparently thinks enough of this place to send people here when they're overflowing with guests; they now have lockers in the dorms, a TV lounge, and kitchens (the women's dorm even has one right inside it). Management will keep your stuff in a safe, but they claim it's a friendly, sharing place to stay.

However, it's not perfect—cleanliness suffers seriously, little socializing goes on here, beds could be better (much better), and it's hardly a palace. In addition, the hostel's located on a very busy and not-always-attractive street (there are prostitutes working windows on it).

Gestalt:
Aye-vengo
Safety:
Hospitality:
Cleanliness:
Party index:

You might stay here for the central location and the good facilities—in a town with hostels this bad, this is certainly passable, just not all that much fun. Watch yourself at night coming home.

How To Get There:

By bus: Call hostel for transit route.

By car: Call hostel for directions.

By train: From Centraal Station, walk straight across bridge to Damark. Turn immediately right, walk a block or 2 to Spuistraat and take a left; continue to hostel on right.

Bob's Hostel 🐷

Nieuwezijds Voorburgwal 92, 1012 SG Amsterdam

Phone: 020-623-0063

Fax: 020-675-6446

Website: bobsyouthhostel.nl

Rates: €19.50–€45 (about $23 US) per person

Credit cards: No

Beds: 150

Private/family rooms: Yes

Kitchen available: No

Season: Open year-round

Office hours: 24 hours

Affiliation: None

Extras: Breakfast, dinner ($), bar, pot, lockers, TV room, games

---

*T*his, quite simply, is one of the cheapest and hardest-partying hostels in town—and since we're in Amsterdam, that's really saying something. We once heard someone describe it as "scummy," and its unclean bathrooms (just one shower per 16 beds?) and tightly packed beds (150 in a very small facility) resemble barracks. The streetcars crank right by the window, too, reducing quiet further. Did we mention the parties?

If you're the right kind of traveler—young and super-easygoing and non–allergic to smoke—it could potentially be a semi-fun place to stay. But those who value cleanliness should look elsewhere.

The reception desk is actually inside a coffee shop (translation: weed house). Through the haze of smoke, you work your way to a huge check-in line, then wait and wait while stoned Brits and Americans fumble for their wallets to pay for another night—or another baggie of grass. Meanwhile, the rave music blasts your eardrums into shrapnel.

There are both coed and female rooms (but no men's). While the dorms here are smaller than those of some coffee shops–turned–hostels, you've probably got to be the type of person who places an awful lot of value in smoking weed as a way of life—or at least tolerate it—to stay here.

And you'd better like padlocks. A'dam's liberal drug policy and the associated riffraff have created a feeling of paranoia and mistrust around town, so nearly every hostel in the city encourages (or requires) the use of lockers for your stuff. When you're sleeping next to people who spend money on drugs and live this cheaply, you'll find they sometimes aren't the most trustworthy. So be forewarned about places with a higher concentration of potheads; it could mean safety trouble.

The 10-bed dorms, to get back to basics, are sometimes clean and sometimes not—a persistent smoke of you-know-what often lingers in the rooms, so check your lungs at the door. Dinner can be obtained for an extra charge, but some hostellers here are so wasted they don't care about anything except "the munchies." The hostel is well placed, though, near the slanting buildings lining little Gravenstraat and not too far a walk from the city's best neighborhood, the Jordaan.

Best bet for a bite:
Deli next door
Insiders' tip:
You might not wanna stay here
What hostellers say:
"(inhaling you-know-what) Aaaaahhhhh . . ."
Gestalt:
Smoke show
Safety:
Hospitality:
Cleanliness:
Party index:

Yes, most people come here to get stoned. It's not the cleanest bed in town, not the dirtiest; bathrooms are poorly lit and not always cleaned, dorms are too packed, and they throw extra bodies on the floor when it's busy. You might even stumble back to discover someone crashed in your bunk by mistake, and they're not moving.

But we have to admit, some people somehow still like it here, and we've seen worse in town. Just be prepared for some awfully weird dudes if you're staying.

How To Get There:
By bus: Call hostel for transit route.
By car: Call hostel for directions.
By train: From Centraal Station, walk across bridge to Damark. Turn immediately right, walk 2 blocks to Spuistraat and turn left; continue to hostel on right.

The Bulldog Hostel

Oudezijds Voorburgwal 220, 1012 GJ Amsterdam

Phone: 020-620-3822

Fax: 020-627-1612

E-mail: info@bulldoghotel.com

Rates: €18–€105 (about $23–$126 US) per person; doubles €90–€129 (about $113–$161 US)

Credit cards: Yes

Beds: 170

Private/family rooms: Yes

Kitchen available: Yes

Season: Open year-round

Affiliation: None

Extras: Meals, TV, DVD player, bar, air-conditioning, breakfast, lockers, Internet access, coffee shop, tourist information, souvenir shop

N ote: There is a 5 percent discount for ISIC holders.

Quite good overall, this hostel with the memorable name and logo is probably what you want, though it does gets its fair share of stoners. Bulldog founder Henk de Vries (Bulldog is also the name of his popular local energy drink and an associated cafe) says this hostel is his "dream come true," and we agree: It's mostly a great, casual place. But skip it if you're anti-drug or hate smoke: The wacky ter-backy gets lit up at all hours.

They give you a free night on your birthday if you pay for at least one other night. And you gotta love the double-entendre motto of the hostel: "Legalized since 1996." Heh-heh. Only drawback? This place is gradually upscaling. Management even calls it a "hotel" now. Rates have risen, as a result—a single room here will cost you over 100 bucks! But dorms are quite reasonable.

What hostellers say:
"Spliffs go great with an energy drink."

Gestalt:
Bulldog bunks

Safety:

Hospitality:

Cleanliness:

Party index:

Located in the heart of Amsterdam's red-light district, close to Dam Square, it's filled with 8- to 12-bed coed dorms that share bathroom facilities, plus a selection of double, triple, and quad rooms with television and en-suite bathrooms. Free breakfast is included with all the beds, as are free lockers; the Energy bar/coffee shop stays open 'til 3 a.m. most nights, serving energy drinks, coffee, and smoky delights.

The surrounding neighborhood, as you might guess, is pretty sketchy—use caution. Inside the hostel, though, the 24-hour front desk is equipped with video security and they won't let stragglers and marginal types get in. Management is also trying to discourage the testosterone factor by refusing to take group bookings of male sports fans and bachelor parties.

How To Get There:
By bus or train: Contact hostel for transit details.
By car: Contact hostel for directions.

Croydon Hostel �˜
Warmoesstraat 75, 1012 HX Amsterdam

> **Phone:** 020-627-6065
> **Rates:** €13-€35 (about $16-$44 US) per person **Credit cards:** Yes
> **Beds:** 20
> **Private/family rooms:** No
> **Kitchen available:** No
> **Season:** Open year-round
> **Office hours:** Vary; call for hours
> **Affiliation:** None
> **Extras:** Breakfast

---

*T*his place just plain sucks, set above a cheap takeout restaurant on one of Amsterdam's suckiest streets. Sorry, but that's the truth—it's the kinda street where drug dealers solicit you in broad daylight.

There are sagging beds here in the usual sad dorms, no kitchen, no laundry, no food, no

Best bet for a bite:
Elsewhere
Insiders' tip:
Avoid guys with gold teeth
What hostellers say:
"What's Dutch for 911?!"
Gestalt:
Bad trip
Safety: ◣
Hospitality: ◣
Cleanliness: ◣
Party index: ◣ ◣

guard, no nothin'—just overpriced beds you pay for at the restaurant and then get no help with afterward. The clientele at this one must be scary indeed to take such desperate measures. We wouldn't stay here if you paid us. How the heck did this place obtain a lodgings permit, anyway?

Take our advice: Avoid it like the plague.

How To Get There:
By bus or train: Call hostel for transit route.
By car: Call hostel for directions.

Durty Nelly's Hostel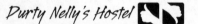
Warmoesstraat 117, 1012 JA Amsterdam

Phone: 020-638-0125
Website: durtynellys.nl
Rates: €28–€50 (about $35–$63 US) per person
Credit cards: Yes
Beds: 42
Private/family rooms: No
Kitchen available: No
Season: Open year-round
Office hours: 24 hours
Affiliation: None
Extras: Bar, breakfast, lockers, restaurant, safe

---

*T*his place is set on the same sleazy Warmoestraat as two other lousy hostels, but it's a cut above them. (Everything's relative, right?) In fact, it has made huge strides since the days when we were practically afraid to walk in the front door without shower shoes.

It's set above an Irish-theme bar that's heavy on cigarette smoke and English beer—a little depressing, we thought. Staff were once extremely, well, hostile, but things are better these days. They claim to have about 40 beds (in mixed-sex dorms of 8, 14, and 20 beds) and they're supercheap beds, yeah—but this is definitely one to put in the not-first-call category, especially with that smoky, loud sports bar downstairs and junkies and sex shops on all sides outdoors. It's also one of the more expensive dorm beds in all of Amsterdam—50 euros for this? In a dorm? No.

At least they've installed key cards for access (thank you) and air-conditioning (good). Now let's see if this one can inch its way upward into the ranks of respectability.

Not there yet.

How To Get There:

By bus or train: Call hostel for transit route.
By car: Call hostel for directions.

> **Best bet for a bite:**
> *Supermarkets*
> **What hostellers say:**
> *"Vast improvement."*
> **Gestalt:**
> *Willy-Nelly*
> **Safety:**
> **Hospitality:**
> **Cleanliness:**
> **Party index:**

Euphemia Hostel

Fokke Simonszstraat 1-9, 1017 TD Amsterdam

Phone: 020-622-9045
Fax: 020-622-9673
E-mail: euphemia-hotel@budgethotel.A2000.nl
Website: euphemiahotel.com
Rates: €15–€40 (about $18–$53 US) per person; doubles €60–€160 (about $75–$200 US)
Credit cards: Yes
Beds: 76
Private/family rooms: Yes
Kitchen available: No
Season: Open year-round
Office hours: 8 a.m.–11 p.m.
Affiliation: None
Extras: Travel library, breakfast ($), TV, lockers, Internet access

---

The Euphemia, a former monastery, down a quiet side alley, is fairly close to Amsterdam's action without being right in the thick of it. It's also around the corner from an Internet

Best bet for a bite:
Albert Heijn Supermarket
Insiders' tip:
Boulangerie Le Mortier bakery on
Vijzelgracht
What hostellers say:
"G'day!"
Gestalt:
Euphoria
Safety:
Hospitality:
Cleanliness:
Party index:

place and a great-smelling bakery. However, as it's chiefly a hotel, only 4 dorm beds are available.

The wheelchair-accessible ground floor has 5 double rooms and a breakfast room with a television, closely spaced round tables, and a little travel library where visitors swap dog-eared guidebooks.

The rest of the place is definitely not wheelchair-accessible; you have to climb a lot of narrow, steep stairs to get to the upper floors and dorm. (They discourage people with kids from lodging on upper floors because of the hazards involved. Smart. But the rest of you will get a workout.) Once up top, the lone quad dorm room is airy and nice, hotel-quality really, with lockers, a television, and a bathroom in the hall.

The other rooms are doubles, triples, and quads—some with views and all quite nice. Being mostly a hotel now, many of these double rooms come with TV and bathroom. It's not luxury, just a one-star hotel that's a decent budget choice for couples. Remember that the price drops in winter and goes up in summer. And in July and August, there's a minimum stay of 2 nights.

Created by some Dutch folks who spent some happy time in New Zealand, there's a vaguely Down Under flavor to the proceedings. Staff will point you anywhere you need: it's a very short walk to both the popular Heineken Brewery and the Rijksmuseum and other museums in the Museumplein complex, which is one of the best things about this place— the position midway between the train station and the museums. You're also just a few steps from two well-known "coffee" shops (Mellow Yellow and Little Coffeeshop), as well as a natural foods store, fruit shop, and several quiet canals.

It has to be said that this hostel used to be better and friendlier, one of the better choices in town, actually. These days it's just a so-so pick, and it's becoming (like a lot of A'dam joints) less and less of a true hostel every year and more of a low-priced hotel.

How To Get There:
By bus: Call hostel for transit route.

By car: Call hostel for directions. Street parking; free overnight.

By train: From Centraal Station, take #16 or #24 streetcar to Weteringcircuit (fifth stop). Turn around and begin walking toward station; hostel is on right.

Flying Pig Downtown Hostel

Nieuwendijk 100, 1012 MR Amsterdam

   Phone: 020-420-6822

   E-mail: downtown@flyingpig.nl

   Website: flyingpig.nl

   Rates: €14.90–€44.90 (about $18–$56 US) per person; doubles €86–€104 (about $108–$125 US)

   Credit cards: Yes

   Beds: 180

   Private/family rooms: Yes

   Kitchen available: Yes

   Season: Open year-round

   Office hours: 24 hours

   Affiliation: None

   Extras: E-mail, breakfast, bar

*A*gainst the odds, the Flying Pig remains a top pick in town—if you come in knowing what to expect. (Hint: A party.)

This huge place, a former hotel easily located by its unmistakable, enormous pig sign on a tawdry strip, is legendary for its laid-back groove. We'll venture to say it's the best-known bunk (at least by North Americans) in the whole city. But is it the best bunk? No. But not the worst. It's actually passable if you can put up with crowds of partying young people and the occasional filth.

The owners came up with this concept while backpacking around Australia (their website tells the whole tale of the pig); this one's actually the second hostel created in the porcine chain, opening a half year after the original Flying Pig first oinked over in the Vondelpark. But it's normally the more popular one of the two; try to book this place well ahead if you really wanna come and experience . . . the experience.

Inside the door from the chaos on the street, you are greeted with—well, more chaos. A harried staff tries to work through bookings while stoned hostellers crash in a chill-out room adjacent to the very popular bar. This kiddie bar is said to be for hostellers only, not locals, and while some order beers and light up purchased-on-the-street pot, others lie in that padded front window area blissing out on the rainbow-colored pads while the world passes them by. Free pitchers of water on the bar help the weed-eaters cleanse the palate.

No wonder the logo here is a pig in an aviator helmet, smoking a huge rasta spliff . . .

Upstairs, a condom machine, beer vending machine, and pinball machine greet you before you've even found your bunk . . . welcome to the dollhouse. Actually, the painted and carpeted halls, restored wooden beams, and numerous windows do display a certain attention to detail on the part of ownership; it's not just a warehouse for your wallet.

The price you pay depends heavily on the size of your room. Get a quad in this maze of a building and you'll pay a premium; camp out in the huge 26-bed room (with wilder hostellers) and it's much cheaper. Even this big room isn't too bad; it's divided into halves and looks up at a neat metal roof that used to be a hotel bar.

They also do rooms of 6, 8, 10, 14, and even 32 beds—and they've also got a few rather plain doubles. These are OK, spruced up with art prints on the walls, but they're still basically 2 smooshed-together twin beds and a spartan bathroom; at least it's a private bathroom. This costs more, of course, but you also get wicker chairs and a bit of worn furniture. All rooms, by the way, have shower, toilet, and lockers, which is nice for a change in this city; many also come with good street views. Mattresses come on ladder-style supports, not the most comfortable.

One outstanding feature here is that this is almost the only hostel in A'dam with a kitchen, a big plus; this kitchen—open to 10 a.m. and noon till midnight—has 2 sets of electric rangetops, plenty of pots and pans, multiple fridges, and a "happy room" to dine in amid a painting of gnomes and nude women frolicking through a magical forest, dude. There's also a more conventional dining room attached to that one with perpetual TV and

Best bet for a bite:
Food surrounds you
Insiders' tip:
*Luggage repair place at
4 Nieuwiezijds Kolk*
What hostellers say:
"Loved it/hated it."
Gestalt:
Central pork
Safety:
Hospitality:
Cleanliness:
Party index:

movies. There are rules, however, on how much you can eat with your breakfast; take more and you've gotta pay extra. Boo!

What else? Internet access in the lobby is wildly popular, even if it doesn't always work properly. Reception does a brisk business selling T-shirts of the pig logo. There are few, if any, rules here; you can work to pay off your stay, and they run movies daily in the "happy room." We'd bet 90 percent of the crowd was American when we dropped by, most of them digging the cigarette machine, video gambling, abundant pot, and beers at the bar. Few were using the piano and pool table, but maybe it was a slow night.

Problems do arise here. A number of hostellers noted problems with cleanliness, comfort, retching late-night hostellers, and useless staffers. These complaints have remained consistent for a decade, so all the amenities here might not mean much to you if you value a good night's sleep and clean bedding and bathrooms. We're giving it a narrow thumbs-up for now, but keeping our eye on 'em. Again, this is not a place to bring a family.

How To Get There:
By bus or train: From Centraal Station, walk straight out front entrance toward Damrak. Pass Victoria hotel, turn right at first alley, and walk to end; look for 100 Nieuwendijk and big pig sign.
By car: Call hostel for directions.

Flying Pig Uptown Hostel
Vossiusstraat 46–47, 1071 AJ Amsterdam
>   **Phone:** 020-400-4187
>   **E-mail:** uptown@flyingpig.nl
>   **Website:** flyingpig.nl
>   **Rates:** €14.90–€42.90 (about $19–$54 US) per person; doubles €68–€92 (about
> $85–$115 US)
>   **Credit cards:** Yes
>   **Beds:** 130
>   **Private/family rooms:** Yes
>   **Kitchen available:** Yes
>   **Season:** Open year-round
>   **Office hours:** 24 hours

Affiliation: None
Extras: E-mail, breakfast, bar

*T*his one's basically the mirror image of its sister hostel, the Flying Pig Downtown (see previous listing): a mellower, more laid-back groove for Flying Piggies who don't want downtown's chaos or a complete party scene. More cultural travelers tend to stay at the Palace over in the Vondelpark—now officially known as the Flying Pig Uptown—while the party crowd camps out at the other one, so it all works out in the end.

> **Best bet for a bite:**
> *Albert Heijn on Overtoom*
> **Insiders' tip:**
> *Lots of car rental places around corner*
> **What hostellers say:**
> *"Not as crazy as the other Pig."*
> **Gestalt:**
> *Piggly wiggly*
> **Safety:**
> **Hospitality:**
> **Cleanliness:**
> **Party index:**

Set in a town house just off the beginning of the big park that A'dammers so love to bike through, it's got all the same stuff as the downtown joint—bar, free e-mail, double rooms, and huge dorms—just fewer beds, that's all. Room prices vary a lot, according strictly to size: A double or quad room is the most expensive, but 6-, 8-, 10-, and 12-bed rooms get progressively cheaper depending on how many people you're willing to sleep with . . . er, alongside.

It's not quite as wonderful as its downtown compadre, but it's pretty darned close. And they have a ton more private and double rooms than the downtown incarnation. Bear that in mind.

If you've seen one Pig, you've seen 'em all; subtract a few stoners, add a few philosophy majors, and you've got the same picture here. Just prepare to feel the noize: Not sure if it's the quality of the hostellers they're letting in, or the thinness of the walls, but we could hear everything going on in the halls and adjacent rooms. Peace and quiet, this is not.

How To Get There:

By bus or train: From Centraal Station, take #1, #2, or #5 tram to Leidseplein stop. Walk across plaza, cross wide busy street, turn left, and walk past Hostelling International sign and park to Vossiusstraat on right. Turn right and walk down to 46 Vossiusstraat.
By car: Call hostel for directions.

Globe Hostel

Oudezijds Voorburgwal 3, 1012 EH Amsterdam

> **Phone:** 020-421-7424
>
> **Fax:** 020-421-7423
>
> **E-mail:** info@hotel-theglobe.nl
>
> **Website:** hotel-theglobe.nl
>
> **Rates:** €12–€36.50 (about $21–$63 US) per person
>
> **Credit cards:** Yes
>
> **Beds:** Number varies
>
> **Private/family rooms:** Yes
>
> **Kitchen available:** No
>
> **Season:** Open year-round
>
> **Office hours:** 24 hours
>
> **Affiliation:** None
>
> **Extras:** Bar, restaurant, pool table, darts, free WiFi, terrace, TVs

*N*ote: Two-day minimum stay required on weekends.

Take an already bad neighborhood (the red-light district), mix in a mediocre-at-best facility with rooms that seem far tinier and scrubbier than the ones depicted on the website, and why would you stay here? You wouldn't. (Well, we had to, but that's not the point.)

Staff are often surly and unhelpful, rooms are either pint-sized or too big. Twenty-two pairs of stoned feet in one room? C'mon, man. And the cleanliness, while slightly improved over previous visits, still doesn't cut it. Facilities are worn and sometimes things are broken.

Positives? A smokeless basement sports bar makes for a convenient beer without setting foot in the dodgy streets surrounding—

Gestalt:
Global
Safety:
Hospitality:
Cleanliness:
Party index:

though, you cannot use it as the hostel common room and just hang out. They don't like that. They also serve bar food such as big burgers for low prices, even if the grub ain't all that great.

The Globe's not the worst place in town—some hostels in A'dam are truly horrific. But this is hardly in even the top half of the selections available, unless you're a huge soccer fan and love to spend your days plunked down in front of the tube watching the footy matches. Save yourself the trouble if you can.

How To Get There:
By car: Contact hostel for directions.
By bus: Contact hostel for directions.
By train: Contact hostel for directions.

Hans Brinker Hostel

Kerkstraat 136–138, 1017 GR Amsterdam

> **Phone:** 020-622-0687
> **E-mail:** sybil@hans-brinker.com
> **Website:** hans-brinker.com
> **Rates:** €18–€35 (about $23–$44 US) per person; doubles €81 (about $101 US)
> **Credit cards:** Yes
> **Beds:** 500
> **Private/family rooms:** Yes
> **Kitchen available:** No
> **Season:** Open year-round
> **Office hours:** 24 hours
> **Affiliation:** None
> **Extras:** Bar, meals ($), club

---

*Y*ou wanna get a handle on this monster-size, one-of-a-kind place before you show up? OK, here's what you've gotta do.

Crank up some later-period U2—you know, *Achtung Baby!* or *Zooropa,* two albums that manage to encapsulate the chaotic and uncertain madness of the new Europe, the one that has torn down most of the old infrastructures and replaced them with cultural diversity, self-expression, and global shrinkage. That, in a nutshell, describes the wild vibe at the Hans Brinker Hostel, basically a hostel on steroids; though the staff shudders at the thought of being labeled among the ranks of lowly hostels, they've got dorms, a nasty attitude, kegs of beer, and weird guests. We say: It's a hostel.

Upon arrival you're greeted by some odd posters that display the motto "Check Out" (as in "Check Out the Hans Brinker Hostel"), with a photo of some poor beat-up guy. It's hard to figure out what the message is: You'll get your butt kicked if you stay here? Possibly.

Back to the objective description. Based on a quiet street, but well within reach of the coffee-shop action, you find this one simply by following your nose to the smell of marijuana—or by following the squads of backpacks to the long check-in line.

Just inside, adjacent to reception, there's a cavernous bar with wooden floors and picnic tables, which transforms at 11 p.m. into a free disco; here, in a dance hall adorned with psychedelic murals, resident DJs spin disco tunes while gweezy guys try out pickup lines on unsuspecting Japanese girls. All vices are catered to here: There are cigarette and beer vending machines, you can send e-mail and get plastered at the bar, and so forth.

Interestingly the population here is not the usual American college girls sprinkling every sentence with the word "like" but rather jaded Euro-types who have been around the block a few times; it's basically a combo of wastoid older guys, dudes with fly shades strapped to their heads, girls who show a lot of navel, and lots of weird beards. A wild crowd, completely European, creating a nutso party atmosphere that goes right off the top end of our party index scale.

Yet the rooms aren't complete junk. You've got many of the amenities you'd seek in a hostel if you were young and Euro (though you can't buy pot on the premises). The 6-bed dorms are extremely tight and raucous, but they're surprisingly clean. They've also got every other size you can imagine—from single rooms to doubles, triples, quads, sevens, eights, and (hell, yes, why not) even tens.

While breakfast is included for free, other meals cost extra. You can also blow some money buying tacky souvenirs at the front desk or save it for whatever floats your boat at the highly acclaimed "smart shop" (drug shop) Conscious Dreams or the cleverly named coffee shop Global Chillage, both just down the block.

The neighborhood is pretty happening in general, and if the hostel meals and crowd don't suit you, there are plenty of Chinese restaurants and other ethnic eateries around. A pricey but good Albert Heijn supermarket on the main street

Insiders' tip:
Bikes will run you down
What hostellers say:
"Tonight, the bottle let me down..."
Gestalt:
Global chillage
Safety:
Hospitality:
Cleanliness:
Party index:

can provide picnic supplies plus a good selection of Dutch cheese, and you can wash your duds at a good laundry (The Clean Brothers) nearby. The area is overtly gay, so there are lots of, um, interesting stores, posters, and bars around.

How To Get There:

By bus: Call hostel for transit route.
By car: Call hostel for directions.
By train: From train station, take #25 or #16 tram to Kerkstraat stop; make a right and walk 1 block to hostel on left.

International Budget Hostel

Leidsegracht 76, 1016 CR Amsterdam

> **Phone:** 020-624-2784
> **Fax:** 020-772-4825
> **E-mail:** info@internationalbudgethostel.com
> **Website:** internationalbudgethostel.com
> **Rates:** €17–€45 (about $21–$56 US) per person
> **Credit cards:** No
> **Beds:** 54
> **Private/family rooms:** Yes
> **Kitchen available:** No
> **Season:** Open year-round
> **Office hours:** 9 a.m.–11 p.m.
> **Affiliation:** None
> **Extras:** Breakfast ($), TV, free WiFi, cat, bike rentals

---

N *ote: Two-night stay required on weekends.*
"But the website looks so nice! . . ."

Um, yeah. About that. When one has been in the hostel-reviewing business as long as we have, one begins to immediately pick up signs that all is not really well beneath an apparently glossy surface—and that first queasy impression usually turns out to be correct.

In the case of the International Budget Hostel, at first glance it seemed like an OK enough place: great, quiet location inside a narrow, renovated 17th-century (yes, really) warehouse, clean and quiet, adequate bathroom facilities. The only downside seems to be getting there: The hostel is set several floors above street level, and there's no elevator. OK. That means walking up several sets of nearly vertical stairs from the street—which could be dangerous for children or people loaded down with very heavy backpacks.

But let's move on. You've got to worry when the staff immediately announce, "We're really nice people." (Red flag: That means they're only nice when you're doing exactly what they want you to do.) They really weren't especially nice; just a couple dudes with a world-weary attitude and not much patience. They charge way too much for a bed—this is one of the two or three most expensive hostel beds in the city, about $50 US a night per person in summer (give us a frigging break). They also charge for breakfast, which is included with your fee in almost every other A'dam hostel, so the cost inches up even higher. No wonder the hostel seemed nearly empty despite it being peak season.

The rooms (which were fairly large, containing 4, 5, or 6 single beds apiece compared with the multi-tibed army-style cots and bunks in other Amsterdam hostels) were fair. But why was the place so empty? Even the chill-out lounge next to reception, which has one of the best views of any hostel room in the city, was deserted. We think we might know why: It's not clean enough, it's not big enough, it's not nice enough, and it's not (despite the owners' protestations) fun enough. If you're staying anyway, check out the great beer hall around the corner. On premises, there's a TV in the lounge, where movies are sometimes played along with a constant stream of music videos. You can satisfy that caffeine craving with coffee dispensed from a machine. But families beware: This hostel sometimes attracts a party crowd, evidenced by the many beer bottles scattered about and a tinge of grass in the air (despite the smoking ban). Escape to the ethnic food options that abound near the Leidseplein area, or just stick to the great restaurants and bars of the hip Jordaan area you're staying in; you won't go hungry or thirsty, though you better be packing some cash—A'dam can be a bit expensive.

The nice beds and decent surrounding neighborhood are almost enough to get our highly coveted thumbs-up recommendation. Almost. Maybe it'll get better over time. We hope so!

Best bet for a bite:
Nepalese cuisine
Insiders' tip:
Great beer hall around corner
What hostellers say:
"Tune in, turn on, drop out."
Gestalt:
Doobie brothers
Safety: ◣
Hospitality: ◣◥
Cleanliness: ◥
Party index: 🔺🔺🔺

How To Get There:
By bus or train: From Centraal Station, take #1, #2, or #5 tram to Leidseplein. Walk back to bridge, turn left at canal, walk down to Leidsegracht, and turn left. Hostel is on right.
By car: Call hostel for directions.

The Meeting Point Hostel
Warmoesstraat 14, 1012 JD Amsterdam

Phone: 020-627-7499
Fax: 020-330-4774
E-mail: info@hostel-meetingpoint.nl
Website: hostel-meetingpoint.nl
Rates: €14–€32 (about $19–$40 US) per person
Credit cards: No
Beds: 100
Private/family rooms: No
Kitchen available: No
Season: Open year-round
Office hours: 24 hours
Affiliation: None
Extras: Lockers ($), bar, pool table, currency exchange, foosball, breakfast ($)

---

*T*his place, which has been just around the corner from Amsterdam's Centraal Station for more than 10 years now, tries hard but still hasn't quite got the hostel formula right. It's worth a shot, though, if other good hostels in town are full—we'd definitely pick it over some of the other scuzzy places in this town, which are so terrible and don't care at all about you except for your wallet. Here, they do appear to care a little, or more than a little. And this is perhaps the cheapest bunk in Amsterdam, in case you're down to your final euros.

A majority of the guests here seem to be Americans or Brits, all congregating behind the locked glass door of the hostellers-only (or so claims management) bar. The bar, painted with murals and decorated with banners from European football (that's soccer to Americans) teams, is clearly the focal point of the establishment and offers a good beer selection, video gambling, long wooden tables, and barstools; loud rave music pumps constantly in this common room beneath a steady stream of Euro-videos. They also sell snacks and fast food here, and it's a good area for mixing. However, a number of hostellers had bought grass on the street and were smoking it in the bar, a practice clearly tolerated by management.

Upstairs, they've got several narrow floors of quite spartan dorms, augmented by worn bathrooms. There are two kinds of dorms here, some with 8 beds and the rest with 18 beds; some coed and some for women only. Some have views—of the main canal, the train station, and downtown—while the more drab rooms contain cot-style beds. The rooms are not cleaned well. These rooms sometimes come with a bit of worn furniture, sometimes not; there are 2 toilets and 2 showers per floor, which is too few considering all the beds they've got here.

Best bet for a bite:
Chinese, maybe?
Insiders' tip:
Cafe Gollem brown cafe on Raam-steeg is cool
What hostellers say:
"I wanna get high, so high . . ."
Gestalt:
Meet 'n' greet
Safety:
Hospitality:
Cleanliness:
Party index:

However, we'll give this to the staff: Rooms on the top floors have knockout views of the city canal and downtown Amsterdam, some of the best in the whole darned city. If you're coming for a canal view, ask for a top-floor front room and hope you get one.

Some of the little touches here are nice—a buzz-in system for security, no curfew, incense in the hallways—and points to the management for its "look before you pay" policy regarding rooms. Always look before you pay. Big locked oil drum–size barrels (that once held orange juice concentrate from South America, by the way) store backpacks in the dorm rooms without fear of theft.

The neighborhood is the usual Amsterdam mix, with a Dutch language school around the corner for those actually here to learn something; in a month or two, they say, you can learn this hard-to-master tongue.

How To Get There:

By bus: Call hostel for transit route.
By car: Call hostel for directions.
By train: From Centraal Station, walk across bridge and turn immediately left. Walk to first right, turn right, and continue to hostel on right.

Shelter City Hostel 🏠🏠

Barndesteeg 21, 1012 BV Amsterdam

Phone: 020-625-3230
Fax: 020-623-2282
E-mail: city@shelter.nl
Rates: €13.50–€38.50 (about $17–$49 US) per person
Credit cards: No
Beds: 160
Private/family rooms: No
Kitchen available: No
Season: Open year-round
Office hours: 7:30 a.m.–2 a.m.
Curfew: Midnight (weekdays); 2 a.m. (weekends)
Affiliation: None
Extras: Breakfast, luggage storage, meals ($), lockers ($), piano, currency exchange, foosball

🍴💲🎉

Tucked among red-light district massage parlors and women standing in windows offering sex 'round the clock, this oasis of calm somehow offers one of the cheapest beds in town despite its location.

There's a catch, though . . . it's a Christian hostel, and though they're not pushy about the message, it's everywhere on the walls. And you may get the cold shoulder if you don't join the God Squad at (nightly) Bible time. However, as a quiet alternative to the crazed city outside, it makes a good detour for families, Bible students, or others who need some sanity.

The ground floor, behind the reception, is fairly pleasant—wicker chairs, a few picnic-style tables, a pool table, and a popular piano. Oh, and religious art and messages are everywhere; note especially the Times Square–style ticker scrolling out messages like "He gave his life for you" . . . "Trust in Him" . . . and so on. You half expect stock quotes and sports scores to roll past next.

Anyway, this area leads to a snack bar serving breakfast, dinner, and snacks—nice place and good food. The real drawing card here, though, is an interior courtyard with lily-pads—a cute place amid the squalor where you can hang out or store your bike.

Up the modern stairs, dorms are mostly 12, 16, and 20 (!) bedded, but there are also some 4- to 8-bed ones—nothing special, but certainly clean and airy, if closely packed. This is by far the city's cleanest bunk. Curtains and big windows add a bit of a homey touch. Try to forget all those snoozing bodies around you.

The front desk sells shampoo, rents towels, doles out lockers for a fee, and provides the useful service of storing luggage behind the front desk during the daytime on well-organized racks. (They also host frequent Bible discussions and screen religious videos, of course.)

Best bet for a bite:
Along the main canal
Insiders' tip:
Avoid Nieumarkt subway stop
What hostellers say:
"Jesu . . ."
Gestalt:
A'dam's apple
Safety:
Hospitality:
Cleanliness:
Party index:

You'll meet hostellers of all stripes here, from nice sane Americans to weird, creepy types. One other surprise: They allow smoking in some parts of the place, despite a general no-booze, no-drugs policy.

How To Get There:
By bus: Call hostel for transit route.
By car: Call hostel for directions.
By train: From Centraal Station, walk to Nieumarkt stop, then walk across square (keep big church on your right), make a left and then an immediate right onto Barndesteeg. Hostel is on right.

Shelter Jordaan Hostel

Bloemstraat 179, 1016 LA Amsterdam
> **Phone:** 020-624-4717
> **Fax:** 020-627-6137
> **E-mail:** jordan@shelter.nl
> **Website:** shelter.nl
> **Rates:** €12–€38.50 (about $15–$49 US) per person
> **Credit cards:** No
> **Beds:** 112

Private/family rooms: No

Kitchen available: No

Season: Open year-round

Office hours: 7:30 a.m.–1 a.m.

Lockout: 10 a.m.–12:30 p.m.

Affiliation: None

Extras: Lockers ($), currency exchange, meals ($), snack shop, breakfast, luggage storage, Bible talks

*T*his is the other Christian hostel in Amsterdam, started over 20 years ago in a quiet canal-side neighborhood to complement the affiliated Shelter Hostel downtown. What's different about this one? Well, the location's a heck of a lot better. And the no-smoking policy (inside, that is) is probably unique in A'dam and quite welcome to nonsmoking hostellers. It's a nice place! Despite (maybe because of) the religious affiliation.

The Shelter Jordaan, formerly called the Eben Haezer, touts itself as the "cheapest bed-and-breakfast in town," and they could add that they have one of the best locations in the whole city.

Granite stairs lead you up to the hostel, pretty much a no-frills affair, bedwise—just 2 floors, each with big single-sex dorms packed tightly with bunks. These 14- to 20-bed rooms contain bunks set on metal frames, and the mattresses don't look terribly comfortable; at least there are lockers in each room and huge, clean gang-style bathrooms nearby. Boys aren't allowed on the girls' floor after 10 p.m., which in retrospect is probably a good thing considering that some people start to wind down about that time and don't want to hear some loudmouth bragging about his great day in Amsterdam while they're saying their prayers.

Though you don't have to carry a Bible and prove you're Christian to stay the night, you do have to be able to tolerate the squeaky-clean crowd that tends to gravitate here. On the other hand, you couldn't ask for a nicer staff—they obviously care about your well-being in a way that most other

Best bet for a bite:

Vliegende Schotel

(Flying Saucer) for veggie

What hostellers say:

"The Lord is my shepherd . . ."

Gestalt:

Hostel heaven

Safety:

Hospitality:

Cleanliness:

Party index:

hostels in town don't. For example, they sell shampoo, toothpaste, postcards, and other stuff at the front desk as well as bus, metro, and tram tickets. And they provide a well-organized info board with details on all aspects of this intriguing city.

There's been lots of work here, and it shows in the blue and red–painted bricks, the pretty patio, and a great cafeteria (which sometimes cranks Christian power pop all day long—you have been warned). Kick-start your day the right way with yogurt, muesli, etc., for breakfast. You can't use the kitchen to cook your own meals, but you can buy your own food and eat it in the dining room; dinner is served for about €4 (about $5 US). They also serve snacks like burgers. They keep an eye on your stuff for free with a locked luggage room and a video camera.

Did we describe the common areas? They have comfy couches, plants, and big windows onto the quiet streets—not to mention a suggestion box and a common room with a TV, library, and games.

Again, it's a really nice Jordaan neighborhood—a bit yuppie, but placed near veggie restaurants, great local bars, and just 300 yards from the Anne Frank House—so this is probably the best-positioned hostel in town. If you want peace, quiet, and the flavor of A'dam without any sleaze, stay here.

There is technically an age limit (you're supposed to be between 15 and 40), but staff reportedly look the other way if you're cool or if it's the low season.

A night security guard keeps the riffraff out, though in the Jordaan that is hardly (if ever) a problem. The real problem here is dealing with the squeaky-cleanness of it all.

Ah, what the hell. Oops. We mean what the heck. Give it a shot.

How To Get There:
By bus or train: From Centraal Station, take #13 or #17 tram to fifth stop (Marnxstraat) and cross street. Turn corner and walk to 179 Bloemstraat.
By car: Call hostel for directions.

Stadsdoelen Hostel
Kloveniersburgwal 97, 1011 KB Amsterdam
   Phone: 020-624-6832
   Fax: 020-639-1035
   E-mail: stadsdoelen@stayokay.com
   Website: stayokay.com

Rates: €18.50–€36 (about $23–$45 US) per HI member; doubles €42–€81 (about $53–$101 US)

Credit cards: Yes

Beds: 176

Private/family rooms: Yes

Kitchen available: Yes

Season: March 1–October 1

Office hours: 7 a.m.–1 a.m.

Curfew: 2 a.m.

Affiliation: Stayokay (Hostelling International–Netherlands)

Extras: Bike storage, Internet access, snacks, bar, lockers, laundry, pool table, darts, bike rentals

*W*e've always liked this place. You won't believe the location of the hostel, or the vibe, when you get here. It's one of the better backpacker-style hostels in town, no question, which is even more amazing because it is a Hostelling International–affiliated shop. Even if it's not as great as it was when it first opened, it's still several notches above almost any other bunk in town. The bland 4-floor building on a canal, a former sailors' home that became a hostel back in the 1940s—thus predating the residential apartments that now surround it—doesn't look like much at first glance. But look again: This is the only hostel in town surrounded on both sides by canals; real estate moguls would kill for a piece of property like this today.

Inside, they really pack the beds in. But one of the interesting features about the architecture here is the way they've used minipartitions to help reduce the noise between bunks and give a little extra privacy to people in these huge rooms; it almost (but not quite) turns that 26-bed behemoth into a manageable, sleepable collection of quad rooms.

You'll also find laid-back management, friendly staff, and good common areas. There are two: a reception area with plenty of couches and chairs for mixin' and minglin' and playin' Monopoly and a really awesome bar out back on the second canal.

You enter the bar and immediately spy art on the walls, green plants hanging in pots, decorative railroad signs (who snuck into the rail yard and took those?), and assorted other memorabilia. It's a colorful place with beers on tap, a dartboard and darts, a big TV, the whole deal. So you sidle up to the big wooden bar and order a beer. The music isn't overpoweringly loud (well, not always, anyway); they sell microwaved soups and snacks as long as the bar is open ('til midnight, usually). And there's a nightly happy hour, when drink prices are reduced.

You get a continental breakfast for free in the morning and have access to two very important extras—the ones you want. We're talking about the kitchen and laundry. The kitchen is big and useful, serving as one of the prime mixing points for newfound friends. The laundry is right in there, too, which we actually liked—kill two tasks with one stone, you know? The staff will find you bikes to rent, then let you stash 'em in the basement for safekeeping.

The dorms? They come in male, female, and coed flavors, all of them too big but all partitioned off as described above. Private-room bookings and families are now accepted, a reversal of this hostel's long-standing policy—and a reason to stay here if you're traveling as a couple or family.

Reception sells long-distance Eurolines bus tickets and keeps track of the active message board without getting preachy about anything, a welcome switch. They'll also direct you around the beautiful little neighborhood where the hostel sits, which itself is tucked just far enough away from the red-light district to be comfortable and 2 minutes from the city's best shopping area, the Kalverstraat. (This is about a 15-minute walk from the train station, as well; avoid taking the Metro because the stop is kind of dangerous.)

What else? Big, backpack-size lockers for your stuff; Internet machines to cruise and write e-mail; modern, clean bathrooms; extra-secure bike storage

Best bet for a bite:
La Place, on Kalverstraat
Insiders' tip:
Kalverstraat
What hostellers say:
"Great base!"
Gestalt:
Love canal
Safety:
Hospitality:
Cleanliness:
Party index:

in the basement. (They've taken aggressive security measures in recent years to combat a dodgy neighborhood nearby.) Even the 2 a.m. curfew is somewhat flexible: Staff reopen the doors hourly afterward throughout the night to let in straggling hostellers.

This place is not perfect. The building could certainly use some upgrading after all these years, and staff aren't as kind or watchful (or cleaning-happy) as they used to be. But this is a lower-priced and much more laid-back alternative to the other "official" hostel in town. And a special winter deal makes it even cheaper, giving you 5 nights for the price of 4.

Gentlepeople, start your hostelling engines.

How To Get There:

By bus or train: From Amsterdam's Centraal Station, take #4, 9, #16, #24, or #25 streetcar to Muntplein stop. Walk back down canal toward city center, along Nieuwe Doelenstraat; after crossing first bridge, take a right to cross another small bridge over canal. Make a left on Kloveniersburgwal; hostel is on right. (Late at night, take a taxi.)

By car: Call hostel for directions.

Vondelpark Hostel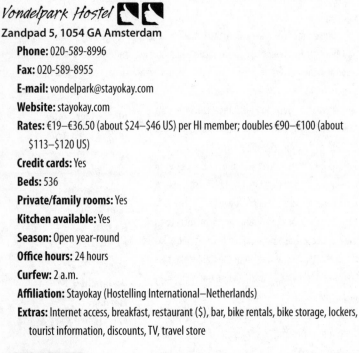

Zandpad 5, 1054 GA Amsterdam

> **Phone:** 020-589-8996
> **Fax:** 020-589-8955
> **E-mail:** vondelpark@stayokay.com
> **Website:** stayokay.com
> **Rates:** €19–€36.50 (about $24–$46 US) per HI member; doubles €90–€100 (about $113–$120 US)
> **Credit cards:** Yes
> **Beds:** 536
> **Private/family rooms:** Yes
> **Kitchen available:** Yes
> **Season:** Open year-round
> **Office hours:** 24 hours
> **Curfew:** 2 a.m.
> **Affiliation:** Stayokay (Hostelling International–Netherlands)
> **Extras:** Internet access, breakfast, restaurant ($), bar, bike rentals, bike storage, lockers, tourist information, discounts, TV, travel store

---

*I*nside a former schoolhouse and bordering the city's biggest and most beautiful park, this Hostelling International entry into the Amsterdam field gets points for quiet and good facilities. In fact, we can say only one semi-negative thing about it: It's too far from the center. (But even that becomes surmountable through the use of public transit. And some of Amsterdam's key museums are actually closer to this hostel than to the train station.)

The dorms and private rooms are good bunks in airy schoolrooms, some with views onto the Vondelpark (which is, yes, a park). This is all the more surprising because, despite its huge size, it doesn't feel like a warehouse at all. There's one really big dorm here, but that's for groups, so don't sweat it. You won't be spending much time in your room anyway. You'll be at one of the 2 e-mail machines or enjoying one of the tons of local discounts you'll get when you flash your receipt or Hostelling International membership card.

Once you do sack out, rooms will have 2, 4, 6, 9, 12, 14, or 24 beds; some doubles have views of the park. Doors feature electronic locks and beds come with "duvies"—thick English-style quilted blankets good for keeping out the persistent damp chill that follows you around the city in bad weather.

Oh, and almost every room—from the tiniest double to the biggest group dorm— has its own bathroom, a nice plus. We met everyone from Euro-teens to Swedish families here, so obviously the word is out big-time about the place.

They serve overly heavy dinners for a fee in the ambitiously named Brasserie Backpackers; skip dinner and head there for happy hour instead, with beer on tap and always a lively crowd of Americans and Europeans with stories to share. Next morning, breakfast—served in rooms named for cities of the world and decorated in appropriate fashion—is actually quite nice: lots of fresh-baked bread, peanut butter, chocolate, cheese, and ham, plus good corn flakes. It's a good effort, especially so because they're not too clucky about your going back for seconds or thirds.

A couple of things to keep in mind: Tons of groups stay here (the other HI joint in town does not take groups), and you'll see them . . . at all hours. Getting giggly in the halls. Singing below your window at 2 in the morning. Hogging the marmalade at breakfast. So get used to it, or move along.

Best bet for a bite:
Overtoom or Leidseplein
Insiders' tip:
FedEx Office on Overtoom
What hostellers say:
"It's getting better all the time."
Gestalt:
Park place
Safety:
Hospitality:
Cleanliness:
Party index:

So, you're in for a good time as long as you can handle the constant parade of Euro-groups and the by-the-book staff. And you're just steps from both the amazing Rijksmuseum (Vermeer, van Gogh, Rembrandt, et al.) and always-hoppin' Leidseplein, a much tamer Times

Square-y alternative to the red-light district. Though it's been somewhat Americanized (Mickey D's, BK, Marriott, etc.) of late, this square is still the best concentration of food and safe street life in town for the money.

Just watch the park area at night; the hostel does a good job of using lots of security measures to protect the place.

How To Get There:
By bus: From bus terminal, take the #12 streetcar to Van Baerlestraat stop and walk straight into park. Go down stairs to hostel on right.
By car: Call hostel for directions. (Note: There is no parking at this hostel.)
By train: From Centraal Station take #1, #2, or #5 streetcar to Leidseplein; walk up to Marriott hotel, turn left on main road, and walk ¼ mile southwest to hostel sign at Zandpad; turn right and walk down walkway to hostel on right.

White Tulip Youth Hostel
Warmoesstraat 87, Amsterdam

> **Phone:** 020-625-5974
> **Fax:** 020-420-1299
> **E-mail:** info@wittetulp.nl
> **Website:** wittetulp.nl
> **Rates:** €11–€37 (about $14–$46 US) per person; doubles €100 (about $125 US)
> **Credit cards:** No
> **Beds:** 81
> **Private/family rooms:** Sometimes
> **Kitchen available:** No
> **Season:** Open year-round
> **Office hours:** 24 hours
> **Affiliation:** None
> **Extras:** Breakfast ($), pub, meals ($), lockers

---

*T*he sweet-sounding White Tulip is actually the former Budget Hostel AVC. That place had crossed the oh-so-fine line from hostel to flophouse, located above a really sleazy bar—the kind Tom Waits would write a song about. The only saving grace was its location if you wanted to party really hard and not have to go too far to reach your bed—or if you needed to make a quick getaway from the station early the next morning.

What hostellers say:
"It's a party . . . "
Safety:
Hospitality:
Cleanliness:
Party index:

Ownership has changed; not much else has. The popular Irish pub is still there. There are 14 rooms containing a total of 72 beds in a series of private rooms (1 to 3 beds), dorms with en-suite bathrooms (4 to 5 beds), and bigger dorms (8 to 10 beds). What else has changed? It's expensive for such a middling place. Security remains as lax as ever. So does the cleaning crew. If there even is one.

The only possible selling point is its proximity to an old church and a nice flower shop (but also the Prostitution Information Center, so there), and that Irish pub everyone comes to drink at. But it's still nowhere near enough to consider, unless you're super desperate.

How To Get There:
By bus or train: Call hostel for transit route.
By car: Call hostel for directions.

	Attractive natural setting		Comfortable beds		Visual arts at hostel or nearby
	Ecologically aware hostel		A particularly good value		Music at hostel or nearby
	Superior kitchen facilities or cafe		Wheelchair-accessible		Great hostel for skiers
	Offbeat or eccentric place		Good for business travelers		Bar or pub at hostel or nearby
	Superior bathroom facilities		Especially well-suited for families		Editors' choice: Among our very favorite hostels
	Romantic private rooms		Good for active travelers		

Key to Icons

Norway

*N*orway is fjord-tough. But seriously, this is some of Europe's most spectacular scenery—and if you're in the area (in other words, Denmark or Sweden), you'd be foolish not to pencil in a couple days up here. The Oslo-to-Bergen train ride has justifiably been called one of the best in the world, and several side trips off that line bring you face to face with even more spectacular fjord-side scenery.

Hotels are very expensive up here, making hostels an attractive option; if you think your dorm bed costs a lot, just pick up a hotel flyer and do the conversion—you'll get down on your knees and thank us immediately.

Practical Details

Norway's country code is 47; Oslo's city code is 22. To dial Oslo hostels from the US, dial 011-47 plus the number AS PRINTED. To dial Oslo hostels from within Norway, also dial the number AS PRINTED.

As we've said, things cost a lot of money. The unit of currency here is the Norwegian krone (NKr). Six kroner equal one US dollar—so that 250 NKr dorm room costs a surprising 40-plus bucks in cold, hard US cash.

OSLO

Most travelers to Norway begin in Oslo; it's the biggest city, the most cultural, and the easiest to reach via overnight train or ferry from Denmark or Sweden. (You can also catch an all-day train from Copenhagen or Göteborg.) This is a place that has long benefited from its position by the water (it was founded in 1050!), but the work of being a port city has given some ground to the arts and big business. Residents zip across the water on ferries to the hidden beaches—and the Viking Ships Museum—of the Bygdøy peninsula. At night, young folks congregate in the hippest nightclubs of the moment. And you're just a short ride from the big mountains of Lillehammer, former venue for the Winter Olympics. It remains a top ski destination for Norwegians—and a great place for a hike in the meadows in summer.

If coming by train you arrive at Oslo Sentral, which faces wide Karl Johans Gate—the main street of the city, which is actually tackier and more commercial than one would hope these days, but it leads you right into the center. To get around, you can use an extensive network of streetcars, buses, or the subway, which is known here (as in Stockholm) as the "T-bana."

Not to be confused with the E- (Eric) Bana, of course.

OSLO HOSTELS AT A GLANCE

	RATING	PRICE	IN A WORD	PAGE
Haraldsheim Hostel		245–470 NKr	modern	p. 339
Anker Hostel		220–620 NKr	central	p. 337

Anker Hostel

Storgata 55, Oslo 0182

> **Phone:** 22-99-7200
> **Fax:** 22-99-7220
> **E-mail:** hostel@anker.oslo.no
> **Website:** ankerhostel.no
> **Rates:** 220–620 NKr (about $37–$103 US) per person; doubles 600–620 NKr (about $100–$103 US)
> **Credit cards:** No
> **Beds:** 108
> **Private/family rooms:** Yes
> **Kitchen available:** Yes
> **Office hours:** 24 hours (summer), 7 a.m.–11:30 p.m. (Sept–Apr)
> **Affiliation:** None
> **Extras:** Breakfast ($), bar, laundry, free WiFi, lockers

*P*art of the extremely bland-looking Anker Hotel, this independent hostel is very central—much more so than Oslo's other hostel, in fact, almost walking distance from its train station. Its chief redeeming value beyond location is its price: You'll find no (reputable) hotel in town to offer a cheaper double room. It is OK, not great, and many hostellers have mixed feelings about the place.

So do we.

The hotel/hostel sits right across the street from a clinic—a good thing in case the lobby bar gets you a little too relaxed. Inside, the place has single and double private rooms,

Best bet for a bite:
Kaffistova (downtown)
for Norwegian food
What hostellers say:
"I guess it'll do."
Gestalt:
Phat Albertine
Safety:
Hospitality:
Cleanliness:
Party index:

plus 4-, 6-, and 8-bed dormitories. The dorms are equipped with handmade wooden bunks; the doubles come with little work desks and lamps. It feels a lot like our college dorm—except that the rooms here have individual bathrooms, which our freshman dorms certainly didn't. All rooms come with duvets, but you've got to either bring your own sheet or pay big bucks to rent theirs. On the downside, you can smell cooking throughout (there are kitchens inside many of the dorm rooms rather than a single, centralized canteen), and security is very lax. Not good in a big-city neighborhood.

With regard to the kitchen, as in many other Scandinavian hostels you have to cart in most of your own utensils; if you don't feel like doing that, a buffet lunch is served on weekdays. The hotel restaurant is also a fun place to pick up the breakfast spread and meet others doing the same. (They serve dinners only to groups, unfortunately.) A laundry, Internet access, lockers, and parking (for a fee) are also welcome additions. However, be prepared to fork over a big (about $30 US) key deposit upon check-in. Not sure why.

While seriously short on personality—the hostel and the surrounding area are Zipsville for character—this place is certainly good enough given its proximity to all the cool downtown stuff Oslo has to offer and the low price. Just don't expect a perfectly secure or social experience.

How To Get There:

By bus: From bus station, take #10, #11, #12, #15, or #17 streetcar to Hausmanns Gate stop, then walk along Storgata to hostel on left.

By car: Take the E18 into Oslo, following signs for Gjøvik. Exit and turn left at the second traffic circle. At the next light, turn right onto Christian Krogh Street and follow it to the end and the Anker Hotel Best Western. Hostel entrance is 20 yards to the left of main hotel entrance.

By bus: From plaza in front of Oslo station, take #12, #13, or #15 streetcar or #30, #31, or #32 bus to Hausmanns Gate stop. Walk along Storgata to hostel on left. Or, from front station entrance, turn right and walk 2 blocks north to Storgata; turn right and continue ½ mile to hostel.

By train: From Oslo station, take #12, #13, or #15 streetcar or #30, #31, or #32 bus to Hausmanns Gate stop. Walk along Storgata to hostel on left. Or, from front station entrance, turn right and walk 2 blocks north to Storgata; turn right and continue ½ mile to hostel.

Haraldsheim Hostel ◣◣

Haraldsheimveien 4, Grefsen (Oslo) 0409

    Phone: 22-222-965

    E-mail: haraldsheim@haraldsheim.oslo.no

    Website: haraldsheim.no

    Rates: 245–470 NKr (about $41–$78 US) per person; doubles 560–640 NKr (about $93–$107 US)

    Credit cards: No

    Beds: 268

    Private/family rooms: Yes

    Kitchen available: Yes

    Season: January 2–December 23

    Office hours: 24 hours

    Affiliation: Hostelling International

    Extras: Laundry, free WiFi, free breakfast, meals ($), parking, luggage storage, lockers, grounds, meeting rooms, TV room

---

*H*ave to say, right out of the gate, this place is awesome. Located 2 to 3 miles north of Oslo's city center, the city's "official" (and big) hostel does lack a bit of atmosphere and is quite a ways out of town. That's the bad. But the rest is a revelation: A-1 hostelling! We can't complain about a single thing here. The surrounding countryside is great looking, this is cheaper than a hotel back in town, and it's incredibly well-run. Just don't plan on doing much in the city at night, because you'll need to budget time to take the bus back out here before it gets too, too late.

Almost all the beds here come in 4-bed dorms (63 of 'em), but there are 8 doubles as well. Some of the newer rooms come with partial shower facilities; others share everything with everyone. There are lots of amenities that families like: a television lounge, a laundry, meals, a kitchen, Internet access, stuff like that. Warning: Staff have been known to enforce a lockout at times.

The breakfasts here are fast becoming legend, and the good kitchen gets a workout too. A television room and Internet terminals provide welcome distractions when the weather turns bad.

How To Get There:

By bus: From station, take #31 bus to Sinsenkrysset stop; turn right and follow signs ½ mile to hostel.

By car: Contact hostel for directions.

By train: From Oslo station, take #17 streetcar to Sinsenkrysset stop; turn right and follow signs ½ mile to hostel.

Best bet for a bite:
Better eat here

What hostellers say:
"Nice view."

Gestalt:
Hark the Haraldsheim

Safety: ◪

Hospitality: ◪

Cleanliness: ◪

Party index: ▲▲

Portugal

*P*ortugal is perched way on the western edge of Europe, so it takes time to get there. But it's well worth the trip: This place is cheap, sunny, and friendly—generally speaking—if a bit more challenging than, say, England.

Hostels in Lisbon are usually not the backpacker's first choice when it comes to accommodation. Why? Because hotels are really cheap compared with the rest of Europe and are more attractive because they don't have the same rules and aren't booked up with teenage school groups. That's not to say that Lisbon and Portuguese hostels are undesirable. They offer many amenities, including meals, and, interestingly, almost every hostel in the country is open year-round—a mighty welcome switch from the norm. But think twice before booking a hostel over a hotel, because you won't save much dough.

Practical Details

Transit in Portugal is a little sketchy, though you can get to Lisbon pretty easily by long-distance or overnight train from Spain. Once you're here, you fan out into the countryside via train or, often, bus or ferry. A train pass isn't really worth buying, as the country is fairly small and tickets are cheap anyway.

Portugal's phone code is 351. To dial Portuguese hostels from the US, dial 011-351 and DROP THE ZERO from the numbers listed. To dial Portuguese hostels from within Portugal, dial the numbers AS LISTED.

The unit of currency in Portugal is the euro.

LISBON

Lisbon—often overlooked on quickie itineraries of Europe because of its remoteness—actually turns out to be one of the most interesting cities on the Continent. If you're coming, though, be prepared for a change: You're leaving the ordered world of a Paris or London and plunging headlong into Moorish, Spanish, and African influences. Twisting streets, weird smells, haggling over prices, and petty thieves are gonna be part of the experience. So buckle up and dive in.

If traveling by train, you'll most likely start your visit at either the Rossio or Santa Apollónia train station. From there, Lisbon's transportation system consists of buses, trams, an underground Metro, funicular stairways, and taxi-boats . . . a lot to take in! But it is economical and useful, so study a map. You buy transit tickets at *Carris* kiosks—a pass for one

Lisbon

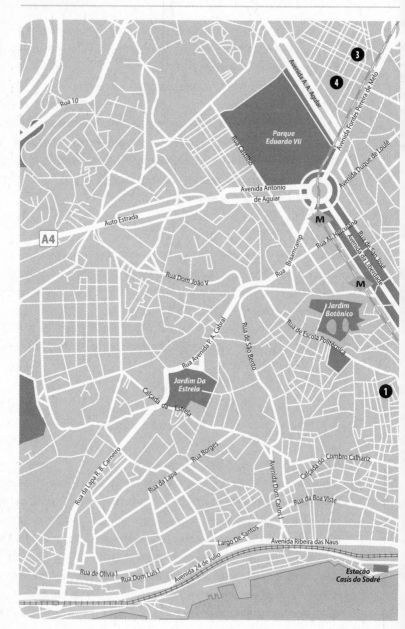

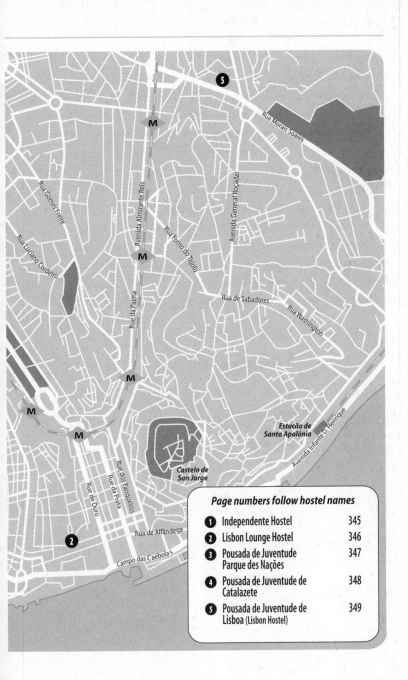

to seven days. These passes cover only buses and trams, however, so you might think about buying a Lisboacard, which gives you unlimited use of the Metro and other transport, plus free or discounted access to about 25 monuments and museums around the city.

To explore the best, start at the Baixa district—it's Portuguese for "low"—down by the water, a carefully designed grid erected in the wake of the devastating 1755 earthquake. Look here for incredibly cheap and good eats, usually some form of grilled meat, chicken, or fish. Veggie eats can be found, too. The hillside Alfama neighborhood is the Baixa's opposite, a warren of streets where you're almost certain to get mixed up. But it's mighty interesting as you pick your way among the steeper-than-steep stairways or flea market stalls that give the area so much character.

Up top, finally, is Bairro Alto, with some of the best music in town and—obviously—the best views, too. The club scene is amazing, beyond belief to anyone but a Euro-clubber; come on the weekend and you'll never think your hometown's "scene" is a scene again.

To get around, use the craziest combination of trolleys, stairways, subways, and ferries you can manage; it won't be any crazier than what anyone else is doing, anyway. You'd be nuts to try driving in this city, so make like the locals and do a Chutes and Ladders tour up and down the hills of this beguiling city.

LISBON HOSTELS AT A GLANCE

	RATING	PRICE	IN A WORD	PAGE
Lisbon Lounge Hostel	★★	€14–€25	awesome	p. 346
The Independente Hostel	★★	€16–€21	fantastic	p. 345
Pousada de Juventude de Lisboa	★	€14–€17	good	p. 349
Pousada de Juventude de Catalazete	★	€11–€13	distant	p. 348
Pousada de Juventude Parque des Nações	★★	€14–€17	central	p. 347

The Independente Hostel 🏴🏴

Rua De São Pedro De Alcântara No. 81, 1250-238 Lisbon

> **Phone:** 0213-461-381
> **Fax:** 0213-478-402
> **E-mail:** reservations@theindependente.pt
> **Rates:** €16–€21 per person (about $20–$26 US)
> **Credit cards:** Yes
> **Beds:** 90
> **Private/family rooms:** Yes
> **Kitchen available:** Yes
> **Season:** Open year-round
> **Office hours:** 24 hours
> **Affiliation:** None
> **Extras:** Free WiFi, free breakfast, meals ($), bar, deck, fax service, bike rentals

🗑️ ❌ 🎖️

*S*upposedly the brainchild of three brothers, the Independente gets everything right. In an Art Deco space of 11 dorms and 4 suites on the border of the Bairro Alto district, this joint was once an ambassador's home, and it looks it.

The hostel features wrought-iron staircases, a popular bar, free breakfast, and nice dinners (with wine) in a great little restaurant for a very small extra charge. There's also a healthy supply of both art and sunlight, and windows aplenty.

Dorms come in configurations of 6, 9, or 12 beds apiece. The 4 suites, as we said, are even better but you really can't go wrong with a bed here. The Tagus River across the way provides the views, history, and tranquility.

This is living large on a beer budget, friends. Book it while you can.

Best bet for a bite:
Right here
Insiders' tip:
Chiado neighborhood
What hostellers say:
"Superb!"
Gestalt:
Fado-lous
Safety: 🏴
Hospitality: 🏴
Cleanliness: 🏴
Party index: 🎉🎉

How To Get There:

By bus: Contact hostel for transit route.
By train: Contact hostel for transit route.
By car: Contact hostel for directions.

Lisbon Lounge

Rua São Nicolau 41, 1100-547 Lisbon

Phone: 0213-462-061
Website: lisbonloungehostel.com
Rates: €14–€25 (about $21 to $38 US) per person; doubles €54–€64 (about $81 to $96 US)
Credit cards: Yes
Beds: 44
Private/family rooms: Yes
Kitchen available: Yes
Season: Open year-round
Office hours: 24 hours
Affiliation: None
Extras: Bike rentals, free breakfast, laundry, free WiFi, free walking tours, movies

Step right up, folks: This here is your top hostel in town, in a great artsy neighborhood to boot.

Nine dorms of 2 to 8 beds apiece fill the town house, plus there's a lounge on each and every floor. Decor is terrific: whitewashed walls befitting the location, art on the walls, great playful Euro-furniture. And the kitchen—with its sturdy wood tables, open concept, and stonework—is one you (or any millionaire) would be proud to have in your own house. Can you tell an artist owns this place?

Everything is kept clean, and staff are hip, professional, helpful, and friendly. They offer

Best bet for a bite:
Rua dos Correeiros restos and supermarket
What hostellers say:
"Best in town. Obrigado."
Gestalt:
Chez Lounge
Safety:
Hospitality:
Cleanliness
Party index:

extras like movies and free walking tours. And the location is aces: in the heart of a warren of historic old buildings, some refurbished with coffee bars, restaurants, and the like.

Not sure what else you could possibly ask of, or want, in a hostel for your 20 bucks. Given the commitment, beauty, and personality here, this is one of the top hostels in Europe.

How To Get There:
By bus: Contact hostel for transit route.
By train: Contact hostel for transit route.
By car: Contact hostel for directions.

Pousada de Juventude Parque des Nações

Rua de Moscavide, Lt 47-101, 1998-011 Lisbon

> **Phone:** 0218-920-890
> **Fax:** 0217-232-101
> **E-mail:** lisboaparque@movijovem.pt
> **Rates:** €14–€17 (about $17–$18 US) per HI member; doubles €30–€42 (about $38–$53 US)
> **Credit cards:** No
> **Beds:** 92
> **Private/family rooms:** Yes
> **Kitchen available:** Yes
> **Season:** Open year-round
> **Office hours:** 8 a.m.–midnight
> **Affiliation:** HI-MOVIJOVEM
> **Extras:** Breakfast, meals ($), laundry, cafe, Internet access, bar, terrace

---

*T*his medium-size hostel serves as a kind of nondescript overflow for the more popular central hostels. It's marketing itself as a fun, family-friendly place. Unfortunately, it's about 6 miles northeast of central Lisbon, and both the friendliness and cleanliness factors are lagging. Sure, it's open year-round and does have a kitchen—the main hostel in town doesn't—but otherwise it's not quite as good and is much farther from the action. The place consists of 10 double bedrooms (2 of which are wheelchair-accessible) and 18 quad rooms. If you do come, expect lots a school groups with a minibus to get them all the way out here. It also, as we said, could be a lot cleaner than it actually is. We'll give it a pass, though it is adequate and the breakfasts are decent.

Since it's near the Plaza of Nations Park, site of the 1998 World Expo, there is a surprising amount of stuff to see, do, and eat around here. We're talking a plethora of cafes and markets where you can pick up picnic supplies or fixin's for dinner. After your little shopping trip, check out Europe's biggest oceanarium—in the park, naturally.

Best bet for a bite:
Park of Nations food court
What hostellers say:
"Obrigado!"
Gestalt:
Expo-sed
Safety:
Hospitality:
Cleanliness:
Party index:

How To Get There:
By bus or train: Call hostel for transit directions.
By car: Call hostel for directions.

Pousada de Juventude de Catalazete

Estrada Marginal (near Inatel), 2780-267 Oeiras (Lisbon)

> **Phone:** 0214-430-638
> **Fax:** 0217-232-101
> **E-mail:** catalazete@movijovem.pt
> **Rates:** €11–€13 (about $14–$17 US) per HI member; doubles €26–€75 (about $33–$94 US)
> **Credit cards:** No
> **Beds:** 86
> **Private/family rooms:** Yes
> **Kitchen available:** Yes
> **Season:** Open year-round
> **Office hours:** 8 a.m.–midnight
> **Lockout:** 2–6 p.m.
> **Curfew:** Midnight
> **Affiliation:** HI-MOVIJOVEM
> **Extras:** Meals ($), laundry, cafe, bar, TV

---

*T*his pleasant, medium-size hostel sits pretty along its own stretch of sandy beach—a relief for those who have tired of the cacophony of the big city. Better yet, it's just a short ride by local train from the craziness of Lisbon and is just beautifully run.

If it's privacy you seek, the hostel sports 14 double rooms and 1 private apartment with full kitchen (it sleeps up to four). Otherwise you'll be sacking out with the young'uns in one of the 6-bed dormitories (there are 9 of those in all). Fortunately, there's a laundry for guest use as well as a cafe and a bar serving ultrastrong coffee. Should you be sampling Lisbon's nightlife, remember that the strict curfew is at midnight and you'll have to plan on a short night. Still, the ace kitchen and clean and friendly demeanor make it well worth considering.

Most people staying here accept the curfew and come for the beach. You should do the same: Leave the club scene for another night and another hostel.

Best bet for a bite:	
Bring your own grub	
Insiders' tip:	
Bring a towel	
What hostellers say:	
"Surf's up!"	
Gestalt:	
Reach the beach	
Safety:	
Hospitality:	
Cleanliness:	
Party index:	

How To Get There:

By bus: From Lisbon's Cais do Sodré Station, take bus to Oeiras. Or contact hostel for transit route.

By car: Call hostel for directions.

By train: From Lisbon's Cais do Sodré Station, take local train to Oeiras. Walk downhill to town, underneath main road and through park; follow signs ½ mile to hostel. Or contact hostel for transit route.

Pousada de Juventude de Lisboa (Lisbon Hostel)

Rua Andrade Corvo 46, 1050-009 Lisbon
  Phone: 0213-532-696
  Fax: 0217-232-101
  E-mail: lisboa@movijovem.pt

Rates: €14–€17 (about $19–$21 US) per Hostellling International member; doubles €40–€44 (about $50–$55 US)

Credit cards: No

Beds: 176

Private/family rooms: Yes

Kitchen available: No

Season: Open year-round

Office hours: 8 a.m.–midnight

Curfew: Midnight

Affiliation: HI-MOVIJOVEM

Extras: Breakfast, meals ($), television, lockers, tourist information, conference room, disco, bar, currency exchange, laundry

*W*ith its central location, Lisbon's only down-town hostel gets good marks for position and upkeep—a surprise, actually. It's not perfect, and staff could take a chill pill every now and then, but it's OK.

They give you a free breakfast, serve meals for very little (though we'd always eat out in this town), and have some private rooms with double beds. The hostel tries to pile on the amenities. There's a "disco" (really? That's so 1975!), bar, television room, and tourist information desk, for starters. There are 14 double rooms—2 of them outfitted to be wheelchair-accessible—plus 19 quads and a dozen 6-bed dorms; you won't have to worry about being shoehorned into a super-huge dorm room for once, which is nice.

This is kind of a blah location, sure, but think of it this way: At least you're in town. And it's gonna be fairly quiet. Third, you're pretty close—especially via the city's Metro subway—to the stuff you actually wanna see, such as the cheap-to-eat "Low Town" or the hard-partying "Upper Town" (we're sparing you the

Best bet for a bite:
Espiral (macrobiotic/veggie) on Praça da Ilha do Faial

Insiders' tip:
Funiculars provide great views of city

What hostellers say:
"I liked it."

Gestalt:
Port authority

Safety:

Hospitality:

Cleanliness:

Party index:

Portuguese names because, well, we can't pronounce them, either). Or some hostellers just head for nearby Eduardo Park, which is fine for a day of doing nothing much (don't hang out there at night, of course); check out the greenhouses full of exotic plants, for a small charge, if you're into green thumbing.

How To Get There:
By bus: Take #44, #45, or #90 bus to Picoas stop, then walk 50 yards to hostel.
By car: Call hostel for directions.
By train: From any station, walk to Rossio Metro stop and take subway to Picoas stop. Cross Avenida Augusto de Aguiar and then cross Rua Pedreira. Continue 50 yards to hostel.
By subway: Take Metro to Picoas stop, cross Avenida Augusto de Aguiar, and then cross Rua Pedreira. Continue 50 yards to hostel.

Spain

*S*unny, peppy, and affordable, Spain's your place if you loathe clouds. You can lie on beaches; gawk at some of Europe's most incredible museums, castles, and historic sites; gorge yourself on fish, paella, tapas, and wine for a pittance; and dance 'til dawn—that's what the Spaniards do. We're talking about a culture where dinner happens around midnight. Really.

The hostel system in Spain is extensive, but you'll have to work to find a true bargain. That's because hotel rooms cost almost the same as a double room at a typical hostel; unless you're traveling alone, it might not make sense to find an out-of-the-way hostel.

Note that the word *hostal* in Spain means a small, European-style hotel (what other countries call a "pension" and we might call a "simple B&B"); it is NOT A HOSTEL. Look for the words *joves* or *juvenil* (youth) and *albergue* (hostel).

Practical Details

It's easy to get to Spain. You can fly direct from the US, London, Paris, and elsewhere. (See the introduction for more on European budget airlines.) Once you're here, Spain's train system is efficient if slow due to the long distances and varied terrain involved in a city-to-city trip. There are some high-speed trains between Madrid and the southern coast that can quicken the journey, but these AVE trains are quite a bit more expensive than regular trains; even Eurail pass holders need to pay a supplemental fee.

Spain's country code is 34; there aren't any special city codes. To dial Spanish hostels from the US, dial 011-34 plus the number AS PRINTED. To dial Spanish hostels from within Spain, dial the number AS PRINTED.

The unit of currency in Spain is the euro.

BARCELONA

Located only a couple hours' train ride from the French border, Barcelona is Spain's most international and cosmopolitan city. Why do you think they awarded this place the Olympics? This is the place to see world-class art and architecture, and the food's pretty darned good, too. It's also pretty flat, making walking easy. And the transit system is top-notch—just hop on a subway to get around. From Sants Station, catch a Red Line train into town (toward Fondo); from França, you can easily walk to the action.

While here, you'll want to see the Modernist architecture of such stars as Gaudí. If you're not into that, check out the amazing nightlife; this city rocks all night. Las Ramblas is the main drag, connecting most of the downtown parts; the elevated Montjuïc (Jewish Mountain) is the location of the Olympic Stadium and palaces. L'Eixample is probably the most interesting neighborhood.

There is one "official" hostel in the city, but it's a pretty hefty trek from the action.

BARCELONA HOSTELS AT A GLANCE

	RATING	PRICE	IN A WORD	PAGE
Itaca Hostel	🐾🐾	€11–€28	best	p. 358
Albergue Mere de Déu	🐾	€17.25–€23.25	faraway	p. 353
Kabul Hostel	🐾	€13–€30	paaaarty	p. 360
Gothic Point Hostel	🐾🐾	€24.50–€27	unusual	p. 357

Albergue Mere De Déu 🐾

Passeig de la Mare de Déu del Coll 41–51, 08023 Barcelona

Phone: 93-210-5151

Fax: 93-210-0798

E-mail: alberg-barcelona@gencat.cat

Rates: €17.25–€23.25 (about $22–$30 US) per HI member

Credit cards: Yes

Beds: 209

Private/family rooms: No

Kitchen available: No

Season: Closed December 24–26

Office hours: 24 hours

Affiliation: HI

Extras: Breakfast, luggage storage, lockers, playground, laundry, information desk, parking, TV room, Internet access, meals ($)

Barcelona

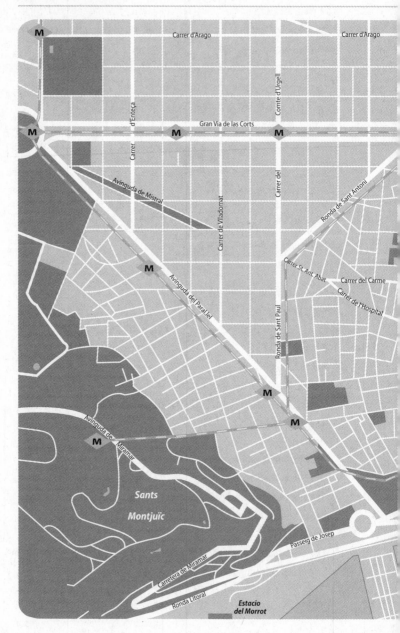

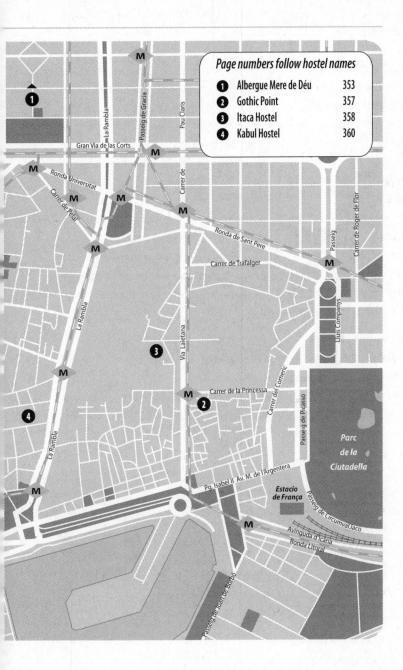

Page numbers follow hostel names

S taff here must be pretty overworked. The first time we called to reserve a room, we were told that they were "full up." *Click.* (That's the sound of a phone hanging up, in case you couldn't figure that out.) The next time we called, still full—and still less than gracious.

To be fair, though, that hasn't happened since. And, better yet the place is not only pretty good once you get here and finish dealing with the staff, but getting better with age. For starters, it's well designed, with homier-than-you'd-expect touches. Rooms are pretty decent, too, if a bit large: 6-, 8-, and 12-bed dorms. Family and double rooms are no longer an option. It's all supplemented by tons of amenities, everything from Internet access to a TV room to meals, lockers, a luggage room, and grounds. Needless to say, Spanish school groups love the place.

Best bet for a bite:
Back in the city
What hostellers say:
"Nice place; too distant."
Gestalt:
Far out
Safety:
Hospitality:
Cleanliness:
Party index:

Drawbacks? It's kind of remote—you're far north of the central city, several miles away, in fact, and though there are certainly some eateries and other distractions, it's really not where you wanna be. Thank goodness for Metro access, if you can figure out how to use it.

How To Get There:

By bus: Take #28 bus from Plaça de Catalunya to hostel.
By car: Contact hostel for directions.
By train: From Sants Station, take Metro Blue Line (#5) toward Horta to Provença Station. Walk through concourse to Diagonal Station, change to Green Line (#3), and continue

Key to Icons

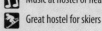
Attractive natural setting
Ecologically aware hostel
Superior kitchen facilities or cafe
Offbeat or eccentric place
Superior bathroom facilities
Romantic private rooms

Comfortable beds
A particularly good value
Wheelchair-accessible
Good for business travelers
Especially well-suited for families
Good for active travelers

Visual arts at hostel or nearby
Music at hostel or nearby
Great hostel for skiers
Bar or pub at hostel or nearby
Editors' choice: Among our very favorite hostels

toward Montbau 3 stops to Vallcarca Station. Walk through Plaça Mons down Avenida Rep. Argentina; cross over Avenida Hospital Hilitar and bear left to hostel.

Gothic Point Hostel

Carrer dels Vigatans 5, 08003 Barcelona

Phone: 93-231-2045

E-mail: infogothic@equity-point.com

Website: gothicpoint.com

Rates: €24.50–€27 (about $31–$34 US) per person

Credit cards: Yes

Beds: 145

Private/family rooms: No

Kitchen available: No

Season: Open year-round

Office hours: 24 hours

Affiliation: None

Extras: Free Internet access, breakfast, bar, tours, lockers ($), laundry

---

*T*his place with the spaceship theme has its ups and its downs. For starters, the bunks are a little strange and quite hard to get into if you're put on a top level—you've got to see what we mean. They're enclosed, which is good, but it's all a bit claustrophobic. We're talking a serious lack of air circulation here. As a result, the dorm rooms (containing 6 to 14 beds apiece) can get sorta hot in summertime, not to mention noisy. There's also a weird drape-like partitioning system. And several hostellers whispered to us that their stuff had been moved or swiped. Security is quite lax, obviously.

The location is ace, though: It's just 150 yards from the Picasso Museum! And the bathrooms are surprisingly good for such a busy hostel; the lounge is fun; and they do serve up a kind of (not very nutritious) breakfast. Thanks for trying, guys. Fun can be had here, and often

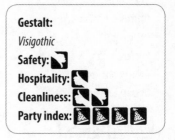

Gestalt:
Visigothic
Safety:
Hospitality:
Cleanliness:
Party index:

is. And the "nodules" get generally good reviews—again, see what we mean. There's also a good attempt to clamp down on security.

It'll do in a pinch, but there are better places in town.

How To Get There:

By car: Contact hostel for directions.

By bus: Take #54 bus from Berlin and Numancia Streets to Gran Via Street. Change to #45 bus and continue to Plaça del Angel. Get off bus and cross Via Laietana Street to Argenteria Street. Take first left onto Vigatans, just past La Caixa (bank). Late at night, take taxi.

By train: From Sants Station, take Metro Blue Line (#5) toward Horta to Verdaguer station; change to Yellow Line (#4) and continue (toward La Pai) to Jaume I station. Follow signs to Argenteria exit and walk 50 yards along Argenteria Street to first left; turn left on Vigatans, just past La Caixa (bank). Late at night, take taxi.

From Catalunya Station, take Red Line (#1) to Urquinaona Station, then change to Yellow Line (#4) and continue to Jaume I Station. Late at night, take taxi.

Itaca Hostel

Carrer de Ripoll 21, 08002 Barcelona

> **Phone:** 93-301-9751
> **E-mail:** pilimili@itacahostel.com
> **Website:** itacahostel.com
> **Rates:** €11–€28 (about $14–$35 US) per person; doubles €60–€70 (about $75–$88 US)
> **Credit cards:** No
> **Beds:** 30
> **Private/family rooms:** Yes
> **Kitchen available:** Yes
> **Season:** Open year-round
> **Office hours:** 24 hours
> **Lockout:** Yes
> **Curfew:** 4 a.m.
> **Affiliation:** None
> **Extras:** Lockers, breakfast

$\mathcal{S}$till the reigning king of Barcelonian hostels, this nice-looking place in the city's so-called Gothic neighborhood is small (and a bit hard to find) but extremely well-kept. It has great positioning working for it: The place is just a short stroll from the Picasso Museum, the Ramblas, the Cathedral, and tons o' Gaudi. Couldn't pick a better spot to situate a hostel if you tried, could you? (Go ahead and try. We're waiting. See?)

And then they go and get the hostelling part of the deal right, too. Rooms here are broken out into 6-, 8-, and 12-bed dorms, and they've also got some private rooms with their own en-suite bathrooms. Amazingly, each room has a balcony, and pastel colors predominate rather than a party ethos. It scores high in all categories with us: friendly, hip, kept clean, and reasonable. All in all, this is an excellent choice. Staff are superb, the place is clean (big points for that), fun, and happy, and you meet cool people staying here. What the heck else do you want?

Yes, there is a kitchen, a breakfast service (you need to pay a little extra for that), and storage lockers with keys; if you're traveling with a family or small group, inquire about the more expensive apartment, which isn't all that spectacular but certainly offers privacy.

> **What hostellers say:**
> *"Amazingly good!"*
> **Safety:** 🗾
> **Hospitality:** 🗾
> **Cleanliness:** 🗾

How To Get There:

By bus: From bus station, take Metro line 1 from Arc de Triomf station to Urquinaona station. Walk along Via Laietana to Avenida de la Catedral, then follow Carrer del Dr. Joaquím Pou to hostel.

By car: Contact hostel for directions.

By train: From train station, walk along Via Laietana to Avenida de la Catedral, then follow Carrer del Dr. Joaquím Pou to hostel.

Or take Metro line 3 to Plaça Catalunya station; walk along Portal del l'Angel to Avenida de la Catedral, turn onto Avenida de la Catedral, and continue to Carrer del Dr. Joaquím Pou and hostel.

By subway: Take Metro line 1 to Urquinaona station, then walk along via Laietana to Avenida de la Catedral, then follow Carrer del Dr. Joaquím Pou to hostel.

Kabul Hostel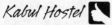

Plaça Reial 17, 08002 Barcelona

> **Phone:** 93-318-5190
> **E-mail:** info@kabul.es
> **Website:** kabul.es
> **Rates:** €13–€30 (about $16–$38 US) per person
> **Credit cards:** No
> **Beds:** 200
> **Private/family rooms:** No
> **Kitchen available:** No
> **Season:** Open year-round
> **Office hours:** 24 hours
> **Affiliation:** None
> **Extras:** Breakfast, bar, restaurant ($), laundry, TV room, Internet access, pool tables

O K, OK, we'll give this place a tentative thumbs-up thanks to massively positive hosteller feedback to us, but with one huge caution: This place is best for one thing—drinking and partying. (OK, that was two things.) You come for a party, not for perfectly clean beds, top management, great food, or peace and quiet. But if you're looking to meet fellow travelers and (did we mention this?) drink with 'em, it's among Europe's best hostels in which to do so. It's not the first or even the second place we'd stay in town, but for youngsters on the prowl, it just can't be beat in this part of the Continent.

The dorm facilities here—with rooms of 4, 8, 10, and 20 beds—are, frankly, kinda beat-up and flimsy. Yes, they've got a laundry, serve meals, run an Internet terminal, and maintain a television lounge, but the main draw at the Kabul is the bar, and that's where everyone eventually gravitates. Management encourages (did we mention this?) drinking, drinking, and more drinking. Heck, there's even a beer vending machine, which actually is kinda cool. But we digress. There's so much merriment here

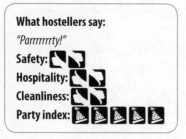

What hostellers say:
"Parrrrrrrty!"
Safety:
Hospitality:
Cleanliness:
Party index:

that things can get out of hand . . . people crashing all over the floor and such. Staff are sometimes OK, sometimes gracious, and sometimes borderline sociopathic. Cleanliness? Not perfect, sometimes pretty good and sometimes lacking.

But the location is decent, on the central Plaça Reial, and we liked the funny murals. Just take care at night, as this isn't the city's safest neighborhood.

How To Get There:
By bus: Contact hostel for transit route.
By car: Call hostel for directions.
By train: Take Metro Green Line (#3) to Liceo stop.

MADRID

Stuck right in the dead center of Spain, the nation's capital takes a lot of traveling to get to from just about anywhere. It's a heavy seven-hour slog from Barcelona, for example, and the scenery along the way isn't all that impressive. It's probably best to take an overnight train from somewhere like Paris, though that option certainly isn't cheap if you want to sleep lying down as opposed to sitting upright.

You'll probably arrive at Chamartín Station, far north of the city center, so you'll need to take the good and cheap Metro subway into town. Once downtown (they call it El Centro), just wander around, checking out all the squares, cathedrals, and museums you'd expect of a capital. Plenty of parks, palaces, and gardens can be found nearby, as well; consult a good map to find them. The Huertas neighborhood is one of the hippest for eating and drinking.

MADRID HOSTELS AT A GLANCE				
	RATING	PRICE	IN A WORD	PAGE
Los Amigos	🔖	€17–€19	OK	p. 367
AJ Richard Schirmann	🔖	€14–€18	marooned	p. 364
AJ Santa Cruz de Marcenado	🔖	€14–€18	fine	p. 362
Barbieri International Hostel	🔖🔖	€10–€20	colorful	p. 365

The Metro is incredibly cheap (costing €1.50–€2/about $2–$2.50 US per ride, or about €12/$16 US for a book of 10 tickets). Study the system first to figure out where you're going, though, as the network can be a little confusing with all those lines.

The city's hostels suffer the same problems experienced by those all over Spain: They're not always centrally located and don't necessarily provide the best possible deals for budget travelers, especially for those over age 26 or those traveling alone. They're also prone to being block-booked by school groups during the school year. Staff can seem indifferent at best and downright snippy at worst. Still, they present a good alternative for diehard hostel fans, and each has enough good points to merit a stay—especially for disabled travelers (whose needs aren't necessarily met by other budget options). Just remember that they're quite popular, so you should make bookings at least 2 weeks in advance. And there's a strict limit of 3 consecutive nights' stay and 6 nights' stay in any 6-month period as well.

Albergue Juvenil Santa Cruz de Marcenado

Calle Santa Cruz de Marcenado 28, 28015 Madrid

Phone: 91-547-4532
Fax: 91-548-1196
Rates: €14–€18 (about $18–$23 US) per person
Credit cards: No
Beds: 72
Private/family rooms: No
Kitchen available: No
Season: Open year-round
Office hours: 8 a.m.–10 p.m.
Curfew: 1:30 a.m.
Affiliation: HI
Extras: Laundry, TV lounge, breakfast, luggage storage, lockers, information desk

*O*f Madrid's 2 "official" hostels, this one is more centrally located—about 2 miles north of the Centro—and thus a better choice for party animals. It's cheap and fairly well run, if a bit boring. Located in the studenty Argüelles neighborhood, the modern, well-equipped facility is easily accessible by Metro or bus. The decor isn't exactly outstanding, but most hostellers who choose to stay here don't bother sticking around much, since the area offers a lot to do.

Inside, they've got 2 double rooms, 6 quads, 2 six-bed dorms, and 4 larger dorms. The place isn't exactly teeming with facilities, but it's clinically and decently run. (Staff could be more tolerant of us non–Español speakers, though.) There is a laundry, lounge with a TV, and a luggage room, and the location more than makes up for anything else it lacks. Fall out of bed one way and you're on the doorstep of the Centro Cultural Conde Duque, a converted 17th-century barracks that hosts concerts and art expositions. Roll a little farther east and you're in the Plaza Dos de Mayo, filled with wonderful cafes and kids by day, the epicenter of student life by night.

This proximity to the activity—and the fact that Argüelles is linked to the rest of the city by 3 efficient Metro lines—means this place scores pretty high on the convenience meter. And if you can't find someone in the hostel who wants to do something, you shouldn't have far to go outside before you find something to do by yourself.

So bring on the Mambo Taxi. Madrid awaits.

Insiders' tip:
Clamores Jazz Club for jazz
What hostellers say:
"Great area!"
Gestalt:
Mambo No. 5
Safety:
Hospitality:
Cleanliness:
Party index:

How To Get There:

By bus: Take #2, #21, #44, or #133 bus. Contact hostel for further details.

By car: Contact hostel for directions.

By train: From the Centro, find Sol, Callao, or Lavapiés Station and take #3 Line north (toward Moncloa) to Argüelles Station. Exit station at Camino Alberto Aguilera exit (on south side) and walk east for 1 block; turn right onto Camino Serrano Jove, then make an immediate left onto Camino Santa Cruz de Marcenado.

From Chamartín Station, take Metro Line #10 toward city center (toward Aluche) 6 stops to Alonso Martínez Station, then change to Line #4 and continue to last station at Argüelles. Exit station at Camino Alberto Aguilera exit (on south side) and walk east for 1 block; turn right onto Camino Serrano Jove, then make an immediate left onto Camino Santa Cruz de Marcenado.

Albergue Juvenil Richard Schirmann

Casa de Campo, s/n, 28011 Madrid

> **Phone:** 91-463-5699 or 91-463-5697
> **Fax:** 91-276-7516
> **Rates:** €14–€18 (about $18–$23 US) per person
> **Credit cards:** No
> **Beds:** 134
> **Private/family rooms:** Yes
> **Kitchen available:** Yes
> **Season:** Open year-round
> **Office hours:** 9 a.m.–10 p.m.
> **Affiliation:** HI
> **Extras:** Laundry, kitchen, TV room, bar, library, parking, meals ($)

lose to a park with facilities for children, plus a swimming pool and jogging areas, this hostel might fit the bill if you're wanting a little less action in a bucolic (though somewhat dodgy) area.

Located in the gigantic Casa de Campo park, west of the downtown core, this place is certainly attractive. Decorations show a detectable IKEA influence, and the place is fabulously equipped (there's both a bar and a library, and how's that for covering all the bases?). It's quiet and bright throughout. Although it's a bit of a

Best bet for a bite:
Casa Mingo on Paseo de la Florida

What hostellers say:
"No, I don't want a date . . ."

Gestalt:
Schir thing

Safety:

Hospitality:

Cleanliness:

Party index:

ways from downtown, you can be downtown in under half an hour if you time your transit connections right. The Teleférico (sky-ride) near the lake is kind of cheesy, but views of the Guadarrama mountains to the north are well worth the *fromage* factor. At least it's something to write home about.

That being said, it has a number of considerable disadvantages. Number one, it's not at all easy to reach. Number two, personal safety is something worth being paranoid about. The Madrid City Council has been encouraging prostitutes and their johns to vacate the city center, and guess where they've ended up? Here. The problem is tolerable during the day, but at night it's downright creepy: Curb-crawling cars can be a pain in the ass, and solo women may not feel comfortable or safe in the area. You'd be well advised to either take a taxi or ask staff about the best way to get back after dark. Number three, unlike the Santa Cruz hostel, individual hostellers can't book beds in advance. You just have to show up or give a call that day.

Still, in the frying-pan heat of a Madrid summer, it may be the best call you make. Just watch out for those school groups and hookers.

How To Get There:

By bus: Take #31, #33, #39, or #45 bus to Casa de Campo, then walk along Paseo de las Castañas, away from the lake.

By car: Contact hostel for directions.

By train: Contact hostel for transit details.

Barbieri International Hostel

Calle Barbieri 15, 2 Piso, 28004 Madrid

> **Phone:** 91-531-0258
> **Website:** barbierihostel.com
> **E-mail:** booking@barbierihostel.com
> **Rates:** €10–€20 (about $13–$25 US) per person; doubles €44–€50 (about $55–$63 US)
> **Credit cards:** Yes
> **Beds:** 38
> **Private/family rooms:** Yes
> **Kitchen available:** Yes
> **Season:** Open year-round
> **Office hours:** 24 hours
> **Affiliation:** None
> **Extras:** Lockers, breakfast, laundry, TV room, air-conditioning, free WiFi, reading room, meals

---

*Y*et another backpackers-style fun spot in Spain, this one gets both raves and raspberries from hostellers far and near. They liked: the combination of fun, hospitality, and amenities. They didn't like: the comfort of the beds, the condition of the rooms, and the cleanliness of the dorms and bathrooms. Staff make mistakes, it gets crowded—but it's a social time.

The Barbieri's located in the center of the city, near the famous Puerta del Sol. Inside, the

What hostellers say:
"Used to be better."
Gestalt:
Madrid about you
Safety:
Hospitality:
Cleanliness:
Party index:

dorms are 2- to 8-bedded—a little tight, but quite clean and somewhat cooled by the air-conditioning that ought to be mandatory in every Spanish hostel. The lounge bops with TV viewers, Internet tweeters, and wine drinkers (they'll sell you a bottle at the desk), while a separate reading area is better for bookworms.

Still, we can't give this place a wholehearted recommendation. It's lacking too much for that.

How To Get There:

By bus: From Méndez Alvaro bus depot, take Metro Light Blue Line (#1) to Gran Via station, turn left on Hortaleza Street and make second right onto Infantas Street; take next left onto Calle Barbieri. Hostel is at #15, on second floor.

By car: Contact hostel for directions.

By train: From Chamartín Station, take Metro Blue Line (#10) to Martinez Metro Station; change to Green Line (#5) and continue to Chueca Station. Exit station, turn right, and continue down Calle Barbieri. Hostel is at #15, on second floor.

By plane: From airport, take Pink Line (#8) to Nuevos Ministerios station; change to blue (#10) and continue to Alonso Martinez Metro Station; change again to Green Line (#5) and continue to Chueca Metro Station. Exit station, turn right, and continue down Calle Barbieri. Hostel is at #15, on second floor.

Los Amigos Hostel

Calle Arenal 26 (4th floor), 28013 Madrid

> **Phone:** 91-559-2472
>
> **E-mail:** reservassol@losamigoshostel.com
>
> **Website:** losamigoshostel.com
>
> **Rates:** €17–€19 (about $21–$24 US) per person; doubles €45–€50 (about $56–$63 US)
>
> **Credit cards:** Yes
>
> **Beds:** Number varies
>
> **Private/family rooms:** Yes
>
> **Kitchen available:** Yes
>
> **Season:** Open year-round
>
> **Office hours:** 24 hours
>
> **Affiliation:** None
>
> **Extras:** Lockers, free Internet access, TV room, games, mail storage, breakfast, bar, airport pickups ($), free continental breakfast

*V*isits at this place vary. Once when we stopped in, it was really nice and clean. Another time, there was nothing going on to speak of. Another time, borderline terrible. But overall it suffices, like all the other places in town (truth be told, there isn't a lot of quality variation). Situated on a calm side street (which is an important late-night consideration in Spain), yet quite close to some old neighborhoods and plazas, Los Amigos is upstairs from the street. Hostellers liked the friendly staff, clean digs, and goodies like free Internet access, a mail-drop service (who gets mail forwarded to a hostel?), and a kitchen.

Gestalt:
Si Amigos

Safety:

Hospitality:

Cleanliness:

Party index:

The furniture in the 6- to 8-bed dorms has simple lines, and rooms are spacious enough and well-kept; big lockers are available in each one for your stuff. The common lounge—where you'll spend most of your time, probably—rocks with its TV, VCR, and games, and the bar kicks in additional cheery atmo. They also serve a very basic breakfast here. There's even an unusual half-day rate if you just need to crash for a bit. Note that front desk security does give you the once-over—and that's a good thing. Again, the vibe here is just so happy that you can't help but leave with new friends (including some of the staff). The central nabe doesn't hurt a bit, either.

Our tip? Book a few days ahead; it's getting a lot of buzz—and deservedly so.

How To Get There:

By bus: Contact hostel for transit details.

By car: Contact hostel for directions.

By train: From Chamartín Station, take #10 line toward Puerta del Sur 9 stops to Principe Pio station. Follow signs to "Ramal Opera-Príncipe Pío" (R) line and continue 1 stop to Opera station. Exit to street level, cross street, and walk 40 yards along Calle Arenal; hostel is on left, at #26, on fourth floor (use elevator). From Atocha Station, take Metro Light Blue Line (#1) 4 stops to Sol station; change to Red Line (#2) and continue to Opera station. Exit to street level, cross street, and walk 40 yards along Calle Arenal; hostel is on left, at #26, on fourth floor (use elevator).

By plane: From airport, take Pink Line (#8) to end of line (Nuevos Ministerios station). Transfer to #10 line and ride toward Puerta del Sur for 5 stops to Principe Pio station. Follow signs to "Ramal Opera-Príncipe Pío" (R) line and continue 1 stop to Opera station. Exit, cross street, and walk 40 yards along Calle Arenal to hostel on left at #26 (take elevator to fourth floor).

Key to Icons

Attractive natural setting	Comfortable beds	Visual arts at hostel or nearby
Ecologically aware hostel	A particularly good value	Music at hostel or nearby
Superior kitchen facilities or cafe	Wheelchair-accessible	Great hostel for skiers
Offbeat or eccentric place	Good for business travelers	Bar or pub at hostel or nearby
Superior bathroom facilities	Especially well-suited for families	Editors' choice: Among our very favorite hostels
Romantic private rooms	Good for active travelers	

SEVILLE (SEVILLA)

The city that gave its name to a whole breed of orange remains one of Spain's prettiest draws. The center is compact enough that you might not need to use the local bus system. While wandering, you'll soon enough find the city's amazing (and amazingly big) cathedral, plus plenty of other wonders—castles, museums, and Barrio Santa Cruz, an attractive warren of tiny streets.

Albergue Juvenil Sevilla

Camino Isaac Peral 2, 41012 Sevilla

> **Phone:** 95-505-6500 or 90-251-0000
> **Fax:** 95-505-6508
> **E-mail:** sevilla.itj@juntadeandalucia.es
> **Rates:** €7.15 (about $9 US) per HI member
> **Credit cards:** Yes
> **Beds:** 294
> **Private/family rooms:** Yes
> **Kitchen available:** Yes
> **Season:** Open year-round
> **Office hours:** 24 hours
> **Affiliation:** HI
> **Extras:** Cafe ($), laundry, meeting rooms, Internet access, TV room, store, luggage storage, game room, breakfast, garden

*I*n recent years, the regional governments of many Spanish provinces have started to fund and run the hostel networks in their area. Andalusia is one example of an area where they got it right: InturJoven, the organization that oversees the hostels in this southern province, has streamlined its operations. It now has about 20 hostels in towns, in cities, and near beaches, and the Seville youth hostel is one of the better places it runs.

The hostel is located in the southern part of town, near Reina Mercedes University. When you approach the hostel, you see that there are actually 2 buildings; one of the university residences is right next door. (Unfortunately, hostel residents don't get to use the basketball or tennis courts that separate the 2 buildings.) Inside the spacious hostel building, the vast majority of rooms are triples, with en-suite bathrooms that take a little getting used to: A strange combination of doors and shower curtains means that you've got to be veeeeery careful your shower doesn't end up submerging the whole floor. If you've forgotten your towel, you can rent one for about a dollar. There are also plenty of doubles, a good thing for couples or families. All the beds include linens, and energetic central heating means no freezing your butt off—if it's working properly. Cleanliness is good.

Best bet for a bite:
Tapas and paella in the Centro
What hostellers say:
"Serviceable."
Gestalt:
Orange you glad you came?
Safety:
Hospitality:
Cleanliness:
Party index:

Management has equipped the place with a number of amenities, including a laundry, kitchen, conference rooms, a game room, a TV lounge, and a cafeteria that serves included breakfast, as well as lunch and dinner for a charge (making up for the strange lack of eateries in the surrounding area). However, don't get the idea this is big fun: It's a zombie-like atmosphere, and not always all that friendly.

A taxi from the center will cost about €4 (about $5 US), or you can walk the distance in about half an hour, enjoying the older, more historic areas of the city—including Plaza de España and Maria Luisa Park. The park, built for the 1929 Ibero-American Exposition (which didn't end up happening), is worth a look just for the insanely ornate architecture and tile work on its buildings.

Otherwise, this hostel isn't close enough to the city center that a party vibe ever really catches on. Most nights it's pretty tame, making this a good place for those who need to get up early for travel or sightseeing.

How To Get There:

By bus: Take #34 bus from Plaza Nueva or #6 bus from front of the Plaza de Armas bus station.
By car: Contact hostel for directions.
By train: From Seville Station, take C2 or #27 bus to hostel, or walk 1 mile.

Sweden

*F*rom Malmö to Lappland, Sweden is a big country and takes in a little bit of everything.
Mostly it's woods and lakes punctuated by small towns of beautiful, healthy people tooling around in their Saabs and Volvos. Stockholm, the capital, is the buttoned-down business center where most of the heavy lifting gets done. Over on the other coast, Gøteborg faces off against Denmark with a salty mixture of port activity, university life, and a bustling arts and music scene.

Practical Details

Sweden's trains are superclean and efficient, but the long travel distances over flat terrain mean you'll spend a lot of time staring out the window at—well, Sweden. Sadly, the awesome ScanRail pass exists no more, but you can buy either point-to-point tickets or a Eurail Sweden pass, which for under-26 travelers costs $200 to $300 for three to eight days in a month, traveling second-class. Over-26ers pay more: $270 to $530 US for the same time periods, depending on first- or second-class travel.

Things are expensive here. The unit of currency is the Swedish krona (SEK); there are 6.5 kronor to one US dollar, a good rate—but that still means your 210 SEK dorm room costs more than 30 bucks.

Sweden's phone code is 46; Stockholm's city code is 08. To dial Stockholm hostels from the US, dial 011-46, then DROP THE ZERO from the number listed. To dial Stockholm hostels from Sweden, dial the number exactly AS LISTED. To dial Stockholm hostels from within Stockholm, DROP THE 08 and dial the number EXACTLY AS PRINTED.

Vandrarhem means hostel in Swedish. Hostels here are uniformly clean and cheaper than the exorbitant hotels—Swedish families think nothing of staying at a hostel when on vacation (and kids get deep discounts). But remember to join HI before coming: The official hostels charge a stiff surcharge (about $8 US) per nonmember per night.

STOCKHOLM

Among Europe's most beautiful cities—especially when you consider the gorgeous oceanside setting—Stockholm simply must be seen on a Scandinavian tour, though it's quite far from most anywhere else and quite hard on your wallet, too. Another interesting fact about

Stockholm

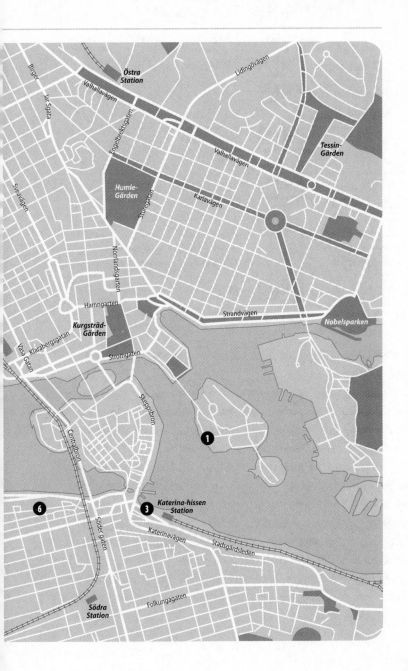

STOCKHOLM HOSTELS AT A GLANCE

	RATING	PRICE	IN A WORD	PAGE
City Backpackers	🐾🐾	190–280 SEK	homey	p. 376
Af Chapman/ Skeppsholmen	🐾🐾	260–590 SEK	interesting	p. 375
Långholmen Vandrarhem	🐾🐾	255–615 SEK	quiet	p. 380
Zinkensdamm Vandrarhem	🐾🐾	235–440 SEK	green	p. 385
Red Boat Mälarens	🐾	260–510 SEK	salty	p. 383
M/S Rygerfjord	🐾	410–680 SEK	cruisin'	p. 382
Gustaf af Klint	🐾🐾	210 SEK	overboard	p. 378

this city: A number of its hostels are located on boats floating in the harbor—a novel way to get to know the city.

Gamla Stan (the Old Town) is the central and logical starting point for a tour. This area is jam-packed with palaces, churches, squares, and statues, not to mention chic restaurants, jazz bars, shops, and the like. The real up-and-coming district, though, is Södermalm, just south of here; this is where the beautiful people bop all night long.

You'll get around best by using the subway, known here as the T-bana; all lines conveniently converge at the station known as T-Centralen, right next to the train station. Subway rides cost around 20 SEK (about $3 US), so to save dough, think about buying an SL Travelcard from the transit authority. It costs 115 SEK (about $18 US) for one day, but only 230 SEK (about $35 US) for three days. Seniors and travelers under 20 get an additional 40 percent discount, making it a steal.

Also take the time at some point to hop a ferry to one of the outlying islands of the Stockholm archipelago—they're very quiet and pretty, and some ferries are discounted or free with Eurail passes.

Af Chapman/Skeppsholmen Hostels ⌐⌐

Flaggmansvägen 8, 11149 Stockholm

> **Phone:** 08-463-2266
> **Fax:** 08-611-7155
> **E-mail:** chapman@stfturist.se
> **Rates:** 260–590 SEK (about $40–$91 US) per HI member; doubles 590 SEK (about $91 US)
> **Credit cards:** Yes
> **Beds:** 280
> **Private/family rooms:** Yes
> **Kitchen available:** Yes
> **Season:** Open year-round
> **Office hours:** 24 hours
> **Lockout:** 11 a.m.–3 p.m. (Af Chapman only)
> **Curfew:** 2 a.m. (Af Chapman only)
> **Affiliation:** HI-STF
> **Extras:** TV room, laundry, luggage storage, lockers, meals ($), parking

🍁👥🍲🛏️🍴

N ote: Half-price discounts for children.

Talk about unique, cool hostelling. This double-barreled hostel covers all the bases, from land to sea, and must be seen to be believed. It's as central to Stockholm's downtown as a hostel could be, making it/them a real steal since you won't need public transit once you're here.

Half the hostel actually floats, just as several others in the city do: It's an 18th-century sailboat moored in the water. Rooms are a little tight, but the place nevertheless fills up months in advance; you'd better call way ahead if you want a bunk. "Skeppsholmen's Van-drarhem," the sister hostel sitting up on the dock, is a little roomier and nicer, a very good place to meet fellow travelers. It used to be a workshop, however, so it's not exactly plush either.

The crowd here ranges from Euro-teenyboppers to Swedish families and even elderly folk day-tripping around the country. Together, the 2 hostels consist of 20 double rooms, 13 triples, 22 quads, 1 five-bed dormitory, 8 six-bed dorms, and 8 even larger dorms. The boat

Best bet for a bite:
Here and now
What hostellers say:
"Floats my boat."
Gestalt:
Ship ahoy
Safety:
Hospitality:
Cleanliness:
Party index:

rooms are a bit cramped and uninspiring—but some come with water views. Obviously. In the bigger, landside wing there's a laundry, kitchen, and meal service; the dry hostel is wheelchair-accessible, too. But if you've gotta pick, why not try both? Sleeping on water is a unique experience, that's for sure.

Views of Stockholm, on all sides of you, are splendid. What's really amazing about this location, though, is the clutch of cool sights in the area. You're closer to the Modern and National museums than anyone sleeping in the city's $500-a-night digs, and you're within walking distance of both the Royal Castle and Parliament. You can catch a ferry to another cool island right from here, walk back into town for upscale shopping and clubbing, or just hang out on the dock or boat when the weather's good. About the only thing lacking is a subway stop, but that's a minor complaint. This is a good place, efficiently run, and so popular that you will want to book miles in advance to stay.

How To Get There:
By bus or train: From Central Station, take #65 bus to Skeppsholmen Island and walk 100 yards to hostel.
By car: Contact hostel for directions.

City Backpackers Hostel

Upplandsgatan 2a, 11123 Stockholm
> **Phone:** 08-206-920
> **Fax:** 08-100-464
> **E-mail:** info@citybackpackers.se
> **Website:** citybackpackers.org
> **Rates:** 190–280 SEK (about $29–$43 US) per person; doubles 650–1,300 SEK (about $100–$200 US)
> **Credit cards:** Yes
> **Beds:** 65
> **Private/family rooms:** Yes

Kitchen available: Yes

Season: Open year-round

Office hours: 7:30 a.m.–noon; 2–7 p.m.

Affiliation: None

Extras: Laundry, sauna ($), free WiFi, TV room, games

*T*he City BackPackers hostel—a big apartment with wooden stairs and wooden doors—is simply one word: awesome. Blessed with a great location within walking distance of the city's central train station, it's situated a hop, step, and a jump from the Old Town, the museums, and oodles of shops, theaters, and cinemas. It's clean, safe, and quite friendly despite a number of rules. And fun! This place has it all: It's the top bunk in what's arguably Europe's best hostel town.

Door security consists of a key code. You walk in between houses in a small backyard; inside, it's all very quiet despite the street traffic. They ask you to take off your shoes, which keeps things clean; then you enter through a sort of reading room decorated with pictures of movie stars and pictures of ABBA and Björn Borg. A big map of the world on the wall reminds you of why you're here: to mix and mingle with others from different places. Staff are thoughtful and have carefully arranged bus timetables and ideas for things to do in the city in the same room. There's a book exchange for free, too, culled from other travelers' leavings.

Rooms consist of 5 doubles, 6 three- to four-bed dorms, and 4 eight-bed dorms. It's not the biggest place, not the most hard-rocking, but it's adequate and central. The kitchen downstairs sure is tiny, but to compensate there's a television room with tables beside it where eating is allowed. The bathrooms are also tucked down here, all kept spic-and-span, and you can rent games like Trivial Pursuit for the night. There's also a laundry and—check this out!—a sauna, though both cost extra.

> **What hostellers say:**
> *"Wonderful place."*
> **Gestalt:**
> *Stockholm sweet Stockholm*
> **Safety:**
> **Hospitality:**
> **Cleanliness:**
> **Party index:**

They don't serve breakfast on site and don't have a bar, but there's a good buffet place within a half mile. In fact, since this is the very heart of Stockholm, there are tons of coffee shops and restaurants of all price ranges. And if you're just falling-down tired after a long flight or train ride, this is perfect—only 5 minutes' walk from the main station. With all those ABBA posters, you'll be humming yourself to sleep in no time to "Dancing Queen" or "Fernando."

Do not miss it.

How To Get There:
By bus: Contact hostel for transit details.
By car: Contact hostel for directions.
By train: From Central Station, walk ¼ mile to hostel.

Gustaf Af Klint Hostel
Stadsgårdskajen Kajplatser 153, 11645 Stockholm
 Phone: 08-640-4077
 E-mail: info@gustafafklint.se
 Website: gustafafklint.se
 Rates: 210 SEK (about $32 US) per person; doubles 540 SEK (about $83 US)
 Credit cards: Yes
 Beds: 152 (summer), 130 (winter)
 Private/family rooms: Yes
 Kitchen available: No
 Season: Open year-round
 Office hours: 24 hours
 Affiliation: None
 Extras: Bar, coffee shop, laundry, breakfast ($), TV, restaurant, Internet access

---

*O*K, now having just described the top place in Europe's top hostel town, we have to say: This place is borderline bad. The first thing we noticed, climbing aboard this hostel, was the "boat smell"—a strong odor of oil and boat polish, great if you're planning on joining the merchant marine but not so great if you've got allergies. We got a little queasy, frankly.

But we soldiered on, heading through an entryway room that has been restyled to look very much like an English pub—an English pub with wooden couches, that is. Music was blaring on the radio, and the receptionist immediately copped a snooty 'tude. Again, we soldiered on.

The boat is very small inside, and dark; even in those rooms with great views of the city through portholes or windows, lighting is a definite problem. But we're getting ahead of ourselves. You climb down into the hostel deck on tiny stairs to find 8 double rooms, 17 four-bed cabins, and a huge dormitory (it can squeeze in as many as 20 hostellers). All of 'em rock on the waves a little, even though the boat's always tied up, a problem we didn't find with any other boat hostels in town. (Maybe they should spring for a new rope? Just wondering.) Some hostellers told us the motion bothered them; others didn't. If you're prone to seasickness, you probably should not stay here.

Rooms are tiny, and tall or claustrophobic people might also want to sleep elsewhere in the city. Despite all that, the boat was pretty clean at least—except for the bathrooms, located in the narrow hallways, which unimpressed us. Somehow they've also squeezed in a bar (where you can drink wine) and a laundry in the place.

There are a few pictures on the walls, but otherwise you won't get much to cheer about here. They don't do any tours or activities, and the information about what you can do in Stockholm was, frankly, lame and outdated. Maybe that's because they want you to stay here: During the summer you can sit out on the deck, and they run a combination restaurant/snack bar year-round (the room with the English-pub decor), which also doubles as the TV room. The breakfast is actually pretty nice—lots to eat, with great views while you do.

What to do in the area? This boat/hostel (boastel?) is tied up right in the middle of the city, surrounded by restaurants, bars, coffee shops, museums, and parks. So there are options. Just remember that the close proximity to busy streets and subway lines sometimes brings night noise.

Cheap? Yes. Recommendable? Er . . . we'll let you read between the lines. LINE no not really LINE.

> **Best bet for a bite:**
> *Fried-fish stands*
> **What hostellers say:**
> *"Shiver me timbers . . ."*
> **Gestalt:**
> *Seasick*
> **Safety:**
> **Hospitality:**
> **Cleanliness:**
> **Party index:**

How To Get There:

By bus: Contact hostel for transit details.

By car: Contact hostel for directions.

By train: From Central Station, take T-bana to Slussen Station; take lower exit and walk 200 yards east to hostel on water.

Långholmen Vandrarhem

Långholmsmuren 20, 10272 Stockholm

> **Phone:** 08-720-8500
>
> **Fax:** 08-720-8575
>
> **E-mail:** vandrarhem@langholmen.com
>
> **Rates:** 255–615 SEK (about $39–$95 US) per HI member; doubles 620–740 SEK (about $95–$114 US)
>
> **Credit cards:** Yes
>
> **Beds:** 272 (summer), 26 (winter)
>
> **Private/family rooms:** Yes
>
> **Kitchen available:** Yes
>
> **Season:** Open year-round
>
> **Office hours:** 24 hours
>
> **Affiliation:** HI-STF
>
> **Extras:** Bar, breakfast ($), TV room, laundry, store, museum, restaurant ($)

---

*N*ote: Half-price discounts for children.

What a great place! The "official" hostel agency STF strikes again. This hostel, hidden in a leafy park on a small island off the beaten path, was a prison until 1975—but you'd hardly know it (if not for the surveillance cameras scanning the grounds). This is probably Stockholm's quietest hostel, and one where you've got a decent shot at actually securing a bed.

The hostel's close to town, but you've got to stroll a ways from the subway station. At least the walk's pleasant, with birds singing and water and greenery all around you. Eventually you come to a stone wall, follow it, and then come to the big blond stone structure. The former guard station is now the reception, where the personable staffers check you in and peddle Swedish T-shirts and postcards.

You sleep in the former cells, which occupy the bottom floor of the building: There are quad rooms, 3-bed rooms, and a mess of doubles down here, though in winter they scale back drastically from more than 250 beds to just 26! Must be the weather. Anyway, many hostellers share bathrooms in the hallway, but you can pay more for a double room—er, cell (really, a cell?)—with its own bathroom, telephone, and small TV. There's a small museum in the big hallway, with exhibits describing the former life of the building; up big stone stairs, you'll find a small but good (and clean) eat-in kitchen. They also serve dinner and breakfast here, both for an extra charge. Other amenities are good as well—a laundry, a bar, and city information.

Best bet for a bite:
Back in Södermalm
What hostellers say:
"Tonight there's gonna be a jailbreak..."
Gestalt:
Soft cell
Safety:
Hospitality:
Cleanliness:
Party index:

They claim not to accept group bookings, which is a huge bonus if you're sick of schoolkiddies roaming the halls starting food fights and such. On the other hand, there's zero party action, and this is one of the most inconvenient hostels to reach in town . . . if they rented bikes, it would be among our top picks in this part of Europe, but it's a bit hard to get here after an evening of nightlife. Take note of a few rules, too: There's no smoking in the dorm rooms, you can stay only a maximum of 5 nights in a row, and you need to pay a small cleaning charge (roughly $3 US) when you check out.

Still, this is a great place and it has been for a long while. Come for the uniqueness of the experience.

How To Get There:
By bus: Contact hostel for transit details.
By car: Contact hostel for directions.
By train: From Central Station, take T-bana to Hornstull Station; walk ½ mile north up Vasterbbron and cross bridge onto island. Continue to hostel.

MVS Rygerfjord Hostel

Södermälarstrand Kajplats 12–14, 11825 Stockholm

> **Phone:** 08-840-830
> **Fax:** 08-840-730
> **E-mail:** hotell@rygerfjord.se
> **Rates:** 410–680 SEK (about $63–$104 US) per person; doubles 895 SEK–1050 SEK (about $137–$162 US)
> **Credit cards:** Yes
> **Beds:** 240
> **Private/family rooms:** Yes
> **Kitchen available:** No
> **Season:** Open year-round
> **Office hours:** 8 a.m.–midnight
> **Affiliation:** None
> **Extras:** Restaurant ($), breakfast ($), TV, musical performances

*A*nother hostel? Again, on a boat? Yep, Stockholm just keeps the bunks and the watery experiences coming. This boat hostel is OK—not great—and a little bigger and more party-hearty than the others in town. But it's expensive.

The first things you see in the entryway are a cigarette machine and then a gambling machine, just like on a cruise boat. That's the feel of the place: fun, but not so much fun that you're dragging yourself out of a puddle of drool at 5 in the morning like an extra from *The Hangover*. A big map of Stockholm hangs on the wall, and red carpets welcome the bedraggled hosteller.

What hostellers say:
"I'm on a boat!"
Gestalt:
Lovely boat
Safety:
Hospitality:
Cleanliness:
Party index:

As with other boats, you descend a stairway to the rooms belowdecks—in this case, though, stairs aren't so small that you'll break your legs in the process. Rooms are small, but they're brightened by small round windows; in all, there are 12 quad rooms, a 12-bed dorm, and tons of single and double rooms. Bathrooms are all in the hallways, and there are sinks with hot and cold water—oh, the luxury—in each dorm as well. All in all, the whole place is pretty well lit and bright-feeling.

The hostel restaurant is big, too, with great views through portholes of Stockholm day or night; they serve meals and breakfast here, and it's one of the few areas where smoking's allowed. (The television lounge is the other.) They also maintain a bar, and during the summer, hostellers sit outside on the deck and watch the city. Sometimes live bands get things rocking.

We'd be remiss if we didn't mention the staff. The owner/manager who gave us the tour is the "captain" of the operation, and he hailed everyone with a friendly hello. He really seems to care about his passengers' well-being, and they felt taken care of in kind. Some staff were a bit less friendly, and we have one minor complaint: Noise really carries on this boat. Really carries. OK, one more complain: You have to pay for towels—and then you have to give them back. Whaaaat? But that's OK. We like it anyway. It's just not as great as some of the other joints in town.

How To Get There:
By bus: Contact hostel for transit details.
By car: Contact hostel for directions.
By train: From Central Station, take T-bana to Mariatorget. Walk to shore, following signs.

Red Boat Mälarens Hostel
Södermälarstrand, Kajplats 6, 11820 Stockholm
    Phone: 08-644-4385
    E-mail: info@theredboat.com
    Rates: 260–520 SEK (about $37–$69 US) per person; doubles 650–750 SEK (about $89–$103 US)
    Credit cards: Yes
    Beds: 90
    Private/family rooms: Yes
    Kitchen available: No
    Season: Open year-round
    Office hours: 24 hours
    Affiliation: None
    Extras: Bar, restaurant, laundry service, breakfast ($), televisions, free WiFi and Internet access

*A*nother hostel on boat? No. Yes. It's amazing to think that Stockholm has more hostels on water than land, but it does.

And this hostel actually consists of not one boat in the water, but two. It's locally known as "the red boat," so you should have absolutely no trouble finding it, and it gets our vote for the coolest decor in Stockholm, if not the cleanest or most comfortable rooms. The boat next door, by the way, is "the white boat" and it's also part of the hostel. (Secret info time: Which boat you pick makes a difference. Go for red. Push for red. Bet on red.)

What hostellers say:
"Can I walk the plank?"
Gestalt:
Captain's crunch
Safety:
Hospitality:
Cleanliness:
Party index:

The entrance to the hostel is small, with a wooden couch you can sit on. Inside, everything is made of wood, and decorations run to the nautical—lamps, ropes, fishing nets, and so forth. Then you climb down very narrow stairs to the rooms. There are 90 beds between the two ships, split up into 32 double rooms (some of which can be converted into very expensive singles), 7 four-bed dorms, and a bigger ten-bedded cabin—though nothing is all that big when you're talking about boats; narrow (and also stuffy) is again pretty much the rule of thumb here. Showers and bathrooms are located in the hallways; showers are bigger than you might expect and kept clean, though the hallway is narrow indeed. All the doors are red, by the way, just like the ship's exterior.

There's no smoking in the rooms, but you can smoke in the lounge or in part of the restaurant, which has more wooden tables with red-and-white tablecloths on them—like a small (floating) Italian restaurant—and more wall hangings: Bits of rope, paintings, buoys—you get the picture. They run this eatery from spring through fall, it doubles as the TV room, and there are both smoking and nonsmoking sections; each has its own television set.

Staff are helpful and will dispense info or send your laundry out to a nearby service; they run a bar as well. Breakfast costs extra—not cheap, as usual. You can also rent a more expensive hotel room here, but it's about twice the price of a double in the hostel. Quite expensive.

We'll give this place a thumbs-up, but barely. There are many better hostels in town, most of them also on (better) boats.

How To Get There:

By bus: Contact hostel for transit details.

By car: Contact hostel for directions.

By train: From Central Station, take T-bana to Slussen Station; exit via lower exit and walk 300 yards west to hostel.

Zinkensdamm Vandrarhem ![icon] ![icon]

Zinkens väg 20, 11741 Stockholm

Phone: 08-616-8100

Fax: 08-616-8120

Website: zinkensdamm.com

Rates: 235–440 SEK (about $36–$68 US) per HI member; doubles 560 SEK–790 SEK (about $86–$122 US)

Credit cards: Yes

Beds: 490

Private/family rooms: Yes

Kitchen available: Yes

Season: Open year-round

Office hours: 24 hours

Affiliation: HI-STF

Extras: Laundry, bike rentals, solarium ($), store, TV room, breakfast ($), sauna ($), grounds

---

*Y*et another great family-friendly hostel in Stockholm, this one—for once—is not on a boat. It's in a leafy locale, a little too far from Södermalm's nighttime action—but excellent if you're bringing a family and/or a car in tow. It's also spotless, perhaps the cleanest joint in a clean city when we visited. It's viably the top pick in town, except for its remoteness.

The big yellow hostel structure was designed on a small-town theme: The reception area is large and looks something like a train station. This is where you check in, purchase postcards and snacks, book tickets, mail letters, and pick up city info. Moving along, each spacious hallway has its own Swedish street name plus street signs directing you around the complex. (A little hokey, but this corn serves a purpose—it's harder to get lost that way.)

Dorm and corridor walls and floors are painted yellow, light blue, and light pink—colors of the Swedish flag, don'cha know—and all are kept absolutely spotless, with each room sporting a mirror and small table. Paintings on the walls enliven the atmosphere even further.

What hostellers say:
"Quiet as a mouse."
Gestalt:
Green machine
Safety:
Hospitality:
Cleanliness:
Party index:

Room sizes vary, with most rooms containing 4 bunks each; there's also a section of larger dorms of 8 beds apiece, and one wing of doubles that serve as private rooms. You can choose from rooms with en-suite bathrooms or those with shared bathrooms, paying less for the latter. The kitchen's clean and bright, with light-blue walls and prominent recycling bins. Even the television lounge is friendly and happy, its '50s-style furniture contrasting with pastel walls, and there's a restaurant with bar, as well. The big backyard is a great spot to hang out on sunny days—or rent a bicycle from reception. The sauna and solarium are also quite popular, as is the laundry.

Of all the city's hostels, this is probably the best-kept, most family-friendly one of all. Only partying types or night owls wouldn't like it: It's too quiet and remote.

How To Get There:

By bus: Contact hostel for transit details.
By car: Contact hostel for directions.
By train: From Central Station, take T-bana to Zinkensdamm Station. Walk down Ringvagen and make a right at STF signs; continue to hostel.

Key to Icons

Attractive natural setting	Comfortable beds	Visual arts at hostel or nearby
Ecologically aware hostel	A particularly good value	Music at hostel or nearby
Superior kitchen facilities or cafe	Wheelchair-accessible	Great hostel for skiers
Offbeat or eccentric place	Good for business travelers	Bar or pub at hostel or nearby
Superior bathroom facilities	Especially well-suited for families	Editors' choice: Among our very favorite hostels
Romantic private rooms	Good for active travelers	

Switzerland

Switzerland is, quite simply, an amazing travel experience. Just don't come expecting warm fuzzies; the notoriously efficient Swiss hostel managers are hardworking, focused on cleanliness, and not really inclined to yuk it up or even show lots of emotion.

But the hostels are almost all decent, if similarly devoid of character. The independent hostels of Switzerland are a happy exception—homey, fun, laid-back, and tucked in quiet scenery.

Practical Details

Swiss International is the national airline, but it's pretty expensive; better to fly into Germany, France, or England instead, then take a train.

Once you're here, SBB—Switzerland's rail company—is as efficient as a Swiss watch; its trains and tracks are world renowned for their comfort and scenery. While these rail systems cross an incredible variety of landscapes, even the iron horse can't get everywhere. It's likely that at some point you will need to supplement your train travel with some form of gondola, lift, bus, cog railway, steam train . . . something. It's all part of the fun.

Swiss Railpasses are one of the best deals in the world. They come in bunches of four, eight, 15, and 30 days; like other country railpasses, they confer free passage on all state railroads and most private ones, too. They get you free passage on terrifically scenic rides like the Glacier Express, Bernina Express, Panorama Express, and more; you pay only for a seat reservation. As a great bonus, they're also good on the postbus system (see bus section below) and ferryboats that ply Swiss lakes. As if that weren't enough, many mountain railways and gondolas—which are not covered by this otherwise amazing pass—will still give you a discount for holding one.

Other similar options from the Swiss have included a Half-Fare Travel Card, which gets you half off all train tickets for a month, a Flexipass, a Swiss Card, a Rail 'n' Drive Pass, and a Family Card. Contact the tourism offices or travel offices listed in this book for the latest pricing info, or just stand in line at any Swiss train station ticket office; the staff are exceptionally knowledgeable about this stuff.

Austrian railpasses are also available in various changing packages, which a travel agent can better fill you in on.

Always remember to punch your train ticket before you get on the train; there will be a machine in every station that stamps the current date and time on the ticket, showing the conductor that it has been "used up."

Oh, and let's not forget this important side note: Train station toilets—marked with a WC—almost always require you to cough up a few francs for the privilege of, well, going. As a bonus (we guess), these same joints sell shampoo, shaving kits, and what have you; use one of the nice sinks and you could even spruce up in one of these places before a big meeting or date. Suddenly that buck isn't hurting quite so much. (Some Swiss train stations even offer inexpensive pay showers.)

Like Austria, Switzerland has a system of "postbuses" taking travelers and locals into inaccessible areas. They're cheap. Punch your ticket for local bus rides on the bus; longer-distance tickets don't need to be punched, just shown to the driver when you get on.

Switzerland's country code is 41. To call Swiss hostels from North America, dial 011-41 and DROP THE ZERO from the numbers printed in this book. To call Swiss hostels from Europe, dial 0041 and DROP THE ZERO. To dial Swiss hostels from within Switzerland, dial the numbers just AS PRINTED. Also remember that it's cheaper to make coin calls at night and that directory assistance is expensive (dial 1818).

You'll need plenty of money—this is one of the most expensive countries in Europe (and the world), so everything from your hostel bed to your train ticket to your groceries will cost more than you expected it to. (Trying to dine out cheaply is a massive challenge, and usually a losing battle; we pack picnics from local grocery stores instead, and the quality of Swiss grocery food is second to none.)

Swiss money consists of solid, heavy change—just as you'd expect from such a prosperous and efficient land—plus a selection of paper bills. The change weighs a ton when you're traveling, so get in the habit of paying for purchases with the coins whenever possible; save a few for lockers at train stations, too, which take only coins. At press time, one Swiss franc (CHF) was almost exactly equal in worth to one US dollar, and has been for quite a while. Here's a quick primer:

Five-franc coins are enormous barbells.

Two-franc coins are smaller but also weighty.

One-franc coins are thinner than the twos.

The half-franc is a tiny oddball, yet worth 50 cents.

Swiss francs get split up into 100 centimes (or *rappen,* in German) for the purposes of making change. The 20-centime pieces are solid but not worth much, just 20 cents each. And the skinny 5- and 10-centime coins aren't worth your time of day; though they're light, give 'em to street musicians—or else be stuck with an ever-growing pocket of souvenirs.

The paper is easier to carry, obviously, and to keep straight in your head. That's because you'll normally be dealing only with the four kinds of bills noted below; ATMs give only the first two. Yes, that long blue 100-franc note is worth about $100 US, obviously—enough for a hostel night and a dinner, about what you'd probably spend in a typical day on the road. The slightly shorter 50-franc note is worth half as much (duh). Twenty-franc notes—shorter again, and pinkish—are worth $20 (stop us if you're sensing a theme), and the yellowish-orange 10-franc notes, which are very short (like Monopoly money), are worth $10 US (OK, now we're just messing with you).

No sweat, right? The real challenge, as we've said, is to keep your balance with all that really heavy change weighing down your pockets.

GENEVA

Set beside a pretty lake, with a decent climate and views of the Alps on a very clear day, Geneva's got some serious advantages when you're considering a travel itinerary. It's very close to France if you're going to or coming from that way. And this city lets its hair down in a way that no other place in Switzerland quite does; that alone makes it worth a stop.

Superb transportation connections mean that you can be in Paris, Zürich, or Italy within a little more than half a day. Once here, getting around is very easy, thanks to a comprehensive network of buses and, especially, streetcars (also called trams) that wind through the alleys, boulevards, hills, and streets. As a bonus, a Swiss Pass will get you free rides on all of 'em. Clear maps of all routes are posted at each stand, and you're never far from one.

Eating and going out to clubs at night are two of the joys of being here. Some tourists want to catch boats and cruise around the lake; that's fine, particularly on a sunny day, but we found the mélange of cultures that have gathered here—most of them speaking French—so interesting that we never got far away. Clubs and bars are numerous, ranging from Anglo to African to Euro-pop in feel. Restaurants, well, there are so many that we can't

GENEVA HOSTELS AT A GLANCE

	RATING	PRICE	IN A WORD	PAGE
City Hostel Geneva		32–66 CHF	central	p. 392
Nouvelle Auberge de Jeunesse		32 CHF	ethical	p. 393

Geneva

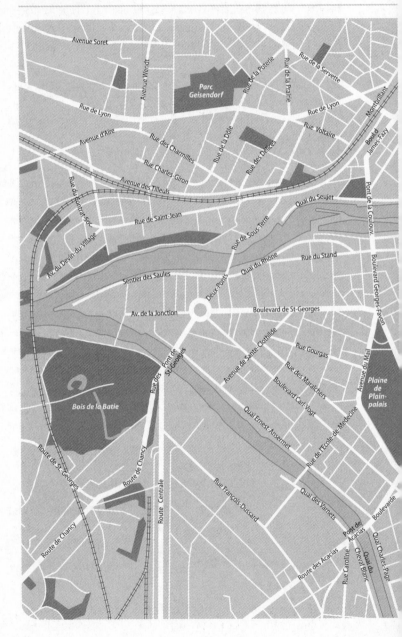

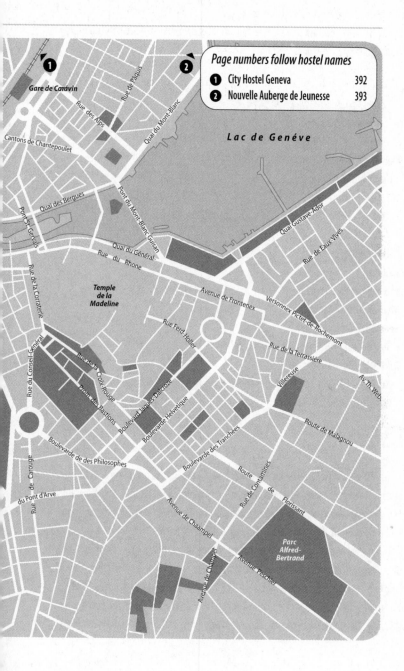

Lac de Genéve

Gare de Caravin

Cantons de Chantepoulet

Rue de Paquis

Rue des Alps

Quai du Mont-Blanc

Quai des Bergues

Pont St-Gervais

Pont du Mont-Blanc Guisan

Quai Gustave-Ador

Quai du Général-

Rue du Rhone

Rue de Eaux-Vives

Rue de la Corraterie

Temple de la Madeline

Avenue de Frontenex

Versonnex Pictet-de-Rochemont

Rue Ferd-Holler

Rue de la Terrassière

Rue du Conseil-Central

Rue de la Croix-Rouge

Villereuse

Av. Th. Web.

Pont des Bastions

Boulevard Jaques-Dalcroze

Boulevarde Helvetique

Route de Malagnou

Boulevarde de des Philosophes

Boulevarde des Tranchées

Rue de Carouge

Boulevarde des Tranchées

Route

Rue de Contamines

de Florissant

du Pont d'Arve

Avenue de Chaampel

Avenue de Champel

Avenue Peschier

Parc Alfred-Bertrand

begin to describe the options. Just know that most are good; the French insistence on quality eats has shaped the town's culinary habits.

An expensive city to eat and play in, sure, but so's all of Switzerland—and this is probably the best food town in the country. So enjoy yourself.

City Hostel Geneva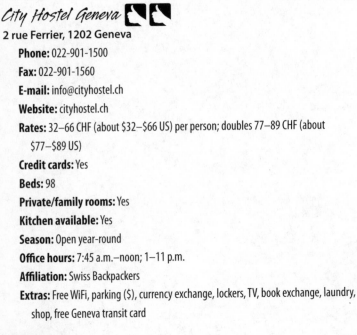

2 rue Ferrier, 1202 Geneva

> **Phone:** 022-901-1500
>
> **Fax:** 022-901-1560
>
> **E-mail:** info@cityhostel.ch
>
> **Website:** cityhostel.ch
>
> **Rates:** 32–66 CHF (about $32–$66 US) per person; doubles 77–89 CHF (about $77–$89 US)
>
> **Credit cards:** Yes
>
> **Beds:** 98
>
> **Private/family rooms:** Yes
>
> **Kitchen available:** Yes
>
> **Season:** Open year-round
>
> **Office hours:** 7:45 a.m.–noon; 1–11 p.m.
>
> **Affiliation:** Swiss Backpackers
>
> **Extras:** Free WiFi, parking ($), currency exchange, lockers, TV, book exchange, laundry, shop, free Geneva transit card

The best (and newest, relatively speaking) entry in the Geneva hostelling sweepstakes has earned its great reviews for friendly management, a good location, and affordable pricing. And they even throw in a Geneva Transport Card—which gets you full public bus and subways rides all over town for as long as you're staying here—for free!

The place is open 24 hours, with no curfew or lockout, yet it doesn't party all night like many independent big-city hostels do. Dormitories here come in various sizes, but none is too, too big; they range from a cheaper 3- or 4-bed room to shared doubles, private doubles (more expensive ones have private bathrooms and television sets in them), and even some single rooms. No matter what you pay, there are always sinks in the rooms and lockers in the halls. They're surprisingly spacious, and cleaner than almost any other backpacker-style hostel around.

There's no included breakfast at the hostel, but there is a coin-op laundry—and tons of eating options almost right outside your door in an interesting ethnic neighborhood. Some are described on the hostel's comprehensive bulletin-board guide to local eats. We also liked the fact that the place claims to invest a small percentage of its profits in a local nonprofit that brings disadvantaged youth to the city. The nonsmoking policy (inside) was even better.

Best bet for a bite:
Any produce market (ask the staff)
What hostellers say:
"Really good place!"
Gestalt:
Swiss please
Safety:
Hospitality:
Cleanliness:
Party index:

Other extras include a currency exchange at the front desk, parking in a private lot, that aforementioned city transit card to get you around town, and Internet terminals for e-mailing the latest on Switzerland back home. Great hostel, and well-run.

How To Get There:
By bus: Contact hostel for transit details.
By car: Contact hostel for directions.
By train: From Cornavin Station, exit and make an immediate left onto busy rue de Lausanne. Walk ¼ mile to motorcycle shop; turn left onto rue Prieure, continue to rue Ferrier on right.

Nouvelle Auberge de Jeunesse (New Geneva Hostel)

30 rue Rothschild, 1202 Geneva
   Phone: 022-732-6260
   Fax: 022-738-3987
   Website: genevahostel.ch
   E-mail: geneve@youthhostel.ch
   Rates: 32 CHF (about $32 US) per HI member; doubles 85–95 CHF (about $85–$95 US)
   Credit cards: Yes
   Beds: 334

Private/family rooms: Yes

Kitchen available: Yes

Season: Open year-round

Office hours: 7–10 a.m.; 2 p.m.–midnight

Lockout: 10 a.m.–4 p.m.

Affiliation: HI

Extras: Breakfast, meals ($), TV, laundry, Internet access, pool table, games, free
  transit card

This hostel's entrance area is typical of French-style hostelling—it's cavernous and dedicated to a variety of activities. One part's been sectioned off to form a "bistro" (read: cafeteria); another, the laundry room; there's a television somewhere in there and, finally, the hosteller kitchen. Though you have to figure out the weird system for using these things—it costs a token (which you buy from the front desk) to cook for 45 minutes and 3 tokens to do laundry—it all actually works quite well once you deduce that you're supposed to put tokens and not money into the machines. Lots of people had trouble with this operation, not surprising since instructions were variously printed in German, French, Italian, or English.

It's a 6-stage building, which actually means 8 floors in American terms: a ground floor, 6 floors above that, and a basement. The rooms are upstairs, and the doubles here are real stunners—two single bunks, a bathroom, a closet, and a concrete balcony overlooking the lake and mountains. Whoever designed these was really thinking.

Dorm rooms aren't bad, divided mostly into 6-bed rooms with bathrooms and sinks. The laundry is good, containing multiple washers and dryers, and the kitchen has a long table and enough burners to accommodate four or five folks at once. A free city transportation card is an amazing bonus. Reception staff get very busy with check-ins and dealing with hosteller issues, but they somehow manage to keep any potential cynicism in check and get the job done smoothly and effectively.

The hostel neighborhood is fun and diverse, meaning that you can nibble kebabs, cruise the Internet, and buy great French bread—all within half a block. You can also walk a block and sun by huge Lake Leman, one of the prettiest we've seen; that's big Mont Blanc looming way off in the distance, while vineyards and France cover the opposite shore. On the way, stroll past the UN's European headquarters, just a stone's throw away in Wilson Palace. (The guy with the Uzi and the earpiece guarding the entrance won't joke around with you. Don't even try.)

For eats you've got a wealth of choices. Back toward the station, in just 10 minutes we found a superific Swiss grocery store, a daily produce market, an Italian grocer, and a hole-in-the-wall veggie joint (where, since this is basically in France, people were smoking inside while they ate the health food!). Penetrating farther into the old city, you'll locate plenty of cafes where people sip coffee or mineral water and eat pastries. That's the most popular pastime around here: eating.

Best bet for a bite:
Public Market, rue de Coutance
Insiders' tip:
Free bikes available on waterfront
What hostellers say:
"C'est beau!"
Gestalt:
Geneva pool
Safety: ◣
Hospitality: ◣
Cleanliness: ◣
Party index: ◮◮◮

How To Get There:

By bus: Take #1 bus to Wilson Palace, then walk less than 50 yards to hostel.
By car: Call hostel for directions.
By train: From front of Geneva Station, turn left and walk down rue de Lausanne about ½ mile. Turn right at hostel sign onto rue Rothschild. Or take #13 or #15 streetcar toward Nations to Butini stop. Walk back toward train station 2 blocks to rue Rothschild. Turn left and continue to hostel.

ZÜRICH

Zürich gets a bad rap from some, but our feeling was that young travelers who want to experience a hip city should come here. Along with Geneva—a very different place, by the way—this town's got the most vibrant nightlife in all Switzerland, one part Berlin/Zoo Station/fly shades and one part Teutonic cool.

The two hostels here are total opposites in character: One's strict, hygienic, pastoral, and staid; the other's central, hopping, noisy, young, and fun. Take your pick.

Zürich's public transit is decent, not great—a network of buses and trams fans out from the train station into the commercial, tourist, and residential areas.

ZÜRICH HOSTELS AT A GLANCE

	RATING	PRICE	IN A WORD	PAGE
Zürich Hostel		42.50–44.50 CHF	strict	p. 398
City Backpacker Hotel Biber		37–77 CHF	social	p. 396

If you think you're going to be hopping around the city doing a lot of sightseeing, one option is the "9 o'clock Travelcard" (in German, *9-Uhr-Tagespass*). It gets you free public transit within city limits on weekdays from 9 in the morning until everything stops running (around 1 a.m. for most lines) and all day long on weekends. It's not cheap, and you'd have to ride a whole lot to make it worth your while. Still, it's something to think about.

There's obviously lots to do around town, including several theater companies, a variety of cruises on Lake Zürich, and huge and impressive department stores right on Bahnhofstrasse outside the train station. If you like movies, the city has an interesting promotion each Monday: big reductions on tickets. The theaters are packed! So get in line early.

The Swiss National Museum, directly behind the train station (and pretty close to the independent hostel), showcases Swiss history—old stoves, weapons, artifacts, and lots of other stuff that traces the story of this fascinating mountain-rimmed land. The Kunsthaus museum downtown exhibits modern art; the Fraumunster church's Chagall stained-glass work is also worth a look.

Mid-August is a good time to come—the city hosts its biggest party, the annual Lake Parade. Begun in 1991, the parade now throws a half-million crazed Germans, locals, traveling Americans, and other visitors into one heaving stewpot. It's a lot of fun as the normally reserved Swiss let loose for a day.

The City Backpacker Hotel Biber

Niederdorfstrasse 5, 8001 Zürich

> **Phone:** 044-251-9015
> **Fax:** 044-251-9024
> **E-mail:** sleep@city-backpacker.ch
> **Website:** city-backpacker.ch

Rates: 37–77 CHF (about $37–$77 US) per person; doubles 118 CHF (about $118 US)
Credit cards: Yes
Beds: 65
Private/family rooms: Yes
Kitchen available: Yes
Season: Open year-round
Office hours: 8 a.m.–noon; 3–10 p.m.
Affiliation: Swiss Backpackers
Extras: Laundry, lockers, travel store, Internet access

♫

*T*his is the poorer of Zürich's two hostels, but it's also the one you're more likely to book into just because it's so central to Zürich's considerable action. Or maybe you'll stay because it's so much looser and more laid-back than its HI counterpart (see below). Yes, it's fun. Yes, we don't need many rules to enjoy our stay. But no, this hostel doesn't do a good enough job of managing itself, cleaning itself, or making the experience of staying positive.

First things first. Its location is smack in the Niederdorf, the city's really fun old town—think dance clubs, cafes, souvenir shops, and poseurs, all crammed into every available square inch of the winding lanes, avenues, and very old town houses that make up the area.

But things start to go downhill when you go upstairs. Stairs? Yep: You're faced with a steep climb up winding stairs to the reception, and then possibly more stairs to get to your room. There's no elevator. (Don't duck into the restaurant kitchen on the first couple of floors by mistake; the cooks might come at you with cutlery. Not really. But don't.)

There are 4 or 5 doubles available, plus about 50 other beds in six-bed dorm rooms and quads. The rooms each have lockers, a bit of furniture, dedicated bathrooms, and—perhaps the best reason for staying here—their own little kitchens featuring fridges, rangetops, dining tables, and windows onto Zürich. Breaking up the kitchen space this way, floor by floor, helps avoid the dinnertime crush that plagues so many city hostels. Still, it doesn't compensate for the crowded, not-completely-clean dormitories and bunks.

As we've said, there are very few rules here: no lockout, no curfew; you come and go as desired. They've got a laundry downstairs and Internet terminals (for a fee) for e-mail–happy hostellers. The little front desk shop sells Swiss army knives and other souvenirs at reasonable (not rip-off) prices. One more bonus: The manager is one of the cofounders of Switzerland's independent association, Swiss Backpackers, so he can brief you (well, in addition to this book) on other backpacker-style digs around the country.

As we've mentioned, the hostel is incredibly convenient to Zürich's main train station—just a 5- to 10-minute walk away—and that means you can day-trip just about anywhere in Switzerland: Geneva, the Alps, and even Italy are only a 3- to 4-hour ride. More likely, though, you'll be hanging out in the place that calls itself "little big city," shopping, drinking, and eating. You can stay right in this neighborhood and get the best of the bars, discos, and other nightlife. Or walk around the area, checking out the city's numerous clock towers. If you have any energy left from climbing those zillion stairs to and within the hostel, that is.

Best bet for a bite:
All along Niederdorfstrasse
What hostellers say:
"Couldn't be more central—this rocks!"
Gestalt:
Zürich man, poor man
Safety:
Hospitality:
Cleanliness:
Party index:

How To Get There:

By bus: Call hostel for transit route.

By car: Call hostel for directions.

By train: From Zürich Station, walk out front entrance and turn immediately left. Walk to river and cross little bridge, then turn right on Limmatquai. Go ½ block, turn left up alley, then turn right onto Niederdorfstrasse. Hostel is on right, above Spaghetti Factory restaurant. Climb stairs up and up to reception.

Zürich Hostel

Mutschellenstrasse 114, 8038 Zürich

> **Phone:** 043-399-7800
>
> **Fax:** 043-399-7801
>
> **E-mail:** zuerich@youthhostel.ch
>
> **Rates:** 42.50–44.50 CHF (about $43–$45 US) per HI member; doubles 128–138 CHF (about $128–$138 US)
>
> **Credit cards:** Yes
>
> **Beds:** 290
>
> **Private/family rooms:** Yes
>
> **Kitchen available:** Sometimes
>
> **Season:** Open year-round

Office hours: 24 hours

Affiliation: HI

Extras: Breakfast ($), meals ($), information desk, laundry, meeting rooms, TV, lockers, garden, table tennis, bike storage, pool table, jukebox, fireplace, snack bar, Internet access

This hostel—in an institutional set of bunker-like, 5-story buildings that could probably withstand a bomb blast—delivers the goods in some ways. It's not convenient to town at all; it's not fun or spic-and-span, but it has enough services for families or backpackers who have cars to survive the night. And it was reconfigured to increase privacy. That was a good thing, 'cuz it's soooo expensive and sooooo distant from the action.

Yeah, you heard right. You've got to get way out of town to get to this place. The entrance area features the usual hanging-out lounge, in this case a huge one with a TV that even has an English-language channel. That room's adjacent to the dining area, where they serve the daily, included breakfast buffet starting at the ungodly hour of 6 a.m. They did serve a good breakfast, we'll give 'em that.

Snacks are served throughout the day, and dinner can be purchased at night in the hostel restaurant; the kitchen claims to be renowned for its Asian buffet, but we wouldn't traipse all the way out here just to eat. Our feeling is that the hostel food and drink are overpriced, especially since you're so far from town that you'll be forced to eat their dinners.

Inside, all dorms contain no more than 6 beds, which is a nice switch from the usual sardine job. In addition to the 5 six-bed rooms with sinks, there are 16 doubles with their own bathrooms and 31 quad rooms (only 10 have en-suite bathroom facilities) that are good for families, couples, or buddies traveling together. Each dorm comes with lockers and one desk. Though staff are as Swissly efficient and impersonal as ever, we were surprised to find the place not all that clean.

Showers, toilets, and hair dryers are available on each floor and sometimes in rooms, too. Other

Best bet for a bite:
Not around here
What hostellers say:
"Pretty good."
Gestalt:
Far and away
Safety:
Hospitality:
Cleanliness:
Party index:

amenities include a courtyard, giant chessboard outside, bike shed, and lots more services—almost like a rustic hotel, really, except with much less charm and attention.

You can tell they're really geared toward groups at this place when you stumble across the huge, 200-seat auditorium; the rec room—yeah, that's a big-screen TV in there, along with foosball, a pool table, and a jukebox—or one of the two seminar rooms. Don't even think about cleaning your bike in there or taking a nap or eating a picnic. They won't like it.

The hostel's far from town but close to Lake Zürich, which is one possible trip. But you didn't come here to see that, did you? Yes? Well, then, this hostel is perfect for you. The only other interesting option around here is the Rote Fabrik cultural center, a showplace for avant-garde art, music, dance, and the like. It's practically next door, lending some much-needed culture to this too-remote place.

All in all, a pretty good place—just miles from the action, which is a damned shame.

How To Get There:

By bus: From Zürich station, take #7 streetcar to Morgental stop and walk ¼ mile north to hostel. Or take #8 S-Bahn (suburban train) to Wollishofen stop, then walk 3 blocks to Mutschellenstrasse; turn right and continue 2 more blocks to hostel, following signs.

By car: Call hostel for directions. Free parking behind hostel.

By subway: Take #8 S-Bahn (suburban train) to Wollishofen stop, then walk 3 blocks to Mutschellenstrasse; turn right and continue 2 more blocks to hostel, following signs.

By train: From Zürich station, take #7 streetcar to Morgental stop and walk ¼ mile north to hostel. Or take #8 S-Bahn (suburban train) to Wollishofen stop, then walk 3 blocks to Mutschellenstrasse; turn right and continue 2 more blocks to hostel, following signs.

Key to Icons

Attractive natural setting	Comfortable beds	Visual arts at hostel or nearby
Ecologically aware hostel	A particularly good value	Music at hostel or nearby
Superior kitchen facilities or cafe	Wheelchair-accessible	Great hostel for skiers
Offbeat or eccentric place	Good for business travelers	Bar or pub at hostel or nearby
Superior bathroom facilities	Especially well-suited for families	Editors' choice: Among our very favorite hostels
Romantic private rooms	Good for active travelers	

United Kingdom (England, Scotland, Wales & Northern Ireland)

*O*nce a great empire, now a fairly small group of islands, the United Kingdom (UK) still casts a huge cultural shadow. But if you've never been, you might need a program to know the players.

England is the land of pubs, chip shops, green, rolling countryside; the Beatles, the Rutles (sorry), Led Zep, Her Majesty the Queen; and (of course) London—which probably still fancies itself capital of the world. It's a great place to go backpacking. England's "second city" is Manchester, a working-class place that suddenly became hip when rave music swept the islands (and, briefly, the Western world). Wales is the most mysterious, wildest part of the UK; people speak Welsh, the identity is distinct, and the combination of farms, quarries, mountains, and fewer people makes this a great place to hike by yourself. Welsh hostels also seem to be among the friendliest in the UK. Scotland can be summarized pretty quickly: bagpipes and beer. Stir in bags of rain, iffy food, and a measured dose of friendliness, and you've pretty much captured the essential Scottish experience. The hostels here are spare and less friendly, but they're beautifully located—some in old stone houses. Finally, Northern Ireland is on an entirely different island, and carries a whole complex box of emotions and histories besides, but it's now and probably forever part of the UK (and they'll never let you forget it). And it's one of the most starkly beautiful places in all of Europe.

Getting There & Getting Around

There are oodles of flights from the US (and everywhere else) to London. In a sea of competitors, shop around vigorously, but we've found that the following are especially worth checking out:

British Airways (britishairways.com) runs the most flights to the States, and outside the summer season these are often the cheapest as BA scrambles to fill planes. In high summer, though, prices escalate.

Virgin Atlantic (virgin-atlantic.com) is often just as cheap, with lots better service and food. They have a good online booking engine, and the website has a fun personality (for an airline).

From Europe, Ryanair's (ryanair.com) fares out of Ireland and London are almost always unbeatably low, though heavy airport taxes can add to the price you're quoted online.

EasyJet (easyjet.com) flies to Luton airport north of London from Europe at competitively low prices.

British trains—overseen by British Rail (britrail.com)—are a traditional way to travel in the UK, though quality varies a lot and the trains don't go everywhere. Remember that the UK is NOT covered by Eurail passes; you'll need to either buy expensive point-to-point tickets or else invest in a BritRail pass before you get there. (Occasionally you can find one at a train station, but don't risk it.) This pass isn't cheap, but it does include free passage on the Heathrow Express, a handy commuter train that zips from Heathrow airport to a Tube stop in downtown London three times hourly. Other passes in the UK include combination passes only valid in Ireland; London-only passes; Scottish passes; and more.

Finally, train schedules can be accessed anywhere in the UK by calling the national info number (08457-484-950). It's a toll call, however. From the US, contact the rail company by simply dialing (866) BRITRAIL.

Buses are by far a cheaper ride than trains, and they're a fine way to go—in fact, they're probably going to be your main mode of transport in the UK, so get used to riding and waiting. The main problem: figuring out what seem like hundreds of local bus lines and their changing schedules. The good news is that there's usually a bus going wherever you're going in England, as long as you don't travel on Sunday or certain Mondays, when some lines run less frequently. It might take you all day to make connections, but most bus drivers in the UK are helpful, so you'll get there eventually.

Between-city buses run constantly, too, and even in the sticks you'll be amazed when a double-decker pulls up in the middle of nowhere to whisk you away to East Twee or somewhere. Look for "coach" in the phone directories.

National Express (08705-808-080; nationalexpress.com) is England's huge, Greyhound-like company; it runs tons of scheduled daily lines along major routes and some weird ones too. If you're seriously wanting to get from Aberdeen to, say, Stratford-upon-Avon, give 'em a call to see if they go there. They well might. Buses are less expensive than the train, but not a lot cheaper with the Express. In return you get a few perks like on-time buses, helpful drivers, toilets, and, sometimes, an attendant walking down the aisle with snacks for sale.

Local buses fill the rest of the gaps, and these can range from incredibly efficient lines to laughable ones. There are literally hundreds of small bus companies in England, sometimes a half dozen in one town or city, so there's no central way to contact them. Just ask at the hostel or bus station when you arrive, or study the posted schedules at the bus stop where you're dropped off.

In Scotland, Scottish Citylink (0871-266-3333, a toll call; citylink.co.uk) brings you from big city to big city efficiently; it now also covers the Isle of Skye as well. To get to really remote places in Scotland, the postbus system is one more potential ally. These buses or station wagons, which really do carry the mail, will carry you, too, for a slight charge. However, they sometimes run as infrequently as once a day or week, so be sure you know the return schedule before you commit. (They don't run at night.) Usually it's no trouble.

The most popular kind of backpacker travel these days, however, is none of the above; it's the "JOJO" (jump on, jump off) minibus service that circles the British Isles like sharks, scooping up backpackers in faraway train stations and depositing them safely in remote, beautiful places. It's also known as "HOHO," which is hop on and hop off.

MacBackpackers (0131-558-9900; macbackpackers.com), a company started by an independent hostel chain, offers various tours of the Land O'Tartan. You've gotta stay in their hostels, like 'em or not. But their drivers are pretty knowledgeable.

You probably won't be using ferries much, unless you're visiting Scotland—in which case you almost certainly will, to see the islands. Caledonian MacBrayne (01475-650-100 or 08000-665-000; calmac.co.uk) runs most of the ferries in Scotland; P&O (poferries.com; 08716-642-121 in the UK; a toll call) runs most of the rest. Other ferries in England, Wales, and Scotland are locally run; consult the local tourism office for information on getting to places like the Orkneys and such.

Money

You'll need money, as everything in the UK is expensive. One English pound equals, at this writing, about $1.50 US. (Check the current exchange rates before your departure for the UK.) To get a rough idea of what something in English pounds would cost you in the US, take the English price and add half of it to itself. Ouch! Yeah, you just paid 30 bucks for that £20 burger and beer in that pub in that oh-so-cute little seaside village.

Look carefully through your coins, because bigger isn't always better. A copper "pence" coin is just like an American penny. Two-pence coins are also copper, only bigger. Ten-pence coins are something like dimes, but larger. Twenty-pence coins look funny, like small stop signs; 50-pence coins look like big stop signs. A pound is a very small, thick coin that's worth a lot (relatively speaking). Two-pound coins are kind of rare; they're two-colored, a gold outside and a silver inside. Bills (or "notes") are more obvious, but look sharp: The number of pounds is printed lightly in the upper-left-hand corner. A 5-pound bill is worth about $7.50 US, a 10-pound bill is worth about $15 US, and so on. In Scotland you'll sometimes receive unusual 1-pound bills. Exchange these for coins or larger bills before you get to France, because they might be suspicious of these.

In Northern Ireland you'll get a slightly different kind of cash: It's still British pounds sterling (again, known simply as pounds), but it looks a little different because it has been printed by banks in Northern Ireland. These bills are worth exactly the same as pounds in England, and a little bit more than Irish pounds. If you're going to England afterward, note that you can't spend Northern Ireland–printed pounds there, so change them all before you leave, if possible. (You can use British or even Scottish pound notes in Northern Ireland with no trouble at all, however.)

Phones

All phone and fax numbers listed in the book are written as dialed from within the UK itself. To call hostels in the UK from North America, dial 011-44 and then DROP THE ZERO from the numbers printed here. To call UK hostels from elsewhere in Europe, dial the long-distance code (usually 00), then 44, then drop the zero. To call them from within the UK, as we've said, dial them just AS PRINTED. To call the hostels from within their home cities, you usually DROP THE CITY CODE (the first part; 0131 for Edinburgh, for example).

BELFAST

Belfast inspired mixed emotions. Despite some recent reminders of "The Troubles," as they call them here, the city remains a peek inside the heart of Northern Ireland.

BELFAST HOSTELS AT A GLANCE

RATING	PRICE	IN A WORD	PAGE
Belfast City Backpackers Hostel	👍👍	£14	great	p. 406
Arnie's Backpackers	👍👎	£13.40–£16.70	iffy	p. 405
Belfast International Hostel	👍👎	£11.50–£31.50	institutional	p. 407
Linen House	👎	£6.50–£20	flailing	p. 408

Arnie's Backpackers

63 Fitzwilliam St., Belfast BT9 6AX

Phone: 028-90-242867
E-mail: info@arniesbackpackers.co.uk
Website: arniesbackpackers.co.uk
Rates: £13.40–£16.70 (about $20–$25 US); doubles £44 (about $66 US)
Credit cards: Yes
Beds: 22
Kitchen available: Yes
Private/family rooms: Yes
Season: Open year-round
Office hours: 24 hours
Affiliation: None
Extras: Fireplace, garden

A redbrick town house on a drab side-street in downtown Belfast, Arnie's is small—very small—and only so-so.

Dorms contain 4 or 8 beds each, and they can make a private double or room at your request—they actually apologize for charging more for these, which they don't need to do—but this isn't your best option in town.

Cleanliness is only OK. It's friendly, yes. But the biggest drawback would be the aging building. Besides a kitchen, there are no mod amenities. It's basically a place to crash, cook a quick meal, and have a break in the back courtyard.

One other caveat: This hostel is located half a block from a huge city hospital. Yes, really. We're not saying you will hear sirens. But you may. On the other hand, you're also only a short walk from the calming Belfast Botanic Gardens.

You're also half a block from University Road and tons of grub.

Best bet for a bite:
Ruba Spice
What hostellers say:
"Bit too small."
Gestalt:
Arnie's army
Safety:
Hospitality:
Cleanliness:
Party index:

How To Get There:

By bus: From bus station, walk south along Great Victoria Street (becomes Bradbury Place) and continue straight ¾ mile (1 km) to Fitzwilliam Street. Turn right and continue ½ block to hostel on right.

By train: From train station, walk south along Great Victoria Street (becomes Bradbury Place) and continue straight ¾ mile (1 km) to Fitzwilliam Street. Turn right and continue ½ block to hostel on right.

By car: Contact hostel for directions.

Belfast City Backpacker Hostel

53-55 Malone Avenue, Belfast BT9 6EP

> **Phone:** 028-9066-0030
>
> **E-mail:** info@ibackpacker.co.uk
>
> **Website:** ibackpacker.co.uk
>
> **Rates:** £14 per person (about $21 US); doubles £40 (about $60 US)
>
> **Credit cards:** Yes
>
> **Beds:** Number varies
>
> **Private/family rooms:** Yes
>
> **Kitchen available:** Yes
>
> **Season:** Open year-round
>
> **Office hours:** 24 hours
>
> **Extras:** Lockers, fax service, ironing boards, laundry, WiFi, bike rentals, TV, games

---

*N*ow this is Belfast's top bunk.

Stocked with good amenities (DVDs, a kitchen, a laundry) and populated by a happy vibe, this indy gets everything right.

The outside is a foreboding redbrick apartment building, but inside there are clean common areas and dorms outfitted in IKEA rugs and furniture. The dining room is school-simple but clean, and the actual cooking facilities rival those in many nice apartments we've seen. The laundry room looks new (though this hostel is not new at all). Bunks are a bit tightly packed together, but the nice bathrooms make up for this shortcoming.

The nabe is the same university-type district as Arnie's (see p. xxx), but this is just a better place to stay.

How To Get There:

By bus: From bus station, walk south along Great Victoria Street (becomes Bradbury Place) and continue straight 1 mile (2 km) on University Road (becomes Malone Road) to Malone Street. Turn right and continue ½ block to hostel.

By train: From train station, walk south along Great Victoria Street (becomes Bradbury Place) and continue straight 1 mile (2 km) on University Road (becomes Malone Road) to Malone Street. Turn right and continue ½ block to hostel.

By car: Contact hostel for directions.

Best bet for a bite:
Malone Road
Insiders' tip:
The Botanic Inn for pub, grub, and music
What hostellers say:
"Great facilities."
Gestalt:
Backpacker in business
Safety:
Hospitality:
Cleanliness
Party index:

Belfast International Hostel

22-32 Donegall Rd., Belfast BT12 5JN

Phone: 028-9031-5435

Fax: 028-9031-5889

E-mail: info@hini.org.uk

Beds: 202

Private/family rooms: Yes

Kitchen available: Yes

Rates: £11.50–£31.50 per HI member (about $18–$48 US); doubles £29–£42 (about $45–$63 US)

Credit cards: Yes

Season: Open year-round

Office hours: 24 hours

Affiliation: Hostelling International-Northern Ireland

Extras: Cafe ($), library, laundry, lockers, Internet access ($), games, TV, currency exchange, bike storage

The city's "official" hostel, the Belfast International has its good points and its bad points. There are quite a variety of digs, from monster (20-bed) dorms to 26 single and double rooms and a good supply of quad rooms, as well. So this is definitely the hostel in town with the most choice for families. It's relatively inexpensive, and friendly to boot. There's a kitchen. And an elevator. (Sorry . . . "lift". 'Cuz that's what it does. Lift.)

The hostel cafe is pretty fly, too—nicer than a real restaurant, and way cheaper.

However, there are lots of reasons to think about a different place to bunk up, especially if you're traveling solo. Why? The place looks and feels like a bad parochial school at times . . . or a jail. It's just not that attractive outside or inside. The bathrooms, in particular, need work and better cleaning. But that's what happens when herds of hostellers and schoolkids use (and beat up) a place. It's somewhat a victim of its own popularity.

Best bet for a bite:
Causeway Cafe right in-house
What hostellers say:
"Not the best. OK."
Gestalt:
Belfast company
Safety:
Hospitality:
Cleanliness:
Party index:

We really do appreciate the efforts most of the staff make here. And that cafe is great. But the boring nabe, plus the institutional feel of this hostel, should make it a backup pick unless you're bringing the entire family, in which case it's probably your only pick.

How to Get There:
By bus: Contact hostel for transit route.
By train: From Botanic Station, walk onto Botanic Avenue and turn right, then left into Shaftesbury Square. Continue past KFC to hostel on left.
By car: Contact hostel for directions.

Linen House Hostel
18 - 20 Kent St., Belfast BT1 2JA
> **Phone:** 028-9058-6400
> **Fax:** 028-9058-6444
> **E-mail:** info@belfasthostel.com
> **Website:** belfasthostel.com

Rates: £6.50–£20 per person (about $10–$30 US)
Credit Cards: Yes
Beds: 130
Private/family rooms: Yes
Kitchen available: Yes
Affiliation: None
Extras: TV, free WiFi, laundry, lockers

---

*Y*ikes. This place just did not float our boat in any possible way.

Well, in one way. The one thing the hostel does have going for it is location. The other three hostels we review in Belfast are all in the same neighborhood, more or less, and it's damned boring. This one isn't. It's a stone's throw from the true downtown heart of Belfast, with its handsome City Hall, the city library, plenty o' churches, a million pubs and bars, and the so-called Titanic Quarter (yes, that ill-fated ship was built and launched here).

But the hostel gets everything else wrong. It's not very clean; it smells kinda bad; water pressure and temp in the bathrooms is an issue; you can drink in the basement "party room," and people do—but they also sometimes take the alcohol and unsteady conversations upstairs into the halls, too. Staff try to be helpful when they're not hanging with the guests, but they just don't really have the situation under control at all.

Summary: Give it a pass. It's dirt-cheap and central, yeah, and if you don't care about cleanliness or noise, you could spend a night. But most of us won't want to.

And that's a wrap.

> **Best bet for a bite:**
> *Pub on the corner*
> **Insiders' tip:**
> *Grab drinks at Crown Liquor Saloon*
> **What hostellers say:**
> *"No. No."*
> **Gestalt:**
> *Unraveled fabric*
> **Safety:**
> **Hospitality:**
> **Cleanliness**
> **Party index:**

How To Get There

By bus: Contact hostel for transit route.
By car: Contact hostel for directions.
By train: Contact hostel for transit route.

CARDIFF

Cardiff, largest city in Wales, is the exception to the rule that Wales is a quiet and somewhat traditional place. This city possesses a thriving (though hardly huge) metropolis with youthful energy, helpful tourist officials, decent food, and one heckuva castle. Try to get away from London, even for a day trip—which is possible, given the fast direct trains from England— to see it.

Cardiff Ty Croeso (Welcome House) Hostel

2 Wedal Rd., Roath Park, Cardiff CF14 3QX

Phone: 0845-371-311
Fax: 029-2046-4571
E-mail: cardiff@yha.org.uk
Rates: £16.50–£18 (about $25–$27 US) per HI member
Credit cards: Yes
Beds: 66
Private/family rooms: Yes
Kitchen available: Yes
Season: Open year-round
Office hours: 7 a.m.–11 p.m.
Affiliation: HI-YHA
Extras: TV, laundry, bicycle shop, dinner ($), bar

It's a couple miles outside the central city, yet Cardiff's brick hostel is still plagued by extremely busy surroundings. Bring some earplugs if you want some rest.

Yet it's a surprisingly decent place, well-run, with good rooms and serving up good meals—even a beer on the side, if you will. The plain-jane dorm lineup consists of 6 quad rooms, an 8-bed dorm, and 2 bigger dorms averaging 17 beds apiece. There are 2 lounges and a telly to occupy the little ones, plus a laundry to occupy the big ones.

While in town most visitors suck down a couple beers before quickly heading out for this beautiful country's rural parks. Cardiff's more interesting than you think, though. For one thing, there's a giant castle perched right at the head of downtown. Eyeball that baby while you're drinking a pint. (Pubs are scattered about.) Second, cheap and surprisingly diverse food options are everywhere. There's a bay to look at. And you can get a bus or train from here to just about anywhere else in Wales you'd want to go.

Need directions? The local tourist office (located in the Cardiff Central train station) is great. We know. They once sent a free taxi to fetch our wayward credit card as we were waiting for a train to leave. Honest.

Best bet for a bite:
Bella Italian
What hostellers say:
"More fun than I expected."
Gestalt:
Score Cardiff
Safety:
Hospitality:
Cleanliness:
Party index:

How To Get There:

By bus: From bus station, go around corner and take #28, #29, or #29B bus (£1.30 exact fare or day transit pass required) to Wedal Road stop and walk 200 yards to hostel.

By car: From M4 take A48M to rotary; exit first left off rotary, follow Whitchurch Road to Fairoak Road, and make a left. Continue to smaller rotary; hostel is at corner of Wedal Road and Fairoak.

By train: From Cardiff Central Station, walk 2½ miles to hostel. Or take #28, #29, or #29B bus (£1.30 exact fare or day transit pass required) to Wedal Road stop and walk 200 yards to hostel.

EDINBURGH

You can't believe just how striking Edinburgh is until you've actually gotten here. Hop off the train and walk up the grueling Waverley Steps . . . hmm. A busy street, no big deal.

But then you turn around and see the castle up on its rock, symbol of Scotland, explore the Royal Mile's pubs and shops, check out how the other half lives in tony but nice New Town, and go for a long walk in the free and beautiful Botanic Gardens. If only the weather would cooperate more often.

Hostels here are generally decent, and most are concentrated close to downtown; all can be reached by a bus ride of up to half an hour. City buses, in fact, are generally excellent, though they do shut down late at night and run less frequently on Sunday. The bus and train stations are very convenient and close together.

Note that there are two train stations here; for downtown hostels, get off at Waverley. For suburban joints, hop off a stop earlier at Haymarket.

Edinburgh

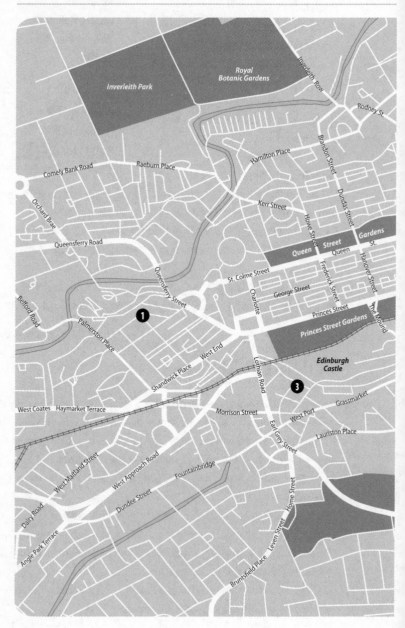

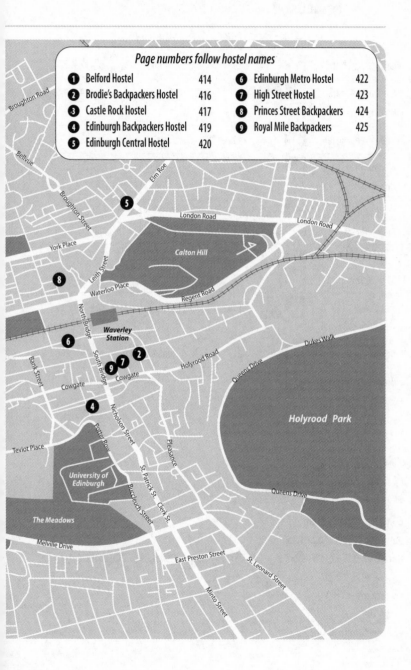

EDINBURGH HOSTELS AT A GLANCE

	RATING	PRICE	IN A WORD	PAGE
Castle Rock Hostel	🐾🐾	£11–£15	primo	p. 417
Edinburgh Central Hostel	🐾🐾	£18–£29.50	modern	p. 420
High Street Hostel	🐾	£11–£28	social	p. 423
Edinburgh Metro Hostel	🐾	£29	good	p. 422
Royal Mile Backpackers	🐾	£13–£15	friendly	p. 425
Princes Street Backpackers	🐾	£11–£15	social	p. 424
Edinburgh Backpackers Hostel	🐾🐾	£11–£21	big	p. 419
Belford Hostel	🐾	£12.50–£29	funkorama	p. 414
Brodie's Backpackers Hostel	🐾	£9–£17	terrible	p. 416

Belford Hostel 🐾

6–8 Douglas Gardens, Edinburgh EH4 3DA

Phone: 0131-220-2200

E-mail: info@hoppo.com

Website: hoppo.com/belford

Rates: £12.50–£29.00 (about $20–$45 US) per person; doubles £40–£82 (about $60–$123 US)

Credit Cards: Yes

Beds: 100

Private/family rooms: Yes

Kitchen available: Yes
Season: Open year-round
Office hours: 7 a.m.–3 a.m.
Affiliation: IBHS
Extras: Laundry, pool table, bar, barbecue, Internet access, TV room, bike rentals, breakfast ($)

*W*e've always filed pretty mixed reviews of this funky place housed in a former church: some good, some not so good. At least it's a little better than it used to be (when it was truly the pits). But it's still not all that great.

Yeah, for starters, it's a church. You won't miss the very tall steeple as you walk downhill (past another church!) in search of the place. The windows still contain stained glass, and it's a bit of a creepy feeling if you're a heathen and you awaken to the sight of it. (Religious hostellers will probably faint with happiness, believing they've gone to heaven.)

Once you get inside, things are extremely secular, though—pretty noisy and lively actually (and smelly). A pool table and bar keep it that way much of the time. There are 5 family rooms for those who seek a bit of extra quiet, and the location's not too bad, but overall this is not a very recommendable place. Renovations occurred in 2010 but rooms remain on the smallish side, not nearly clean or fresh-smelling or bright enough, and staffers sometimes often have attitude issues. How come? This is a freaking church, dudes. We don't get it.

> **What hostellers say:**
> *"Get da funk out my face."*
> **Gestalt:**
> *Holy smokes*
> **Safety:**
> **Hospitality:**
> **Cleanliness:**
> **Party index:**

How To Get There:

By plane: Catch airport express bus #100 to Haymarket Station; walk along Haymarket to second left, at Starbucks. Turn left onto Palmerston Place and pass cathedral. Continue to end of street; hostel is inside church at bottom of hill (look for tall steeple).

By train: From Waverley Train Station, exit to Waverley Bridge and turn right. Walk to top of street. Cross Princes Street and turn left; walk along Princes Street to Lothian Road but stay on Princes Street (becomes Shandwick Place). At Starbucks coffee shop, turn right onto Palmerston Place and walk downhill past St. Mary's Cathedral to end of street. Hostel is inside church on right-hand corner at bottom of hill, just before bridge. Or take taxi (about $6 US). From Haymarket Train Station, exit via main exit to Haymarket Terrace. Cross road and turn right; continue to Palmerston Place (at Starbucks) and turn left. Pass St. Mary's Cathedral and continue to the end of the street Hostel is in church at bottom of hill, before bridge.

By bus: From St. Andrews Square, exit station, turn left, and continue down to Princes Street. Turn right onto Princes Street and follow train directions above.

Brodie's Backpackers Hostel

93 High St., Edinburgh EH1 1SG

Phone: 0131-556-2223

Website: brodieshostels.co.uk

Rates: £9–£17 (about $14–$25 US) per person; doubles £47–£75 (about $71–$113 US)

Credit Cards: Yes

Beds: 50

Private/family rooms: No

Kitchen available: Yes

Season: Open year-round

Office hours: 7 a.m.–midnight

Affiliation: None

Extras: Laundry, stereo

*W*ow. This place, once one of the coolest hostels in the old town, has gone right off the deep end—it's now so bad that it's a borderline turkey. Brodie (whoever you are), say it ain't so!

Incredibly central, it used to be pretty happenin' and well managed. Something must've gone terribly wrong. Because now this place rots.

Best bet for a bite:
Tempting Tatties

Insiders' tip:
Drink at the Tass (pub)

Gestalt:
Jekyll & Hide

Safety:

Hospitality:

Cleanliness:

Party index:

Bunkrooms are mostly big, with dorms ranging from 4 to 16 beds, but they feel smaller than that due to their unkemptness. (Note to women: Several of these dorms are coed. Ask when booking.) Rooms that once housed spacious, glorious bunks have now turned into mosh pits of malfeasance. Bathrooms are still in short supply, the kitchen is scuzzier than ever, and even the fun factor seems mostly to have deserted the place as the cool hostellers have picked up and moved on to greener pastures.

How To Get There:

By bus: From bus station walk to Princes Street and turn left onto it after crossing to the other side; turn right at North Bridge, cross the bridge, then turn immediately left onto High Street (Royal Mile). Continue a few blocks to hostel on right.

By car: Call hostel for directions.

By train: From Waverley Station, exit onto Princes Street; turn right, then right again to North Bridge, and cross the bridge to High Street (Royal Mile). Turn left and continue a few blocks to hostel on right.

Castle Rock Hostel

15 Johnston Terrace, Edinburgh EH1 2PW

Phone: 0131-225-9666

Website: castlerockedinburgh.com

Rates: £11–£15 (about $17–$23 US) per person; doubles £45 (about $69 US)

Credit Cards: Yes

Beds: 220

Private/family rooms: No

Kitchen available: Yes

Season: Open year-round

Office hours: 24 hours

Affiliation: None

Extras: Free WiFi, breakfast ($), laundry, bar, pool table, movies, TV, lockers, piano, fireplace, jukebox, free walking tours

*N*ow this is more like it. A biggish hostel operated by the folks in the Scotland's Top Hostels (aka MacBackpackers) chain, this place hit the ground running on day one and has just gotten better and better over the years—living up, for once, to the name "Top." And dig that location: you're literally right beneath the famous Edinburgh castle that symbolizes all things Scottish, so start right here. Take a snapshot of you, outside the hostel, and e-mail it home to your buds. Wait five minutes. Massive jealousy ensues.

I mean, this place features a piano and a fireplace. A piano. And a fireplace! C'mon.

Best bet for a bite:
Helios Fountain in Grassmarket
Gestalt:
No-hassle castle
Safety:
Hospitality:
Cleanliness:
Party index:

There's a kitchen, so you don't have to pay outrageous British dinner prices if you don't want to. There's a jukebox. There's a pool table. There's a "no stag or hen parties" rule. (Translation: No bachelor/bachelorette parties. Heh.) It's artistically designed. There are hairdryers in the bathrooms. Double bunks are sturdy and classy.

And the place is hip. These guys are so cool they arrange free walking tours of the central city for you. And they're so green the owners of the mini-chain actually bought a plot of woods in the countryside to offset the carbon their minibuses belch. Believe it.

Just down a long set of stairs from the hostel, you're deep in the heart of student heaven. The University of Edinburgh and an art school make their homes around here, and the Grassmarket area is home to many a cool restaurant or other diversion. So, although

Key to Icons

Attractive natural setting	Comfortable beds	Visual arts at hostel or nearby
Ecologically aware hostel	A particularly good value	Music at hostel or nearby
Superior kitchen facilities or cafe	Wheelchair-accessible	Great hostel for skiers
Offbeat or eccentric place	Good for business travelers	Bar or pub at hostel or nearby
Superior bathroom facilities	Especially well-suited for families	Editors' choice: Among our very favorite hostels
Romantic private rooms	Good for active travelers	

this hostel is not on the main drag (i.e., Royal Tourist Trap), that actually means it's mostly immune to the hordes of wide-eyed American tourists dying to get their pictures taken next to the guy wheezing away on his bagpipes up on the Mile.

Nice view of that castle, plus Internet access, a fun place, and a fun crowd. Score. You'll love it.

How To Get There:

By bus: From bus station, turn left and walk down to Princes Street; cross street, turn right, and walk to Waverley Bridge; turn left and cross bridge. Climb up to Royal Mile (High Street), then turn right and walk uphill to Johnson Terrace on left. Bear left and walk downhill to hostel on left.

By car: Call hostel for directions.

By train: From Haymarket Station, walk up ramp to Waverley Bridge and turn left; cross bridge, climb up to Royal Mile (High Street). Turn right on High Street and walk uphill to Johnson Terrace on left; bear left and walk downhill to hostel on left.

Edinburgh Backpackers Hostel

65 Cockburn St., Edinburgh EH1 1BU

Phone: 0131-220-2200

Website: hoppo.com/edinburgh

Rates: £11–£21 (about $17–$32 US) per person; doubles £49–£60 (about $75–$90 US)

Credit Cards: Yes

Beds: 110

Private/family rooms: Yes

Kitchen available: Yes

Season: Open year-round

Office hours: 24 hours

Affiliation: IBHS

Extras: Meals ($), Internet access, pub crawls, TV, storage

---

*T*his big hostel's located on too-hip-for-its-own-good Cockburn Street, which winds downhill from the famous Royal Mile. From the main train station, it's much easier to access from a ramp that ends at the Waverley Bridge than by the torturous Waverley Steps.

Again, location is everything here if you're looking to get pierced or tattooed. The drill's the same as at the other indie hostels—a more lax attitude toward cleanliness and an emphasis on having a good time. It's very noisy here, and bunks (in rooms of 5 to 14 beds apiece) are kinda flimsy, but it's hardly a terrible place. The 3 private rooms on the top floor—calling this section a penthouse is a stretch, since you've gotta walk up, like, five flights of stairs, but still—are even better.

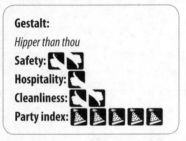

Gestalt:

Hipper than thou

Safety:

Hospitality:

Cleanliness:

Party index:

For all of you who thrive on the famous HI-SYHA sterility, you'll not appreciate the vibes here. The building is standardly Victorian in architecture but wedged near the aforementioned tattoo parlor as well as an S&M shop, a hemp shop, and a half dozen pubs in which to wet your whistle.

How To Get There:

By bus: Exit terminal and turn left. Walk downhill to Princes Street; cross over and walk toward Waverley Bridge. Turn left and cross bridge, then cross Market Street and walk uphill. Hostel is near top of the hill on left.

By car: Call hostel for directions.

By train: From Waverley Station, follow signs uphill to Waverley Bridge. Follow ramp to bridge; turn left and walk to the end of the bridge. Cross Royal Mile at Market Street and walk uphill. Hostel is near top of street on left.

Edinburgh Central Hostel

9 Haddington Place, Edinburgh EH7 4AL

> **Phone:** 0131-524-2090
>
> **E-mail:** central@syha.org.uk
>
> **Website:** edinburghcentral.org
>
> **Rates:** £18–£29.50 (about $27–$45 US) per HI member; doubles £50–£109 (about $75–$165 US)

Credit cards: Yes
Beds: 302
Private/family rooms: Yes
Kitchen available: Yes
Season: January 7–October 31
Office hours: 24 hours
Affiliation: HI-SYHA
Extras: TV room, DVD, Internet access, cafe ($), lockers ($), laundry, conference room

*T*his is a really excellent and, obviously, central hostel despite first appearances: a modern and decent place concealed within an uninspiring, warehouse–slash–French train station–like shell . . . a real surprise given that this is an "official" (SYHA) Edinburgh hostel.

Rooms are entered with a key card (welcome to the modern age, hostels—finally). Rooms range from single and double up to 8-bed dorms, all with lockers and their own bathrooms. It's pretty close to both Waverley Station (Edinburgh's central hub) and famous Princes Street.

What hostellers say:
"Great place."
Gestalt:
Central perk
Safety:
Hospitality:
Cleanliness:
Party index:

Like all HI-SYHA hostels, this one has a hostel kitchen for your own cooking pleasure—but it also has a little cafe. Both continental and Scottish-style (heartier) breakfasts can be purchased, as well as lunches and dinners.

Large-screen televisions are scattered about the lobbies, and yeah, they've got WiFi access. Pay Internet terminals are also set up near the lobby; a handy laundry is a boon. Big and clean, if uninspiring. Good job.

How To Get There:

By bus: From St. Andrews Bus Station, exit onto York Place. Walk along York Place to the Picardy Place rotary. Turn left and continue along Leith Walk ¼ mile to hostel on corner of Haddington Place.
By car: Follow signs into city center and Queen Street; follow Queen Street to York Place. At rotary, take first exit onto Leith Walk. Hostel is ¼ mile beyond, on left. Street parking and garages nearby.

By train: From Waverley Station, exit onto Princes Street. Cross street and turn right; continue to St. James's shopping center and turn left. Walk along Leith Street to the Picardy Place rotary. Turn left and continue on Leith Walk about ¼ miles to hostel on corner of Haddington Place.

Edinburgh Metro Hostel

1½ Robertson's Close, Cowgate, Edinburgh EH1 1LY

> **Phone:** 0131-556-8718
> **Rates:** £29.50 (about $45 US) per HI member; doubles £99–£109 (about $150–$165 US)
> **Beds:** 285
> **Credit Cards:** Yes
> **Private/family rooms:** Yes
> **Kitchen available:** Yes
> **Season:** July 13–August 27
> **Office hours:** 24 hours
> **Affiliation:** HI-SYHA
> **Extras:** Laundry

---

*B*elieve it or not, this overflow annex to the city's "official" hostels consists entirely of private rooms. That's because it's an Edinburgh University dormitory during the academic year. In summer, though, it morphs into a sterile but comfy hostel.

It's great if you're traveling with a family, not so hot if you want atmosphere or lotsa mixing and mingling (and alcohol) . . . 'cuz it's a pretty square place, frankly. At least you're in atmospheric digs, and the price is way less than you'd pay at a B&B or hotel in town. But 285 single bunks? Hmm. Seems more like a capsule hotel than a hostel. And it's pricey: nearly 50 bucks a room. Ouch.

> **Gestalt:**
> *Schooooool's out! For summer!*
> **Safety:**
> **Hospitality:**
> **Cleanliness:**
> **Party index:**

Oh yeah, and then there's this: It's open only for 6 weeks each summer. Grab it while it lasts. If you like hanging out alone.

How To Get There:

By car: Contact hostel for directions.
By bus: Contact hostel for directions.
By train: Contact hostel for directions.

High Street Hostel

8-18 Blackfriars St., Edinburgh

   Phone: 0135-557-3984
   Website: highstreethostel.com
   Rates: £11–£28 (about $17–$42 US) per person; doubles £40–£68 (about $60–$102 US)
   Credit cards: Yes
   Beds: 75
   Private/family rooms: Yes
   Kitchen available: Yes
   Season: Open year-round
   Office hours: 24 hours
   Affiliation: IBHS
   Extras: laundry, luggage storage, free WiFi

*I*n a handsome, 500-year-old (!) stone building on a little street, this hostel is superbly placed—right around the corner from the Royal Mile, for gosh sakes, yet slightly insulated from the noise and traffic of it. And it's clean, friendly, and nicely outfitted too? Are we dreaming?

Some dorms here are as small as 6 beds each, while others are quite a bit bigger. People seem to have a really good time here, which is a good sign, and you're within a mile of more than 100 pubs, we'd guess. Another good thing here is that it has a unique personality, as so many other hostels (particularly in Scotland, sorry to say it) do not.

Yes, they have double rooms; yes, there's WiFi; and they claim they're the only hostel in the world that puts the mattresses through a washing machine. Sweet.

Gestalt:
High times
Safety:
Hospitality:
Cleanliness:
Party index:

It's also nice to be able to shuttle back and forth between this hostel and the affiliated Royal Mile Backpackers (see p. xxx) and check out their different vibes—though "fun" is the operative word at both.

How To Get There:

By bus: From bus station, walk to Princes Street; cross street and turn right down South Bridge. Cross bridge and continue to High Street (Royal Mile). Turn left and walk down High Street to Blackfriars.

By car: Call hostel for directions.

By train: From Waverley Station walk to Princes Street; turn right, then right again on South Bridge, and cross bridge to High Street (Royal Mile). Turn left and walk down High Street to Blackfriars.

Princes Street Backpackers

5 West Register St., Edinburgh EH2 2AA

Phone: 0131-556-6894
Fax: 0131-557-3236
Website: edinburghbackpackers.com
Rates: £11–£15 (about $17–$23 US) per person; doubles £30 (about $45 US)
Credit cards: Yes
Beds: 120
Private/family rooms: No
Kitchen available: Yes
Season: Open year-round
Office hours: 24 hours
Affiliation: None
Extras: Laundry, TV, VCR, free Internet access, meals ($), pool table, game room, shop

---

*N*ote: No children under 18.

This hostel's tucked into a decidedly unhip part of town. Still, it's not far from the pub action on Rose Street. In fact, there's a pub just beneath it. And it has one distinct advantage over its many competitors: It's the cheapest bunk in town, especially if you're looking for a double room.

Dorms run from 4 to 12 beds, and rates include sheets. Things aren't completely spic-and-span, but they're not bottom-of-the-barrel, either. Staff are extremely helpful, breakfast is served extremely inexpensively, and there are not one but two kitchens if you wanna cook your own grub. And get this: On Sunday nights, dinner is free. Free. You read that correctly. Free.

Gestalt:
Beer blast
Safety: ◳◳
Hospitality: ◳
Cleanliness: ◳◳
Party index: 🍕🍕🍕🍕

There's a lot to do at the hostel if it happens to be raining out, too—not that that ever happens in Scotland, right?—such as a movie room that purports to have 400 films on tap. We didn't actually count 'em, mind you. We're taking their word for it on this one.

Check out the interesting room-numbering (actually lettering) system, too. All things considered, it's pretty easy to have a good time here . . . unless you're a clean freak, maybe.

How To Get There:

By bus: From bus station, walk down to Princes Street and make a right, then another immediate right onto West Register Street. Hostel is on right, above pub.

By car: Call hostel for directions.

By train: From Waverley Station, walk across Princes Street to West Register and turn onto it. Hostel is on right, above pub.

Royal Mile Backpackers

105 High St., Edinburgh EH1 1NE

Phone: 0135-557-6120

E-mail: royalmile@scotlandstophostels.com

Website: royalmilebackpackers.com

Rates: £13–£15 (about $20–$23 US) per person

Credit cards: Yes

Beds: 100

Private/family rooms: No

Kitchen available: Yes

Season: Open year-round

Office hours: 6:30 a.m.–3 a.m.

Affiliation: IBHS

Extras: Breakfast ($), laundry, luggage storage, free WiFi

ou couldn't ask for a better location than this when in Edinburgh: The hostel's right on the city's High Street (what people in the US call Main Street), also known here of course as the Royal Mile, above a cafe.

Smallish but good, it's well kept. The kitchen, dorms, common rooms, and lounge are all clean and quite convivial. Dorms contain 6 to 12 beds apiece—no private rooms here; the place is too compact. The owner, that little chain of hostels/tour operators known as Scotland's Top Hostels (and, confusingly, also known as MacBackpackers), is getting the job done right, as you'll see elsewhere in this section. You can even store your bike at the good sister High Street Hostel (see p. xxx), just around the corner, if you want. Basically it's the same vibe, minus the historic building. Thumbs-up all around.

> **Gestalt:**
> *Royal plush*
> **Safety:**
> **Hospitality:**
> **Cleanliness:**
> **Party index:**

How To Get There:

By bus: From bus station walk to Princes Street; cross street and turn right down South Bridge. Cross bridge and continue to High Street (Royal Mile). Turn left and walk down High Street. Hostel is on left, above cafe.

By car: Call hostel for directions.

By train: From Waverley Station walk to Princes Street; turn right, then right again on South Bridge and cross bridge to High Street (Royal Mile). Turn left and walk down High Street. Hostel is on left, above cafe.

GLASGOW

Definitely Scotland's second city, Glasgow is experiencing an arts boom of late: Filmmakers, musicians, and the like are pouring in, and this place now knows an energy that it hasn't felt in decades. Make that centuries. Once denizens of an industrial town, today Glaswegians live in one of the most exciting, changing scenes that Scotland has to offer.

Glasgow Hostel

8 Park Terrace, Glasgow G3 6BY

> **Phone:** 0141-332-3004
>
> **Rates:** £15–£19 (about $24–$32 US) per HI member; doubles £38–£47 (about $57–$71 US)
>
> **Credit cards:** Yes
>
> **Beds:** 149
>
> **Private/family rooms:** Yes
>
> **Kitchen available:** Yes
>
> **Season:** Open year-round
>
> **Office hours:** 24 hours
>
> **Affiliation:** HI-SYHA
>
> **Extras:** Store, laundry, meals ($), TV room

A really nice facility close to a green park, Glasgow's official Hostelling International joint is good and trending toward "great"—something of a shock, given how blah/prim/controlling most of HI-SYHA's other properties are.

This historic building was renovated and features meals, a laundry, and even a kitchen now. It's still showing a lot of wear and tear, though. The television lounge is a hit. Dorms consist mostly of 4- and 6-bed rooms, with a few smaller and a few bigger.

The university-side neighborhood in which the hostel sits is attractive and safe, a far cry from Glasgow's industrial areas, and this working-class city is also enjoying a renaissance as a hotbed of arts and music. Ask a local or hostel staffer to direct you toward some of the cool stuff.

> **Gestalt:**
> *Great Scot*
> **Safety:**
> **Hospitality:**
> **Cleanliness:**
> **Party index:**

How To Get There:

By bus: From Buchanan Bus Station, take #44 or #44A bus (toward Knightswood or Cowdenhill Road) to Woodlands Road. Follow signs uphill to hostel.

By car: From M8 highway westbound, take Junction 18 (Charing Cross and Kelvingrove) and follow signs to hostel. Or, traveling eastbound, take Junction 17 (Dumbarton) and merge left onto A81 highway; turn left at first set of lights, then make next right onto Woodlands Road. Follow signs to hostel. Parking at hostel free on weekends and at night; metered during weekdays.

By train: From Queen Street Station, walk to Cathedral Street and take #11 bus to Woodlands Road; walk to hostel. From Central Station, take #44 or #44A bus toward Knightswood or Cowdenhill Road to Woodlands Road; get off and follow signs uphill to hostel.

LONDON

London's one happenin' place these days. A melting pot since forever, it seems, the city has only improved in recent years. The incredible selection of ethnic food options, the all-night dance scene, the history staring you in the face everywhere you go—it's almost enough to make you forget the dreary weather and air pollution so bad that it still leaves you coughing up black stuff.

The hostels here are strange—some come and go each summer (mostly run by skanky hotels trying to make a fast buck off desperate budget travelers), but the legitimate ones are pretty good. Especially considering the way student types storm London by force so reliably each summer that hostels could charge 50 bucks for a sleeping bag on the floor and probably get away with it. Instead, most of them pass the minimum test for cleanliness, friendliness, and fun. They're also mostly well located, almost all close to some cool neighborhood or a train station.

The exceptions are some of Hostelling International's various London joints (they run more here than they do in any other city in the world); some of them are quite a long way from the center of London, though they can be nice as green suburban getaways. YHA's hostels are as humdrum here as they are elsewhere, but the Oxford Street and Earl's Court joints are two very welcome exceptions to the usual rule.

Subway rides on the Tube are expensive; get a pass. For maximum transit value, order a London Visitor Travelcard ahead of time. This handy-dandy pass—good for a number of consecutive days—gets you unlimited travel on the Tube, the city bus system, most regional British Rail trains, and the Docklands Light Railway (as if you needed that).

Just remember that you've gotta buy the pass before you get to England. Call BritRail at (866) BRITRAIL (in the US) for more information.

If you forget, buy regular Travelcards in London at any Tube station as soon as you get to town. A one-day pass costs £11 (about $16 US) for four zones, or just £9 (about $14 US)

LONDON HOSTELS AT A GLANCE

	RATING	PRICE	IN A WORD	PAGE
St. Pancras Hostel		£26–£30	great	p. 445
Oxford Street Hostel		£33	central	p. 440
Holland Park Hostel		£18–£19	quiet	p. 437
Earl's Court Hostel		£22–£28	OK	p. 435
City of London/ St. Paul's Hostel		£25–£28	downtown	p. 432
International Student House		£21–£50	popular	p. 439
Thameside Hostel		£17–£28	remote	p. 446
St. Christopher's Village Hostel		£14.50–£39	hoppin'	p. 443
Generator Hostel		£24.75–£30	hip	p. 436
Curzon House Hostel		£20–£60	unkempt	p. 433
Piccadilly Backpackers		£12–£50.50	iffy	p. 442

if you're staying downtown and don't need to get out to the burbs. Weekend and weekly passes are even cheaper (per day, that is); all quickly pay for themselves if you make at least three hops per day, which you're guaranteed to do unless you're a total couch potato.

YHA London hostels include linens in the price of your stay. You are required to have an HI membership card, best purchased through your home organization.

Though England is generally quite safe, certain parts of London—such as the King's Cross/St. Pancras area, the docks, and Brixton—need to be treated with caution. Really, so does anywhere that's deserted at night. So be careful, especially if you're traveling alone or venturing out after dark.

London

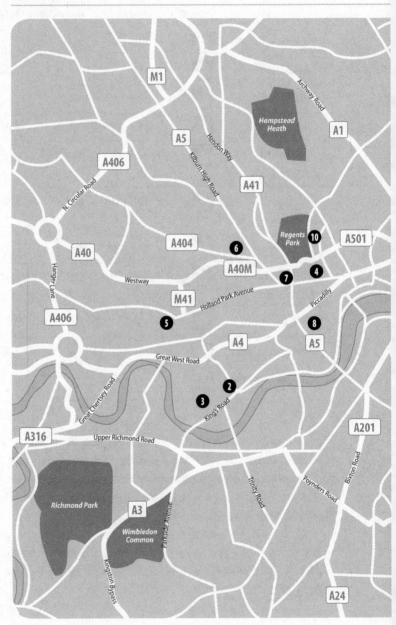

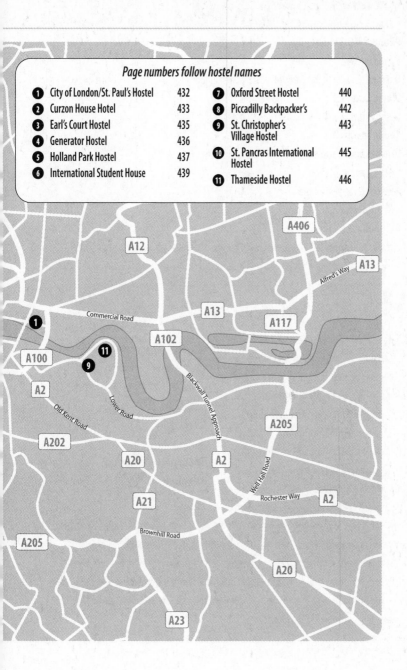

A406

A12

A13

Alfred's Way

Commercial Road

A13

A117

1

A102

A100

11

9

A2

Old Kent Road

Lower Road

Blackwall Tunnel Approach

A205

A202

A20

A2

Well Hall Road

Rochester Way

A2

A21

Brownhill Road

A205

A20

A23

City of London/St. Paul's Hostel

36 Carter Ln., London EC4V 5AB

Phone: 0845-371-9012

E-mail: stpauls@yha.org.uk

Rates: £25–£28 (about $39–$42 US) per HI member

Credit cards: Yes

Beds: 210

Single rooms: Yes

Private/family rooms: Yes

Kitchen available: No

Season: Open year-round

Office hours: 7 a.m.–11 p.m.

Affiliation: HI-YHA

Extras: TV, laundry, breakfast, meals ($), bureau de change, shop, video games, Internet access, luggage storage

Once a choir school for beautiful St. Paul's Cathedral, this hostel would seem to have one of the best locations of any hostel in London—it's right smack in the financial district, near several other cool areas and St. Paul's church. Downside to that? The highish prices (for a hostel) reflect this high-rent district—and they're only getting higher. During the daytime this area hops with bankers, museumgoers, and bridge-gawkers, plus people looking up at tremendously inspiring St. Paul's Cathedral (where Charles and Lady Di got married, as a side note).

What hostellers say:
"Staff really helped me."

Gestalt:
Paulished

Safety:

Hospitality:

Cleanliness:

Party index:

However, keep in mind that this area becomes a ghost town at night because nobody actually lives here; everyone heads home or to Bloomsbury or the West End, so you'll be hard pressed to find excitement after hours and will need to either use to Tube to go to Soho or else make your own party in the place.

And it's not a party place. Not surprisingly, it tends to draw families and elderly travelers, who pile into dorm rooms that range from 4 to 15 beds. Quad rooms are slightly more expensive; "economy dorms," with 15 beds, are cheaper. There's the usual kitchen and TV lounge—heck, some rooms even have TVs! No breakfast is included with your night's sleep, but upper-floor rooms are blessed with great views of downtown London. There's a decent restaurant here, plus video games and a very friendly, fairly hip front desk staff. They go the extra mile for hostellers with unusual needs, too.

The beds and bathrooms are not great—good, not great. But all in all, this hostel grades out as decent and quiet, if boring. Hey, at least you're almost on top of that cathedral and a few pubs.

How To Get There:
By Tube: Take Central Line to St. Paul's or Circle and District Lines to Blackfriars stop. From Blackfriars, walk 2 blocks north on New Bridge, then make a right onto Carter Lane; from St. Paul's, walk down Godliman Street, then right onto Carter Lane.

Curzon House Hostel
58 Courtfield Gardens, London SW5 0NF

   Phone: 020-7581-2116

   Fax: 020-7581-1319

   E-mail: info@curzonhousehotel.co.uk

   Website: curzonhousehotel.co.uk

   Rates: £20–£60 (about $30–$90 US) per person; doubles £55–£100 (about $83–$150 US)

   Credit cards: Yes

   Beds: 88

   Private/family rooms: Yes

   Kitchen available: Yes

   Season: Open year-round

   Office hours: Vary; call for hours

   Affiliation: None

   Extras: Breakfast, TV, free WiFi

Good views would seem to be the only reason to even consider this place, which has somehow remained pretty popular with your rucksacking set—those types who blow into London with a smile and not much else, fresh from a junket to Tasmania—and we never could figure out why. 'Cuz this place is bad, bad, bad.

Rooms have windows and 4 to 6 beds each. Some have views of a local church; some look out onto the quiet square known as Courtfield Gardens. Great; unfortunately, the rooms are consistently broken down and dirty, and staff and management have major personality issues, too. What's your problem, buddy? When a place is this bad, people are going to complain. Deal with it.

A continental breakfast is supplied with your stay, plus access to a small kitchen. But the upkeep is just so awful. Too bad, 'cause staff and guests here actually used to be fairly cool. Not anymore. Do not stay.

What hostellers say:
"What's British for 911?"
Gestalt:
Curzon! Foiled again!
Safety:
Hospitality:
Cleanliness:
Party index:

How To Get There:
By Tube: Take Tube to Gloucester Road stop. From station, turn right onto Courtfield Road, then right again on Courtfield Gardens.

Key to Icons

 Attractive natural setting
Ecologically aware hostel
Superior kitchen facilities or cafe
Offbeat or eccentric place
Superior bathroom facilities
Romantic private rooms

 Comfortable beds
A particularly good value
Wheelchair-accessible
 Good for business travelers
Especially well-suited for families
Good for active travelers

Visual arts at hostel or nearby
Music at hostel or nearby
Great hostel for skiers
Bar or pub at hostel or nearby
Editors' choice: Among our very favorite hostels

Earl's Court Hostel

38 Bolton Gardens, London SW5 0AQ

> **Phone:** 0845-371-9114
> **E-mail:** earlscourt@yha.org.uk
> **Rates:** £22–£28 (about $33–$42 US) per HI member
> **Credit cards:** Yes
> **Beds:** 186
> **Private/family rooms:** Yes
> **Kitchen available:** Yes
> **Season:** Open year-round
> **Office hours:** 24 hours
> **Affiliation:** HI-YHA
> **Extras:** Breakfast, laundry, bureau de change, TV, garden, bike storage, video games, kitchen, Internet access

*H*andy and well placed, this handsome Earl's Court joint looks like a good deal to us, if plain—and predictably stuffed to the gills in high summer season. It's sometimes kinda unclean, but overall, it gets the job done in a section of London where it's usually impossible to find a bed, never mind a cheap one.

The hostel is a town house located in a quiet and pretty neighborhood, safe and very near all sorts of other good things—nightlife, sights, and so forth. Dorms come with 4 to 6 beds per bunkroom, with a few in the 7- to 10-bed range. Things get tight as a tick sometimes, as this is a pretty popular location. However, they've resorted to using some triple bunk beds—3 bunks on one frame. Needless to say, this can be a major pain if you're on the bottom and one or two inebriated bunk mates show up late-night. This crowding takes a slight toll on the cleanliness and general condition of the bathrooms and kitchen.

Still, we liked the exceptionally nice kitchen and courtyard garden, not to mention the access to airport buses and great Kensington museums. (Lots of newer twin rooms add an escape valve for couples.)

Best bet for a bite:
Shish kebab stands in the area
What hostellers say:
"Cool, man."
Gestalt:
Duke of Earl's
Safety:
Hospitality:
Cleanliness:
Party index:

How To Get There:

By Tube: Take Tube to Earl's Court stop; exit right onto Earl's Court and make a left onto Bolton Gardens.

Generator Hostel

37 Tavistock Place, London WC1H 9SE

    Phone: 0207-388-7666
    Rates: £24.75–£30 (about $38–$45 US) per person
    Credit cards: Yes
    Beds: 844
    Private/family rooms: Yes
    Kitchen available: No
    Season: Open year-round
    Office hours: 24 hours
    Affiliation: None
    Extras: Restaurant ($), bar, Internet access

---

*S*orry, we know there's new management of the Generator chain, but this place still just is not cutting it. This wild, huge party hostel is definitely one of the weirder (and bigger) joints in all of Europe. It's a monstrous brick building on a side street just off Russell Square—which itself is practically on top of the world-famous (and free!) British Museum—in a quiet neighborhood of Camden. The hostel logo is a guy with a cyberhelmet on. Or is that a cyberface? Who knows?

Anyway, this enormous hostel packs in more than 800 beds. Yes, 800. Some are

Best bet for a bite:
Safeway
Insiders' tip:
Nice park nearby
What hostellers say:
"Moooo."
Gestalt:
Big Generator
Safety:
Hospitality:
Cleanliness:
Party index:

occupied by long-termers—you know, people living here while they look for a job—and others are taken up by huge tour groups. More and more regular hostellers are beginning to show up, too. It's a basic place, to be sure, but for drunken debauchery and not much else. It is what it is, a place to get hip with Generation Y-ers from all over Europe.

Definitely not the place to choose if you don't like dyed hair, rave clothing, tattoos, piercings, trust-fund hippies, guys with ties . . . hey, who let them in here?

(On the other hand, if you don't feel comfortable with all that other stuff, we've got just one question: Why the heck are you in London in the first place?)

The bar and cafeteria here seem to focus the socializing. There's a serious herd feeling and loads o' dirt, so if you can stand that, it's an OK bunk. We can't. And we won't. Better luck next year, guys.

How To Get There:

By Tube: Take Tube to Russell Square stop, then walk down Bernard Street to Marchmont; turn left and continue to Tavistock Place. Turn left at Compton Place shortly afterward; hostel is at end of short street.

Holland Park Hostel

Holland Walk, Kensington, London W8 7QU

> **Phone:** 0845-371-9122
> **E-mail:** hollandpark@yha.org.uk
> **Rates:** £18–£19 (about $27–$29 US) per HI member; doubles £62 (about $93 US)
> **Credit cards:** Yes
> **Beds:** 200
> **Private/family rooms:** Off-season only
> **Kitchen available:** Yes
> **Season:** Open year-round
> **Office hours:** 7 a.m.–11:30 p.m.
> **Affiliation:** HI-YHA
> **Extras:** Laundry, lockers, breakfast, TV, bureau de change, dinner ($), kitchen, games, bike rentals

---

N ote: Must be a member of Hostelling International to stay.

The biggest advantage to this Hostelling International joint is its very quiet location: It's stuck smack in the middle of gorgeous Holland Park and not too far from Kensington's artsy offerings and upscale shopping. We liked that, but some hostellers didn't like having to hike to the fun stuff—and noticed that some guests tend to stay here a looooong time. Ah, well. It's still just fine, and there's no lockout either.

Half the place is a roomy Jacobean mansion (as YHA will remind you again and again),

though take note: When you get there, you could well get put in the newer concrete annex across the outdoor walkway instead—and that's more like a barracks than a palace, definitely a little less glamorous than what you might have been expecting.

It feels a bit like a barracks, too. Dorms vary wildly in size, from 4 to 20 beds per room (be fore-warned that most contain at least a dozen bunks), and they can be a tight squeeze; that's one draw-back here. A handful of private rooms are possible but almost never available, as group leaders get first dibs on 'em.

The kitchen here is pretty good, dinners aren't bad, and they give you a sizable breakfast. Front desk staff are good at orienting you; they will also sell guidebooks (though, sadly, not this one), useful Travelcards for the Tube, and other stuff. A separate laundry building is a bonus.

While we didn't have any problems, the friendly staff recommend that you be careful walking through the park if you're arriving by night. There are two ways to come by Tube. At night, get off at the High Street Kensington stop. In daytime, use the Holland Park stop instead, though you'll need to look sharp for the sign marking the entrance to the park on your right.

The good security system requires everyone to be buzzed in by a security guard after 4:30 in the afternoon—a bit annoying, but a better idea than letting psychos roam in freely. Why so early? It's already dark by then in winter, that's why.

Best bet for a bite:
Marks & Spencer
Insiders' tip:
Beware of pigeons; keep windows closed!
What hostellers say:
"Not heavenly."
Gestalt:
Goin' Dutch
Safety:
Hospitality:
Cleanliness:
Party index:

How To Get There:

By Tube: At night, take Tube to High Street Kensington. Exit station, cross street, and turn left. Walk several blocks to Holland Park entrance on right. Turn right onto Holland Walk, pass field, enter park on left, then take a right to hostel. In daytime, you can take the Tube to Holland Park. Exit station, cross street, and turn left. Walk down street away from convenience store; turn right into park entrance, and walk down pathway to hostel entrance on right.

International Student House

229 Great Portland St., London W1W 5PN

> **Phone:** 020-7631-8300 or 020-7631-8310
> **Fax:** 020-7631-8307
> **E-mail:** accom@ish.org.uk
> **Website:** ish.org.uk
> **Rates:** £21–£50 (about $32–$75 US) per person; private rooms £74 (about $111 US)
> **Credit cards:** Yes
> **Beds:** 550
> **Private/family rooms:** Yes
> **Kitchen available:** Yes
> **Season:** Open year-round
> **Office hours:** 7:45 a.m.–10:30 p.m.
> **Affiliation:** None
> **Extras:** Laundry, breakfast, restaurant ($), bar, gym, free WiFi, bureau de change, events, TV, jukebox

---

*N*ote: *Discounts available for ISIC cardholders.*

This hostel's well equipped to cater to students (duh), hence it's very, very popular—full, in other words—most of the time. You'll certainly need to book in advance, especially during summer.

The hostel actually consists of 3 separate facilities: 2 buildings here on Great Portland Street, a university residence hall that opens its doors to travelers during the summer, and a nearby annex. Among the extra goodies are an Internet cafe, a gym/fitness center, a bar, a restaurant, and a laundry. Breakfast comes with your bed almost all the time, and the staff run a potpourri of activities and events.

On the other hand, upkeep has slid in recent years; the building is starting to say "beat-up" rather than "vintage cool" to us.

Another drawback? This place costs a lot of quid: This is one of the most expensive hostels in London, unless you're an ISIC cardholder (a student, in other words), and then you get a discount.

We'll still recommend it as a potential pick, but no longer with our highest rating. Investigate other options first.

What hostellers say:
"Thought it would be better."
Gestalt:
School daze
Safety:
Hospitality:
Cleanliness:

How To Get There:

By bus or train: Call hostel for transit route.
By car: Call hostel for directions.
By plane: Two airports are outside London; take A2 airbus to hostel.
By Tube: Take Tube to Great Portland Street stop; walk across street to hostel.

Oxford Street Hostel

14 Noel St., London W1F 8GJ

Phone: 0845-371-9133
E-mail: oxfordst@yha.org.uk
Rates: £33 (about $50 US) per HI member; doubles £80 (about $120 US)
Credit cards: Yes
Beds: 75
Private/family rooms: Yes
Kitchen available: Yes
Season: Open year-round
Office hours: 7 a.m.–11 a.m.
Affiliation: HI-YHA
Extras: TV, lockers, bureau de change, breakfast ($), laundry, kitchen, Internet access

---

N *ote: Children not allowed.*

How on earth did YHA snag such a primo hostel location? It's smack in the heart of London's hippest addresses, Soho and Covent Garden and the West End—incredible. The pub, club, and schmooze scene here arguably rivals that of any-place in the world.

And the hostel's great, too—especially considering how many folks are clamoring to squeeze in here for a night or three. Yes, this is a really small hostel (in a bland building), with smallish dorm rooms; expect a bit of a squeeze plus lots of stairs to hike up first, and a wait for the bathrooms. Deal with that, though, and you've scored one of London's very best bunks—in its best location (for our money).

Best bet for a bite:
Mildred's, on Lexington Street
Insiders' tip:
Famous people hang in Soho Square
What hostellers say:
"This neighborhood is so cool."
Gestalt:
West End girls
Safety:
Hospitality:
Cleanliness:
Party index:

Oh, the deets. Rooms mostly contain 2 to 4 beds each. Management and staff are friendly. The kitchen's compact but useful and it's kept quite clean. The hostel laundry is an extremely welcome addition in a town where just finding a place to wash your clothes can be a bothersome chore.

Hostellers come here for the extremely hip location, so you've got to book very early ahead. Some hostellers hang out in the enormous television room. One thing this place ain't is quiet as a mouse—with all the clubbing at hand, you might wind up sandwiched between an Aussie and a brewski, but that's totally all right with us.

By the way, this hostel's on Noel Street. Was Noel Street named for Noel Gallagher? Just wondering. 'Cuz this place is . . . wait for it . . . an oasis.

How To Get There:

By Tube: Take Tube to Oxford Circus. Walk east on Oxford Street, turn right on Poland, and then turn left on Noel.

Piccadilly Backpackers

12 Sherwood St., Piccadilly, London W1F 7BR

Phone: 0207-434-9009

Fax: 0207-434-9010

E-mail: bookings@piccadillybackpackers.com

Website: piccadillybackpackers.com

Rates: £12–£50.50 (about $18–$76 US) per person; doubles £53–£67.50 (about $80–$100 US)

Credit cards: Yes

Beds: 700

Private/family rooms: Sometimes

Kitchen available: No

Season: Open year-round

Office hours: 24 hours

Affiliation: None

Extras: Ticket office, laundry, travel store, breakfast ($), bar, lockers, Internet access ($), fax, TV, activities

Best bet for a bite:
Chip shop across street

What hostellers say:
"Abort, abort! Ripcord! Ripcord!"

Gestalt:
Picked clean

Safety:

Hospitality:

Cleanliness:

Party index:

Is this the worst hostel in London. Aye, it is. Hands down. And we do mean down.

Just a minute (literally) from Piccadilly Circus, this huge (700 beds) hostel boasts an incredibly ace location—but that is the only promise it delivers on. Sometimes location is not everything, you know what we mean?

Doubtless this is one of the best-situated hostels in the city: Leicester Square (the theater district), Trafalgar Square, Big Ben, hip Soho, and the London Eye are all spread out before you, within 10 minutes' walk. Nobody's arguing that, and if you're here to sightsee and won't be in your hostel more than 6 hours to get some shut-eye, it might be doable. But we don't think so.

Because once you step inside, things begin to diverge from the Web hype. Things smell bad. Staff are standoffish. The elevator takes forever, forcing you to possibly walk up 5 flights of stairs with your pack. The 'Net connections are frequently on the blink. And so on. Rooms range from small to biggish, with some wooden bunks and some odd "pod" bunks that feel a little too cozy; it can get drafty, and cleanliness was terrible during repeat visits. Also, be aware that many dorms here are coed—that means guys 'n' gals bunking together.

There isn't a full kitchen, so be prepared to go out scavenging for takeout. They do allow 24-hour access to microwave ovens here—better than nothing, for sure, but still not the same thing as having a proper stovetop. The free lockers (bring your own padlock or buy one at the desk) are pretty small, although the chill-out hosteller bar has to be counted as a positive. There's no smoking throughout this hostel, not even in the Moroccan-theme lounge, but there's also no curfew; if you're a late-nighter intent on raving it up in Soho, that's a good thing.

By the way, while you're out there in the city, stock up on chow—breakfast here is a big disappointment. As was this hostel. It's not the worst we've seen, but we'd stay in a lot of other places first.

How To Get There:

By Tube: From Piccadilly station, take Exit 1 up to Glasshouse Street; cross onto Sherwood Street, and walk to yellow entrance of hostel.

St. Christopher's Village Hostel
161–165 Borough High St., Southwark, London SE1 1HR

> **Phone:** 0207-407-1856
> **Fax:** 0207-403-7715
> **E-mail:** bookings@interpub.co.uk
> **Website:** st-christophers.co.uk
> **Rates:** £14.50–£39 (about $22–$60 US) per person; doubles £49–£50 (about $74–$75 US)
> **Credit cards:** Yes
> **Beds:** 165
> **Private/family rooms:** Yes
> **Kitchen available:** No

Season: Open year-round

Office hours: 24 hours

Affiliation: None

Extras: Laundry, bar, TV, roof patio, job board, breakfast, meals ($), pinball, hot tub, sauna

*T*he name on the Web page says it all: The Hostel With Attitude. And let's face it: The reason most hostellers roll in here is (a) the cheap price; (b) the attached pub; (c) see (b).

Yes, a typical Brit pub. And what a deal! For half what some hostels in London charge, you get a free continental breakfast, meal discounts, and access to a good private lounge. No wonder many (all?) the guests here spend a predominant amount of their time imbibing.

Dorms come 2 to 14 beds per room, but you won't spend much time in there. You'll likely be in the pub, shooting pool or trying out your karaoke voice. Noise can be a real problem when rock bands play late in the club, though; best to bring your earplugs. Also, smoke from the bar curls upward inevitably to the dorm rooms. If it bugs you, this might not be the place to stay. On the other hand, the rooftop hot tub and sauna just might keep you here.

The staff here seem to go the extra mile, with advice on getting through the hoops of money-changing, visas, and so forth—it seems to attract people who've landed in London to work for a while. They also do wake-up calls. Other amenities include a laundry; that private hostellers' lounge with bar, pinball machine, and 40-channel TV (yippee); a job board; and a mail-forwarding service. We were also impressed with security measures: Each room here is accessed with a key card.

However, we can't recommend the dirty bathrooms, useless storage facilities, and Lilliputian beds. This place is what you make of it, and what you expect of it: If you want luxury or quiet or cleanliness, though, don't bother staying. Party types out for a good time, on the other hand, could have a blast.

Best bet for a bite:
On-site pub grub

What hostellers say:
"Fill 'er up!"

Gestalt:
Brew hotel

Safety:

Hospitality:

Cleanliness:

Party index:

Just 200 yards from London Bridge, the hostel straddles a blue-collar area and sparkly sights. Keep in mind that it's on the much-less-nice South Bank of the Thames, but there are fewer crowds here. Try a dance club like The Ministry of Sound for something different.

Note that several annexes of this hostel have opened around town in Camden, Greenwich, Shepherd's Bush, and near this one.

How To Get There:
By Tube: Call hostel for directions.

St. Pancras International Hostel

79–81 Euston Rd., London NW1 2QE

   Phone: 0845-371-9344

   E-mail: stpancras@yha.org.uk

   Rates: £26–£30 (about $39–$45 US) per HI member

   Credit cards: Yes

   Beds: 186

   Private/family rooms: Yes

   Kitchen available: Yes

   Season: Open year-round

   Office hours: 7 a.m.–11 p.m.

   Affiliation: HI-YHA

   Extras: TV, bike storage, laundry, dinner ($), breakfast, kitchen, free WiFi

*O*ne of London's youngest, freshest Hostelling International joints isn't in London's greatest neighborhood, but it's close to a number of fine attractions and extremely well equipped. If you're traveling with a car or as a family, think about it. Young'uns out to mix and mingle should avoid it, maybe.

The hostel is placed near St. Pancras train station, an area that gets seedy at night and isn't recommended for the solitary female traveler at all. On the other hand, facilities are very nice. Dorm rooms contain 2 to 5 beds apiece, and everything's almost new. The outside and inside are decked out in modern touches like chrome trim.

The train station couldn't be closer, and you're an incredibly short walk from the British Library as well as several Tube stops. The Camden Town area hops despite the sleaze factor, offering bargain shops by day and lots of live music and pubbing by night. We love us some Camden.

How To Get There:

By train: From St. Pancras Station, turn right onto Euston Road, cross Judd Street; hostel is second building on right after crossroad.

By Tube: Take Tube to King's Cross Station. Turn right onto Euston Road and cross Judd Street; hostel is second building on right after crossroad.

Best bet for a bite:
Along Drummond Street, near Euston Square
What hostellers say:
"Scary at night, but great place."
Gestalt:
Saint in the city
Safety:
Hospitality:
Cleanliness:
Party index:

Thameside Hostel

20 Salter Rd., London SE16 5PR

> **Phone:** 0845-371-9756
>
> **Fax:** 020-7237-2919
>
> **E-mail:** thameside@yha.org.uk
>
> **Rates:** £17–£28 (about $26–$42 US) per HI member
>
> **Credit cards:** Yes
>
> **Beds:** 320
>
> **Private/family rooms:** Yes
>
> **Kitchen available:** Yes
>
> **Season:** Open year-round
>
> **Office hours:** 24 hours
>
> **Affiliation:** HI-YHA
>
> **Extras:** Laundry, bureau de change, breakfast ($), travel shop, TV, dinner ($), Internet access, bar, free WiFi

*Y*ou'll hear this well-equipped place touted as being just a mile from the Tower Bridge and steps from the Tube, but truth be told we're a bit skeptical about that info. It's in the Docklands, distant from most attractions—and the Tube—and not heavily foot-trafficked at night, either. The 24-hour desk security made us feel better once we'd arrived, but the hostel is not as over-the-top-wonderful as it's cracked up to be. Atmosphere is lacking and you'll likely spend very little time here doing anything other than sleeping.

Rooms are small—lots of double units here, so there's one good point in its favor—and all of them do contain en-suite bathrooms. Staff are straightforward, rather than peppy, but at least things are kept fairly clean. But you need to allow lots of time to get to this not-exactly-perfect location, which isn't so much seedy as blah. And the hostel gives you no reason to want to stay way out here. It's a decent place, and quiet, but that's it.

Best bet for a bite:
Elsewhere
What hostellers say:
"Pass the Geritol."
Gestalt:
Dry dock
Safety:
Hospitality:
Cleanliness:
Party index:

How To Get There:

By bus: Take East London Tube line to Rotherhithe. From station, walk along Brunel Road to Salter or take taxi to hostel. From Waterloo Station, take P11 bus to hostel.
By Tube: Take East London Tube line to Rotherhithe. From station, walk along Brunel Road to Salter or take taxi to hostel.

Attractive natural setting	Comfortable beds	Visual arts at hostel or nearby
Ecologically aware hostel	A particularly good value	Music at hostel or nearby
Superior kitchen facilities or cafe	Wheelchair-accessible	Great hostel for skiers
Offbeat or eccentric place	Good for business travelers	Bar or pub at hostel or nearby
Superior bathroom facilities	Especially well-suited for families	Editors' choice: Among our very favorite hostels
Romantic private rooms	Good for active travelers	

Key to Icons

MANCHESTER

All right, we'll go ahead and confess to it: We're mad for Madchester. This city surprised the heck out of us. Sure, it's got a rap as a grimy, industrial place—and that's true—but there's a lot of cultural life here in the North. We came away feeling like this was one of our favorite cities, and not just because the Stone Roses and other seminal Brit-pop bands formed here.

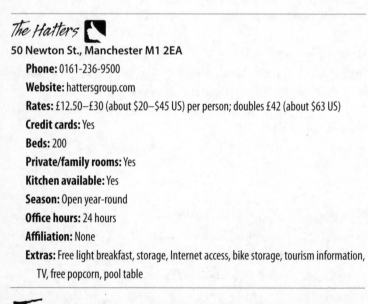

MANCHESTER HOSTELS AT A GLANCE

	RATING	PRICE	IN A WORD	PAGE
Manchester Hostel		£23	plush	p. 449
The Hatters		£12.50–£30	heady	p. 448

The Hatters

50 Newton St., Manchester M1 2EA

Phone: 0161-236-9500

Website: hattersgroup.com

Rates: £12.50–£30 (about $20–$45 US) per person; doubles £42 (about $63 US)

Credit cards: Yes

Beds: 200

Private/family rooms: Yes

Kitchen available: Yes

Season: Open year-round

Office hours: 24 hours

Affiliation: None

Extras: Free light breakfast, storage, Internet access, bike storage, tourism information, TV, free popcorn, pool table

This indy hostel opened in a former Manchester hat factory in 2003, and it has been really nicely renovated inside. A big brick building with arched windows, it seems to have gotten a complete once-over. Dorm rooms contain 2 to 10 beds, and they've got singles as well. It's certainly OK, all in all, not nearly as dirty or noisy as many other indy hostels around the country and Continent.

The location is fairly central, a little north of town but not too, too far, and they've equipped the place with amenities such as a pool table and Internet access.

Staff makes free popcorn to accompany movie viewing in the TV lounge, and a key-card system ensures better security. Staff are pretty cool. A good place.

Gestalt:
Hats off
Safety:
Hospitality:
Cleanliness:
Party index:

How To Get There:

By car: Contact hostel for directions.
By bus: Contact hostel for transit route.
By train: Contact hostel for transit route.

Manchester Hostel

Potato Wharf, Castlefield, Greater Manchester M3 4NB

Phone: 0845-371-9647
E-mail: manchester@yha.org.uk
Rates: £23 (about $40 US) per HI member
Credit cards: Yes
Beds: 136
Private/family rooms: Yes
Kitchen available: Yes
Season: Open year-round
Office hours: 24 hours
Affiliation: HI-YHA
Extras: TV, game room, laundry, meals ($), lockers, conference rooms, cafe, game room

---

*S*ome call this the best hostel in the world, or at least in Europe. And we've got to agree that YHA's Manchester joint certainly deserves all the thumbs up we can muster. It

Manchester

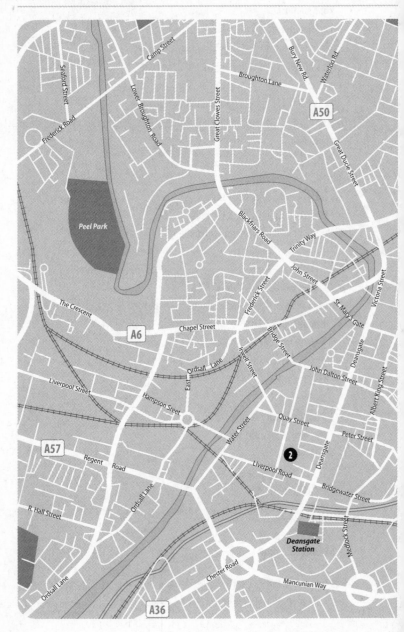

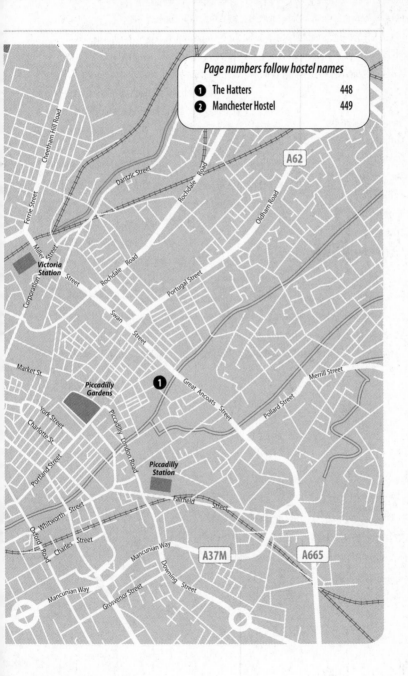

remains as great (or nearly so) as ever, even upon repeat viewings and bunkings, and we don't know how they do it. But this place is just, as they say in Britain, "class."

Lots of thought seems to have gone into the joint, which is almost like a sleek modern hotel. There are plenty of private rooms, for starters, and even the dorms never have more than 6 beds. Every room has its own en-suite bathroom, a rarity in the world of Euro-hostel-ling. Some of the rooms are wheelchair-accessible, too, and some have televisions. Staff are incredibly friendly, the place is spotless, good meals are served—and you can actually have fun here in the common rooms talking with people! It's so unlike a YHA hostel, we almost fell over in surprise.

As a bonus, it's right across the road from the good Museum of Science and Industry, which charts the Industrial Revolution and central England's crucial role in it.

Best bet for a bite:
Rusholme neighborhood (Indian)
Gestalt:
Manchester, united
Safety:
Hospitality:
Cleanliness:
Party index:

As a city, Manchester's definitely on the comeback trail after years of industrial gray. Despite the smog and bricks, you can find tons of veggie eats, pubs, gay culture, and bars, as well as a pumpin' music scene. The raves that the likes of Madonna once dropped in for at the Hacienda dance club nearby (which sadly has since closed) are mostly gone now, but you can

Key to Icons

Attractive natural setting	Comfortable beds	Visual arts at hostel or nearby
Ecologically aware hostel	A particularly good value	Music at hostel or nearby
Superior kitchen facilities or cafe	Wheelchair-accessible	Great hostel for skiers
Offbeat or eccentric place	Good for business travelers	Bar or pub at hostel or nearby
Superior bathroom facilities	Especially well-suited for families	Editors' choice: Among our very favorite hostels
Romantic private rooms	Good for active travelers	

drink beers at any of a hundred pubs (the Ox Noble and the White Lion next door are great), gardens, universities, a Roman fort . . . the list goes on and on. You might even see some of the dudes in Oasis (or ex-Oasis, now that they've broken up. Again).

Tack on Europe's best Indian food—a mile-long strip of curry houses—and you'll be sticking around at least a night or two. We love Madchester, and love this hostel.

How To Get There:
By bus: From Piccadilly Gardens, take #33 bus to hostel. From main bus station, walk 1 mile to hostel, behind Castlefield Hotel. Or take Metro to G-Mex Centre and walk along Liverpool Road to Potato Wharf on left; turn left and walk to hostel on left. Take cab at night.
By car: Call hostel for directions.
By train: From Deansgate Station, walk to Chester Road then turn left at Liverpool Road; take next left. Hostel is on left, behind Castlefield Hotel. From Piccadilly Station, walk 1 mile through city center, following signs to Castlefield/Museum of Science and Industry. Or take Metrolink to G-Mex Station and walk 2 blocks up Bridgewater and Liverpool to hostel. Hostel is behind Castlefield Hotel. Take cab at night.

Paul's Picks*

(*with the help of thousands of others)

TEN GREAT EUROPEAN CITY HOSTELS

Af Chapman/Skeppsholmen Hostel,
Stockholm, Sweden 375

Århus Pavillonen Hostel,
Århus, Denmark 103

The Beehive,
Rome, Italy 280

Boathouse Hostel,
Prague, Czech Republic 81

Circus Hostel,
Berlin, Germany 168

Långholmen Hostel,
Stockholm, Sweden 380

Lisbon Lounge Hostel,
Lisbon, Portugal 346

Manchester Hostel,
Manchester, England 449

Sir Toby's Hostel,
Prague, Czech Republic 94

Wombat's Backpackers,
Vienna, Austria 56

TEN HARD-ROCKIN'
EUROPEAN PARTY HOSTELS

Index